GRENDEL TALES

THE DEVIL MAY CARE

Written by
TERRY LABAN

Illustrated by
PETER DOHERTY

Lettered by
RICHARD STARKINGS

Cover pencilled by
PETER DOHERTY
and painted by
MATT WAGNER

Chapter cover art by
PETER DOHERTY

Grendel created and owned by Matt Wagner

DARK HORSE COMICS®

Editor
DIANA SCHUTZ

Collection designer
CARY GRAZZINI

Publisher
MIKE RICHARDSON

Published by Dark Horse Comics, Inc.
10956 SE Main
Milwaukie, OR 97222

First edition: December 2002
ISBN: 1-56971-796-6

1 3 5 7 9 10 8 6 4 2

This book collects issues one through six of the Dark Horse comic-book series
Grendel Tales: The Devil May Care.

CHAPTER ONE

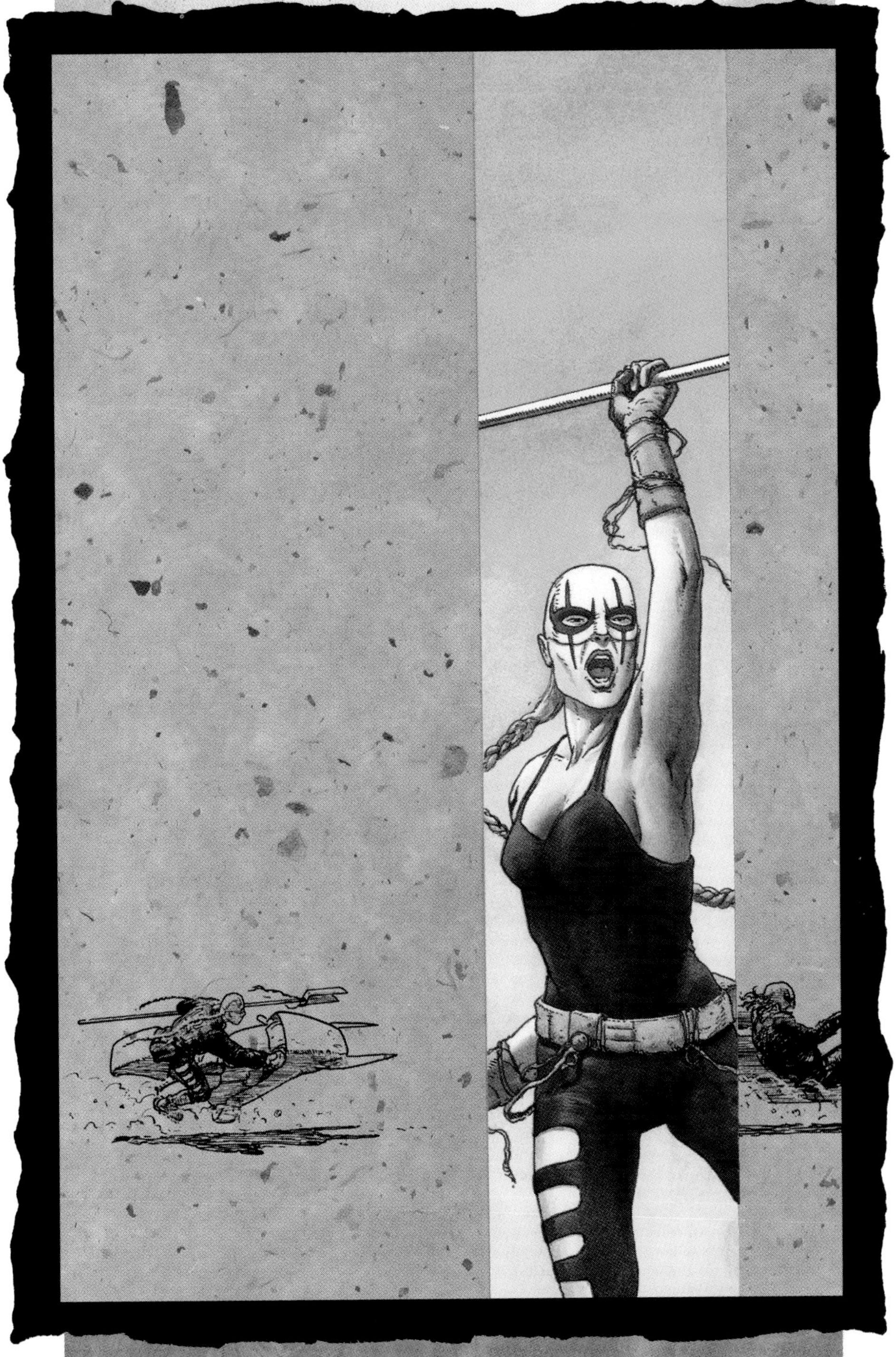

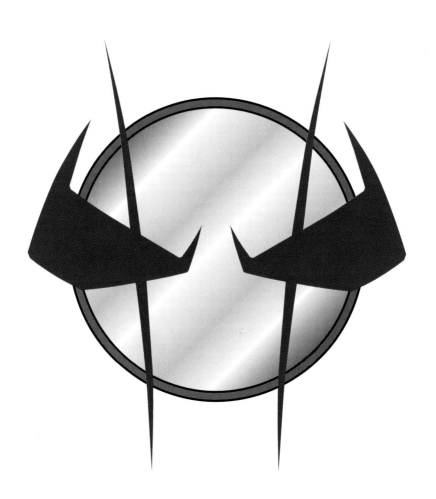

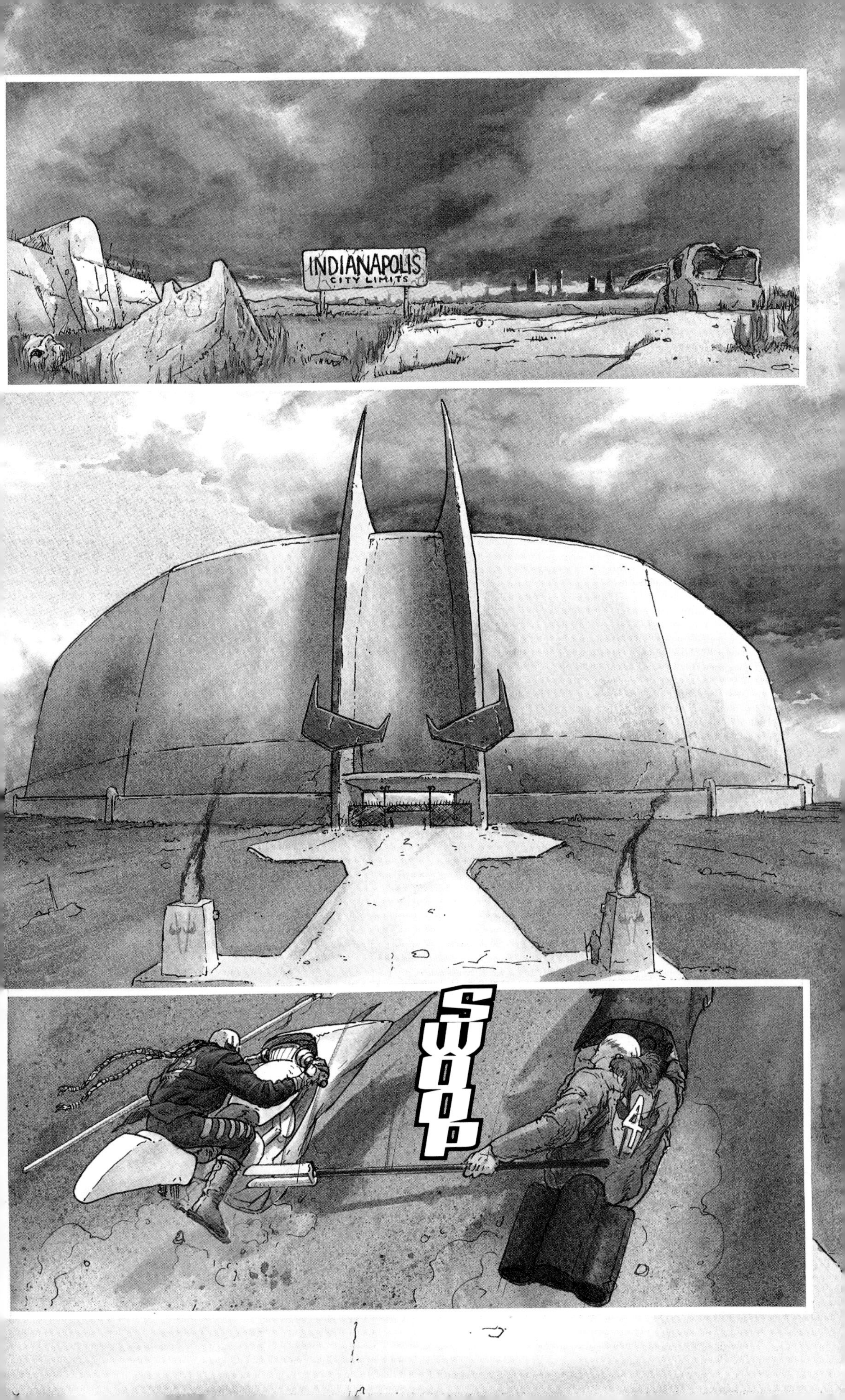
INDIANAPOLIS
CITY LIMITS
SWOOP

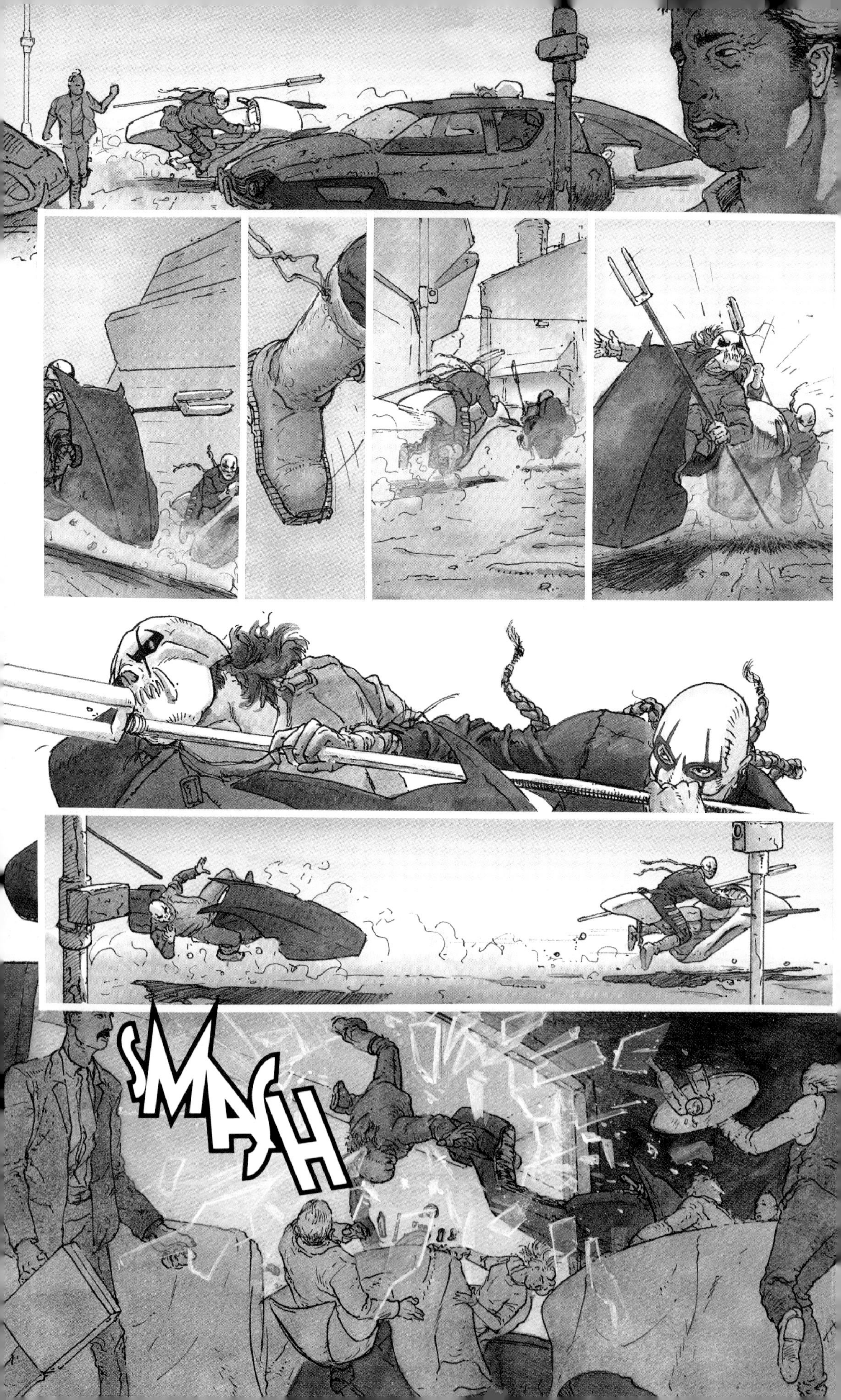
SMASH

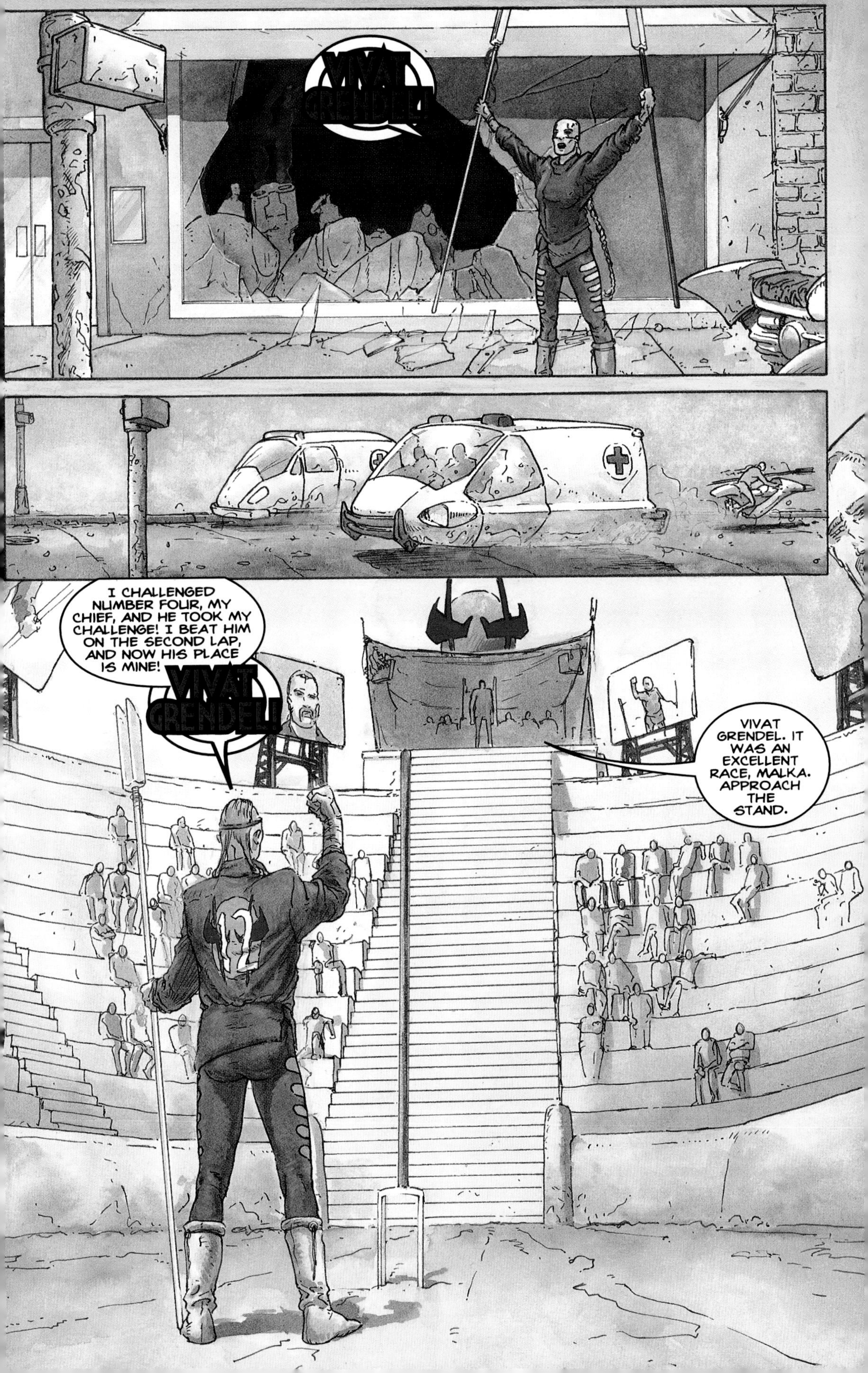
VIVAT GRENDEL!
I CHALLENGED NUMBER FOUR, MY CHIEF, AND HE TOOK MY CHALLENGE! I BEAT HIM ON THE SECOND LAP, AND NOW HIS PLACE IS MINE!
VIVAT GRENDEL!
VIVAT GRENDEL. IT WAS AN EXCELLENT RACE, MALKA. APPROACH THE STAND.

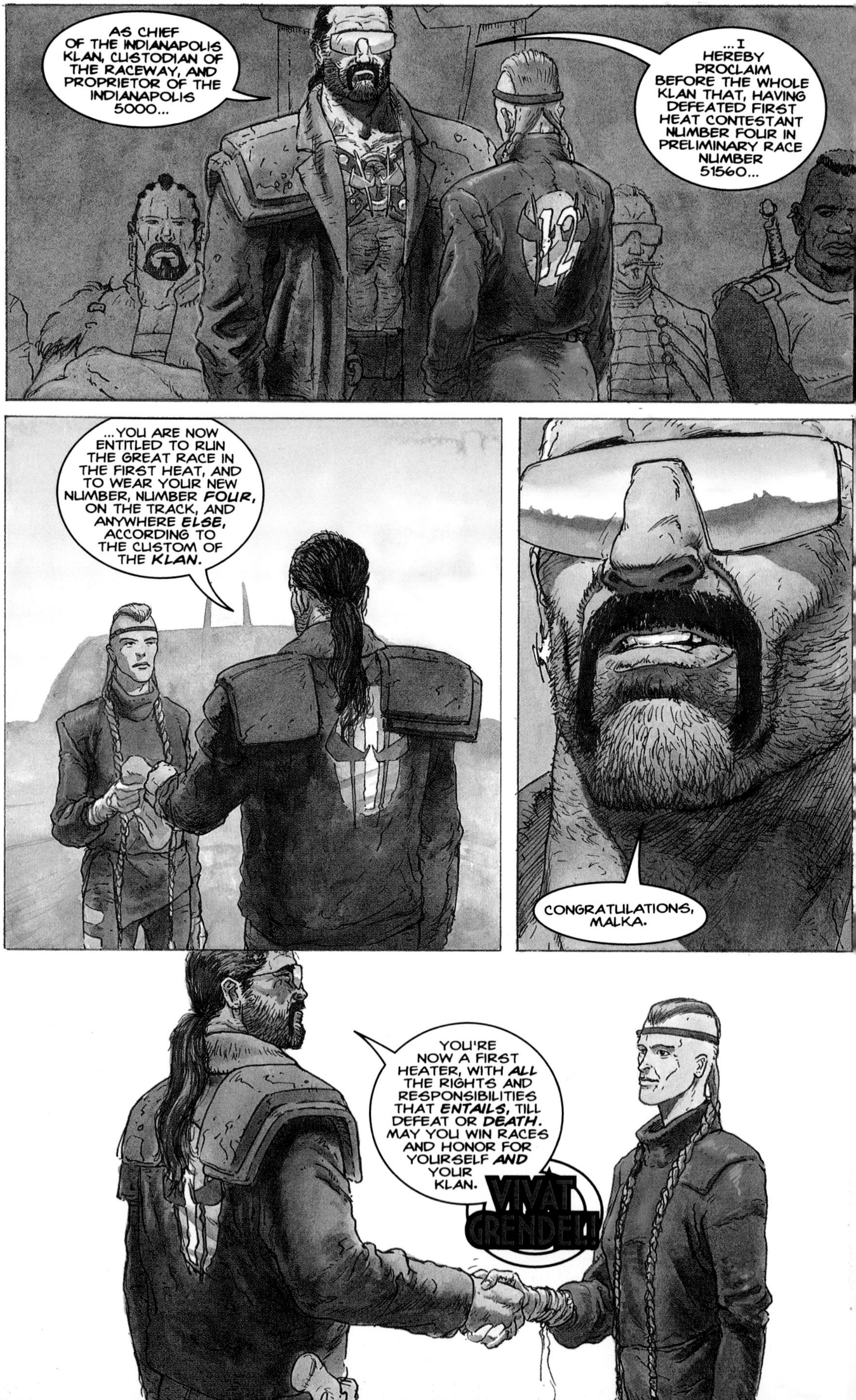
AS CHIEF OF THE INDIANAPOLIS KLAN, CUSTODIAN OF THE RACEWAY, AND PROPRIETOR OF THE INDIANAPOLIS 5000...
...I HEREBY PROCLAIM BEFORE THE WHOLE KLAN THAT, HAVING DEFEATED FIRST HEAT CONTESTANT NUMBER FOUR IN PRELIMINARY RACE NUMBER 51560...
...YOU ARE NOW ENTITLED TO RUN THE GREAT RACE IN THE FIRST HEAT, AND TO WEAR YOUR NEW NUMBER, NUMBER FOUR, ON THE TRACK, AND ANYWHERE ELSE, ACCORDING TO THE CUSTOM OF THE KLAN.
CONGRATULATIONS, MALKA.
YOU'RE NOW A FIRST HEATER, WITH ALL THE RIGHTS AND RESPONSIBILITIES THAT ENTAILS, TILL DEFEAT OR DEATH. MAY YOU WIN RACES AND HONOR FOR YOURSELF AND YOUR KLAN.
VIVAT GRENDEL!

VIVAT GRENDEL!

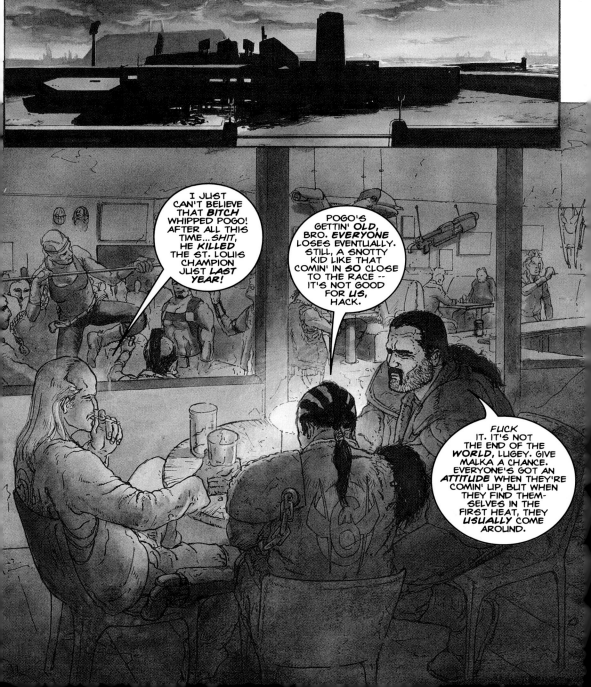

I JUST CAN'T BELIEVE THAT *BITCH* WHIPPED POGO! AFTER ALL THIS TIME... *SHIT,* HE *KILLED* THE ST. LOUIS CHAMPION JUST *LAST YEAR!*

POGO'S GETTIN' *OLD,* BRO. *EVERYONE* LOSES EVENTUALLY. STILL, A SNOTTY KID LIKE THAT COMIN' IN SO CLOSE TO THE RACE -- IT'S NOT GOOD FOR *US,* HACK.

FUCK IT. IT'S NOT THE END OF THE *WORLD,* LUGEY. GIVE MALKA A CHANCE. EVERYONE'S GOT AN *ATTITUDE* WHEN THEY'RE COMIN' UP, BUT WHEN THEY FIND THEM-SELVES IN THE FIRST HEAT, THEY *USUALLY* COME AROUND.

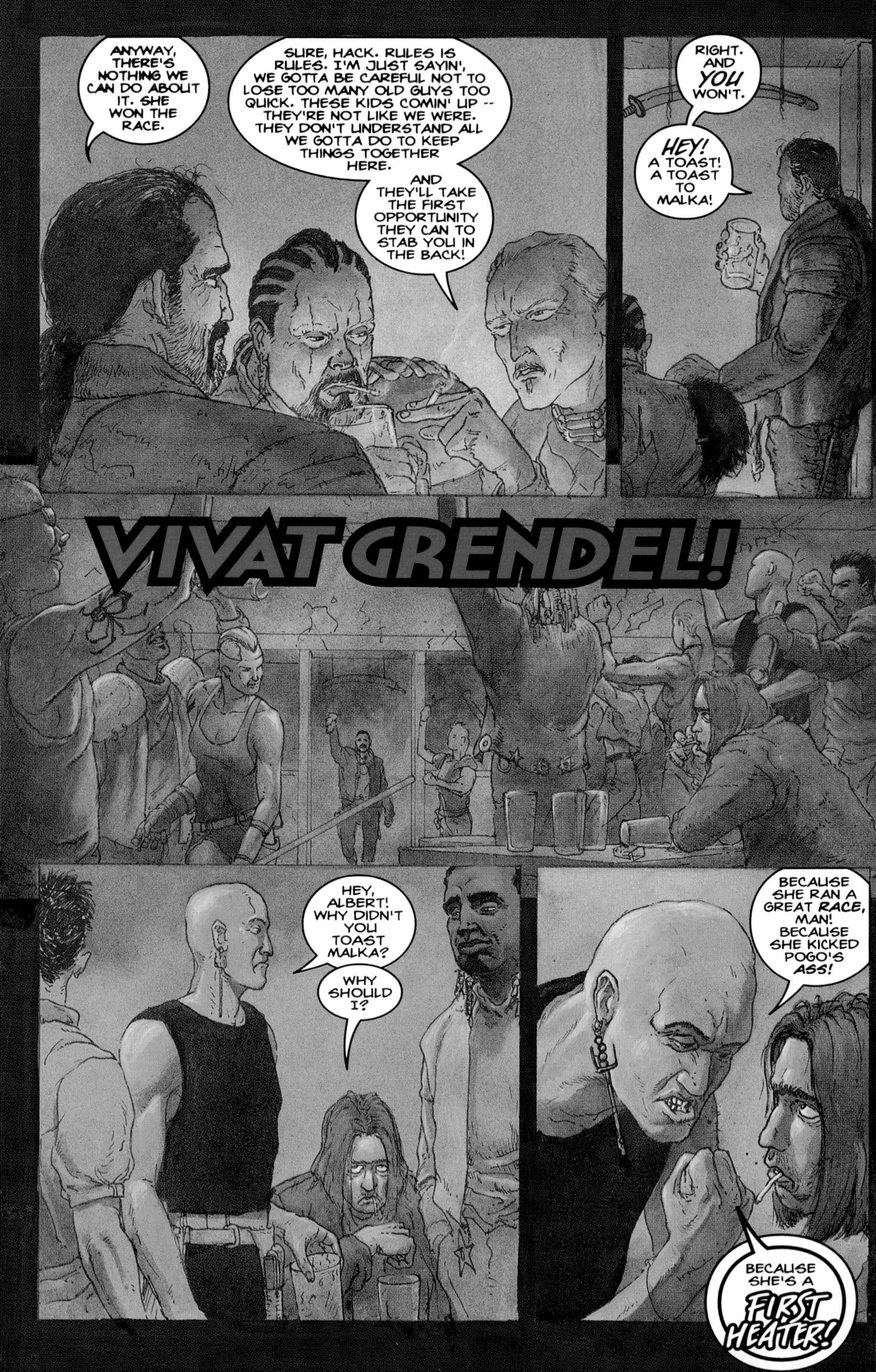

ANYWAY, THERE'S NOTHING WE CAN DO ABOUT IT. SHE WON THE RACE.
SURE, HACK. RULES IS RULES. I'M JUST SAYIN', WE GOTTA BE CAREFUL NOT TO LOSE TOO MANY OLD GUYS TOO QUICK. THESE KIDS COMIN' UP -- THEY'RE NOT LIKE WE WERE. THEY DON'T UNDERSTAND ALL WE GOTTA DO TO KEEP THINGS TOGETHER HERE.
AND THEY'LL TAKE THE FIRST OPPORTUNITY THEY CAN TO STAB YOU IN THE BACK!
RIGHT. AND YOU WON'T.
HEY! A TOAST! A TOAST TO MALKA!
VIVAT GRENDEL!
HEY, ALBERT! WHY DIDN'T YOU TOAST MALKA?
WHY SHOULD I?
BECAUSE SHE RAN A GREAT RACE, MAN! BECAUSE SHE KICKED POGO'S ASS!
BECAUSE SHE'S A FIRST HEATER!

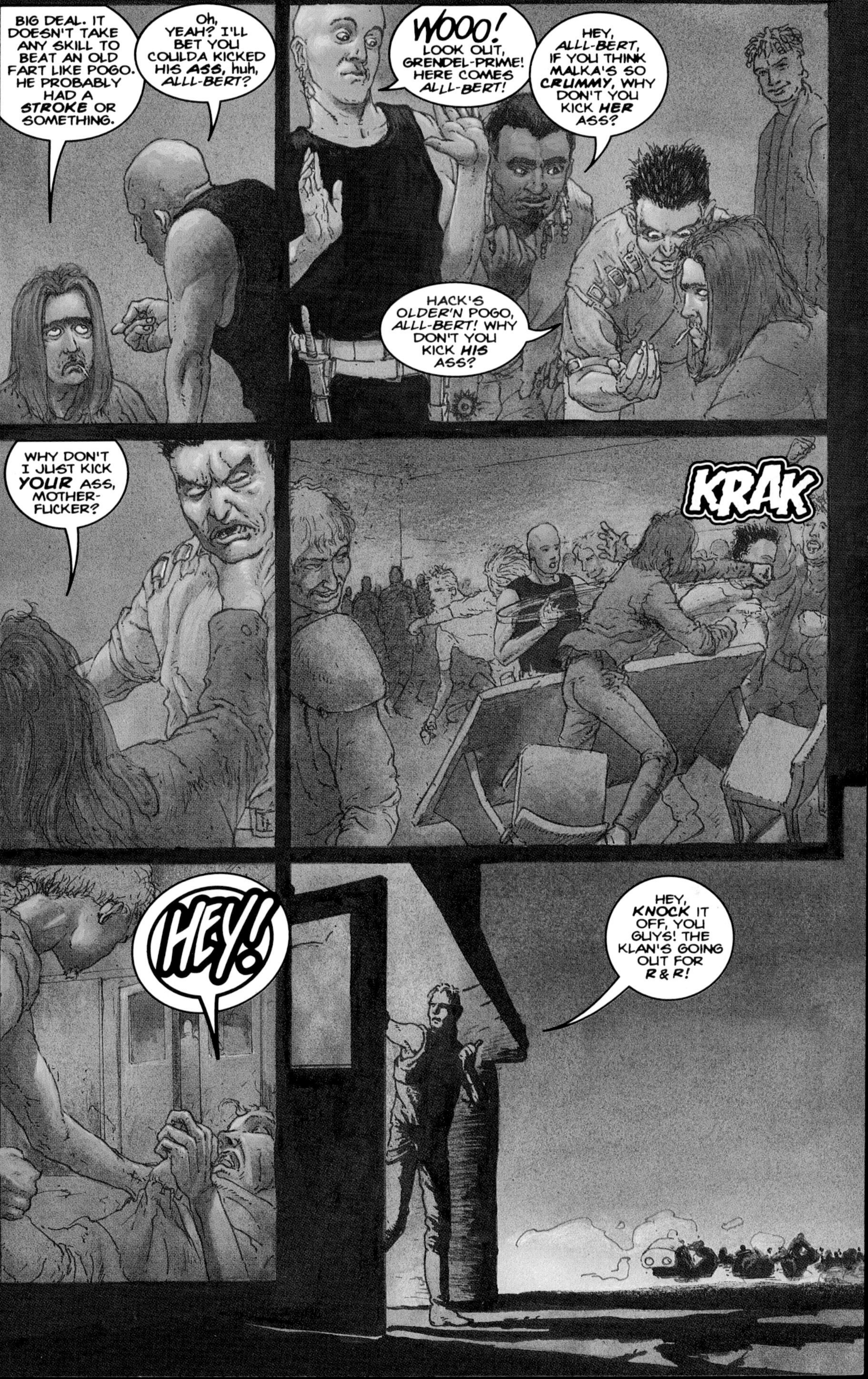
BIG DEAL. IT DOESN'T TAKE ANY SKILL TO BEAT AN OLD FART LIKE POGO. HE PROBABLY HAD A STROKE OR SOMETHING.
Oh, YEAH? I'LL BET YOU COULDA KICKED HIS ASS, huh, ALLL-BERT?
WOOO! LOOK OUT, GRENDEL-PRIME! HERE COMES ALLL-BERT!
HEY, ALLL-BERT, IF YOU THINK MALKA'S SO CRUMMY, WHY DON'T YOU KICK HER ASS?
HACK'S OLDER'N POGO, ALLL-BERT! WHY DON'T YOU KICK HIS ASS?
WHY DON'T I JUST KICK YOUR ASS, MOTHER-FLICKER?
KRAK
HEY!
HEY, KNOCK IT OFF, YOU GUYS! THE KLAN'S GOING OUT FOR R & R!

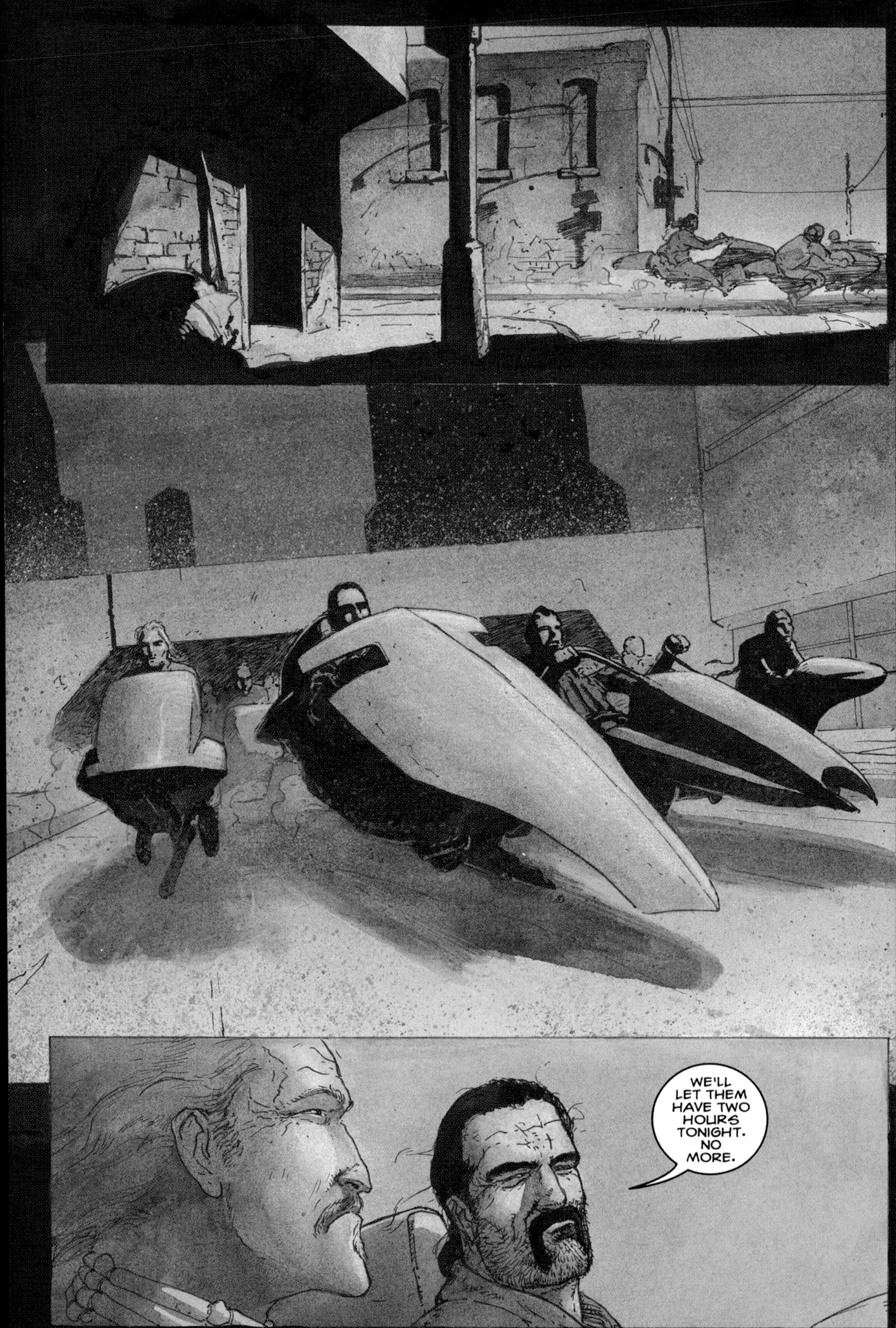
WE'LL LET THEM HAVE TWO HOURS TONIGHT. NO MORE.

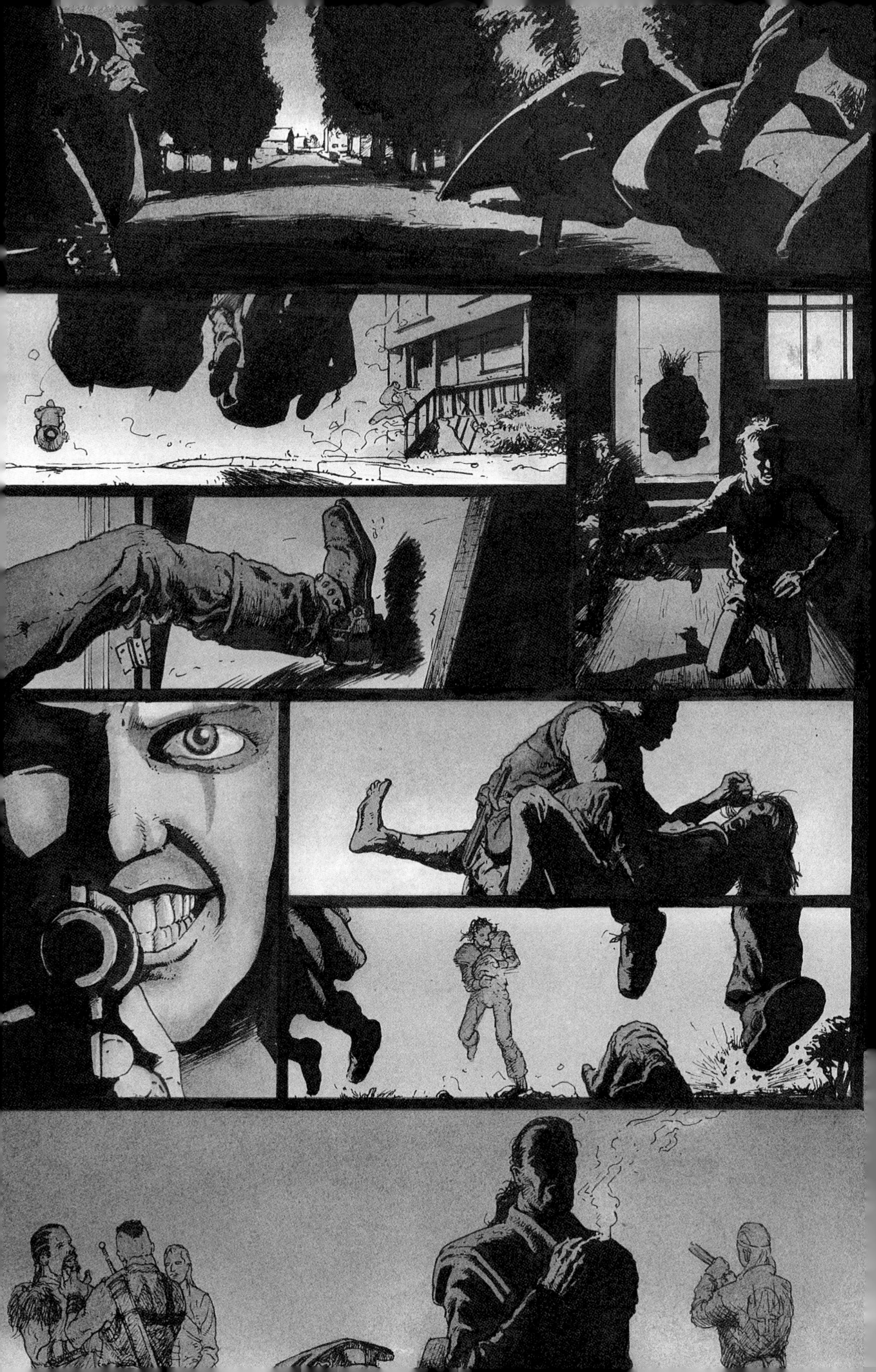

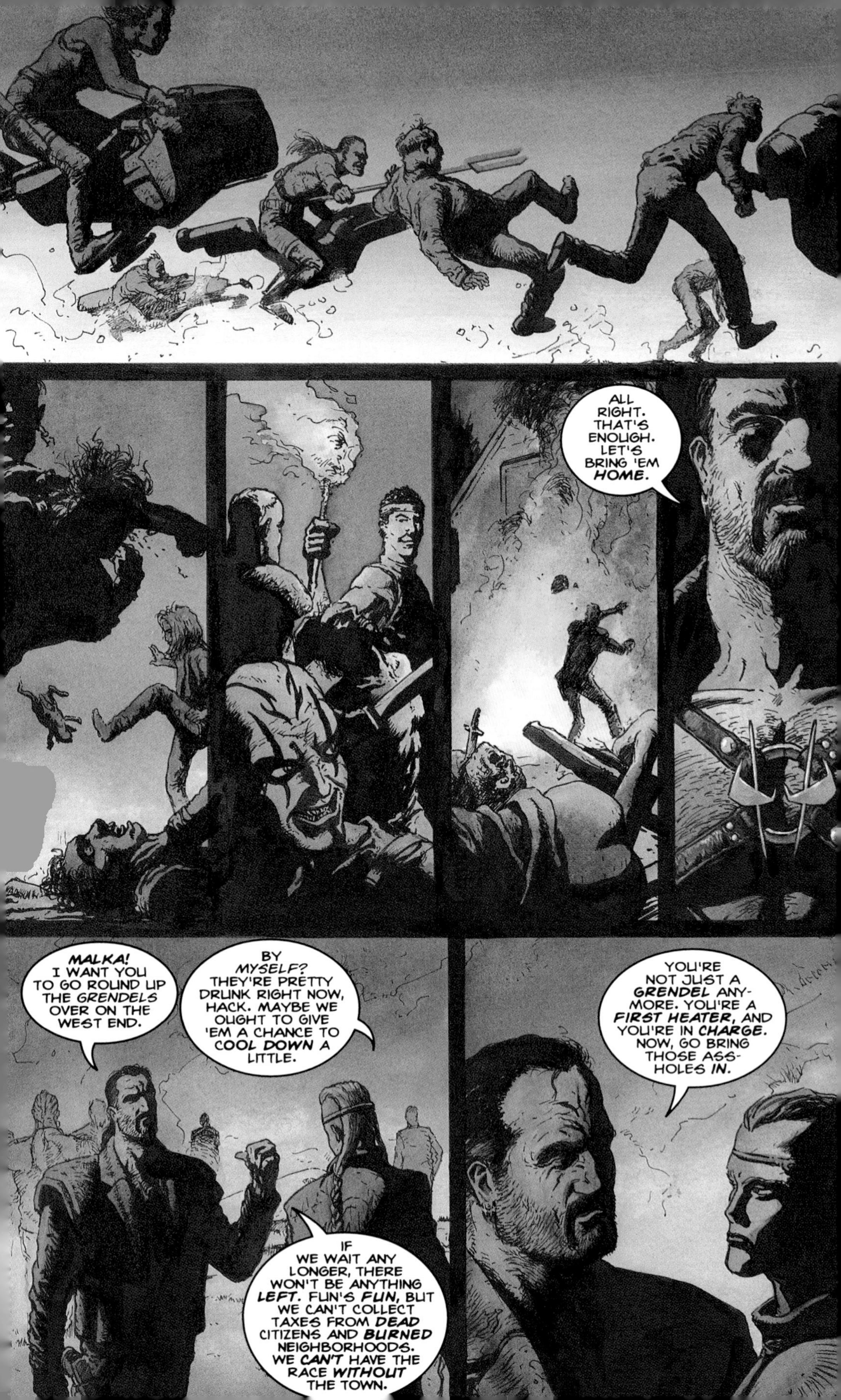
ALL RIGHT. THAT'S ENOUGH. LET'S BRING 'EM HOME.
MALKA! I WANT YOU TO GO ROUND UP THE GRENDELS OVER ON THE WEST END.
BY MYSELF? THEY'RE PRETTY DRUNK RIGHT NOW, HACK. MAYBE WE OUGHT TO GIVE 'EM A CHANCE TO COOL DOWN A LITTLE.
IF WE WAIT ANY LONGER, THERE WON'T BE ANYTHING LEFT. FUN'S FUN, BUT WE CAN'T COLLECT TAXES FROM DEAD CITIZENS AND BURNED NEIGHBORHOODS. WE CAN'T HAVE THE RACE WITHOUT THE TOWN.
YOU'RE NOT JUST A GRENDEL ANYMORE. YOU'RE A FIRST HEATER, AND YOU'RE IN CHARGE. NOW, GO BRING THOSE ASSHOLES IN.

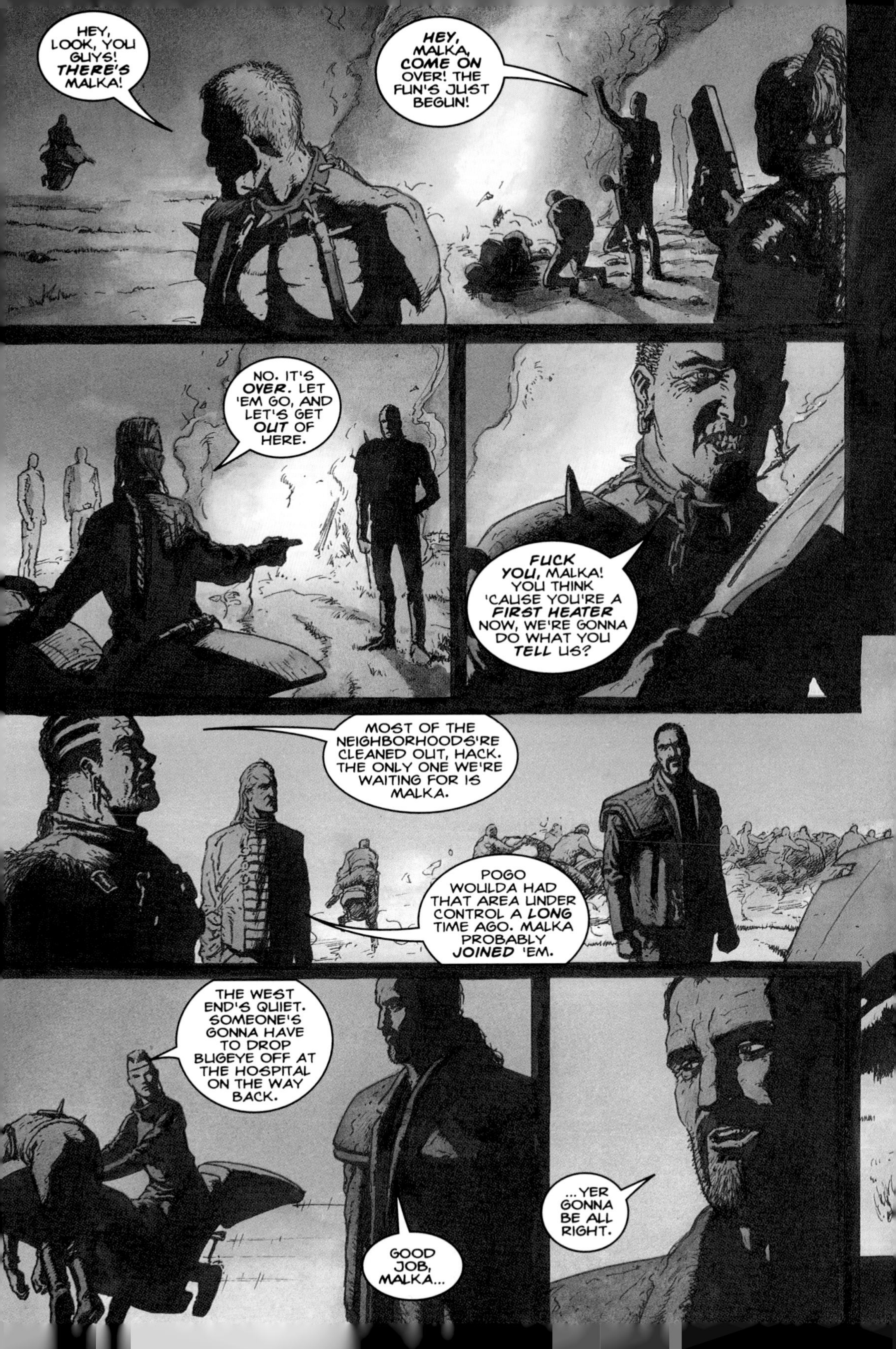
HEY, LOOK, YOU GUYS! THERE'S MALKA!
HEY, MALKA, COME ON OVER! THE FUN'S JUST BEGUN!
NO. IT'S OVER. LET 'EM GO, AND LET'S GET OUT OF HERE.
FUCK YOU, MALKA! YOU THINK 'CAUSE YOU'RE A FIRST HEATER NOW, WE'RE GONNA DO WHAT YOU TELL US?
MOST OF THE NEIGHBORHOODS'RE CLEANED OUT, HACK. THE ONLY ONE WE'RE WAITING FOR IS MALKA.
POGO WOULDA HAD THAT AREA UNDER CONTROL A LONG TIME AGO. MALKA PROBABLY JOINED 'EM.
THE WEST END'S QUIET. SOMEONE'S GONNA HAVE TO DROP BUGEYE OFF AT THE HOSPITAL ON THE WAY BACK.
GOOD JOB, MALKA...
...YER GONNA BE ALL RIGHT.

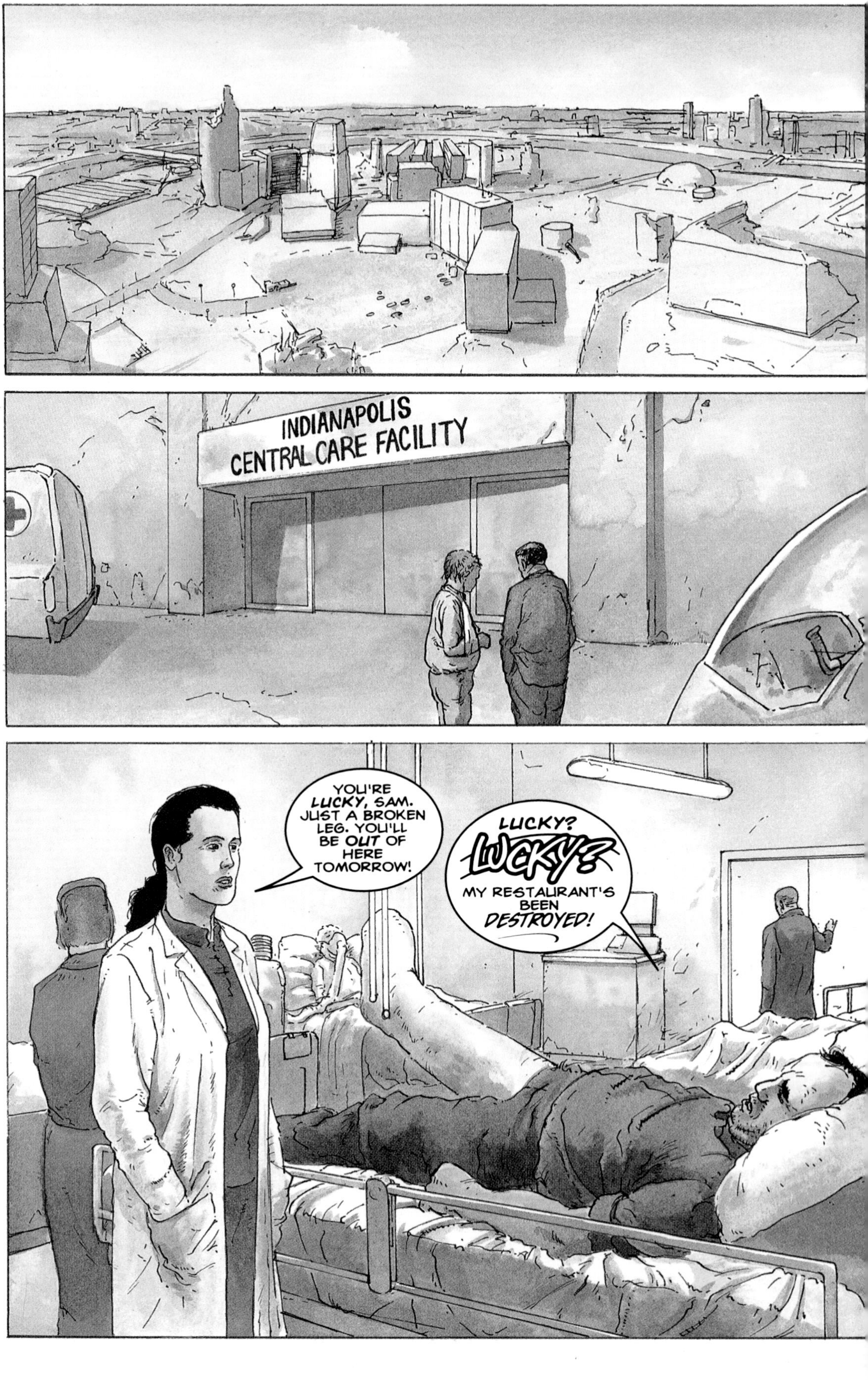
INDIANAPOLIS
CENTRAL CARE FACILITY
YOU'RE LUCKY, SAM. JUST A BROKEN LEG. YOU'LL BE OUT OF HERE TOMORROW!
LUCKY? LUCKY?
MY RESTAURANT'S BEEN DESTROYED!

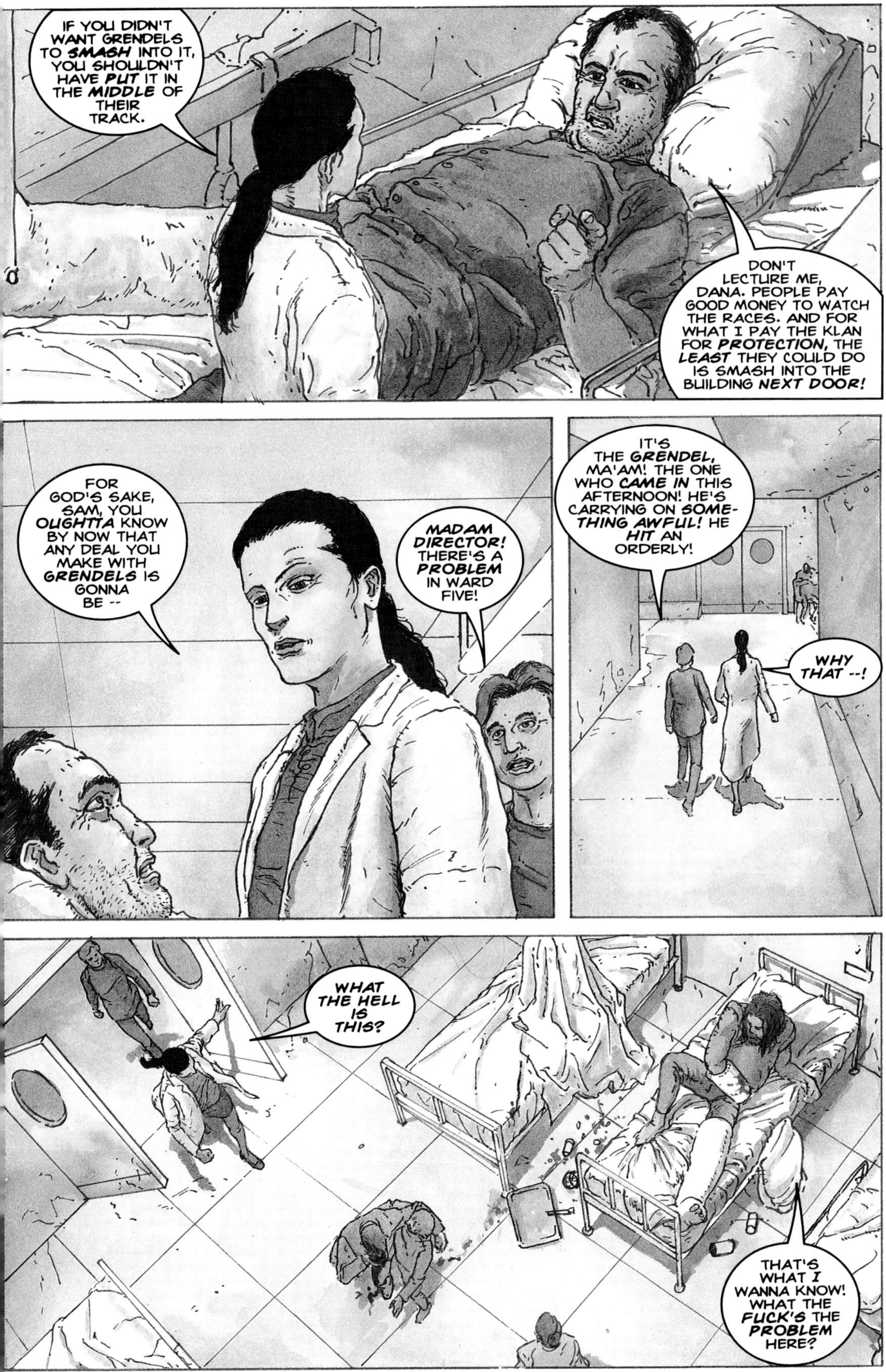
IF YOU DIDN'T WANT GRENDELS TO SMASH INTO IT, YOU SHOULDN'T HAVE PUT IT IN THE MIDDLE OF THEIR TRACK.
DON'T LECTURE ME, DANA. PEOPLE PAY GOOD MONEY TO WATCH THE RACES. AND FOR WHAT I PAY THE KLAN FOR PROTECTION, THE LEAST THEY COULD DO IS SMASH INTO THE BUILDING NEXT DOOR!
FOR GOD'S SAKE, SAM, YOU OUGHTTA KNOW BY NOW THAT ANY DEAL YOU MAKE WITH GRENDELS IS GONNA BE --
MADAM DIRECTOR! THERE'S A PROBLEM IN WARD FIVE!
IT'S THE GRENDEL, MA'AM! THE ONE WHO CAME IN THIS AFTERNOON! HE'S CARRYING ON SOME-THING AWFUL! HE HIT AN ORDERLY!
WHY THAT --!
WHAT THE HELL IS THIS?
THAT'S WHAT I WANNA KNOW! WHAT THE FUCK'S THE PROBLEM HERE?

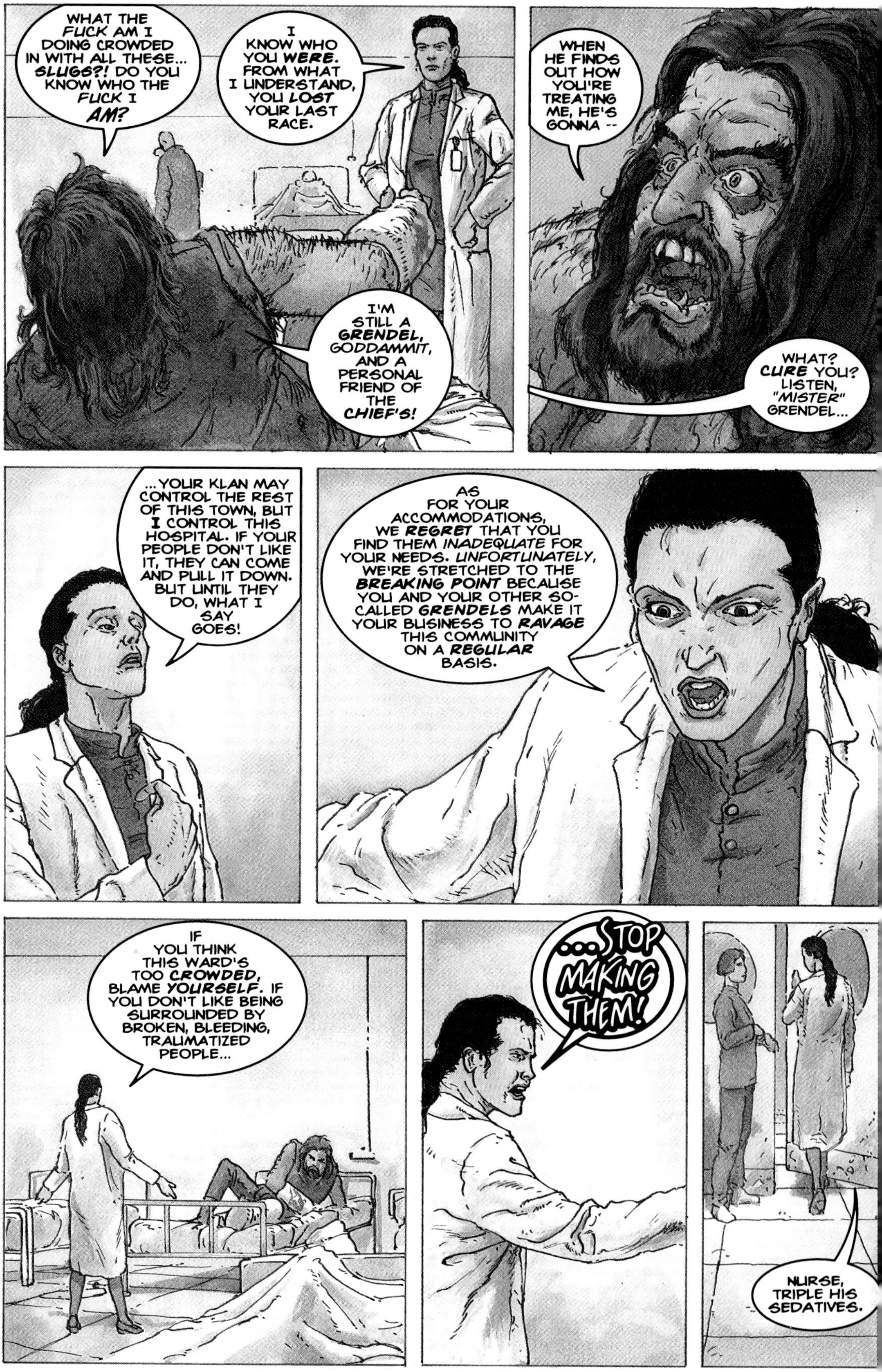

WHAT THE FUCK AM I DOING CROWDED IN WITH ALL THESE... SLUGS?! DO YOU KNOW WHO THE FUCK I AM?
I KNOW WHO YOU WERE. FROM WHAT I UNDERSTAND, YOU LOST YOUR LAST RACE.
I'M STILL A GRENDEL, GODDAMMIT, AND A PERSONAL FRIEND OF THE CHIEF'S!
WHEN HE FINDS OUT HOW YOU'RE TREATING ME, HE'S GONNA --
WHAT? CURE YOU? LISTEN, "MISTER" GRENDEL...
...YOUR KLAN MAY CONTROL THE REST OF THIS TOWN, BUT I CONTROL THIS HOSPITAL. IF YOUR PEOPLE DON'T LIKE IT, THEY CAN COME AND PULL IT DOWN. BUT UNTIL THEY DO, WHAT I SAY GOES!
AS FOR YOUR ACCOMMODATIONS, WE REGRET THAT YOU FIND THEM INADEQUATE FOR YOUR NEEDS. UNFORTUNATELY, WE'RE STRETCHED TO THE BREAKING POINT BECAUSE YOU AND YOUR OTHER SO-CALLED GRENDELS MAKE IT YOUR BUSINESS TO RAVAGE THIS COMMUNITY ON A REGULAR BASIS.
IF YOU THINK THIS WARD'S TOO CROWDED, BLAME YOURSELF. IF YOU DON'T LIKE BEING SURROUNDED BY BROKEN, BLEEDING, TRAUMATIZED PEOPLE...
...STOP MAKING THEM!
NURSE, TRIPLE HIS SEDATIVES.

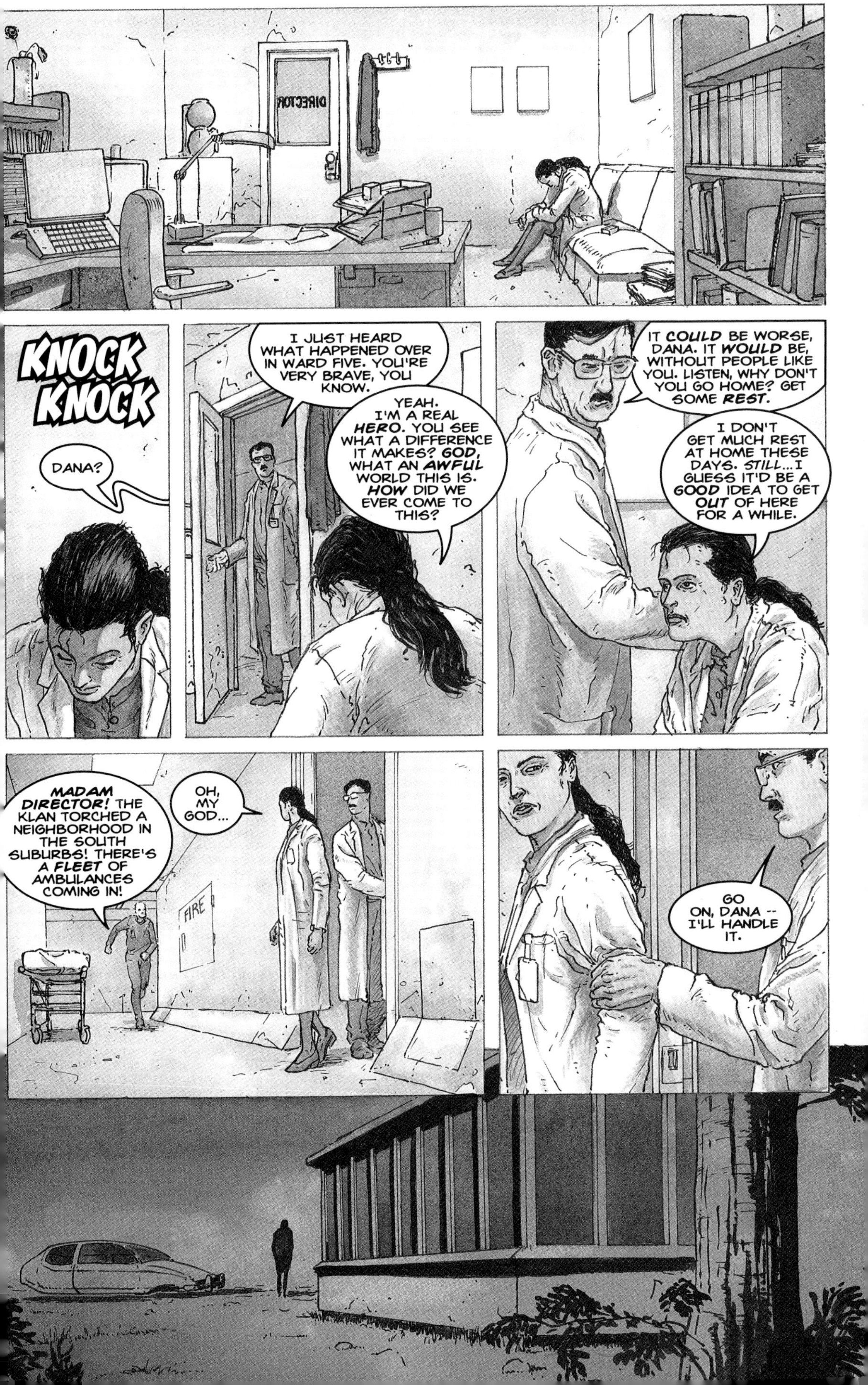
KNOCK KNOCK
DANA?
I JUST HEARD WHAT HAPPENED OVER IN WARD FIVE. YOU'RE VERY BRAVE, YOU KNOW.
YEAH. I'M A REAL HERO. YOU SEE WHAT A DIFFERENCE IT MAKES? GOD, WHAT AN AWFUL WORLD THIS IS. HOW DID WE EVER COME TO THIS?
IT COULD BE WORSE, DANA. IT WOULD BE, WITHOUT PEOPLE LIKE YOU. LISTEN, WHY DON'T YOU GO HOME? GET SOME REST.
I DON'T GET MUCH REST AT HOME THESE DAYS. STILL...I GUESS IT'D BE A GOOD IDEA TO GET OUT OF HERE FOR A WHILE.
MADAM DIRECTOR! THE KLAN TORCHED A NEIGHBORHOOD IN THE SOUTH SUBURBS! THERE'S A FLEET OF AMBULANCES COMING IN!
OH, MY GOD...
GO ON, DANA -- I'LL HANDLE IT.

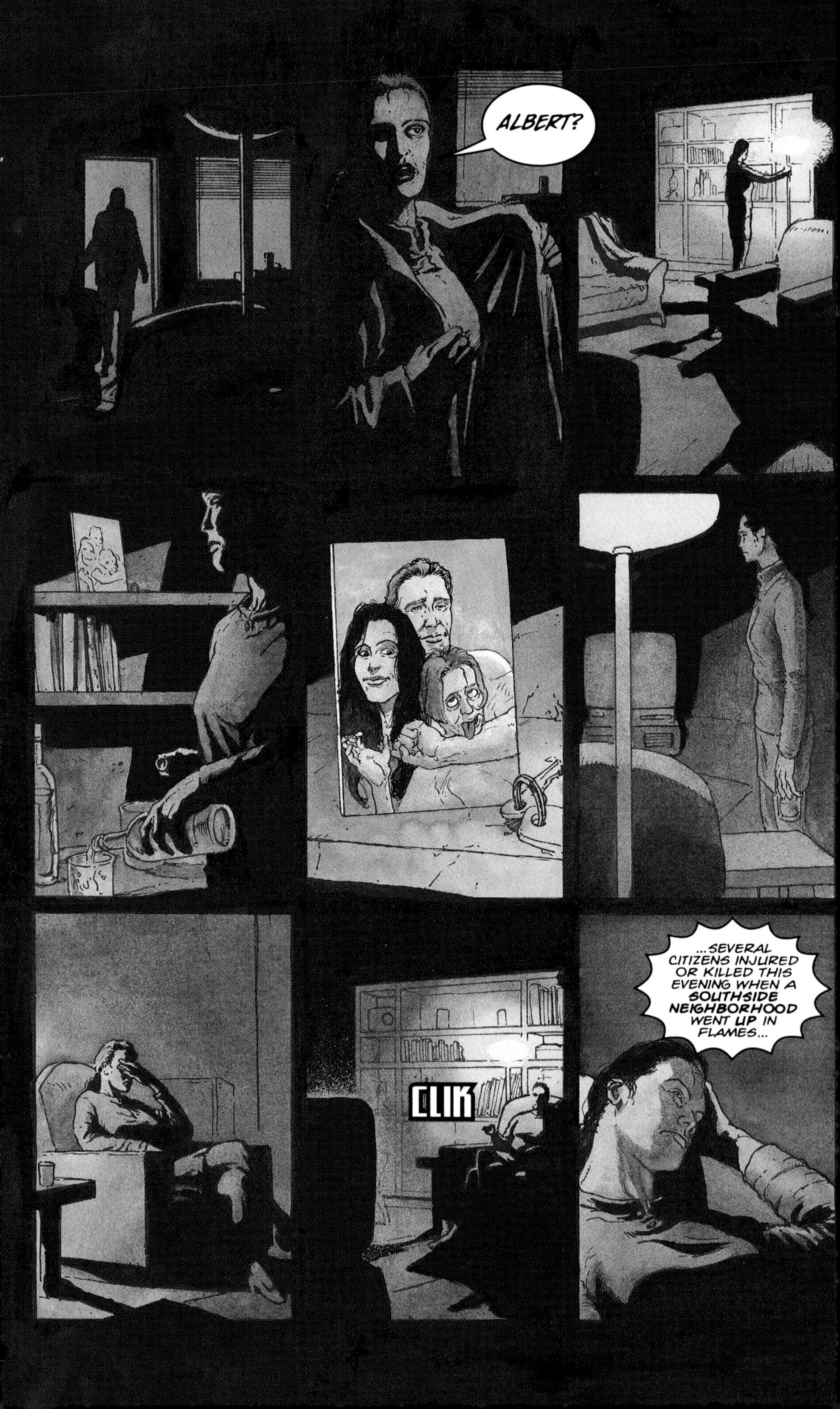
ALBERT?
CLIK
...SEVERAL CITIZENS INJURED OR KILLED THIS EVENING WHEN A SOUTHSIDE NEIGHBORHOOD WENT UP IN FLAMES...

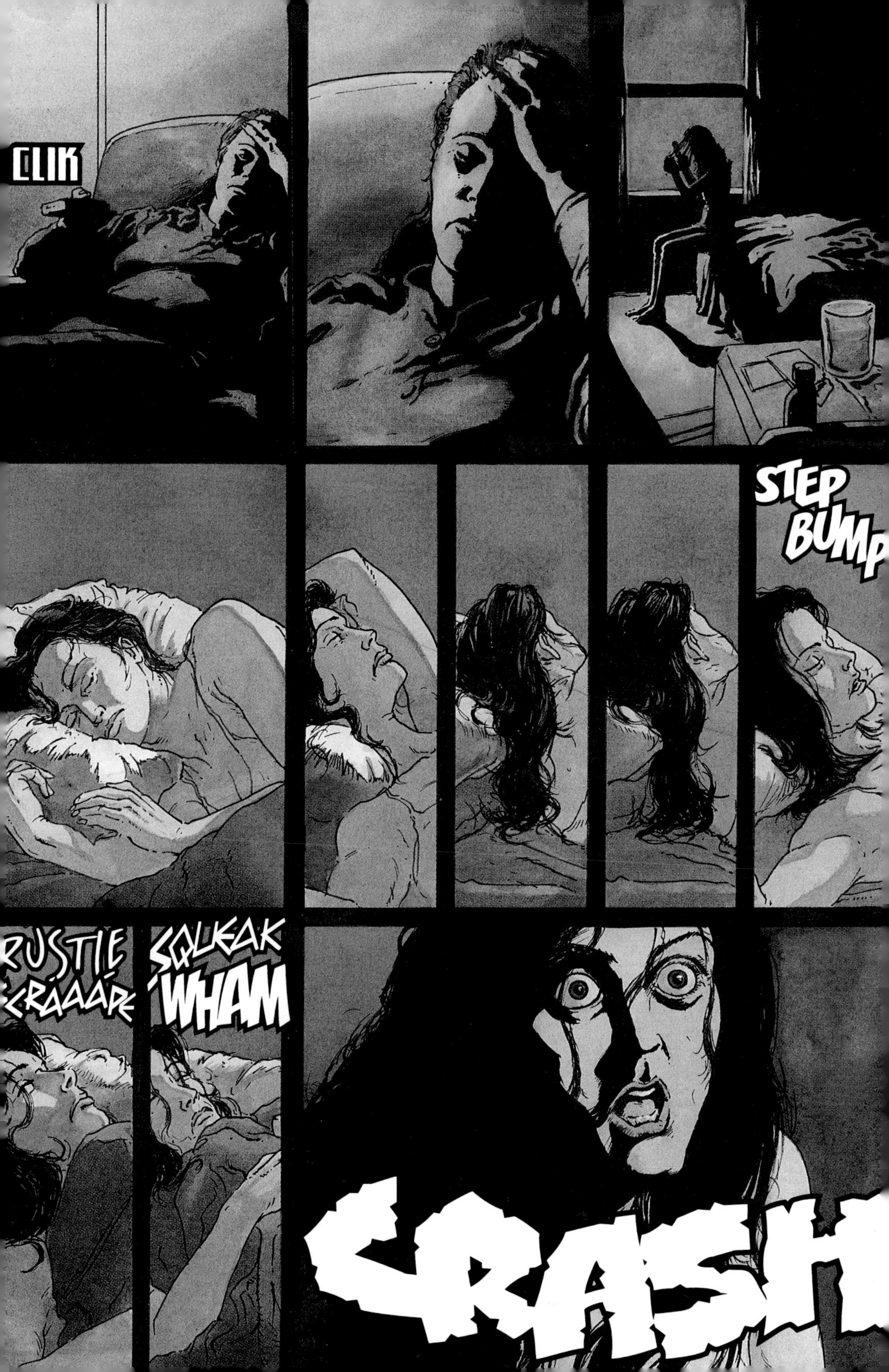
CLIK
STEP
BUMP
RUSTLE
CRAAARE
SQUEAK
WHAM
CRASH

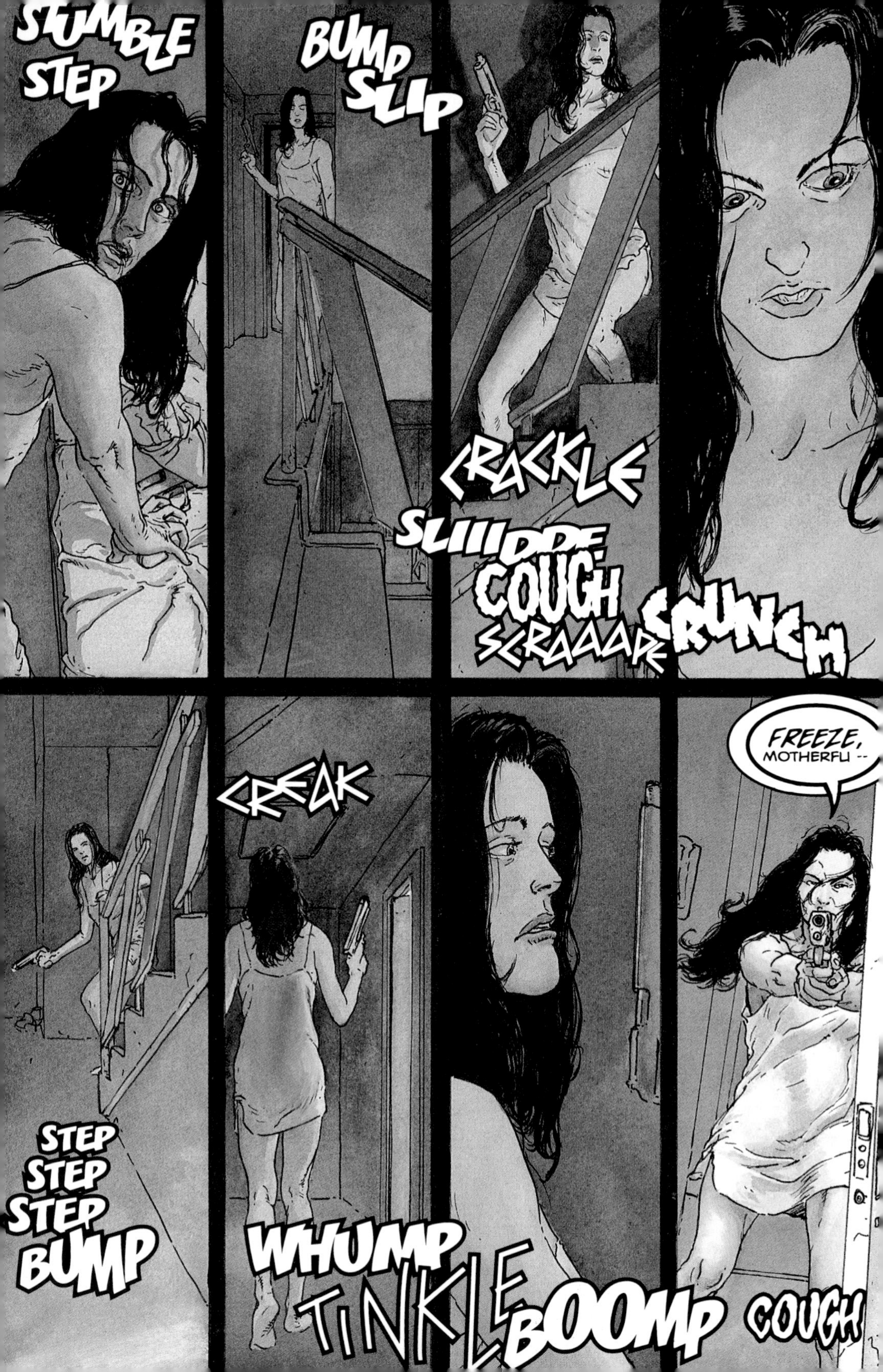
STUMBLE
STEP
BUMP
SLIP
CRACKLE
SLIIIDDE
COUGH
SCRAAAPE
CRUNCH
CREAK
STEP
STEP
STEP
BUMP
WHUMP
TINKLE
BOOOMP
FREEZE, MOTHERFU --
COUGH

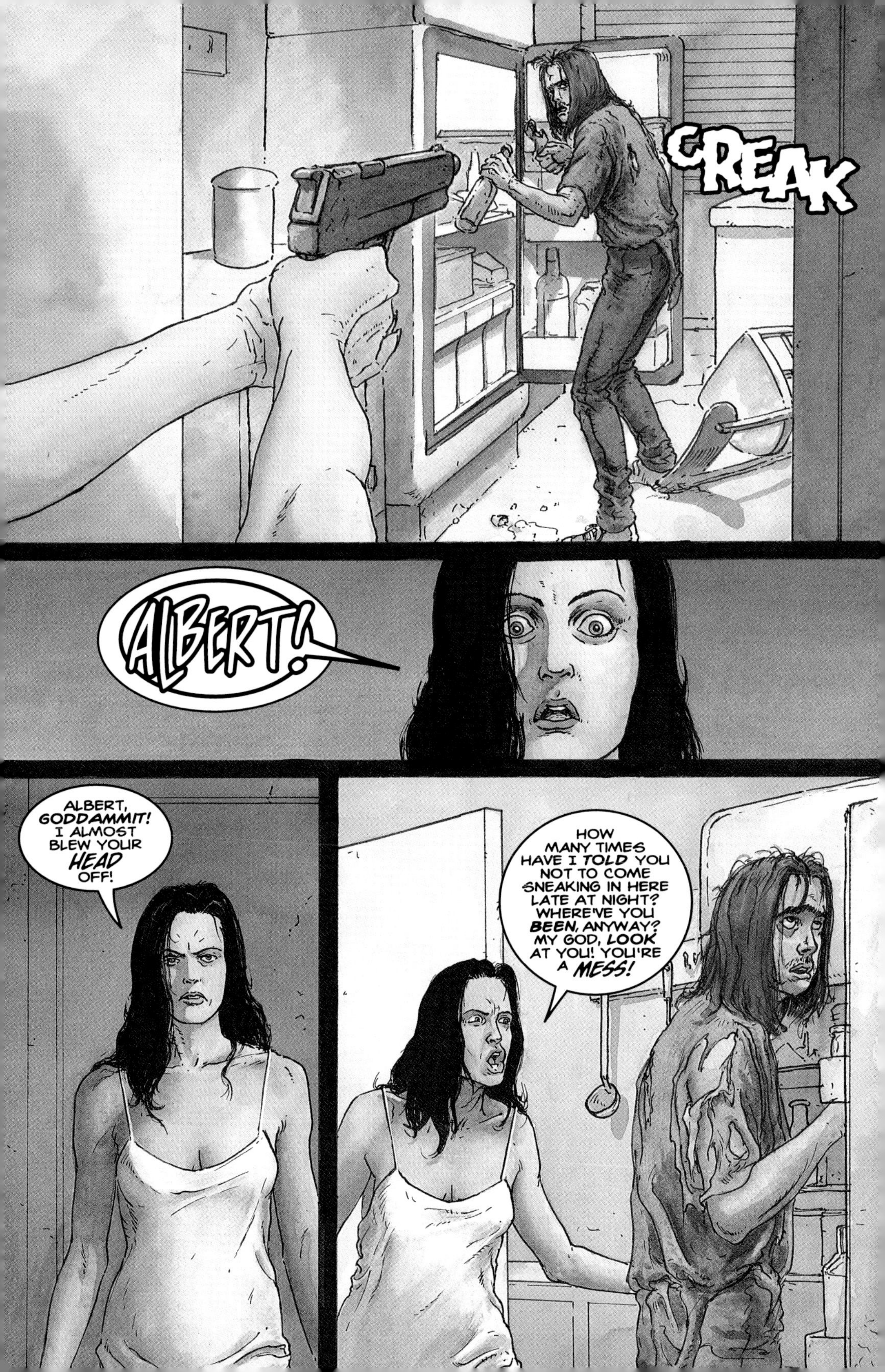
CREAK
ALBERT!
ALBERT, GODDAMMIT! I ALMOST BLEW YOUR HEAD OFF!
HOW MANY TIMES HAVE I TOLD YOU NOT TO COME SNEAKING IN HERE LATE AT NIGHT? WHERE'VE YOU BEEN, ANYWAY? MY GOD, LOOK AT YOU! YOU'RE A MESS!

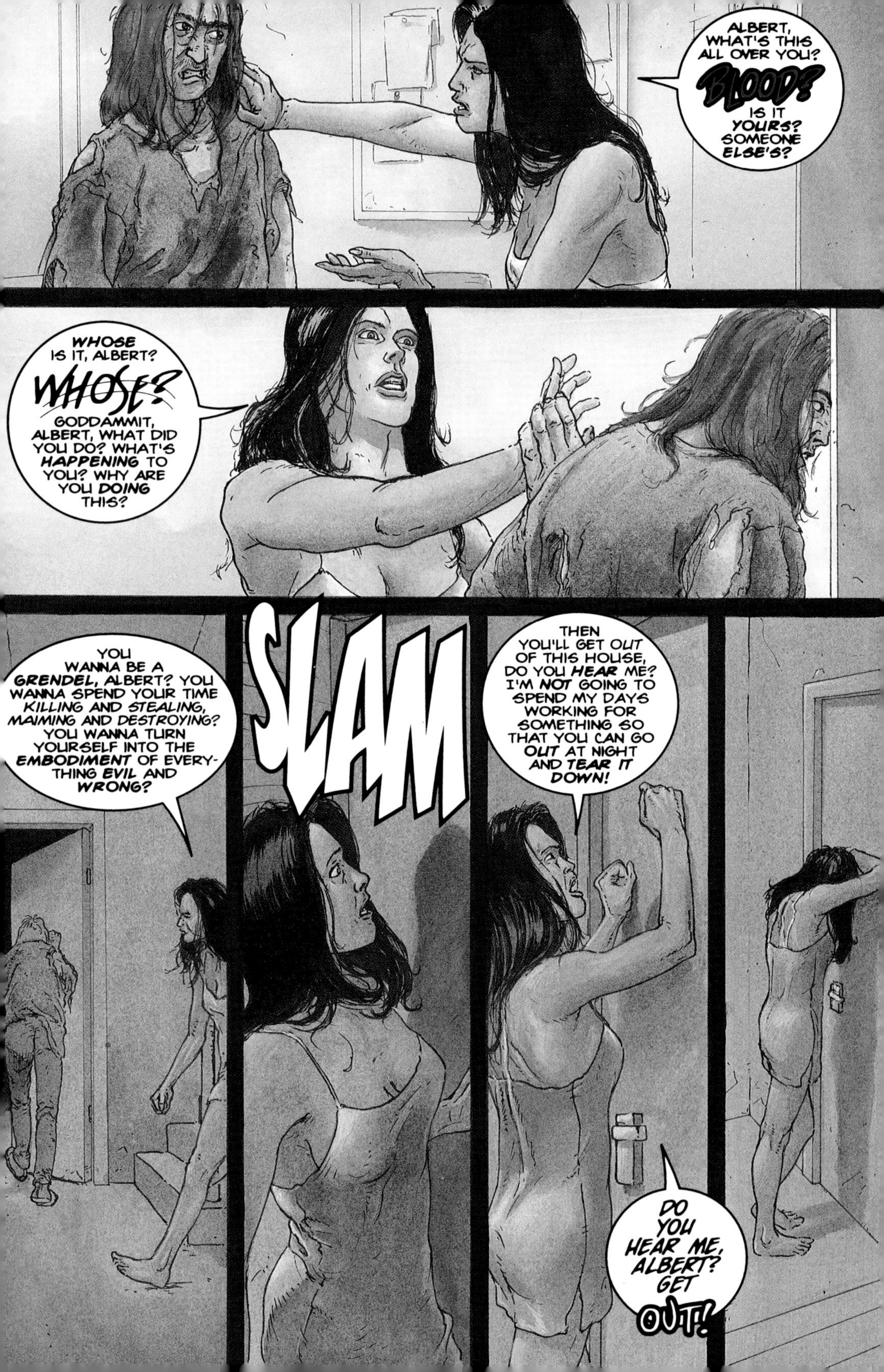

ALBERT, WHAT'S THIS ALL OVER YOU? BLOOD? IS IT YOURS? SOMEONE ELSE'S?
WHOSE IS IT, ALBERT? WHOSE? GODDAMMIT, ALBERT, WHAT DID YOU DO? WHAT'S HAPPENING TO YOU? WHY ARE YOU DOING THIS?
YOU WANNA BE A GRENDEL, ALBERT? YOU WANNA SPEND YOUR TIME KILLING AND STEALING, MAIMING AND DESTROYING? YOU WANNA TURN YOURSELF INTO THE EMBODIMENT OF EVERY-THING EVIL AND WRONG?
SLAM
THEN YOU'LL GET OUT OF THIS HOUSE, DO YOU HEAR ME? I'M NOT GOING TO SPEND MY DAYS WORKING FOR SOMETHING SO THAT YOU CAN GO OUT AT NIGHT AND TEAR IT DOWN!
DO YOU HEAR ME, ALBERT? GET OUT!

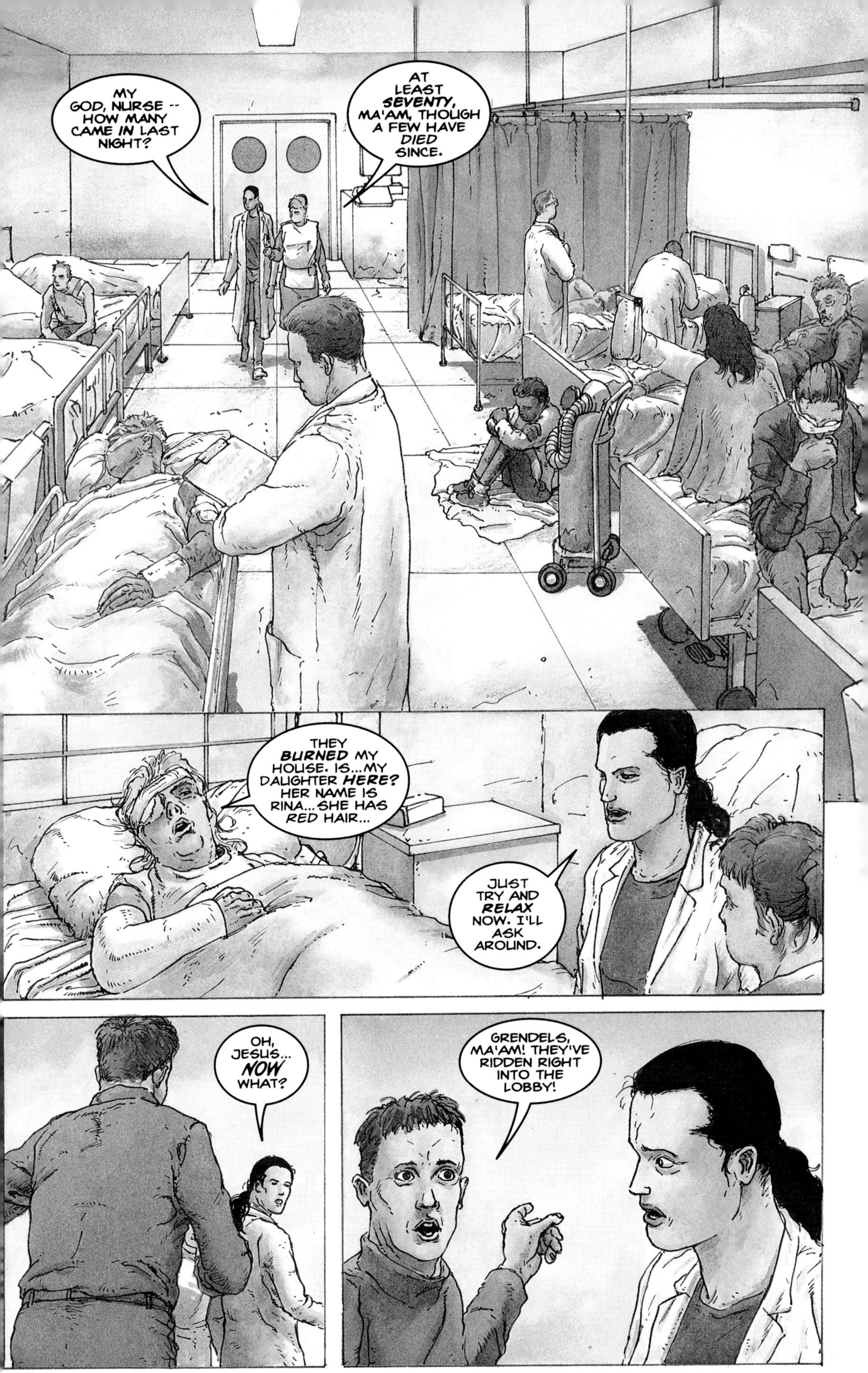

MY GOD, NURSE -- HOW MANY CAME *IN* LAST NIGHT?
AT LEAST *SEVENTY,* MA'AM, THOUGH A FEW HAVE *DIED* SINCE.
THEY *BURNED* MY HOUSE. IS...MY DAUGHTER *HERE?* HER NAME IS RINA...SHE HAS *RED* HAIR...
JUST TRY AND *RELAX* NOW. I'LL ASK AROUND.
OH, JESUS... *NOW* WHAT?
GRENDELS, MA'AM! THEY'VE RIDDEN RIGHT INTO THE LOBBY!

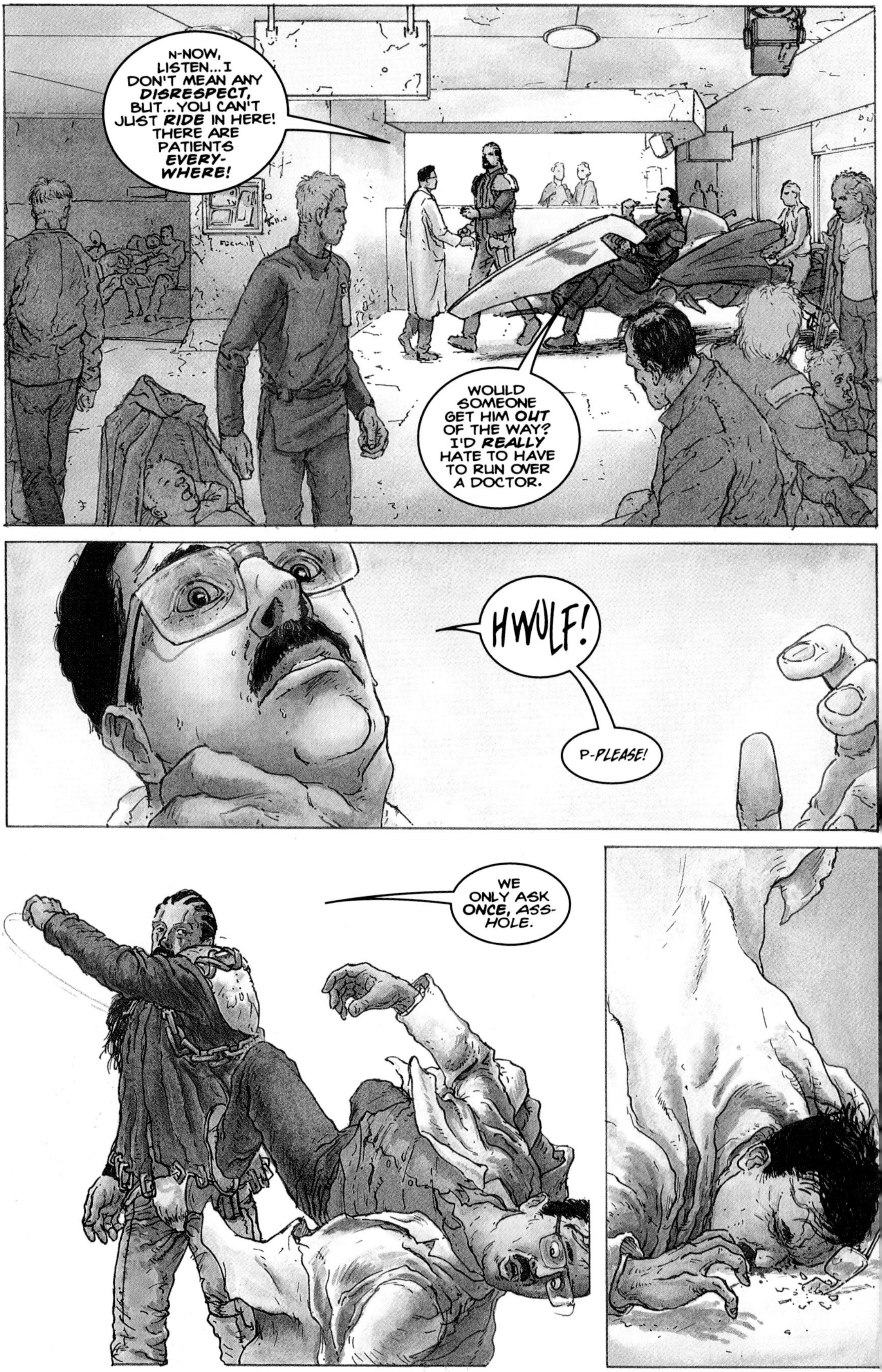
N-NOW, LISTEN... I DON'T MEAN ANY DISRESPECT, BUT... YOU CAN'T JUST RIDE IN HERE! THERE ARE PATIENTS EVERY-WHERE!
WOULD SOMEONE GET HIM OUT OF THE WAY? I'D REALLY HATE TO HAVE TO RUN OVER A DOCTOR.
HWULF!
P-PLEASE!
WE ONLY ASK ONCE, ASS-HOLE.

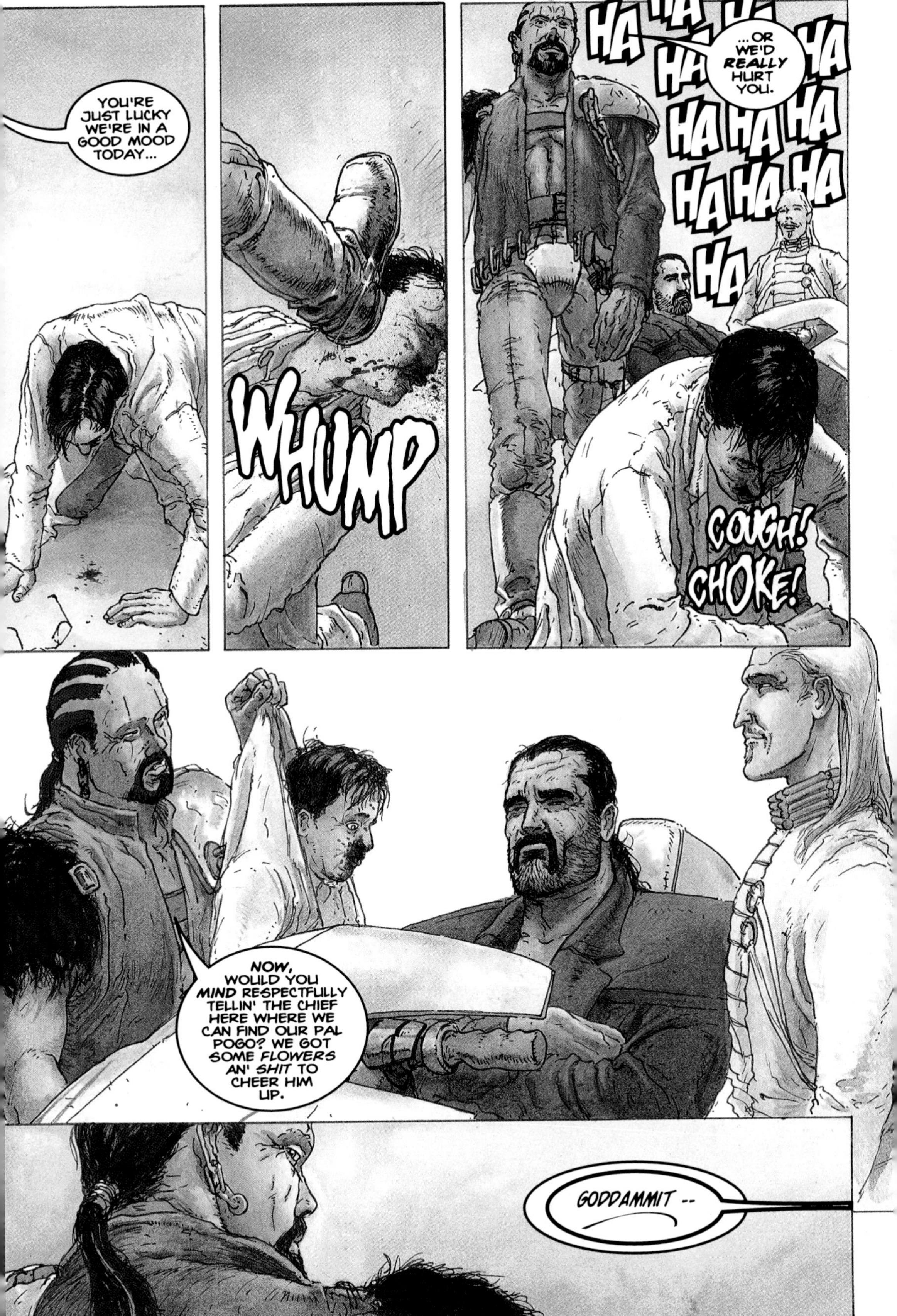
YOU'RE JUST LUCKY WE'RE IN A GOOD MOOD TODAY...
WHUMP
HA HA HA HA HA HA HA HA HA HA HA HA
...OR WE'D REALLY HURT YOU.
COUGH! CHOKE!
NOW, WOULD YOU MIND RESPECTFULLY TELLIN' THE CHIEF HERE WHERE WE CAN FIND OUR PAL POGO? WE GOT SOME FLOWERS AN' SHIT TO CHEER HIM UP.
GODDAMMIT --

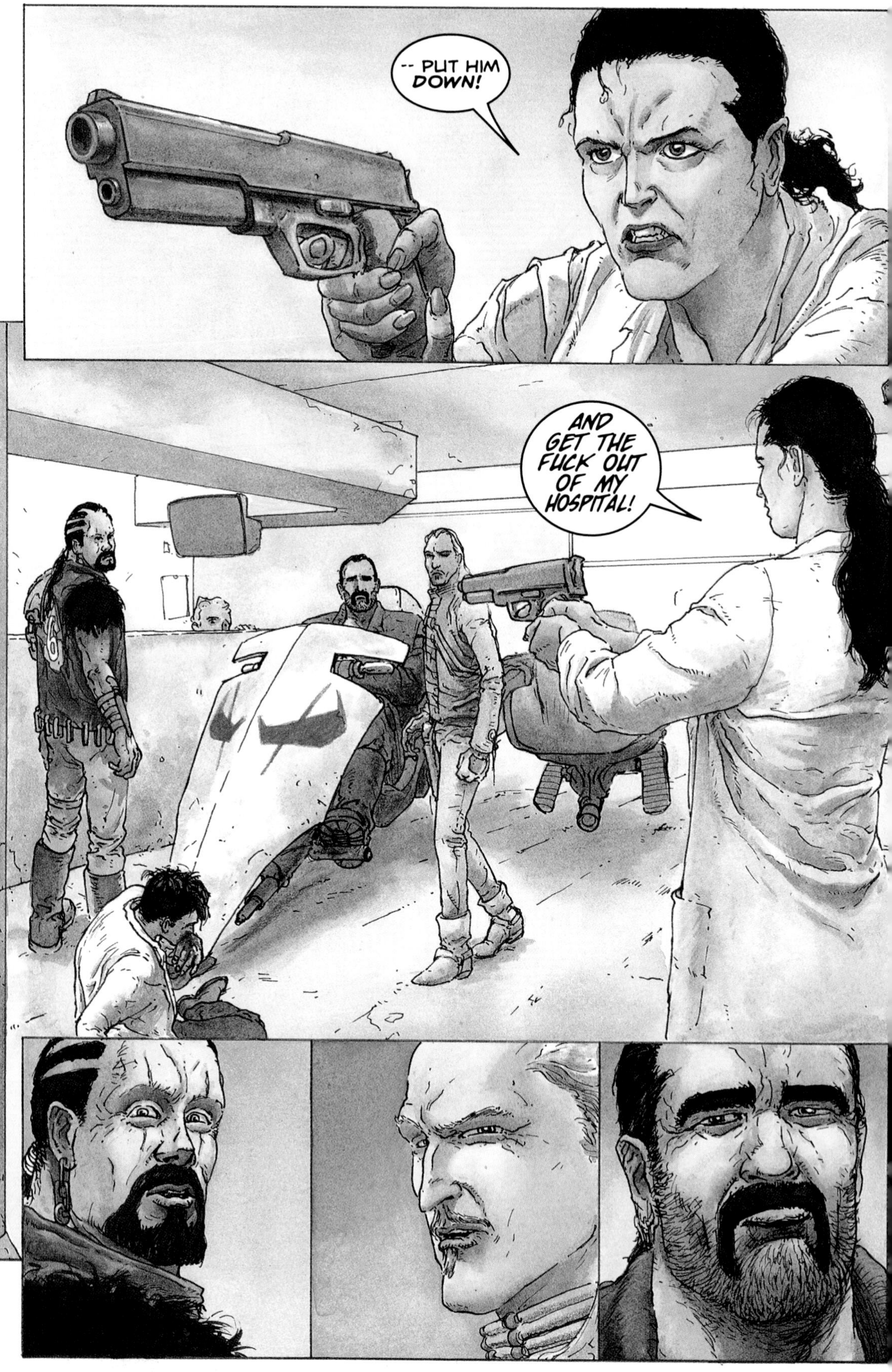
-- PUT HIM DOWN!
AND GET THE FUCK OUT OF MY HOSPITAL!

Chapter Two

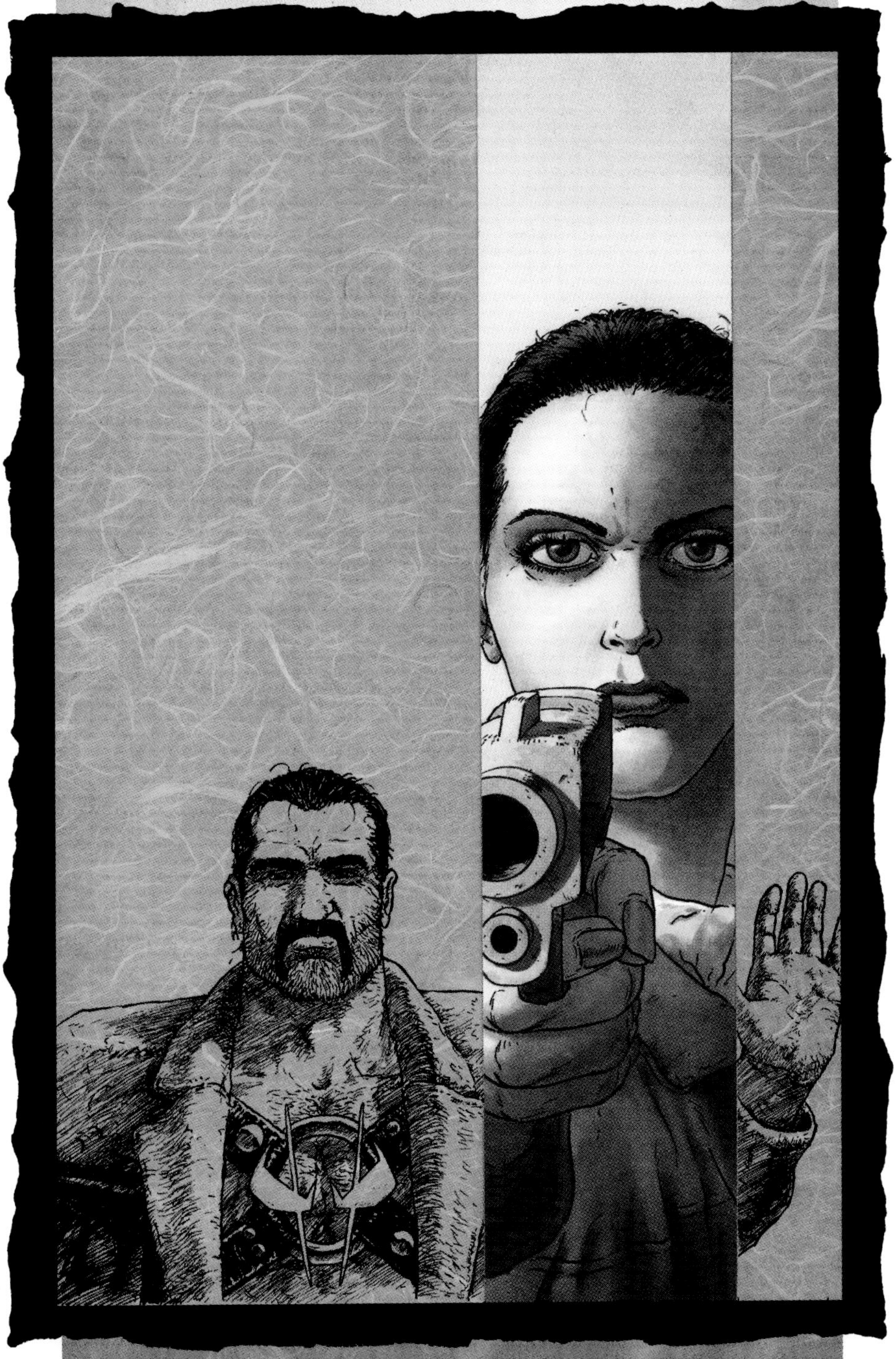

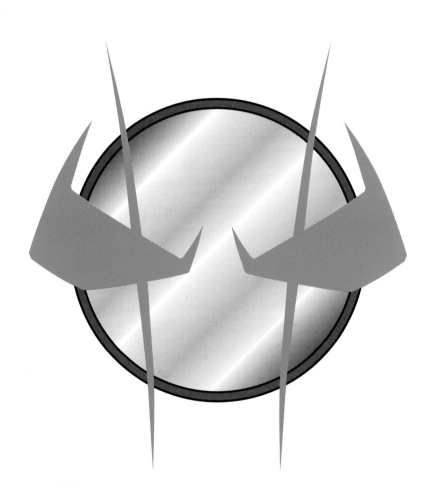

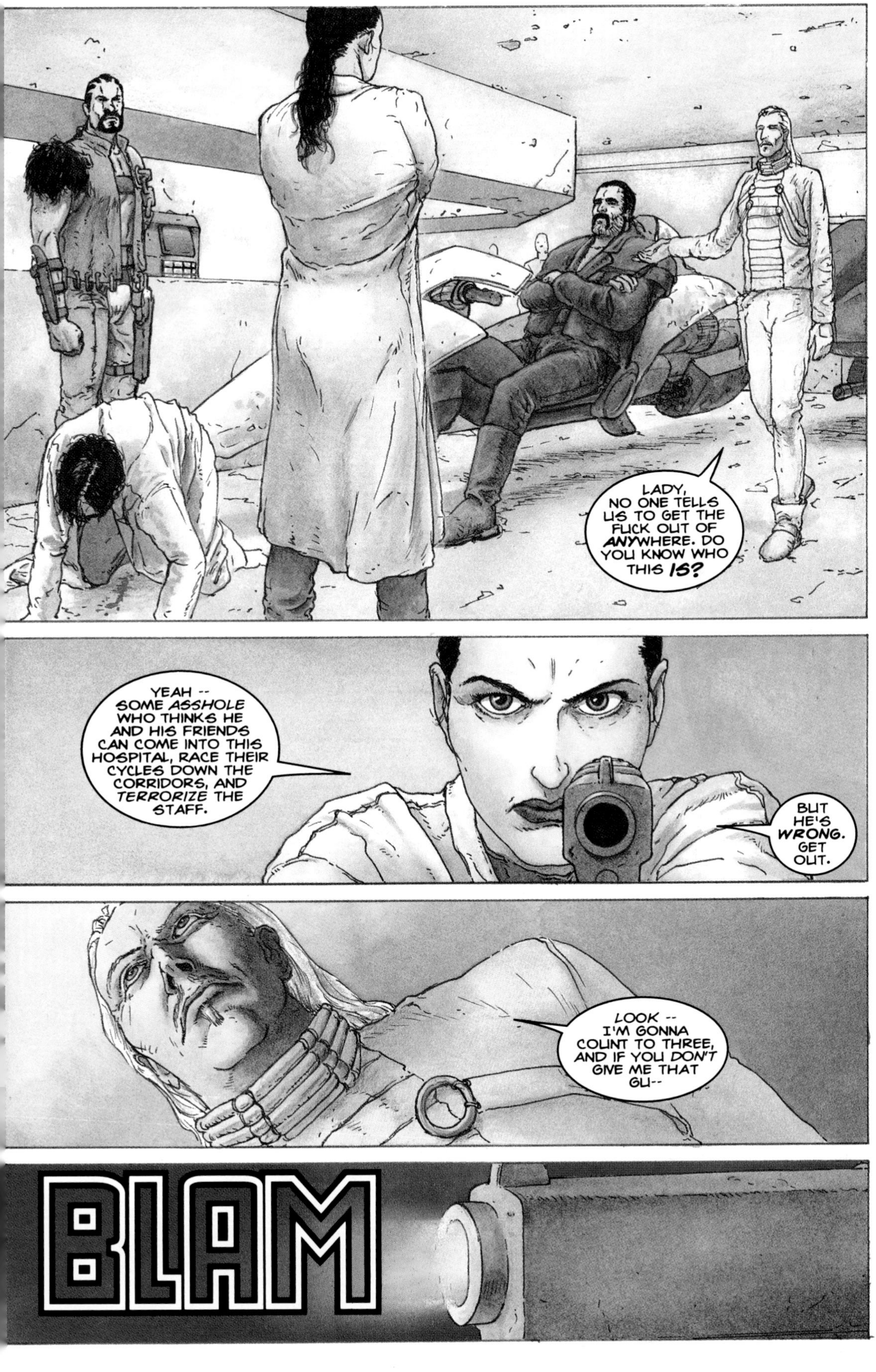
LADY, NO ONE TELLS US TO GET THE FUCK OUT OF ANYWHERE. DO YOU KNOW WHO THIS IS?
YEAH -- SOME ASSHOLE WHO THINKS HE AND HIS FRIENDS CAN COME INTO THIS HOSPITAL, RACE THEIR CYCLES DOWN THE CORRIDORS, AND TERRORIZE THE STAFF.
BUT HE'S WRONG. GET OUT.
LOOK -- I'M GONNA COUNT TO THREE, AND IF YOU DON'T GIVE ME THAT GU--
BLAM

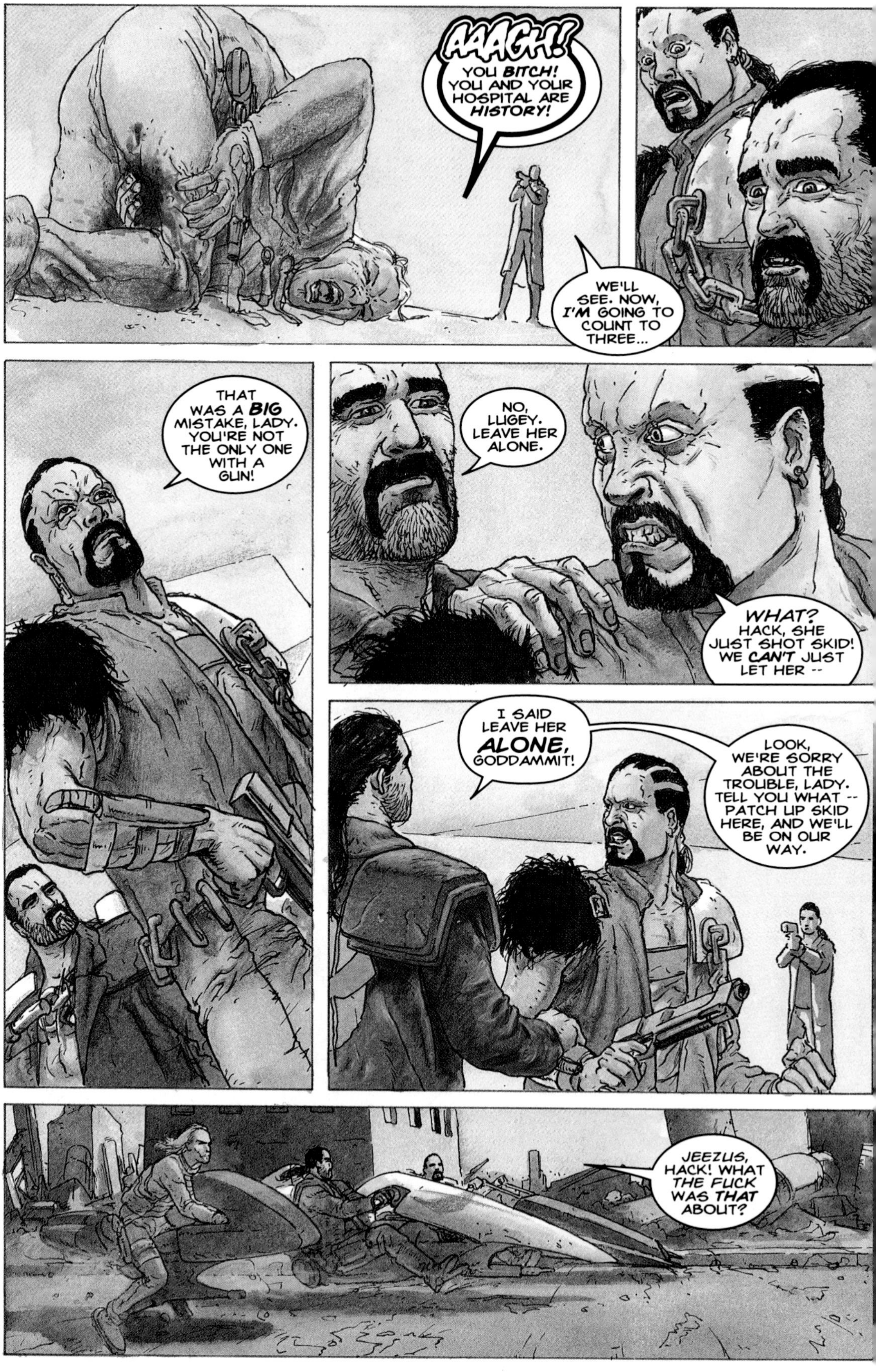
AAAGH!
YOU BITCH! YOU AND YOUR HOSPITAL ARE HISTORY!
WE'LL SEE. NOW, I'M GOING TO COUNT TO THREE...
THAT WAS A BIG MISTAKE, LADY. YOU'RE NOT THE ONLY ONE WITH A GUN!
NO, LUGEY. LEAVE HER ALONE.
WHAT? HACK, SHE JUST SHOT SKID! WE CAN'T JUST LET HER --
I SAID LEAVE HER ALONE, GODDAMMIT!
LOOK, WE'RE SORRY ABOUT THE TROUBLE, LADY. TELL YOU WHAT -- PATCH UP SKID HERE, AND WE'LL BE ON OUR WAY.
JEEZUS, HACK! WHAT THE FUCK WAS THAT ABOUT?

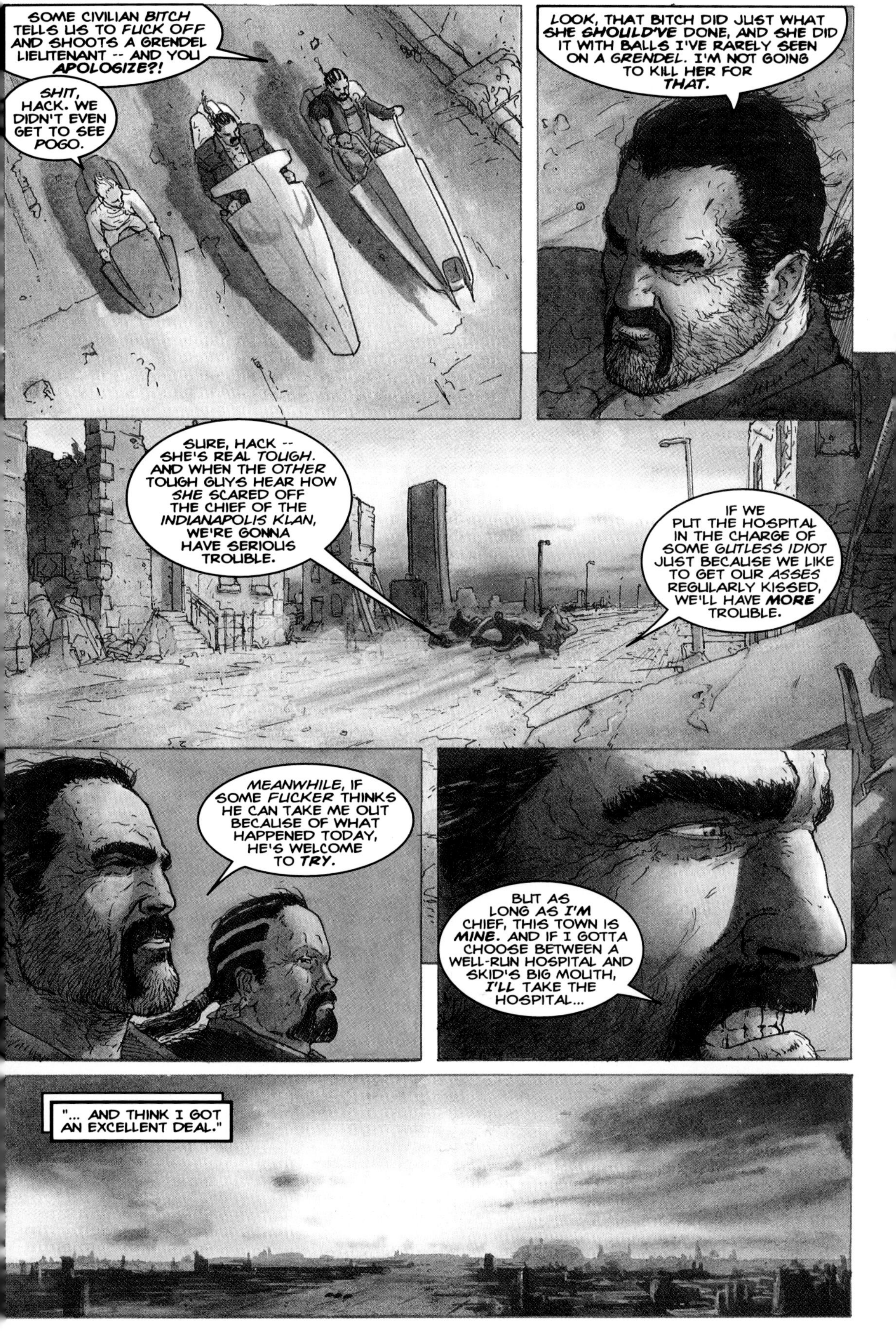
SOME CIVILIAN BITCH TELLS US TO FUCK OFF AND SHOOTS A GRENDEL LIEUTENANT -- AND YOU APOLOGIZE?!
SHIT, HACK. WE DIDN'T EVEN GET TO SEE POGO.
LOOK, THAT BITCH DID JUST WHAT SHE SHOULD'VE DONE, AND SHE DID IT WITH BALLS I'VE RARELY SEEN ON A GRENDEL. I'M NOT GOING TO KILL HER FOR THAT.
SURE, HACK -- SHE'S REAL TOUGH. AND WHEN THE OTHER TOUGH GUYS HEAR HOW SHE SCARED OFF THE CHIEF OF THE INDIANAPOLIS KLAN, WE'RE GONNA HAVE SERIOUS TROUBLE.
IF WE PUT THE HOSPITAL IN THE CHARGE OF SOME GUTLESS IDIOT JUST BECAUSE WE LIKE TO GET OUR ASSES REGULARLY KISSED, WE'LL HAVE MORE TROUBLE.
MEANWHILE, IF SOME FUCKER THINKS HE CAN TAKE ME OUT BECAUSE OF WHAT HAPPENED TODAY, HE'S WELCOME TO TRY.
BUT AS LONG AS I'M CHIEF, THIS TOWN IS MINE. AND IF I GOTTA CHOOSE BETWEEN A WELL-RUN HOSPITAL AND SKID'S BIG MOUTH, I'LL TAKE THE HOSPITAL...
"... AND THINK I GOT AN EXCELLENT DEAL."

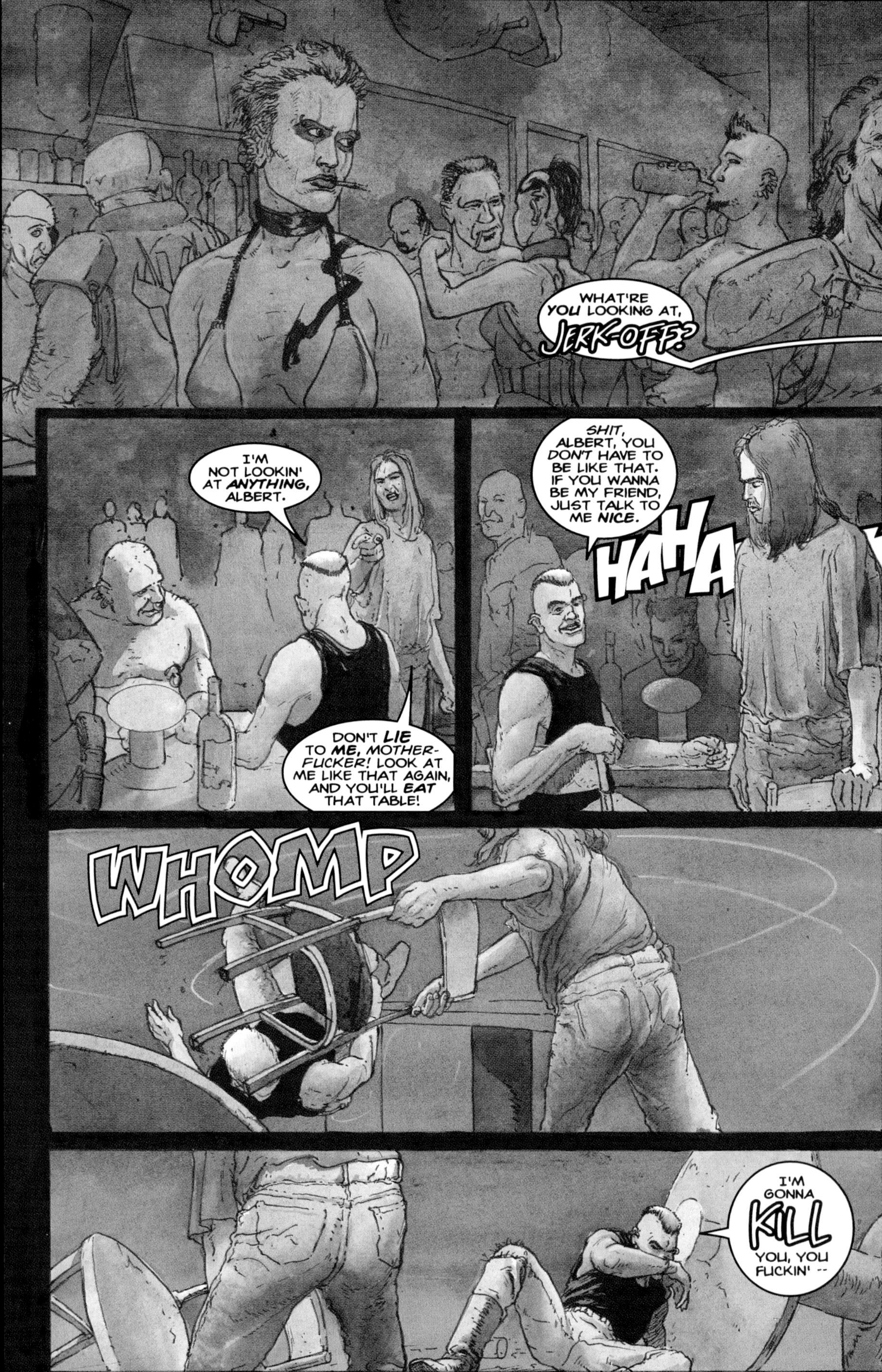
WHAT'RE YOU LOOKING AT, JERK-OFF?
I'M NOT LOOKIN' AT ANYTHING, ALBERT.
DON'T LIE TO ME, MOTHER-FUCKER! LOOK AT ME LIKE THAT AGAIN, AND YOU'LL EAT THAT TABLE!
SHIT, ALBERT, YOU DON'T HAVE TO BE LIKE THAT. IF YOU WANNA BE MY FRIEND, JUST TALK TO ME NICE.
WHOMP
I'M GONNA KILL YOU, YOU FUCKIN' --

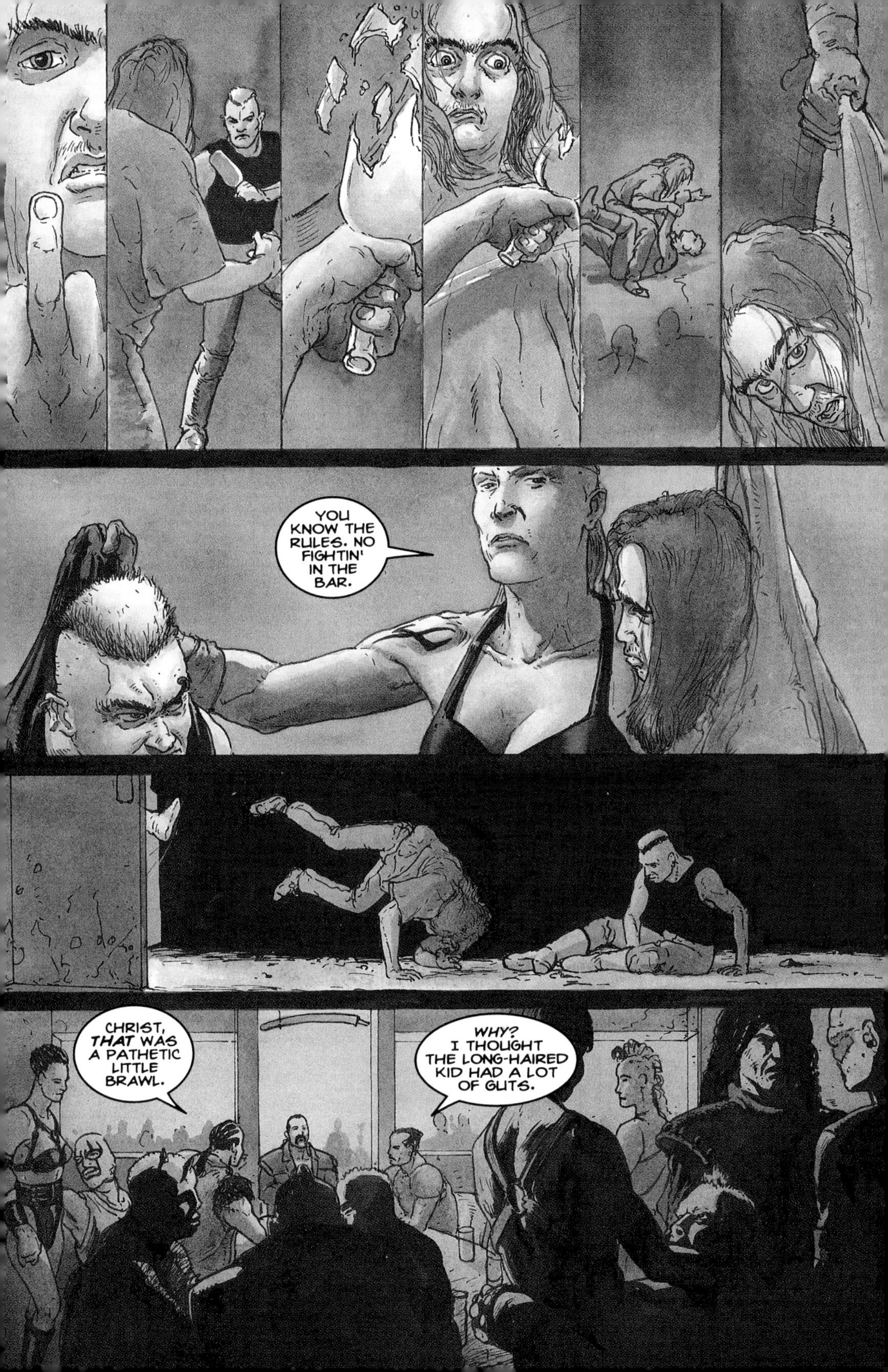
YOU KNOW THE RULES. NO FIGHTIN' IN THE BAR.
CHRIST, *THAT* WAS A PATHETIC LITTLE BRAWL.
WHY? I THOUGHT THE LONG-HAIRED KID HAD A LOT OF GUTS.

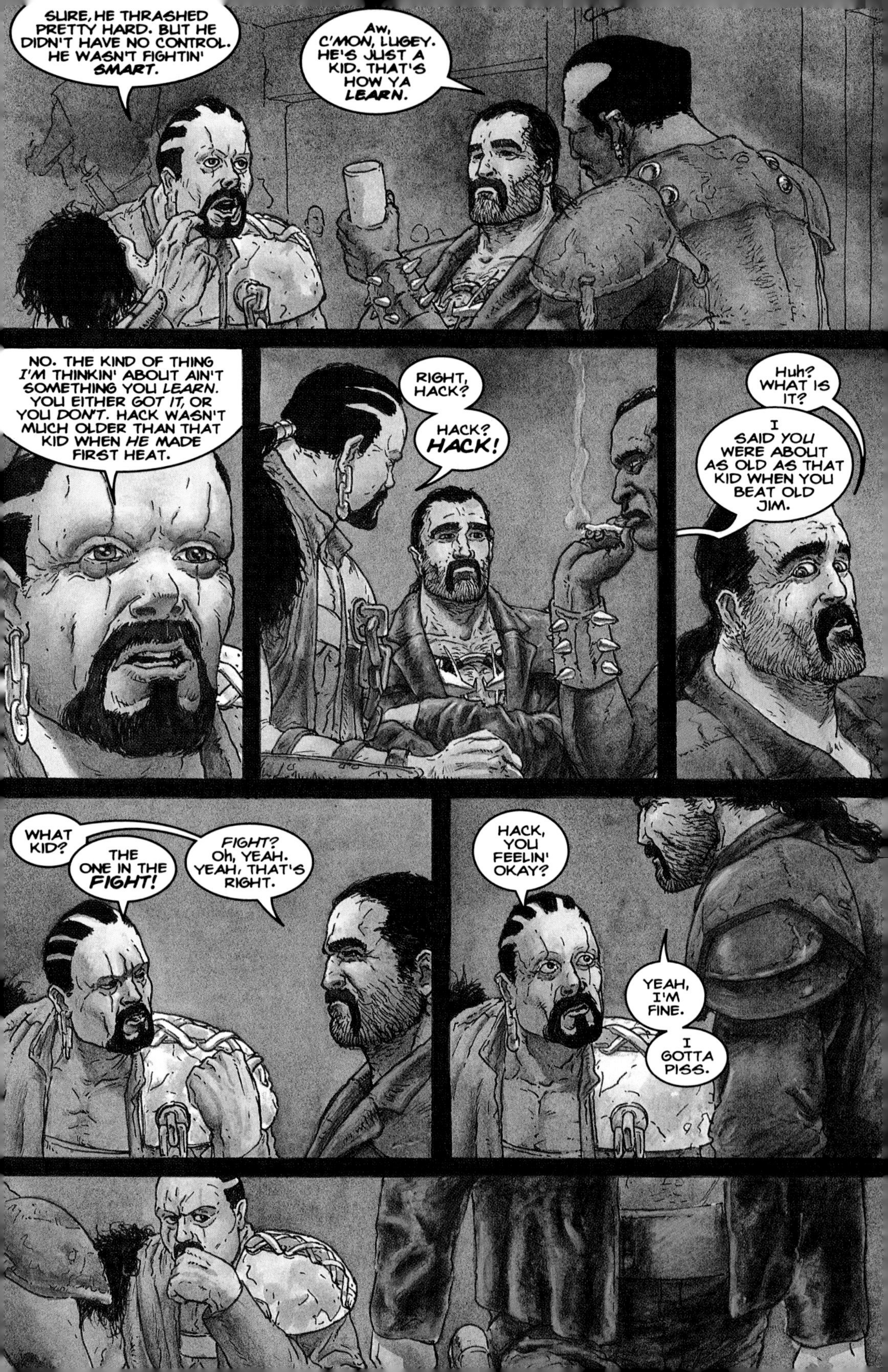
SURE, HE THRASHED PRETTY HARD. BUT HE DIDN'T HAVE NO CONTROL. HE WASN'T FIGHTIN' SMART.
AW, C'MON, LUGEY. HE'S JUST A KID. THAT'S HOW YA LEARN.
NO. THE KIND OF THING I'M THINKIN' ABOUT AIN'T SOMETHING YOU LEARN. YOU EITHER GOT IT, OR YOU DON'T. HACK WASN'T MUCH OLDER THAN THAT KID WHEN HE MADE FIRST HEAT.
RIGHT, HACK?
HACK? HACK!
HUH? WHAT IS IT?
I SAID YOU WERE ABOUT AS OLD AS THAT KID WHEN YOU BEAT OLD JIM.
WHAT KID?
THE ONE IN THE FIGHT!
FIGHT? OH, YEAH. YEAH, THAT'S RIGHT.
HACK, YOU FEELIN' OKAY?
YEAH, I'M FINE.
I GOTTA PISS.

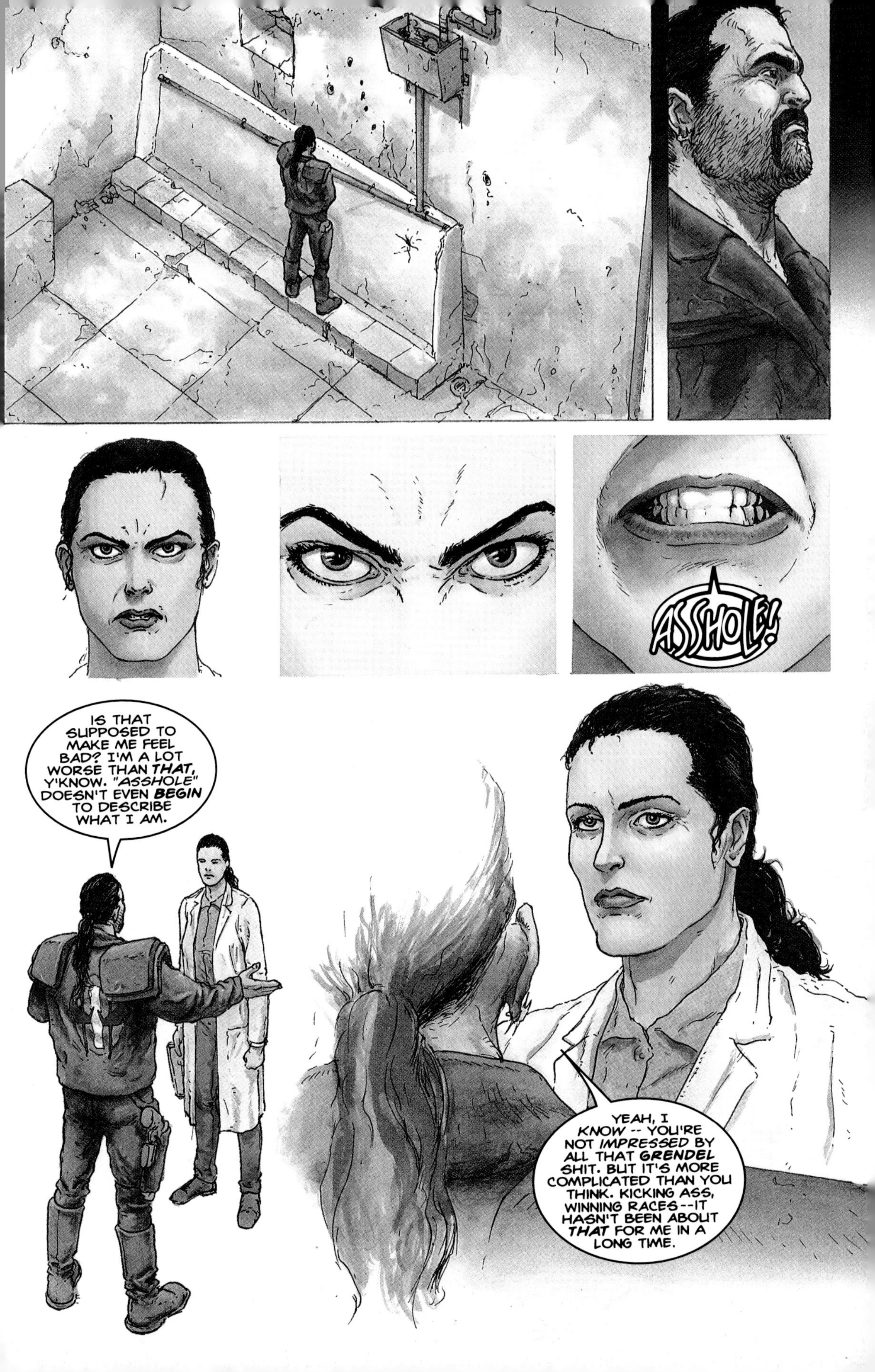
ASSHOLE!
IS THAT SUPPOSED TO MAKE ME FEEL BAD? I'M A LOT WORSE THAN THAT, Y'KNOW. "ASSHOLE" DOESN'T EVEN BEGIN TO DESCRIBE WHAT I AM.
YEAH, I KNOW -- YOU'RE NOT IMPRESSED BY ALL THAT GRENDEL SHIT. BUT IT'S MORE COMPLICATED THAN YOU THINK. KICKING ASS, WINNING RACES--IT HASN'T BEEN ABOUT THAT FOR ME IN A LONG TIME.

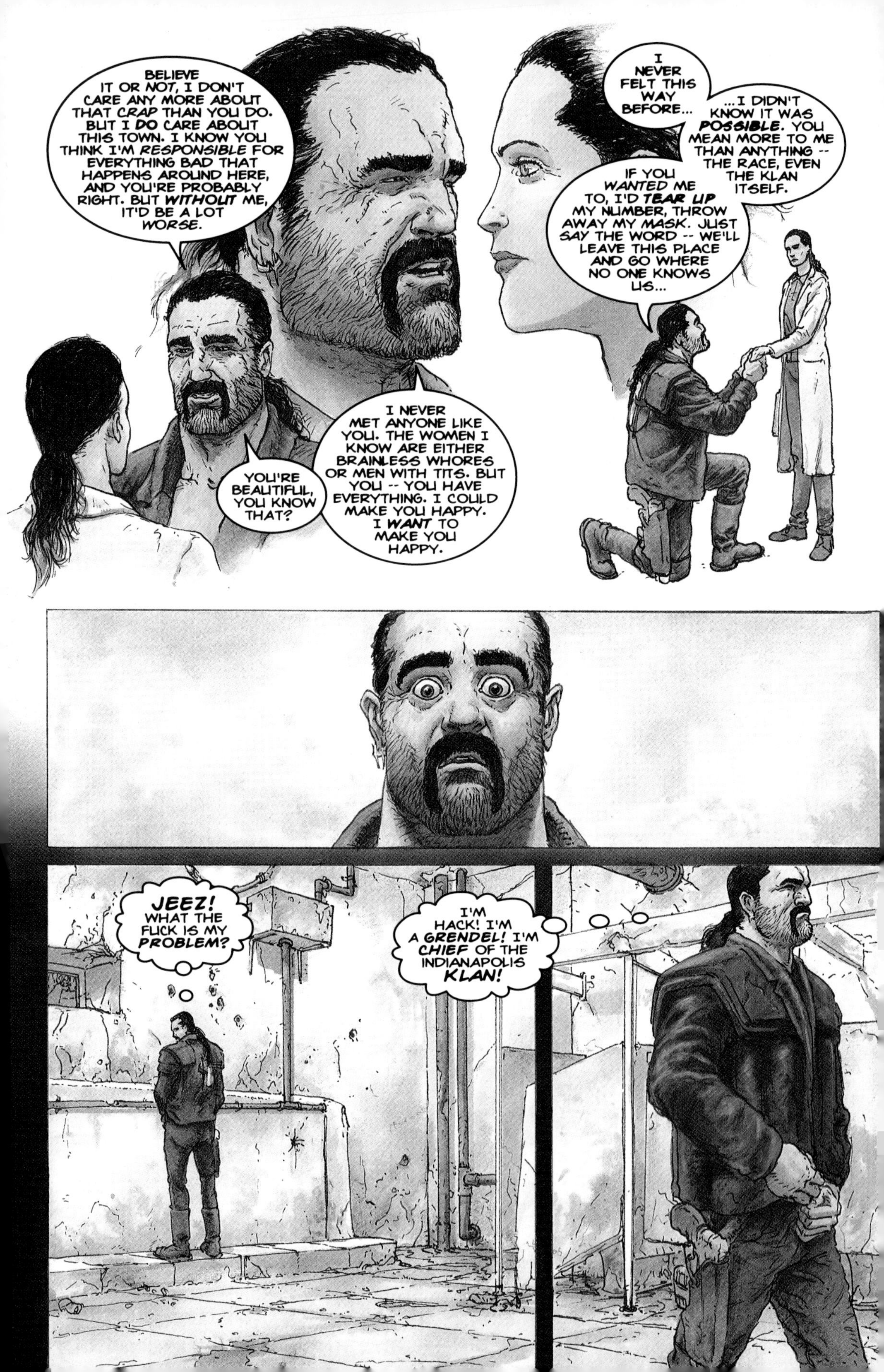
BELIEVE IT OR NOT, I DON'T CARE ANY MORE ABOUT THAT CRAP THAN YOU DO. BUT I DO CARE ABOUT THIS TOWN. I KNOW YOU THINK I'M RESPONSIBLE FOR EVERYTHING BAD THAT HAPPENS AROUND HERE, AND YOU'RE PROBABLY RIGHT. BUT WITHOUT ME, IT'D BE A LOT WORSE.
YOU'RE BEAUTIFUL, YOU KNOW THAT?
I NEVER MET ANYONE LIKE YOU. THE WOMEN I KNOW ARE EITHER BRAINLESS WHORES OR MEN WITH TITS. BUT YOU -- YOU HAVE EVERYTHING. I COULD MAKE YOU HAPPY. I WANT TO MAKE YOU HAPPY.
I NEVER FELT THIS WAY BEFORE...
...I DIDN'T KNOW IT WAS POSSIBLE. YOU MEAN MORE TO ME THAN ANYTHING -- THE RACE, EVEN THE KLAN ITSELF.
IF YOU WANTED ME TO, I'D TEAR UP MY NUMBER, THROW AWAY MY MASK. JUST SAY THE WORD -- WE'LL LEAVE THIS PLACE AND GO WHERE NO ONE KNOWS US...
JEEZ! WHAT THE FUCK IS MY PROBLEM?
I'M HACK! I'M A GRENDEL! I'M CHIEF OF THE INDIANAPOLIS KLAN!

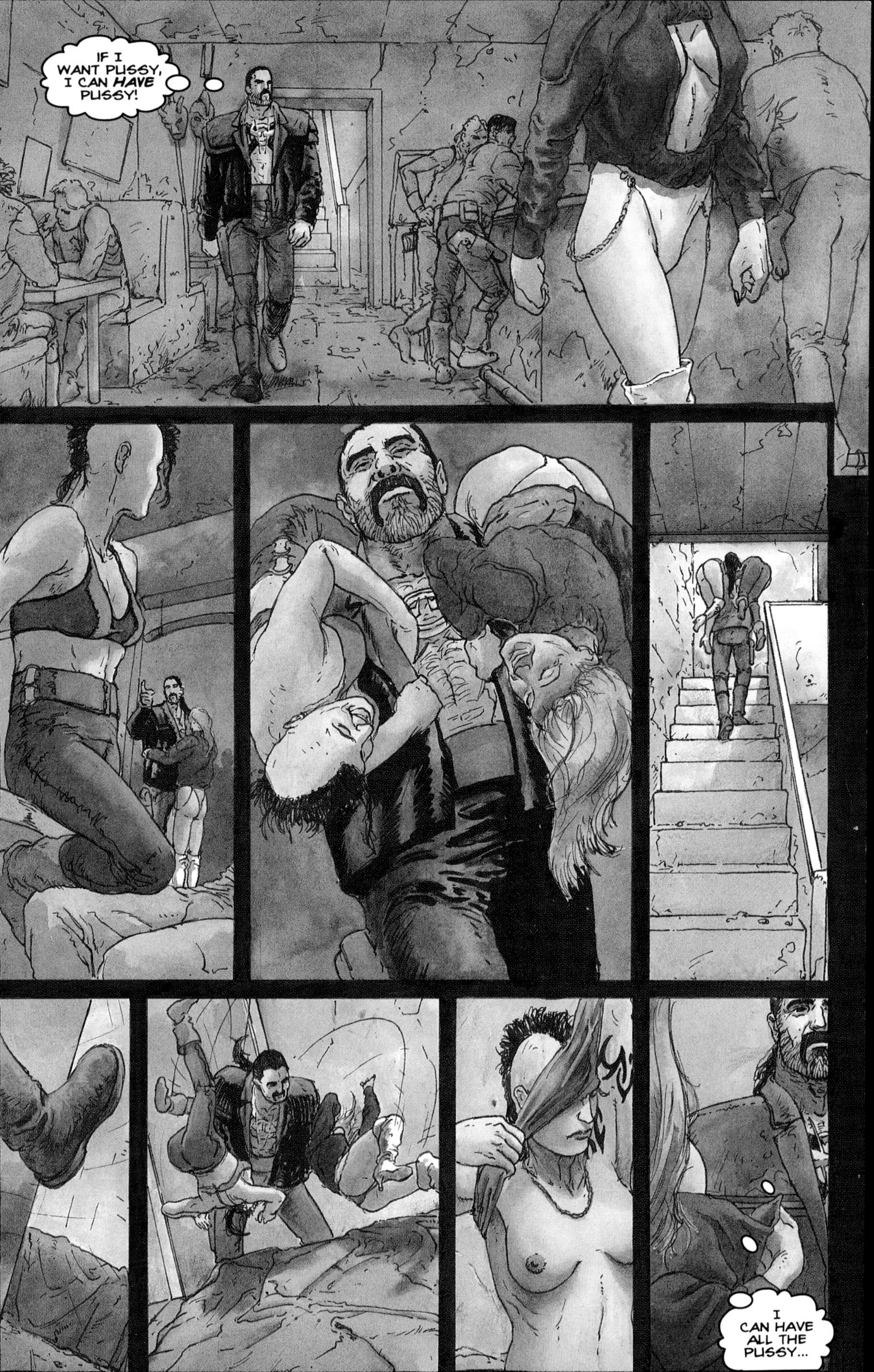
IF I WANT PUSSY, I CAN *HAVE* PUSSY!
I CAN HAVE ALL THE PUSSY...

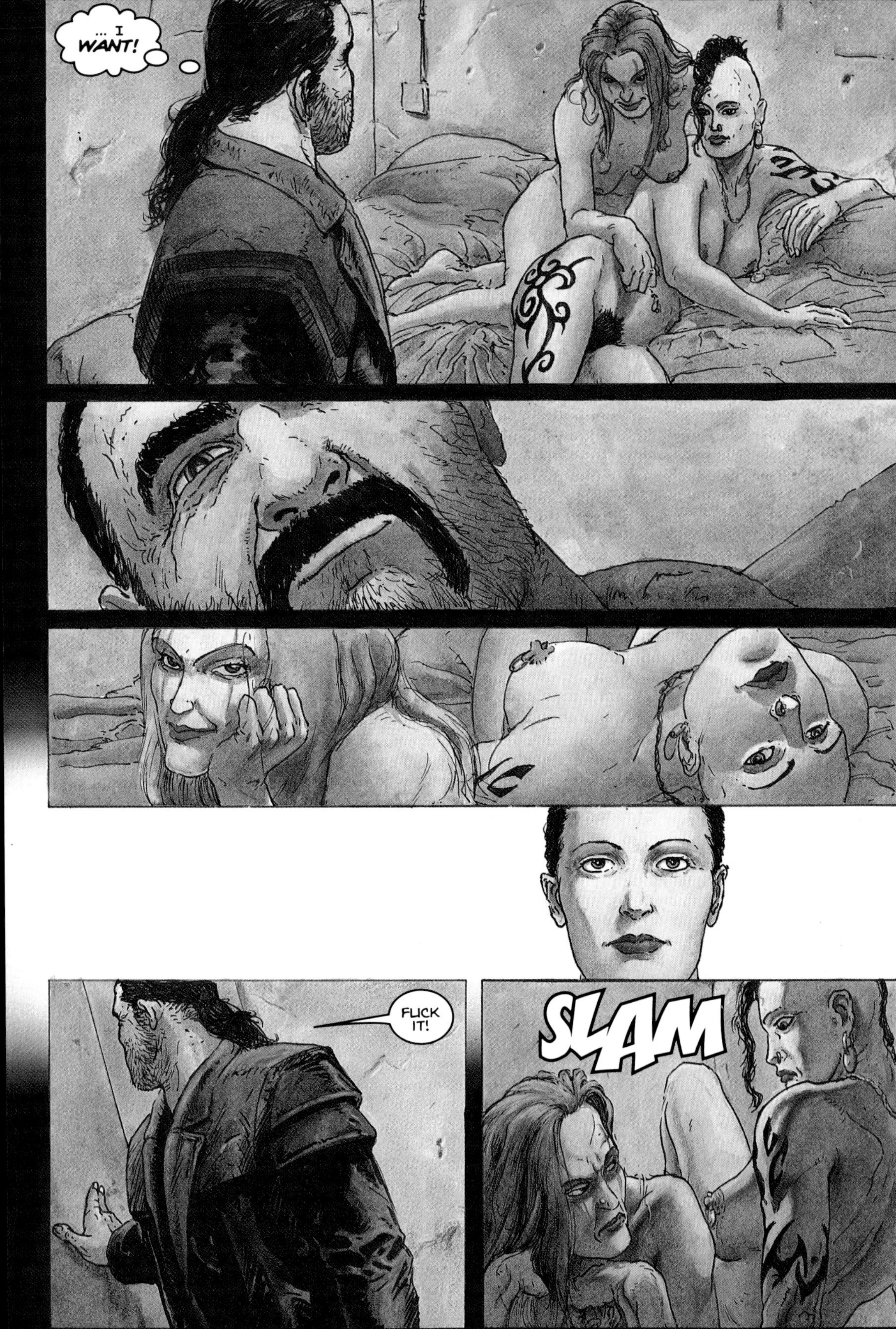
... I WANT!
FUCK IT!
SLAM

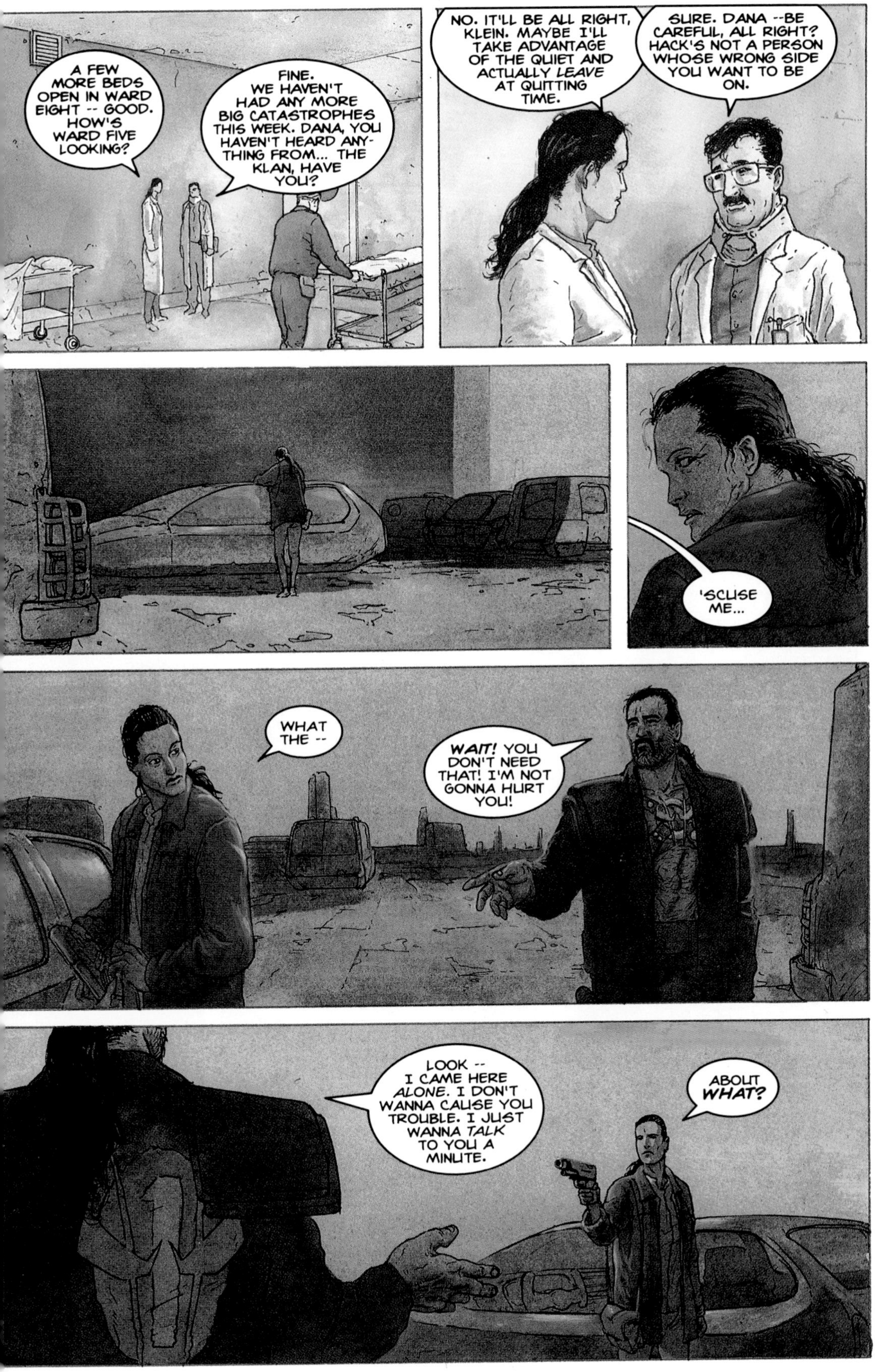
A FEW MORE BEDS OPEN IN WARD EIGHT -- GOOD. HOW'S WARD FIVE LOOKING?
FINE. WE HAVEN'T HAD ANY MORE BIG CATASTROPHES THIS WEEK. DANA, YOU HAVEN'T HEARD ANYTHING FROM... THE KLAN, HAVE YOU?
NO. IT'LL BE ALL RIGHT, KLEIN. MAYBE I'LL TAKE ADVANTAGE OF THE QUIET AND ACTUALLY *LEAVE* AT QUITTING TIME.
SURE. DANA --BE CAREFUL, ALL RIGHT? HACK'S NOT A PERSON WHOSE WRONG SIDE YOU WANT TO BE ON.
'SCUSE ME...
WHAT THE --
WAIT! YOU DON'T NEED THAT! I'M NOT GONNA HURT YOU!
LOOK -- I CAME HERE *ALONE*. I DON'T WANNA CAUSE YOU TROUBLE. I JUST WANNA *TALK* TO YOU A MINUTE.
ABOUT **WHAT?**

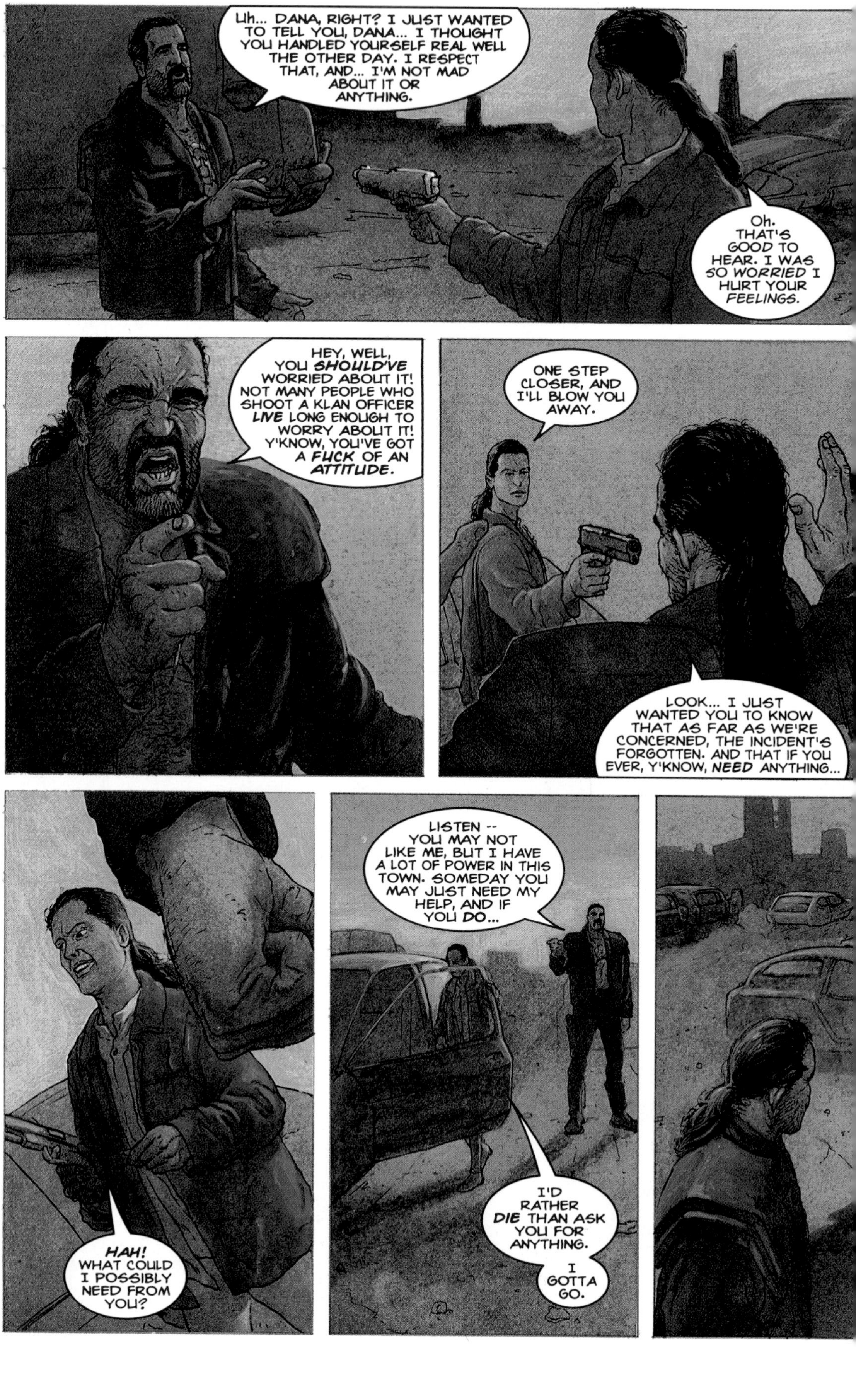
UH... DANA, RIGHT? I JUST WANTED TO TELL YOU, DANA... I THOUGHT YOU HANDLED YOURSELF REAL WELL THE OTHER DAY. I RESPECT THAT, AND... I'M NOT MAD ABOUT IT OR ANYTHING.
OH. THAT'S GOOD TO HEAR. I WAS SO WORRIED I HURT YOUR FEELINGS.
HEY, WELL, YOU SHOULD'VE WORRIED ABOUT IT! NOT MANY PEOPLE WHO SHOOT A KLAN OFFICER LIVE LONG ENOUGH TO WORRY ABOUT IT! Y'KNOW, YOU'VE GOT A FUCK OF AN ATTITUDE.
ONE STEP CLOSER, AND I'LL BLOW YOU AWAY.
LOOK... I JUST WANTED YOU TO KNOW THAT AS FAR AS WE'RE CONCERNED, THE INCIDENT'S FORGOTTEN. AND THAT IF YOU EVER, Y'KNOW, NEED ANYTHING...
HAH! WHAT COULD I POSSIBLY NEED FROM YOU?
LISTEN -- YOU MAY NOT LIKE ME, BUT I HAVE A LOT OF POWER IN THIS TOWN. SOMEDAY YOU MAY JUST NEED MY HELP, AND IF YOU DO...
I'D RATHER DIE THAN ASK YOU FOR ANYTHING.
I GOTTA GO.

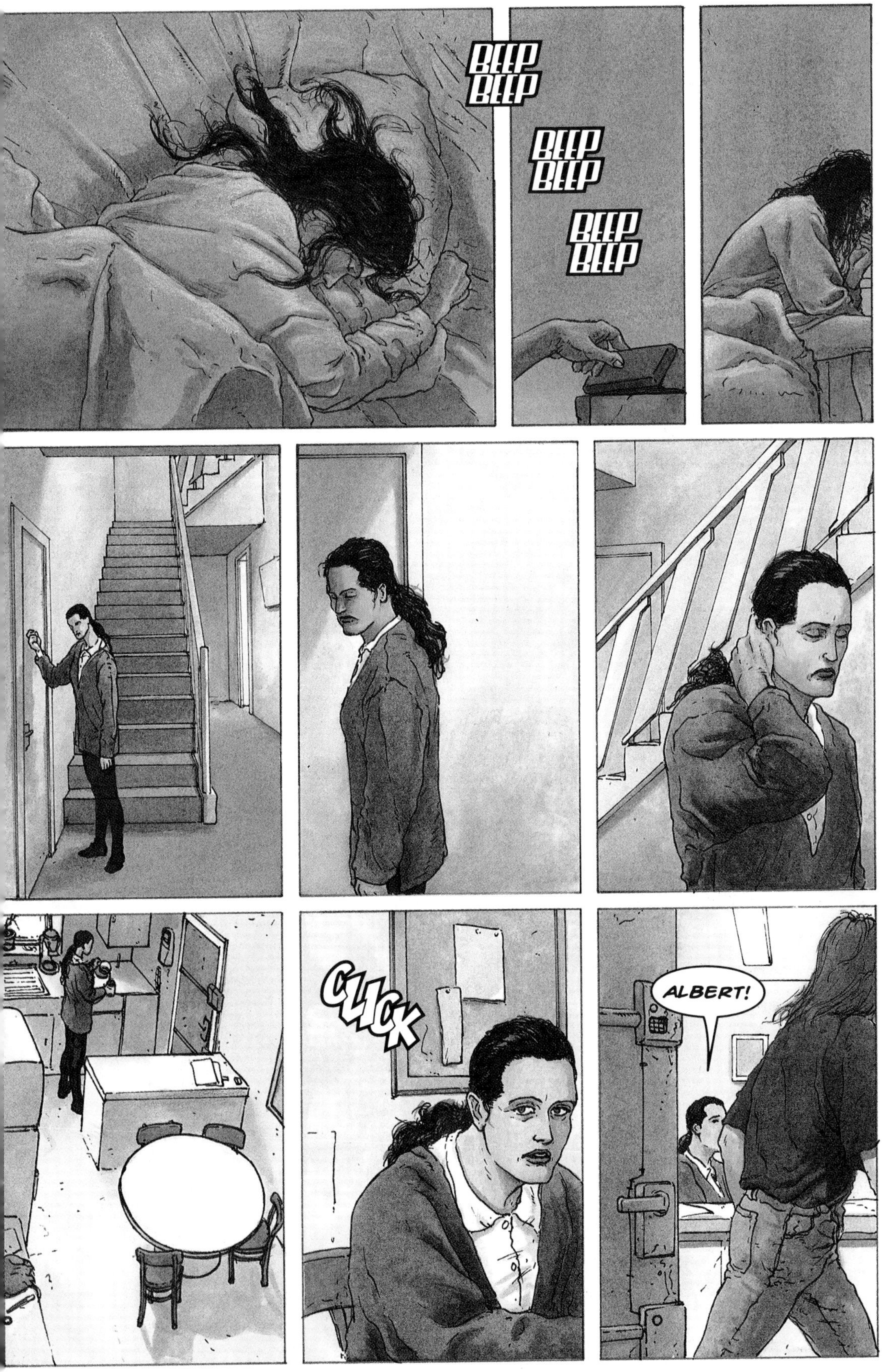
BEEP BEEP
BEEP BEEP
BEEP BEEP
CLICK
ALBERT!

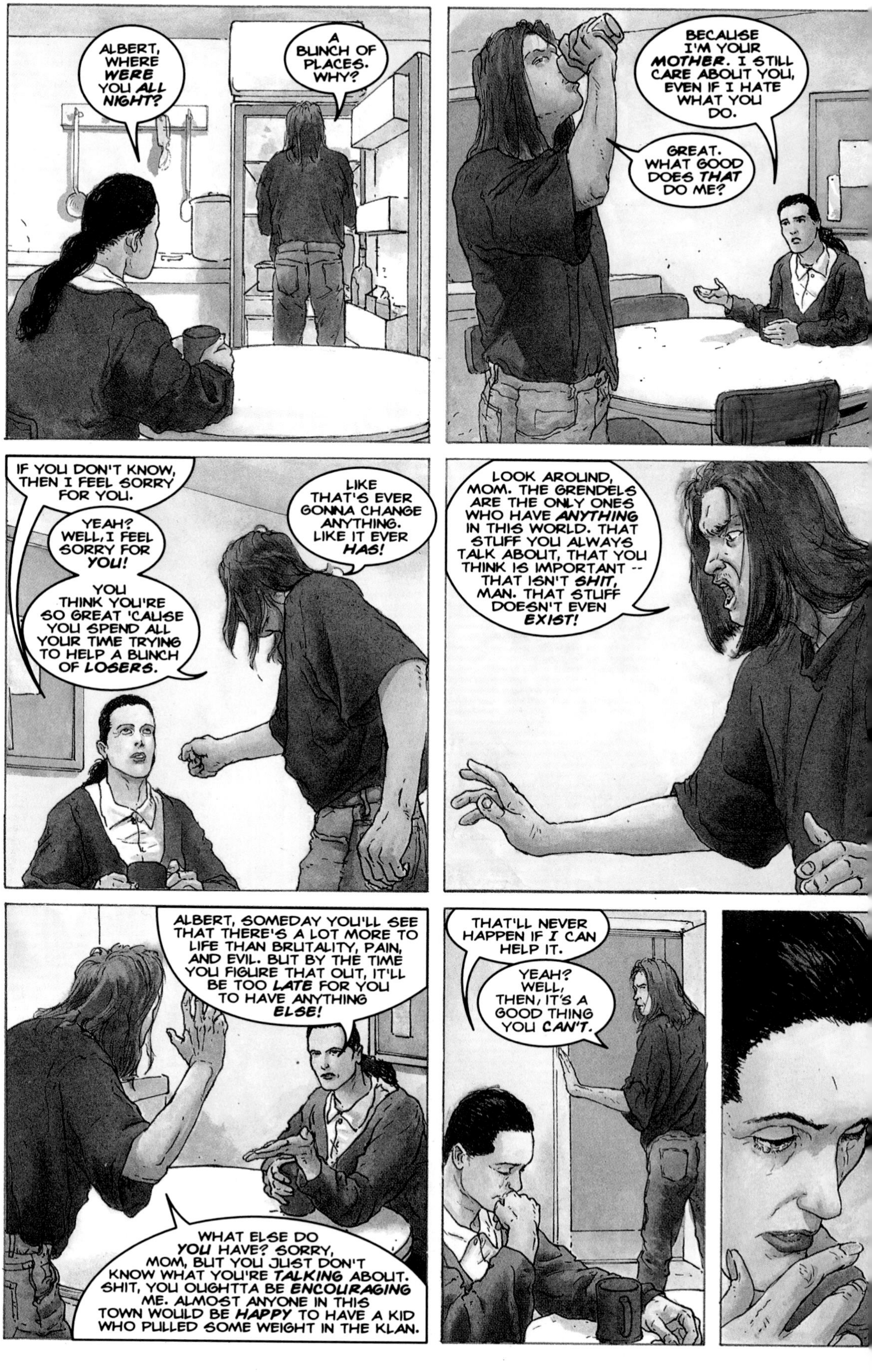

ALBERT, WHERE WERE YOU ALL NIGHT?
A BUNCH OF PLACES. WHY?
BECAUSE I'M YOUR MOTHER. I STILL CARE ABOUT YOU, EVEN IF I HATE WHAT YOU DO.
GREAT. WHAT GOOD DOES THAT DO ME?
IF YOU DON'T KNOW, THEN I FEEL SORRY FOR YOU.
YEAH? WELL, I FEEL SORRY FOR YOU!
YOU THINK YOU'RE SO GREAT 'CAUSE YOU SPEND ALL YOUR TIME TRYING TO HELP A BUNCH OF LOSERS.
LIKE THAT'S EVER GONNA CHANGE ANYTHING. LIKE IT EVER HAS!
LOOK AROUND, MOM. THE GRENDELS ARE THE ONLY ONES WHO HAVE ANYTHING IN THIS WORLD. THAT STUFF YOU ALWAYS TALK ABOUT, THAT YOU THINK IS IMPORTANT -- THAT ISN'T SHIT, MAN. THAT STUFF DOESN'T EVEN EXIST!
ALBERT, SOMEDAY YOU'LL SEE THAT THERE'S A LOT MORE TO LIFE THAN BRUTALITY, PAIN, AND EVIL. BUT BY THE TIME YOU FIGURE THAT OUT, IT'LL BE TOO LATE FOR YOU TO HAVE ANYTHING ELSE!
WHAT ELSE DO YOU HAVE? SORRY, MOM, BUT YOU JUST DON'T KNOW WHAT YOU'RE TALKING ABOUT. SHIT, YOU OUGHTTA BE ENCOURAGING ME. ALMOST ANYONE IN THIS TOWN WOULD BE HAPPY TO HAVE A KID WHO PULLED SOME WEIGHT IN THE KLAN.
THAT'LL NEVER HAPPEN IF I CAN HELP IT.
YEAH? WELL, THEN, IT'S A GOOD THING YOU CAN'T.

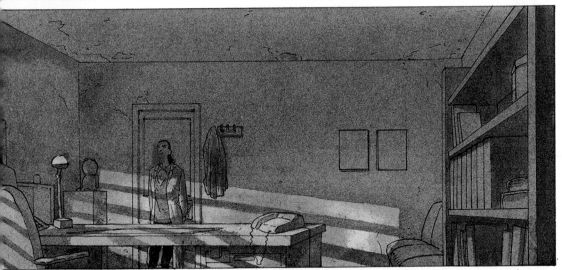

HELLO? I'D LIKE TO SPEAK TO *HACK*, PLEASE.

Oh... WELL, COULD I LEAVE HIM A *MESSAGE*?

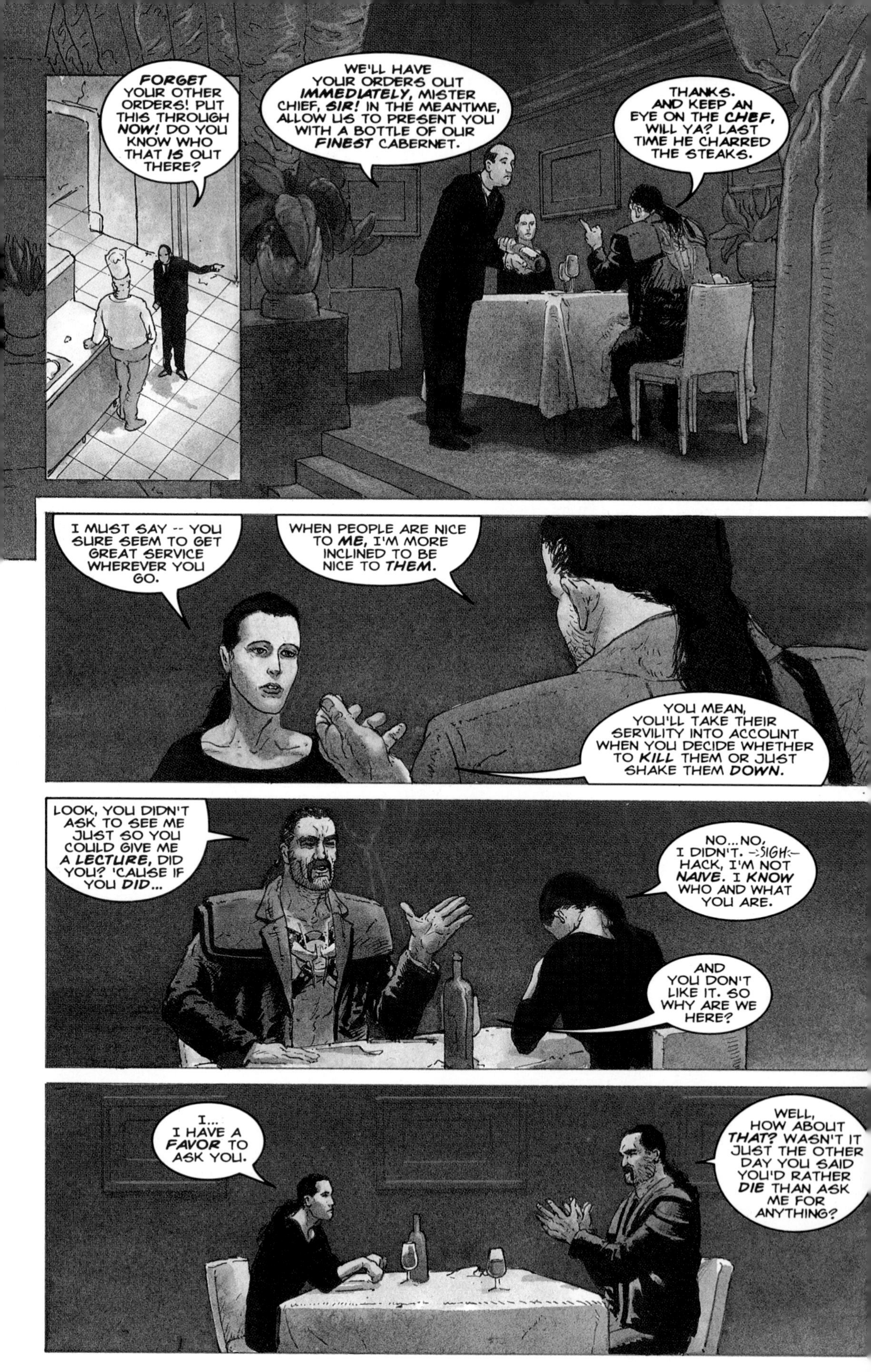
FORGET YOUR OTHER ORDERS! PUT THIS THROUGH NOW! DO YOU KNOW WHO THAT IS OUT THERE?
WE'LL HAVE YOUR ORDERS OUT IMMEDIATELY, MISTER CHIEF, SIR! IN THE MEANTIME, ALLOW US TO PRESENT YOU WITH A BOTTLE OF OUR FINEST CABERNET.
THANKS. AND KEEP AN EYE ON THE CHEF, WILL YA? LAST TIME HE CHARRED THE STEAKS.
I MUST SAY -- YOU SURE SEEM TO GET GREAT SERVICE WHEREVER YOU GO.
WHEN PEOPLE ARE NICE TO ME, I'M MORE INCLINED TO BE NICE TO THEM.
YOU MEAN, YOU'LL TAKE THEIR SERVILITY INTO ACCOUNT WHEN YOU DECIDE WHETHER TO KILL THEM OR JUST SHAKE THEM DOWN.
LOOK, YOU DIDN'T ASK TO SEE ME JUST SO YOU COULD GIVE ME A LECTURE, DID YOU? 'CAUSE IF YOU DID...
NO...NO, I DIDN'T. -SIGH- HACK, I'M NOT NAIVE. I KNOW WHO AND WHAT YOU ARE.
AND YOU DON'T LIKE IT. SO WHY ARE WE HERE?
I... I HAVE A FAVOR TO ASK YOU.
WELL, HOW ABOUT THAT? WASN'T IT JUST THE OTHER DAY YOU SAID YOU'D RATHER DIE THAN ASK ME FOR ANYTHING?

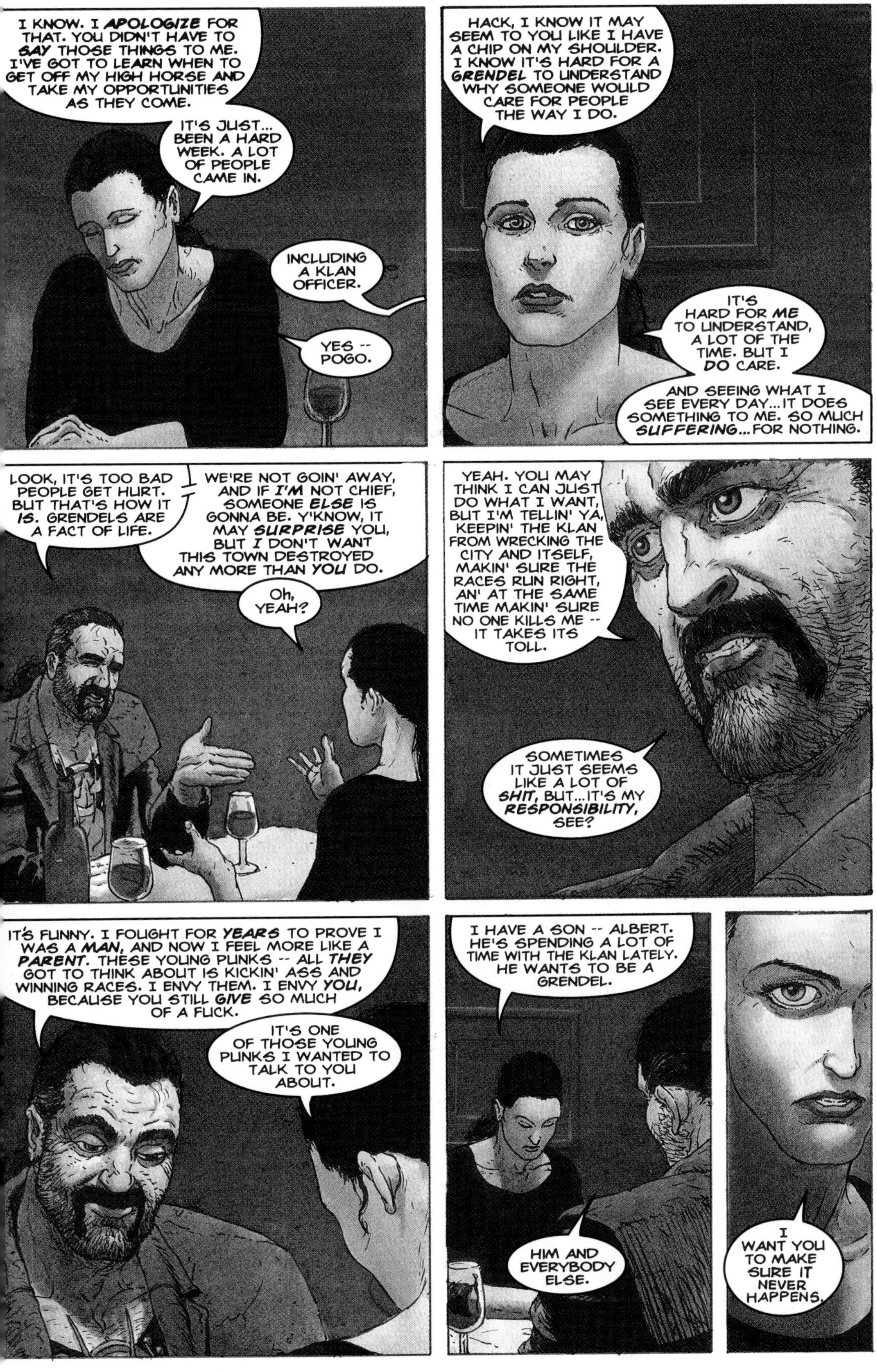
I KNOW. I APOLOGIZE FOR THAT. YOU DIDN'T HAVE TO SAY THOSE THINGS TO ME. I'VE GOT TO LEARN WHEN TO GET OFF MY HIGH HORSE AND TAKE MY OPPORTUNITIES AS THEY COME.
IT'S JUST... BEEN A HARD WEEK. A LOT OF PEOPLE CAME IN.
INCLUDING A KLAN OFFICER.
YES -- POGO.
HACK, I KNOW IT MAY SEEM TO YOU LIKE I HAVE A CHIP ON MY SHOULDER. I KNOW IT'S HARD FOR A GRENDEL TO UNDERSTAND WHY SOMEONE WOULD CARE FOR PEOPLE THE WAY I DO.
IT'S HARD FOR ME TO UNDERSTAND, A LOT OF THE TIME. BUT I DO CARE.
AND SEEING WHAT I SEE EVERY DAY...IT DOES SOMETHING TO ME. SO MUCH SUFFERING...FOR NOTHING.
LOOK, IT'S TOO BAD PEOPLE GET HURT. BUT THAT'S HOW IT IS. GRENDELS ARE A FACT OF LIFE.
WE'RE NOT GOIN' AWAY, AND IF I'M NOT CHIEF, SOMEONE ELSE IS GONNA BE. Y'KNOW, IT MAY SURPRISE YOU, BUT I DON'T WANT THIS TOWN DESTROYED ANY MORE THAN YOU DO.
Oh, YEAH?
YEAH. YOU MAY THINK I CAN JUST DO WHAT I WANT, BUT I'M TELLIN' YA, KEEPIN' THE KLAN FROM WRECKING THE CITY AND ITSELF, MAKIN' SURE THE RACES RUN RIGHT, AN' AT THE SAME TIME MAKIN' SURE NO ONE KILLS ME -- IT TAKES ITS TOLL.
SOMETIMES IT JUST SEEMS LIKE A LOT OF SHIT, BUT...IT'S MY RESPONSIBILITY, SEE?
IT'S FUNNY. I FOUGHT FOR YEARS TO PROVE I WAS A MAN, AND NOW I FEEL MORE LIKE A PARENT. THESE YOUNG PUNKS -- ALL THEY GOT TO THINK ABOUT IS KICKIN' ASS AND WINNING RACES. I ENVY THEM. I ENVY YOU, BECAUSE YOU STILL GIVE SO MUCH OF A FUCK.
IT'S ONE OF THOSE YOUNG PUNKS I WANTED TO TALK TO YOU ABOUT.
I HAVE A SON -- ALBERT. HE'S SPENDING A LOT OF TIME WITH THE KLAN LATELY. HE WANTS TO BE A GRENDEL.
HIM AND EVERYBODY ELSE.
I WANT YOU TO MAKE SURE IT NEVER HAPPENS.

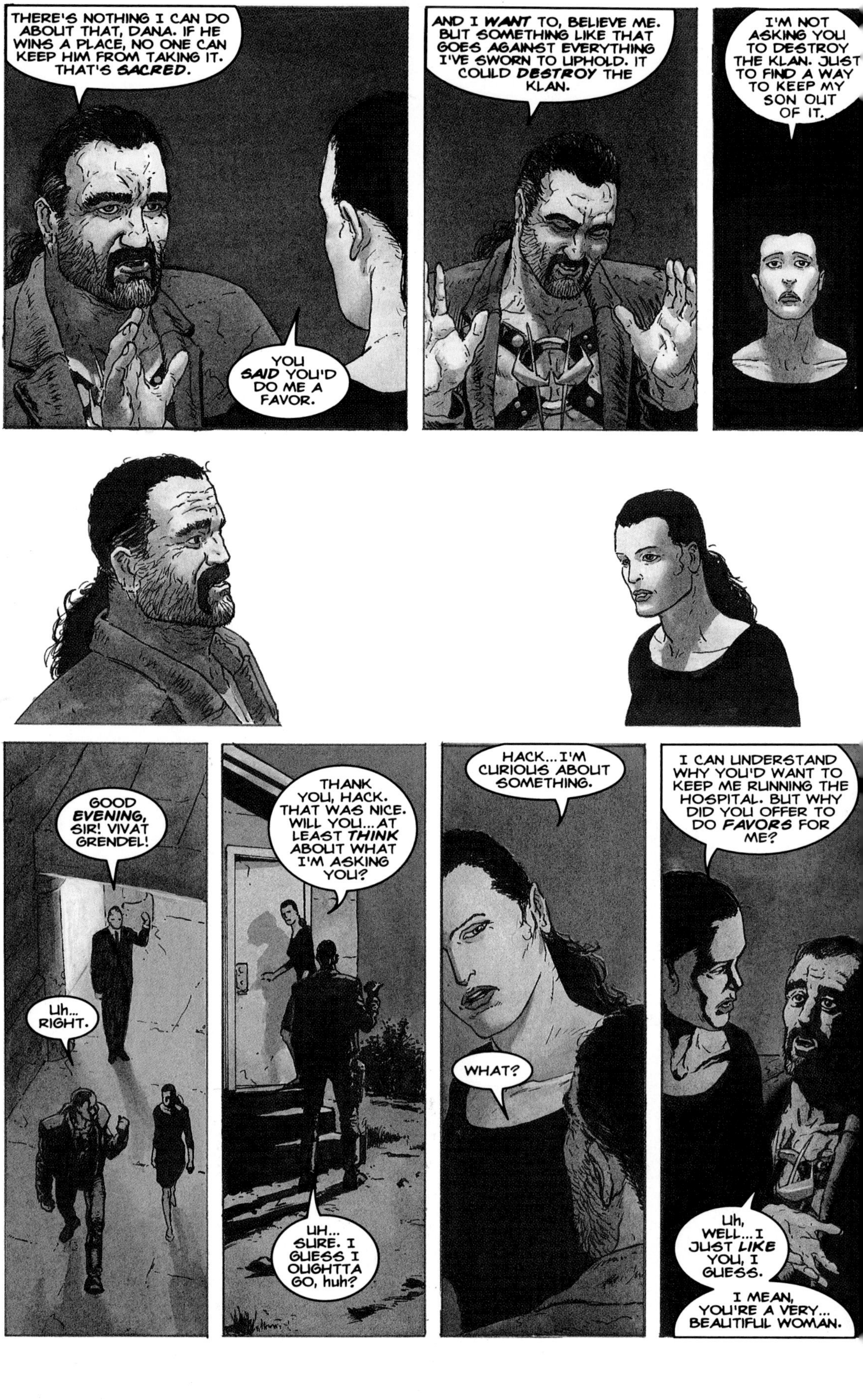
THERE'S NOTHING I CAN DO ABOUT THAT, DANA. IF HE WINS A PLACE, NO ONE CAN KEEP HIM FROM TAKING IT. THAT'S SACRED.
YOU SAID YOU'D DO ME A FAVOR.
AND I WANT TO, BELIEVE ME. BUT SOMETHING LIKE THAT GOES AGAINST EVERYTHING I'VE SWORN TO UPHOLD. IT COULD DESTROY THE KLAN.
I'M NOT ASKING YOU TO DESTROY THE KLAN. JUST TO FIND A WAY TO KEEP MY SON OUT OF IT.
GOOD EVENING, SIR! VIVAT GRENDEL!
Uh... RIGHT.
THANK YOU, HACK. THAT WAS NICE. WILL YOU...AT LEAST THINK ABOUT WHAT I'M ASKING YOU?
UH... SURE. I GUESS I OUGHTTA GO, huh?
HACK...I'M CURIOUS ABOUT SOMETHING.
WHAT?
I CAN UNDERSTAND WHY YOU'D WANT TO KEEP ME RUNNING THE HOSPITAL. BUT WHY DID YOU OFFER TO DO FAVORS FOR ME?
Uh, WELL...I JUST LIKE YOU, I GUESS.
I MEAN, YOU'RE A VERY... BEAUTIFUL WOMAN.

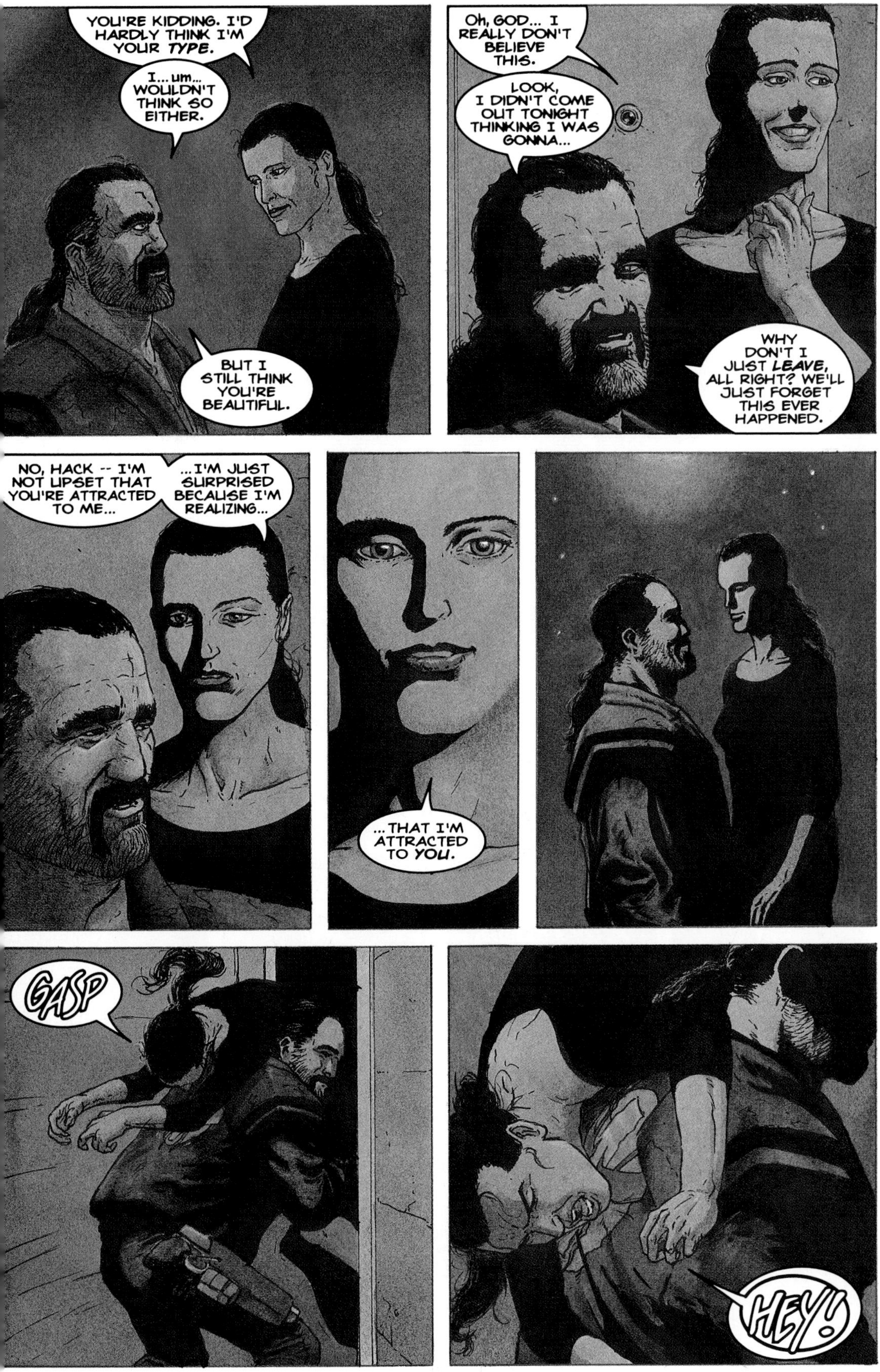

YOU'RE KIDDING. I'D HARDLY THINK I'M YOUR *TYPE.*
I... um... WOULDN'T THINK SO EITHER.
BUT I STILL THINK YOU'RE BEAUTIFUL.
Oh, GOD... I REALLY DON'T BELIEVE THIS.
LOOK, I DIDN'T COME OUT TONIGHT THINKING I WAS GONNA...
WHY DON'T I JUST *LEAVE,* ALL RIGHT? WE'LL JUST FORGET THIS EVER HAPPENED.
NO, HACK -- I'M NOT UPSET THAT YOU'RE ATTRACTED TO ME...
...I'M JUST SURPRISED BECAUSE I'M REALIZING...
...THAT I'M ATTRACTED TO *YOU.*
GASP
HEY!

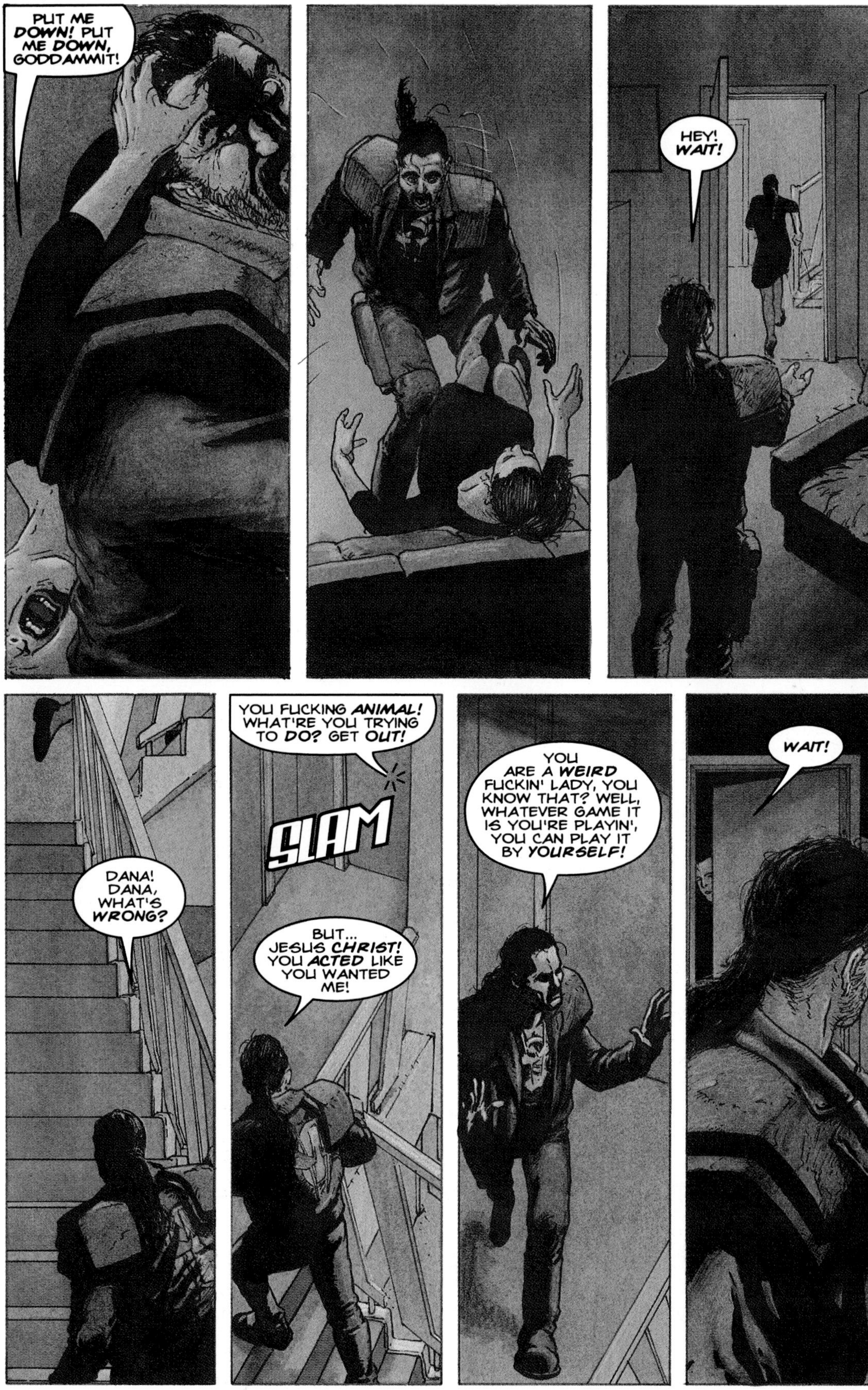
PUT ME DOWN! PUT ME DOWN, GODDAMMIT!
HEY! WAIT!
DANA! DANA, WHAT'S WRONG?
YOU FUCKING ANIMAL! WHAT'RE YOU TRYING TO DO? GET OUT!
SLAM
BUT... JESUS CHRIST! YOU ACTED LIKE YOU WANTED ME!
YOU ARE A WEIRD FUCKIN' LADY, YOU KNOW THAT? WELL, WHATEVER GAME IT IS YOU'RE PLAYIN', YOU CAN PLAY IT BY YOURSELF!
WAIT!

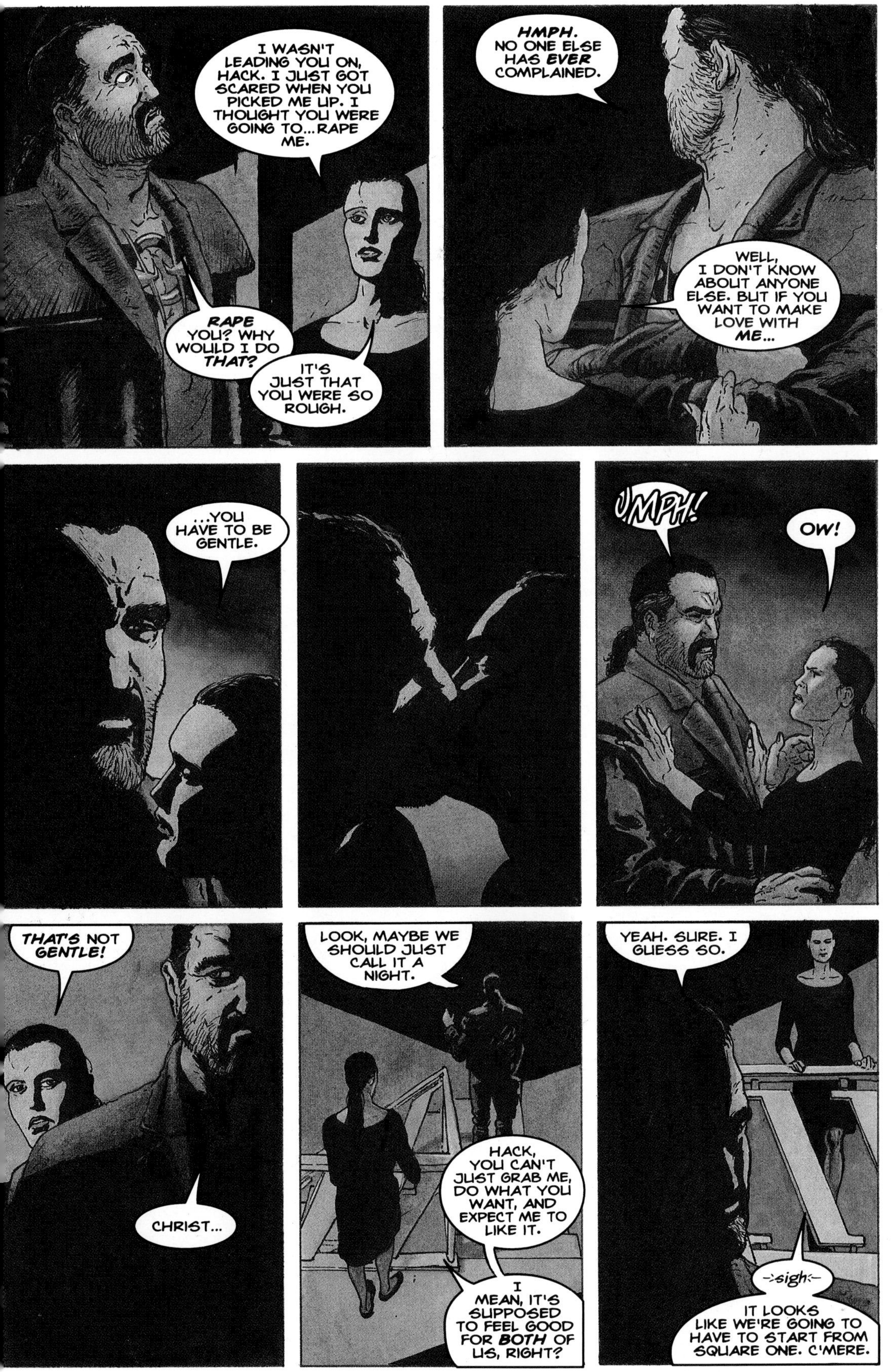
I WASN'T LEADING YOU ON, HACK. I JUST GOT SCARED WHEN YOU PICKED ME UP. I THOUGHT YOU WERE GOING TO...RAPE ME.
RAPE YOU? WHY WOULD I DO THAT?
IT'S JUST THAT YOU WERE SO ROUGH.
HMPH. NO ONE ELSE HAS EVER COMPLAINED.
WELL, I DON'T KNOW ABOUT ANYONE ELSE. BUT IF YOU WANT TO MAKE LOVE WITH ME...
...YOU HAVE TO BE GENTLE.
UMPH!
OW!
THAT'S NOT GENTLE!
CHRIST...
LOOK, MAYBE WE SHOULD JUST CALL IT A NIGHT.
HACK, YOU CAN'T JUST GRAB ME, DO WHAT YOU WANT, AND EXPECT ME TO LIKE IT.
I MEAN, IT'S SUPPOSED TO FEEL GOOD FOR BOTH OF US, RIGHT?
YEAH. SURE. I GUESS SO.
-sigh-
IT LOOKS LIKE WE'RE GOING TO HAVE TO START FROM SQUARE ONE. C'MERE.

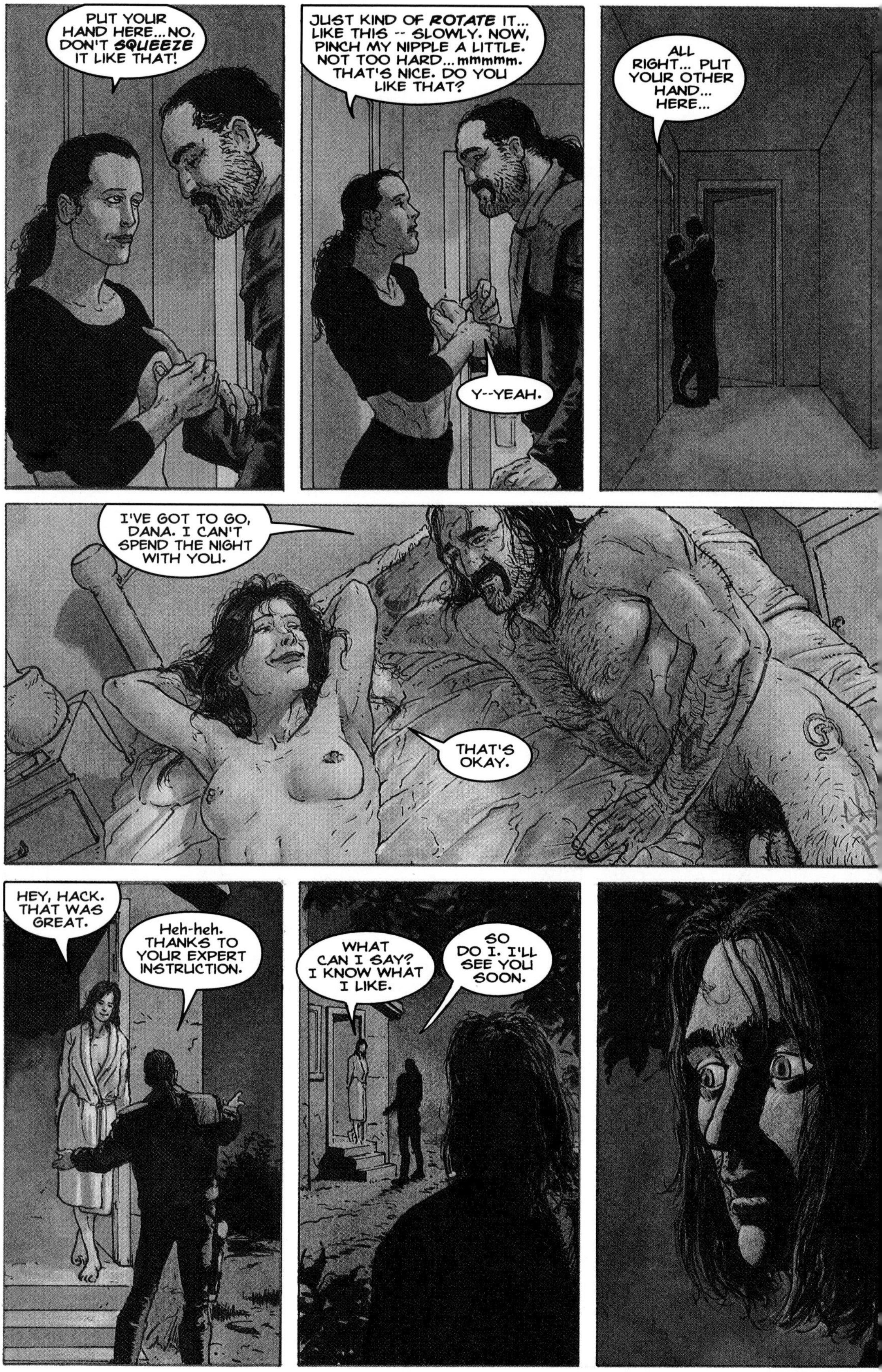
PUT YOUR HAND HERE...NO, DON'T SQUEEZE IT LIKE THAT!
JUST KIND OF ROTATE IT... LIKE THIS -- SLOWLY. NOW, PINCH MY NIPPLE A LITTLE. NOT TOO HARD...mmmmm. THAT'S NICE. DO YOU LIKE THAT?
Y--YEAH.
ALL RIGHT... PUT YOUR OTHER HAND... HERE...
I'VE GOT TO GO, DANA. I CAN'T SPEND THE NIGHT WITH YOU.
THAT'S OKAY.
HEY, HACK. THAT WAS GREAT.
Heh-heh. THANKS TO YOUR EXPERT INSTRUCTION.
WHAT CAN I SAY? I KNOW WHAT I LIKE.
SO DO I. I'LL SEE YOU SOON.

DANA, WHEN YOU GET A CHANCE, WE NEED AN OKAY TO DO AN AMPUTATION ON THAT PATIENT IN WARD SEVEN.

DANA? HEY, *DANA!* IS SOMETHING WRONG?

NO. NO, I'M SORRY, KLEIN. I'M FINE. I WAS JUST... UP KIND OF *LATE* LAST NIGHT.

LEMME GO! I'LL *KILL* YOU, ASSHOLE!

C'MERE! JUST *C'MERE!*

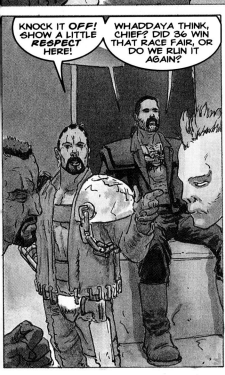

KNOCK IT *OFF!* SHOW A LITTLE *RESPECT* HERE!

WHADDAYA THINK, CHIEF? DID 36 WIN THAT RACE FAIR, OR DO WE RUN IT AGAIN?

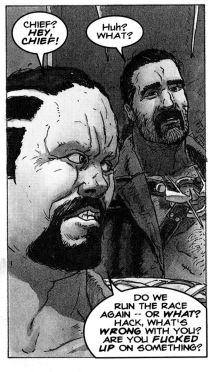

CHIEF? *HEY, CHIEF!*

Huh? WHAT?

DO WE RUN THE RACE AGAIN -- OR *WHAT?* HACK, WHAT'S *WRONG* WITH YOU? ARE YOU *FUCKED UP* ON SOMETHING?

NO, I'M NOT FUCKED UP ON *ANYTHING!*

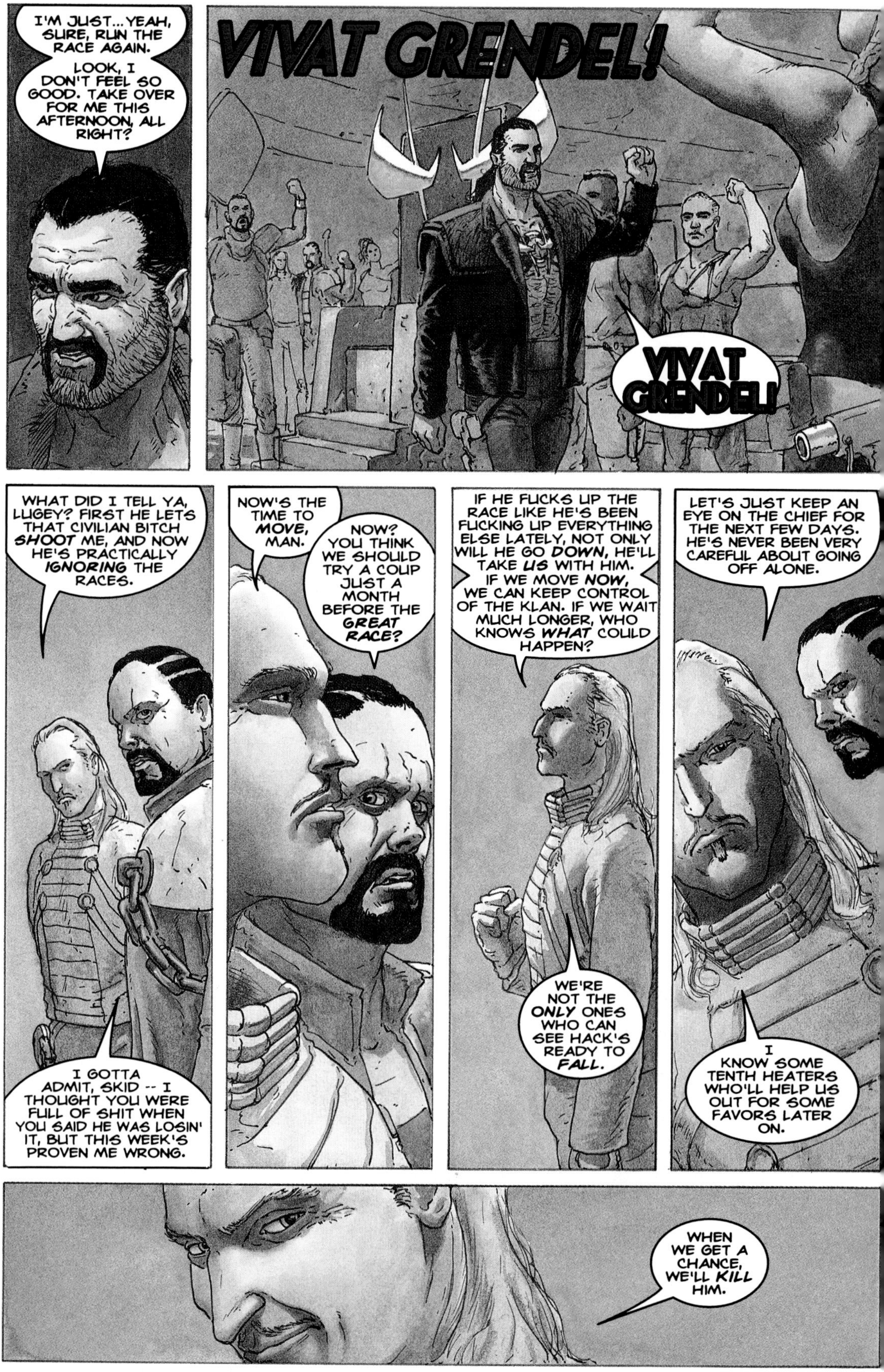

I'M JUST... YEAH, SURE, RUN THE RACE AGAIN.
LOOK, I DON'T FEEL SO GOOD. TAKE OVER FOR ME THIS AFTERNOON, ALL RIGHT?
VIVAT GRENDEL!
VIVAT GRENDEL!
WHAT DID I TELL YA, LUGEY? FIRST HE LETS THAT CIVILIAN BITCH SHOOT ME, AND NOW HE'S PRACTICALLY IGNORING THE RACES.
I GOTTA ADMIT, SKID -- I THOUGHT YOU WERE FULL OF SHIT WHEN YOU SAID HE WAS LOSIN' IT, BUT THIS WEEK'S PROVEN ME WRONG.
NOW'S THE TIME TO MOVE, MAN.
NOW? YOU THINK WE SHOULD TRY A COUP JUST A MONTH BEFORE THE GREAT RACE?
IF HE FUCKS UP THE RACE LIKE HE'S BEEN FUCKING UP EVERYTHING ELSE LATELY, NOT ONLY WILL HE GO DOWN, HE'LL TAKE US WITH HIM.
IF WE MOVE NOW, WE CAN KEEP CONTROL OF THE KLAN. IF WE WAIT MUCH LONGER, WHO KNOWS WHAT COULD HAPPEN?
WE'RE NOT THE ONLY ONES WHO CAN SEE HACK'S READY TO FALL.
LET'S JUST KEEP AN EYE ON THE CHIEF FOR THE NEXT FEW DAYS. HE'S NEVER BEEN VERY CAREFUL ABOUT GOING OFF ALONE.
I KNOW SOME TENTH HEATERS WHO'LL HELP US OUT FOR SOME FAVORS LATER ON.
WHEN WE GET A CHANCE, WE'LL KILL HIM.

CHAPTER THREE

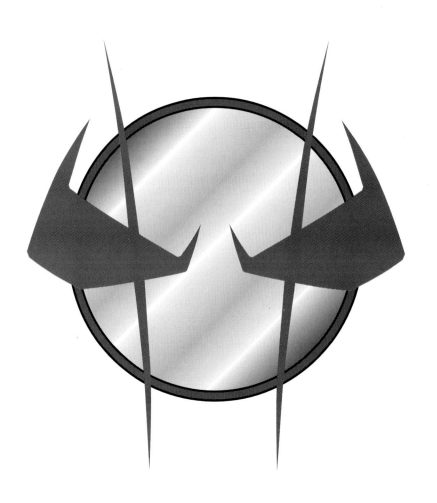

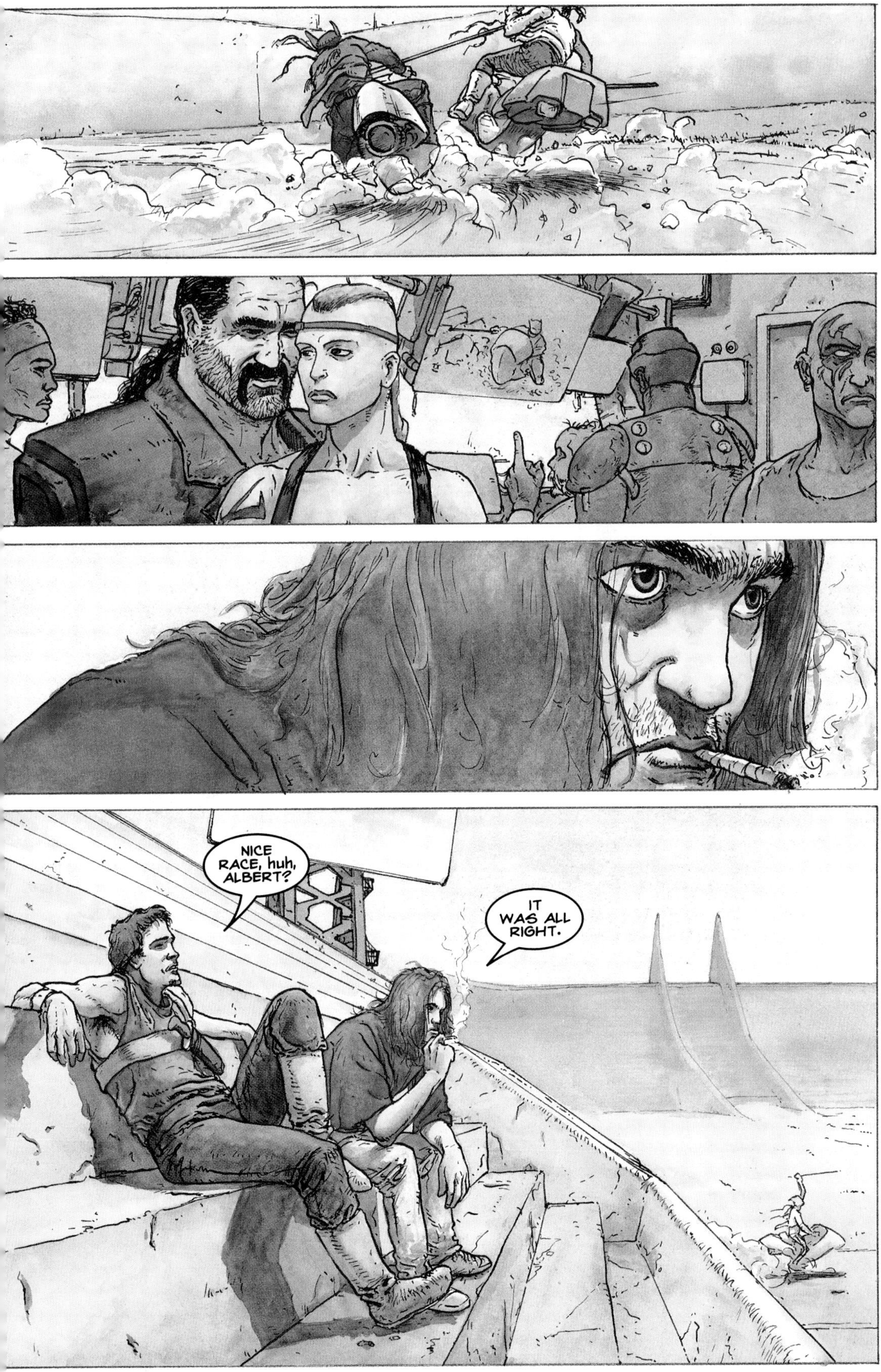
NICE RACE, huh, ALBERT?
IT WAS ALL RIGHT.

ALL RIGHT? FUCK, DOES *ANYTHING* IMPRESS YOU?

YEAH. LOTS OF THINGS.

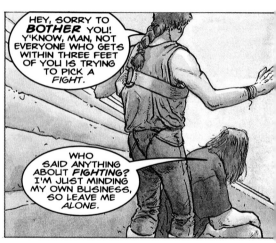

HEY, SORRY TO *BOTHER* YOU! Y'KNOW, MAN, NOT EVERYONE WHO GETS WITHIN THREE FEET OF YOU IS TRYING TO PICK A *FIGHT*.

WHO SAID ANYTHING ABOUT *FIGHTING?* I'M JUST MINDING MY OWN BUSINESS, SO LEAVE ME ALONE.

I'M TELLIN' YA -- THAT ALBERT'S GETTIN' ON MY *FUCKIN'* NERVES. IT'S LIKE HE *WANTS* EVERYONE TO HATE HIM!

AW, HE'S JUST CRABBY 'CAUSE HE WAS UP ALL NIGHT LISTENIN' TO HACK FUCK HIS MOM.

NO SHIT! WHERE'D YOU HEAR *THAT?*

EVERYONE KNOWS! HIS MOM *DOES* HACK EVERY NIGHT! AIN'T THAT RIGHT, STERNO?

THAT'S WHAT THEY *SAY!* FIRST HACK, THEN SKID AND LUGEY...

...I HEAR SHE'S WORKIN' HER WAY THROUGH THE WHOLE *FIRST HEAT!*

RIGHT! THEN SHE'LL DO THE *SECOND* AND THE *THIRD...*

...EVENTUALLY, SHE'LL GET TO *US!*

HEY, ALLL-BERT! HEAR IT'S JUST A DAY OR TWO TILL WE GET TO FUCK YOUR *MOM!*

WHAT DID YOU SAY?

I SAID, IF SHE'S GOOD ENOUGH FOR THE *CHIEF*, SHE'S GOOD ENOUGH FOR *ME!*

I'M GONNA *KILL* YOU!

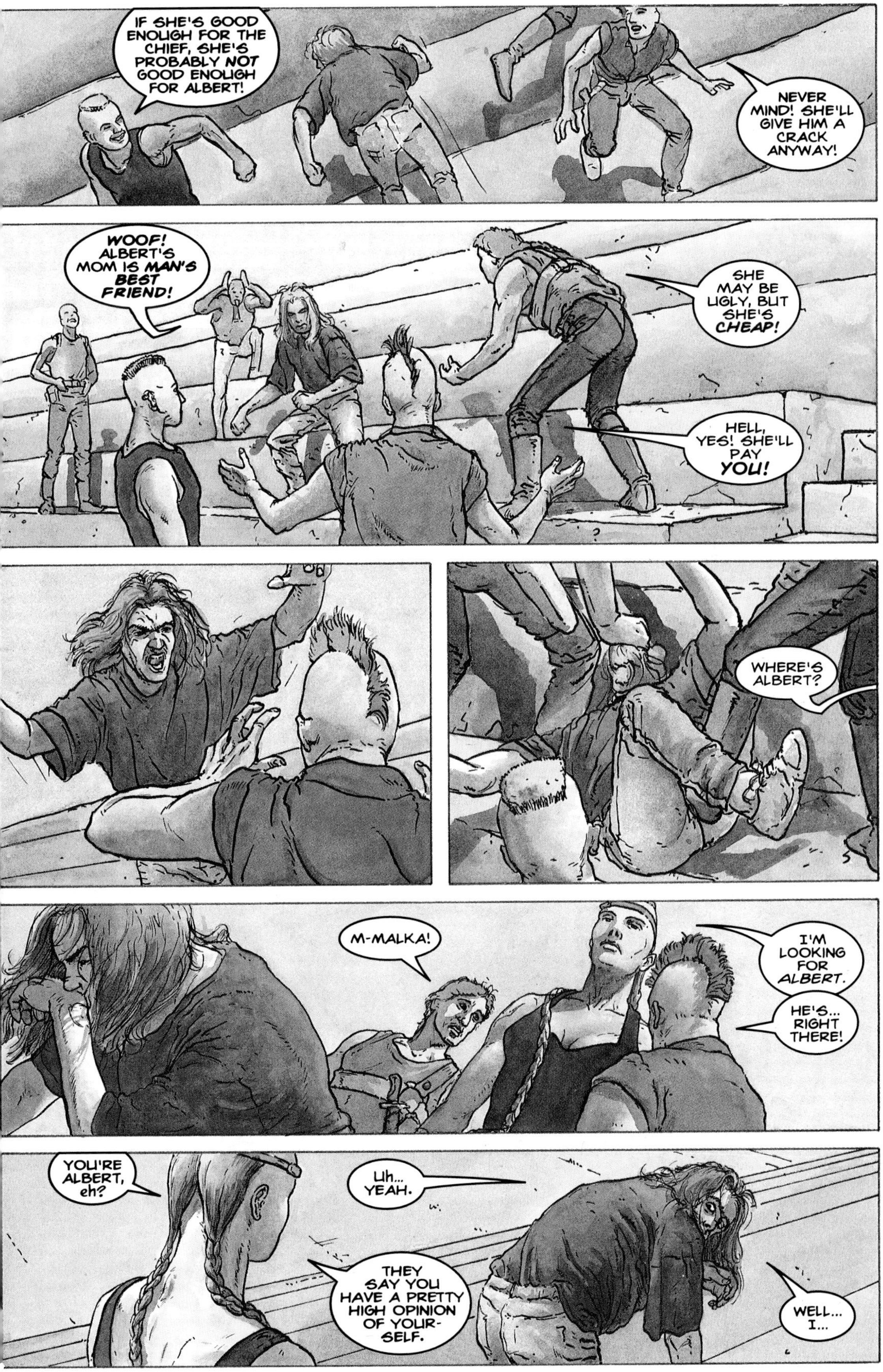
IF SHE'S GOOD ENOUGH FOR THE CHIEF, SHE'S PROBABLY NOT GOOD ENOUGH FOR ALBERT!
NEVER MIND! SHE'LL GIVE HIM A CRACK ANYWAY!
WOOF! ALBERT'S MOM IS MAN'S BEST FRIEND!
SHE MAY BE UGLY, BUT SHE'S CHEAP!
HELL, YES! SHE'LL PAY YOU!
WHERE'S ALBERT?
M-MALKA!
I'M LOOKING FOR ALBERT.
HE'S... RIGHT THERE!
YOU'RE ALBERT, eh?
UH... YEAH.
THEY SAY YOU HAVE A PRETTY HIGH OPINION OF YOUR-SELF.
WELL... I...

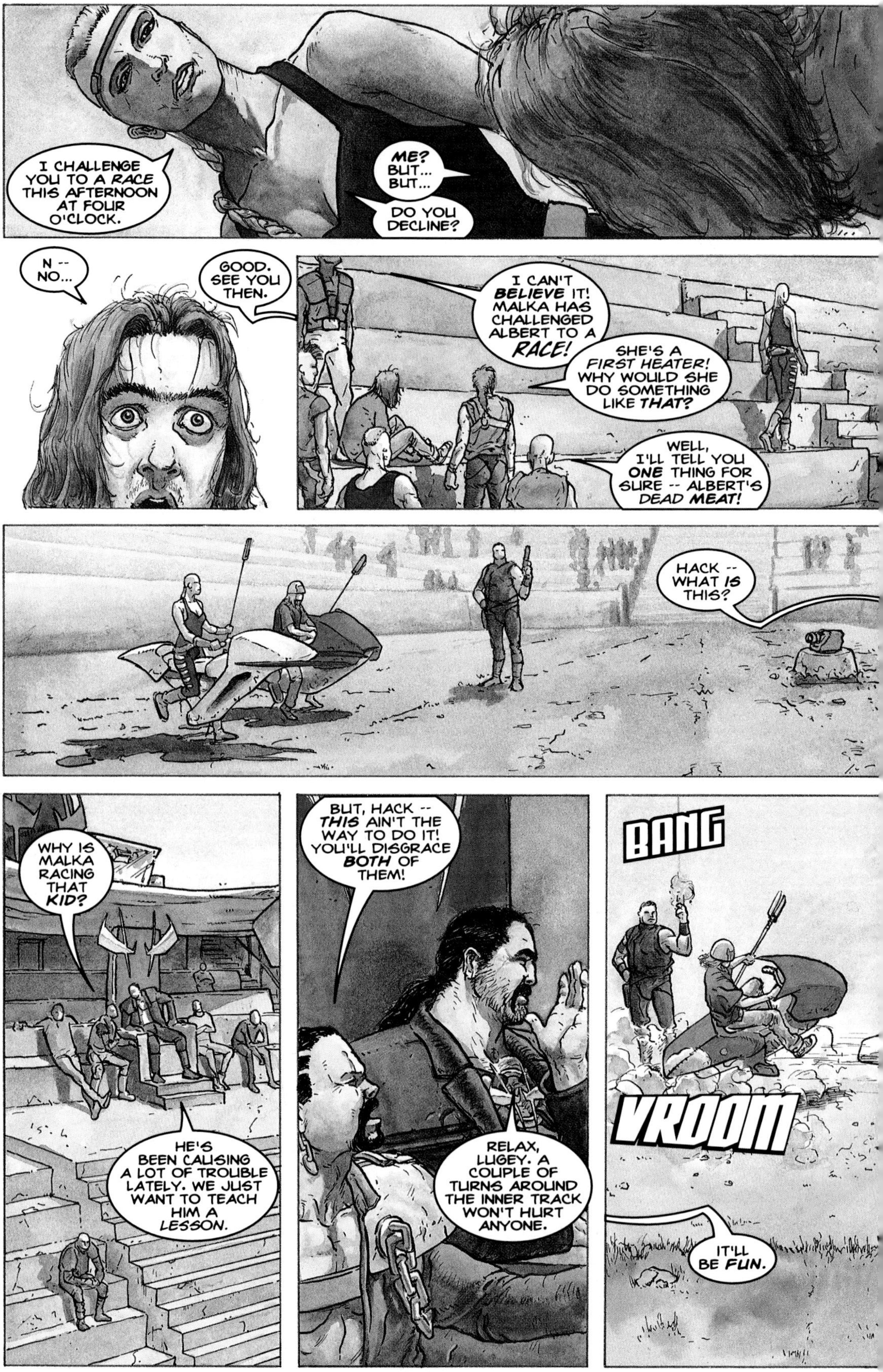
I CHALLENGE YOU TO A *RACE* THIS AFTERNOON AT FOUR O'CLOCK.
ME? BUT... BUT...
DO YOU DECLINE?
N -- NO...
GOOD. SEE YOU THEN.
I CAN'T *BELIEVE* IT! MALKA HAS CHALLENGED ALBERT TO A *RACE!*
SHE'S A *FIRST HEATER!* WHY WOULD SHE DO SOMETHING LIKE *THAT?*
WELL, I'LL TELL YOU **ONE** THING FOR SURE -- ALBERT'S *DEAD* ***MEAT!***
HACK -- WHAT *IS* THIS?
WHY IS MALKA RACING THAT ***KID?***
HE'S BEEN CAUSING A LOT OF TROUBLE LATELY. WE JUST WANT TO TEACH HIM A *LESSON.*
BUT, HACK -- ***THIS*** AIN'T THE WAY TO DO IT! YOU'LL DISGRACE ***BOTH*** OF THEM!
RELAX, LUGEY. A COUPLE OF TURNS AROUND THE INNER TRACK WON'T HURT ANYONE.
BANG
VROOM
IT'LL BE ***FUN.***

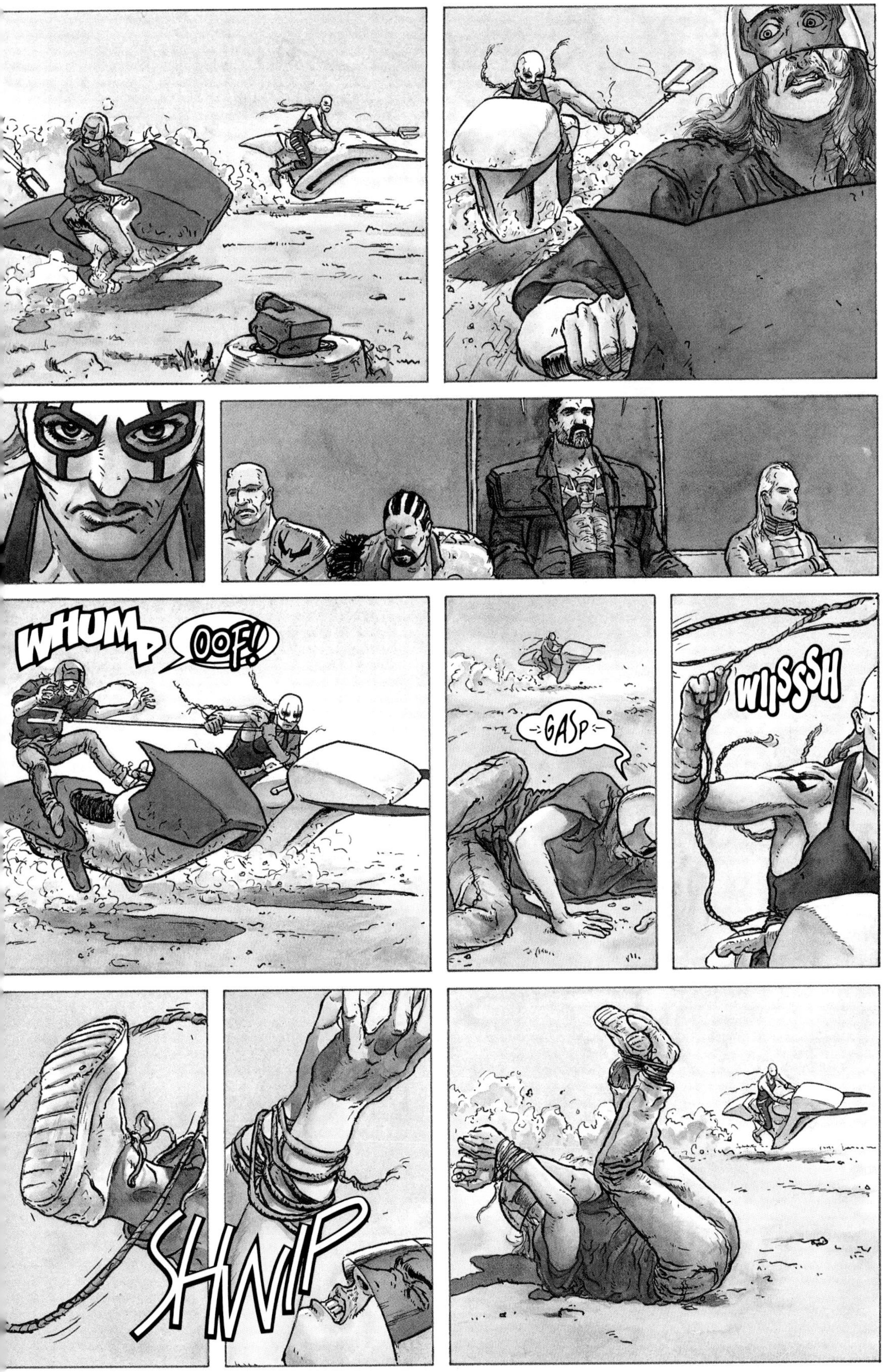
WHUMP
OOF!
GASP
WIISSSH
SHWIP

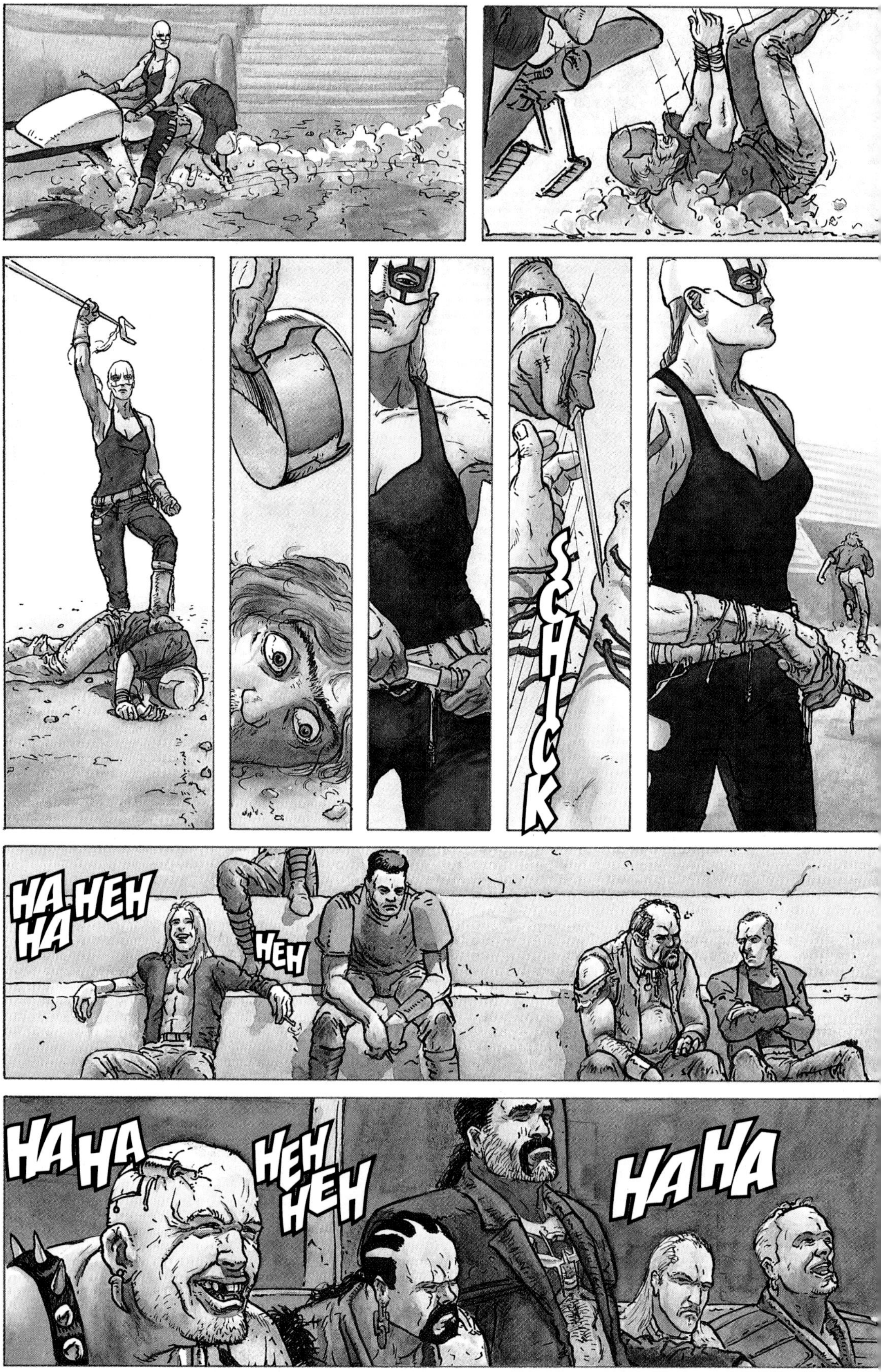
SCHICK
HA HA HEH
HEH
HA HA
HEH HEH
HA HA

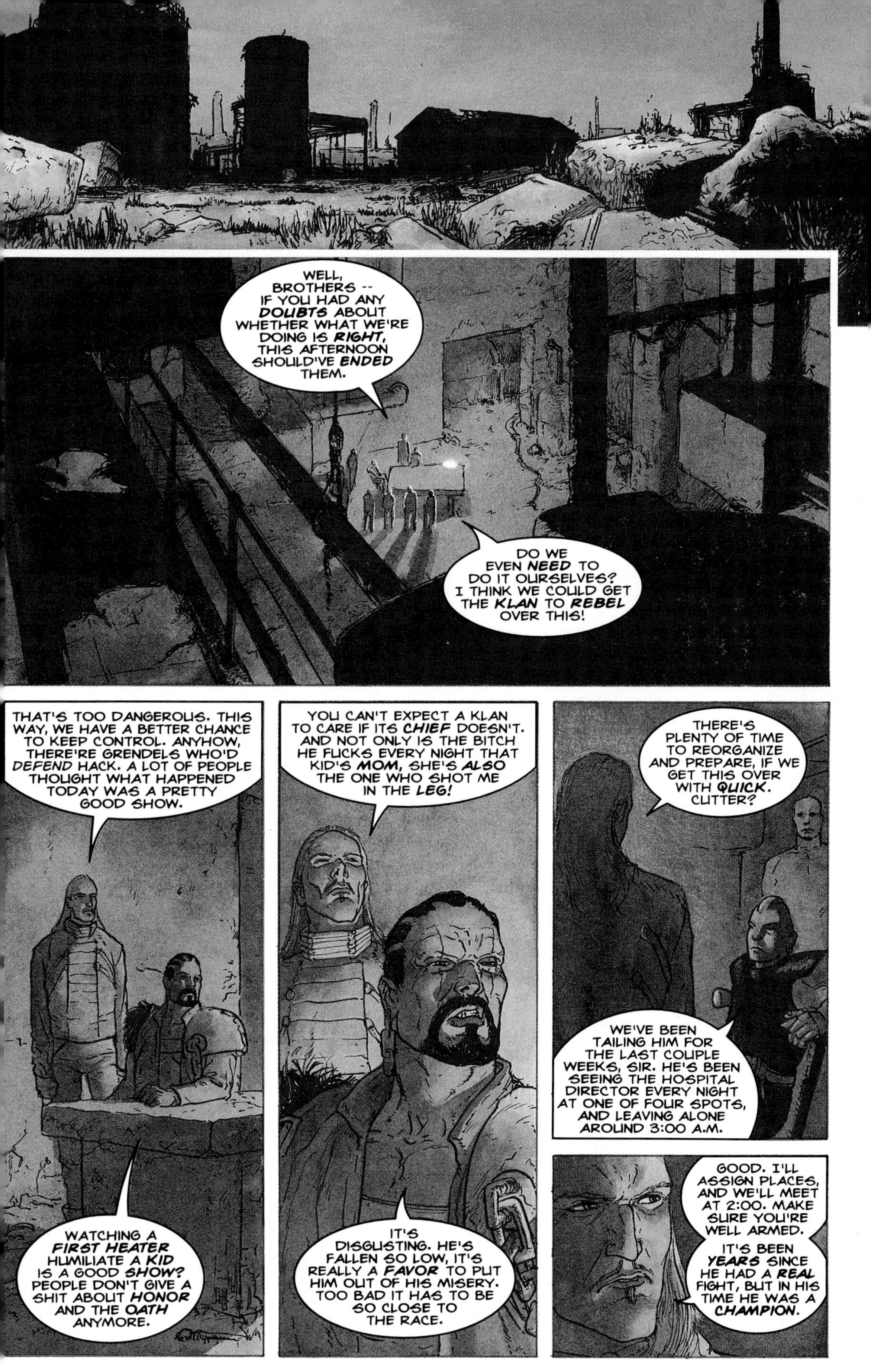
WELL, BROTHERS -- IF YOU HAD ANY DOUBTS ABOUT WHETHER WHAT WE'RE DOING IS RIGHT, THIS AFTERNOON SHOULD'VE ENDED THEM.
DO WE EVEN NEED TO DO IT OURSELVES? I THINK WE COULD GET THE KLAN TO REBEL OVER THIS!
THAT'S TOO DANGEROUS. THIS WAY, WE HAVE A BETTER CHANCE TO KEEP CONTROL. ANYHOW, THERE'RE GRENDELS WHO'D DEFEND HACK. A LOT OF PEOPLE THOUGHT WHAT HAPPENED TODAY WAS A PRETTY GOOD SHOW.
WATCHING A FIRST HEATER HUMILIATE A KID IS A GOOD SHOW? PEOPLE DON'T GIVE A SHIT ABOUT HONOR AND THE OATH ANYMORE.
YOU CAN'T EXPECT A KLAN TO CARE IF ITS CHIEF DOESN'T. AND NOT ONLY IS THE BITCH HE FUCKS EVERY NIGHT THAT KID'S MOM, SHE'S ALSO THE ONE WHO SHOT ME IN THE LEG!
IT'S DISGUSTING. HE'S FALLEN SO LOW, IT'S REALLY A FAVOR TO PUT HIM OUT OF HIS MISERY. TOO BAD IT HAS TO BE SO CLOSE TO THE RACE.
THERE'S PLENTY OF TIME TO REORGANIZE AND PREPARE, IF WE GET THIS OVER WITH QUICK. CUTTER?
WE'VE BEEN TAILING HIM FOR THE LAST COUPLE WEEKS, SIR. HE'S BEEN SEEING THE HOSPITAL DIRECTOR EVERY NIGHT AT ONE OF FOUR SPOTS, AND LEAVING ALONE AROUND 3:00 A.M.
GOOD. I'LL ASSIGN PLACES, AND WE'LL MEET AT 2:00. MAKE SURE YOU'RE WELL ARMED.
IT'S BEEN YEARS SINCE HE HAD A REAL FIGHT, BUT IN HIS TIME HE WAS A CHAMPION.

TOMORROW WE'LL ANNOUNCE THAT *LUGEY* IS CHIEF BEFORE ANY-ONE KNOWS WHAT'S HAPPENED.

WE'LL NEED YOUR HELP TO PUT DOWN THE CHALLENGES. IF WE'RE STILL THERE WHEN THE SMOKE CLEARS, YOU'LL BE MORE THAN HAPPY YOU HELPED US OUT.

TO THE *GLORY* OF THE KLAN AND TO *VICTORY* IN THE RACE...

VIVAT GRENDEL!

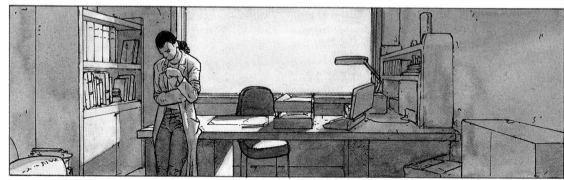

KNOCK KNOCK

COME IN.

DANA! THERE YOU ARE! I'VE BEEN PAGING YOU -- DIDN'T YOU HEAR? ARE YOU ALL RIGHT? YOU DON'T LOOK WELL.

I'M JUST A LITTLE TIRED TODAY.

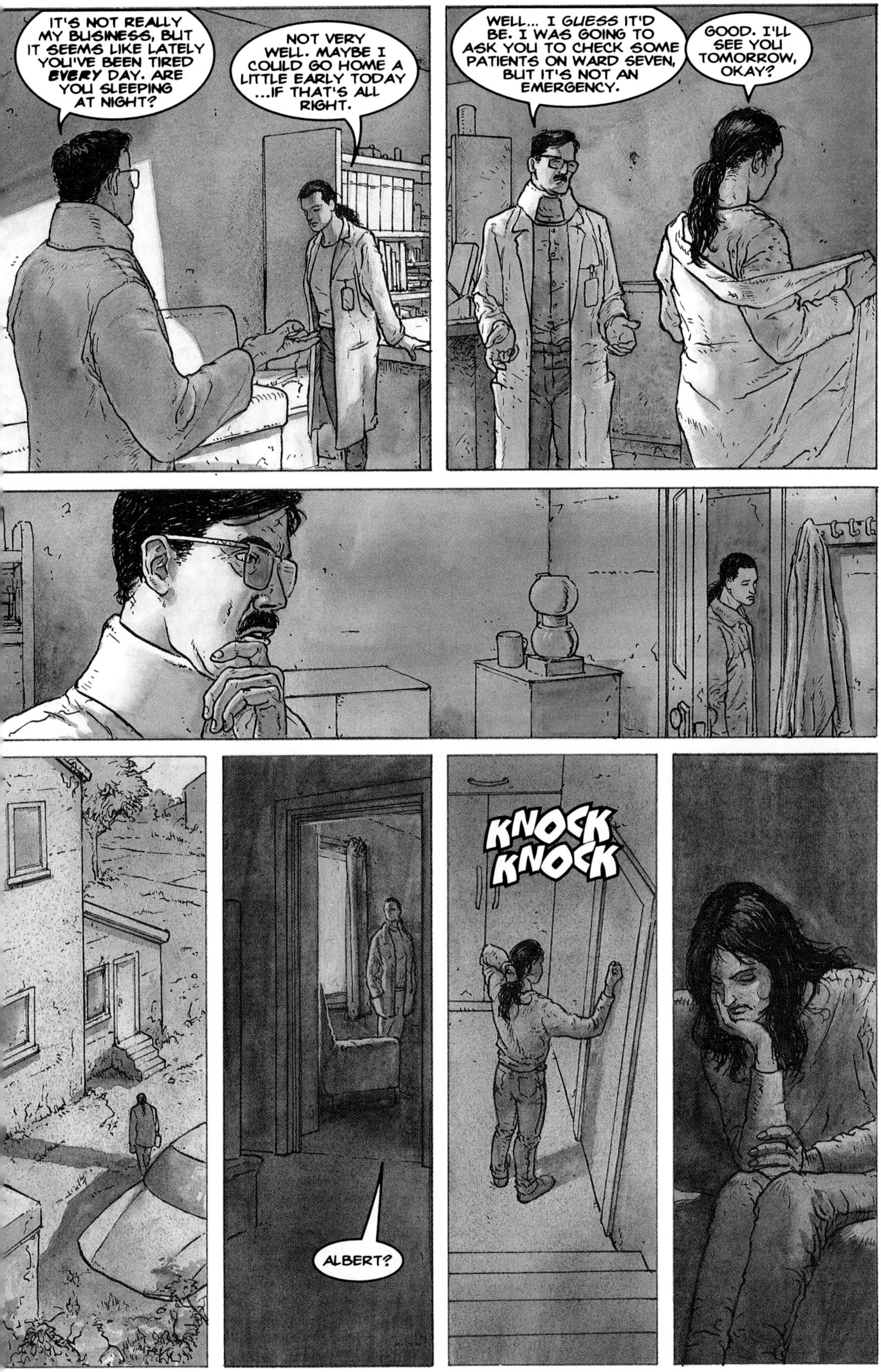

IT'S NOT REALLY MY BUSINESS, BUT IT SEEMS LIKE LATELY YOU'VE BEEN TIRED EVERY DAY. ARE YOU SLEEPING AT NIGHT?
NOT VERY WELL. MAYBE I COULD GO HOME A LITTLE EARLY TODAY ...IF THAT'S ALL RIGHT.
WELL... I GUESS IT'D BE. I WAS GOING TO ASK YOU TO CHECK SOME PATIENTS ON WARD SEVEN, BUT IT'S NOT AN EMERGENCY.
GOOD. I'LL SEE YOU TOMORROW, OKAY?
ALBERT?
KNOCK KNOCK

WAS THAT ALL RIGHT?

YES. IT WAS WONDERFUL.

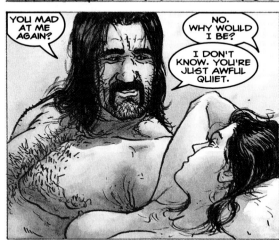

YOU MAD AT ME AGAIN?

NO. WHY WOULD I BE?

I DON'T KNOW. YOU'RE JUST AWFUL QUIET.

IT ISN'T YOU. I'M WORRIED ABOUT ALBERT. I HAVEN'T SEEN HIM IN A DAY AND A HALF. IT'S HAPPENED BEFORE, BUT STILL...

WELL, YOU DON'T HAVE TO WORRY THAT HE'S HANGING AROUND WITH GRENDELS. I DID WHAT YOU ASKED ME TO.

WHAT DO YOU MEAN?

I MADE SURE HE'LL NEVER JOIN THE KLAN. THAT'S WHAT YOU WANTED, ISN'T IT?

Y-- YES. BUT HOW?

DON'T WORRY, DANA. HE'S FINE -- OR AT LEAST HE WAS THE LAST TIME I SAW HIM. I'M SURE HE'LL SHOW UP IN A DAY OR SO. THEN YOU CAN PUT HIM TO WORK CLEANING BEDPANS OR SOMETHING.

WHAT'S THAT SUPPOSED TO MEAN?

NOTHING.

Y'KNOW, I'M STARTING TO THINK MAYBE WE'RE SPENDING TOO MUCH TIME TOGETHER. PEOPLE ARE STARTING TO TALK.

ARE YOU TELLING ME YOU'RE RUINING YOUR REPUTATION BY ASSOCIATING WITH SOMEONE WHO'S RESPECTABLE?

THEY'RE TALKING ABOUT ME, NOT YOU. THEY'RE SAYING I DON'T CARE ABOUT THE KLAN ANY-MORE, THAT I'VE GONE OLD AND SOFT. THERE'S PROBABLY SOMEONE TRYING TO FIGURE OUT THE BEST WAY TO KILL ME RIGHT NOW.

WELL... IF YOU'RE AFRAID SOMEONE'S GOING TO KILL YOU...

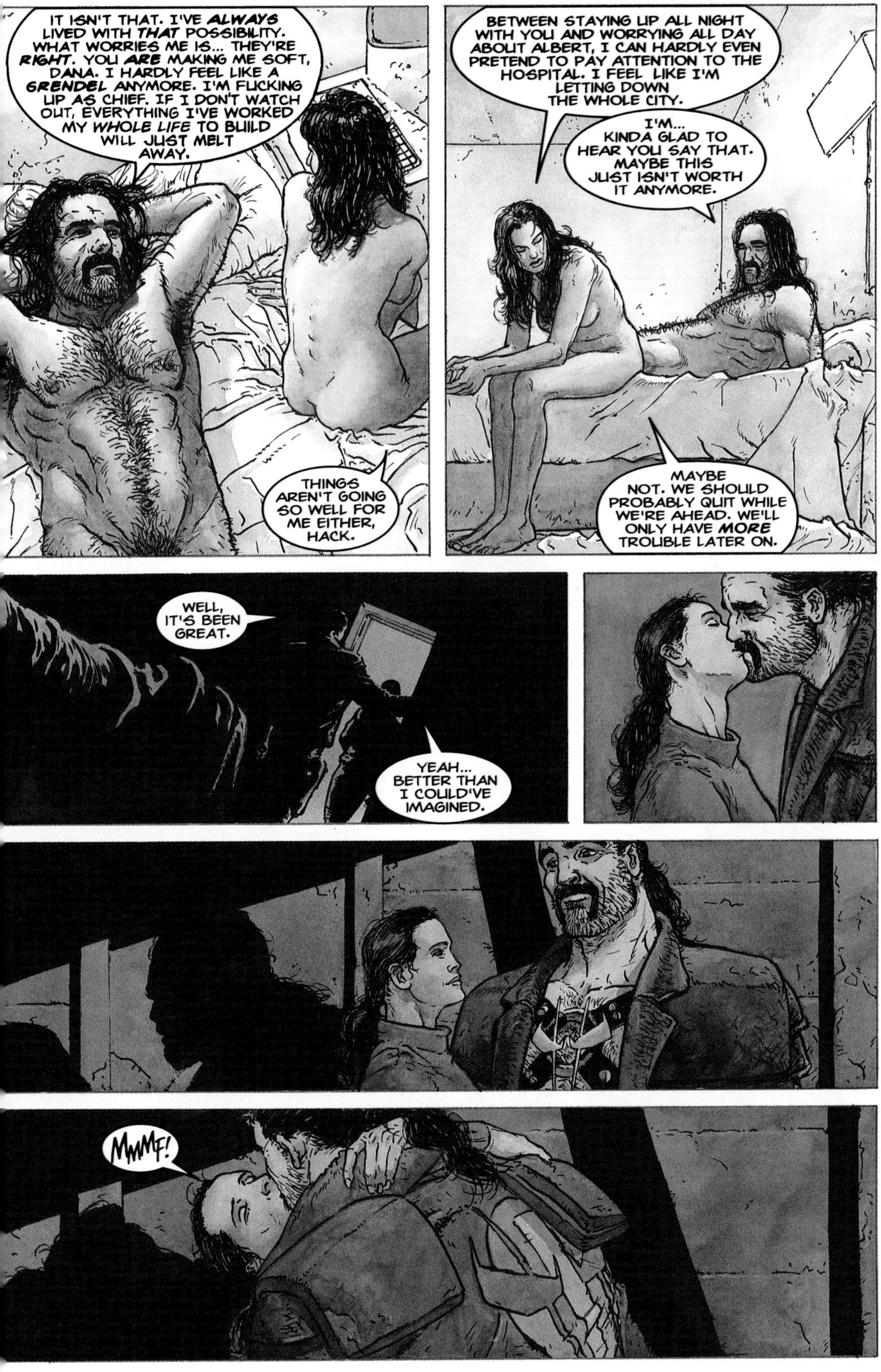
IT ISN'T THAT. I'VE ALWAYS LIVED WITH THAT POSSIBILITY. WHAT WORRIES ME IS... THEY'RE RIGHT. YOU ARE MAKING ME SOFT, DANA. I HARDLY FEEL LIKE A GRENDEL ANYMORE. I'M FUCKING UP AS CHIEF. IF I DON'T WATCH OUT, EVERYTHING I'VE WORKED MY WHOLE LIFE TO BUILD WILL JUST MELT AWAY.
THINGS AREN'T GOING SO WELL FOR ME EITHER, HACK.
BETWEEN STAYING UP ALL NIGHT WITH YOU AND WORRYING ALL DAY ABOUT ALBERT, I CAN HARDLY EVEN PRETEND TO PAY ATTENTION TO THE HOSPITAL. I FEEL LIKE I'M LETTING DOWN THE WHOLE CITY.
I'M... KINDA GLAD TO HEAR YOU SAY THAT. MAYBE THIS JUST ISN'T WORTH IT ANYMORE.
MAYBE NOT. WE SHOULD PROBABLY QUIT WHILE WE'RE AHEAD. WE'LL ONLY HAVE MORE TROUBLE LATER ON.
WELL, IT'S BEEN GREAT.
YEAH... BETTER THAN I COULD'VE IMAGINED.
MMMF!

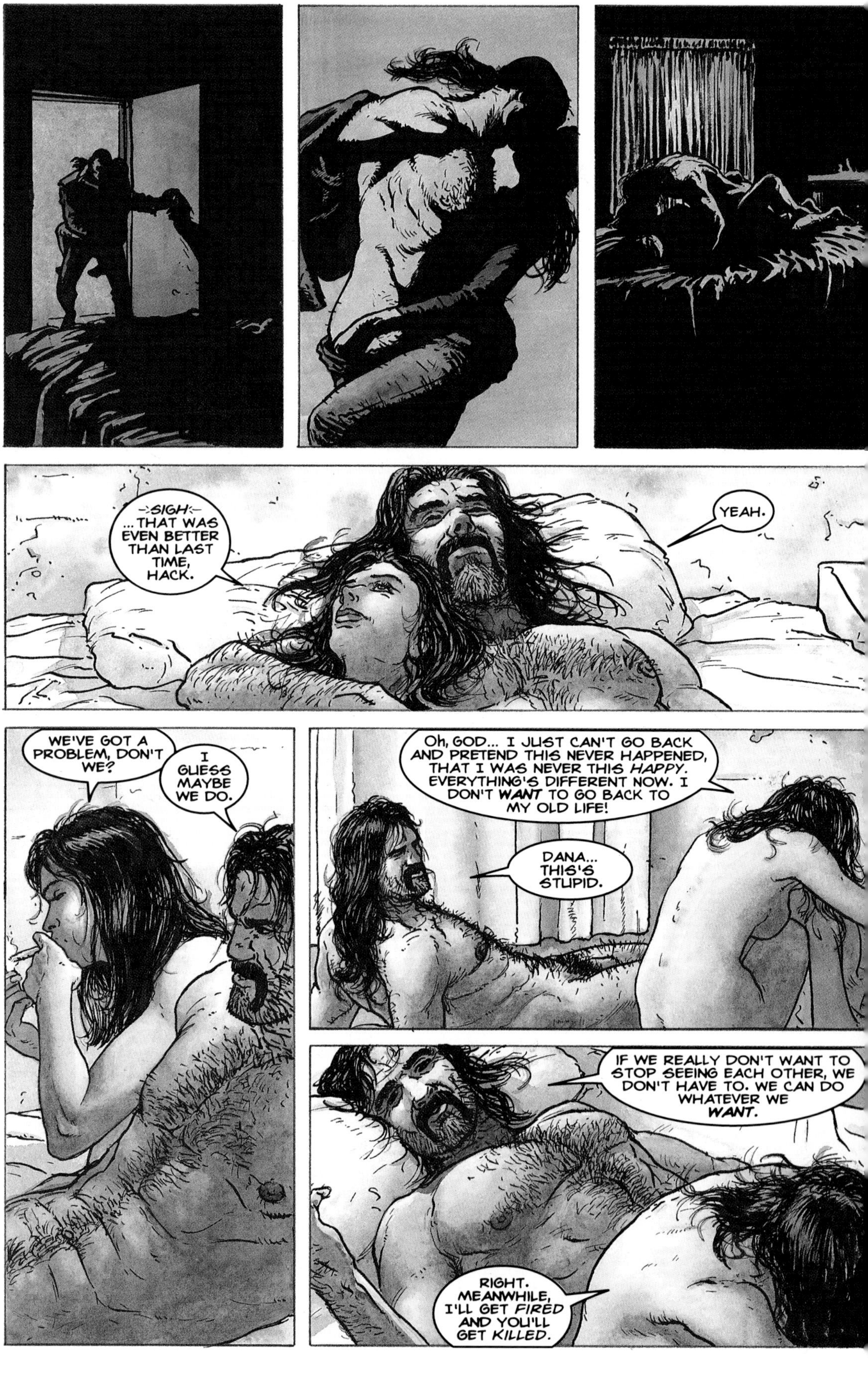

-SIGH- ...THAT WAS EVEN BETTER THAN LAST TIME, HACK.
YEAH.
WE'VE GOT A PROBLEM, DON'T WE?
I GUESS MAYBE WE DO.
Oh, GOD... I JUST CAN'T GO BACK AND PRETEND THIS NEVER HAPPENED, THAT I WAS NEVER THIS HAPPY. EVERYTHING'S DIFFERENT NOW. I DON'T WANT TO GO BACK TO MY OLD LIFE!
DANA... THIS'S STUPID.
IF WE REALLY DON'T WANT TO STOP SEEING EACH OTHER, WE DON'T HAVE TO. WE CAN DO WHATEVER WE WANT.
RIGHT. MEANWHILE, I'LL GET FIRED AND YOU'LL GET KILLED.

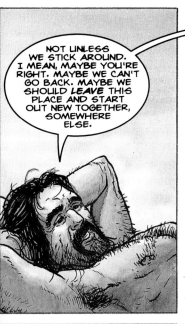

NOT UNLESS WE STICK AROUND. I MEAN, MAYBE YOU'RE RIGHT. MAYBE WE CAN'T GO BACK. MAYBE WE SHOULD *LEAVE* THIS PLACE AND START OUT NEW TOGETHER, SOMEWHERE ELSE.

LEAVE INDIANAPOLIS? I DON'T KNOW, HACK. I'VE LIVED HERE ALL MY LIFE. EVERYTHING I *HAVE* IS HERE. AND MY SON...

YOU CAN'T TAKE CARE OF HIM FOREVER. *SHIT*, NEITHER OF US IS YOUNG -- WE WON'T GET ANOTHER CHANCE. Y'KNOW, I HEAR THERE'RE ISLANDS DOWN SOUTH WHERE LAND IS CHEAP -- WHERE IT'S WARM ALL YEAR ROUND.

NO WINTER. THAT'D BE NICE. BUT... EVEN *I* KNOW A GRENDEL CAN'T JUST LEAVE HIS KLAN. HAVEN'T YOU TAKEN AN OATH?

YEAH. BUT... THE FACT IS, ALL I HAVE TO LOOK FORWARD TO NOW IS A GLORIOUS DEATH, AND SUDDENLY THAT DOESN'T SEEM WORTH STICKING AROUND FOR. I JUST WANNA MAKE SURE THE KLAN GETS THROUGH THE GREAT RACE ALL RIGHT, AND THEN...

...WE CAN JUST SLIP AWAY INTO THE NIGHT.

Oh, HACK... IT'S SO NICE TO THINK ABOUT. DO YOU THINK WE COULD REALLY *DO* IT?

HEY -- IT'S A FREE COUNTRY, ISN'T IT? C'MON -- I'LL TAKE YOU HOME.

GOOD NIGHT, HACK. BE CAREFUL.

I WILL. GOOD NIGHT.

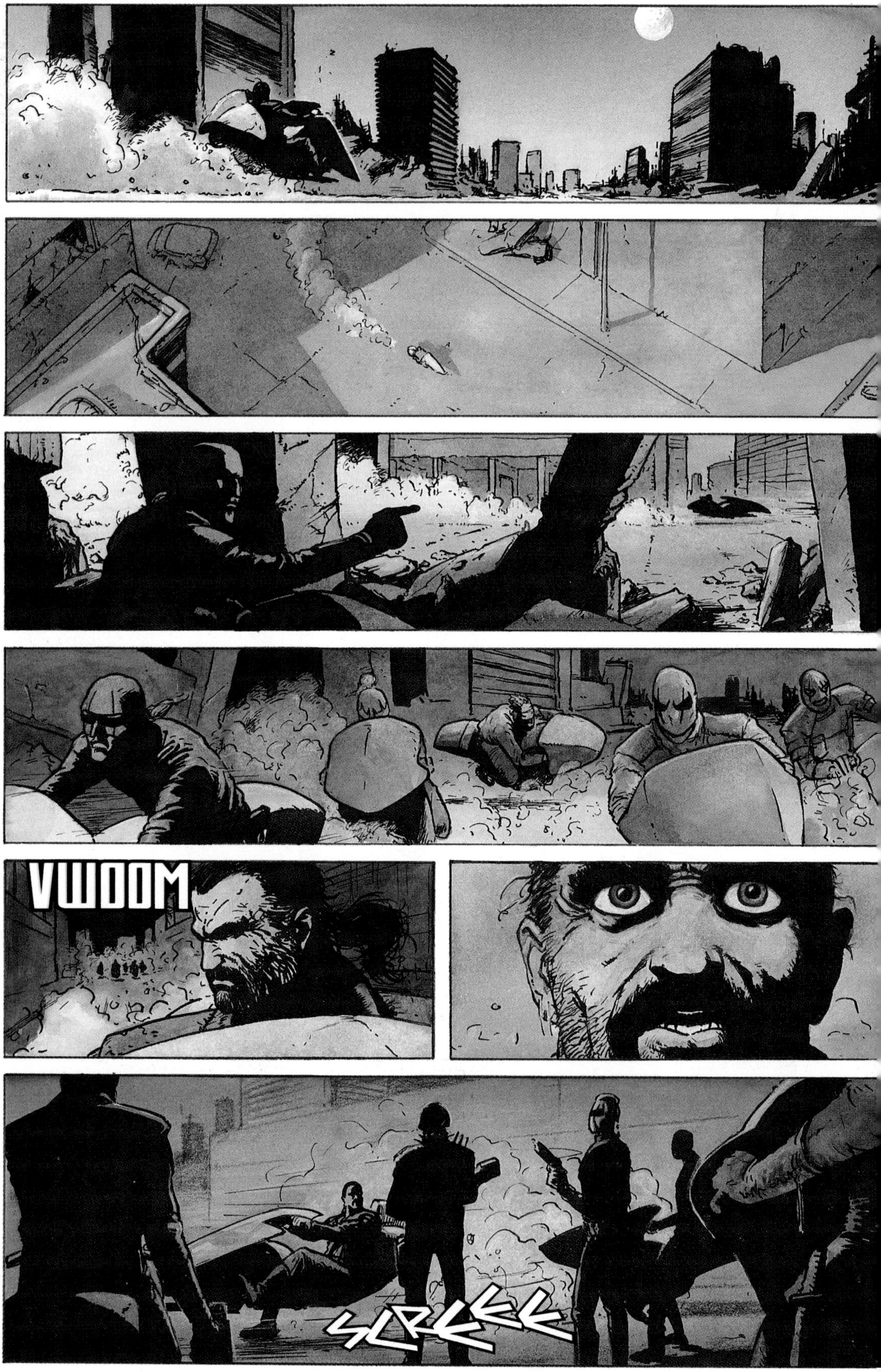
VWOOM
SCREEE

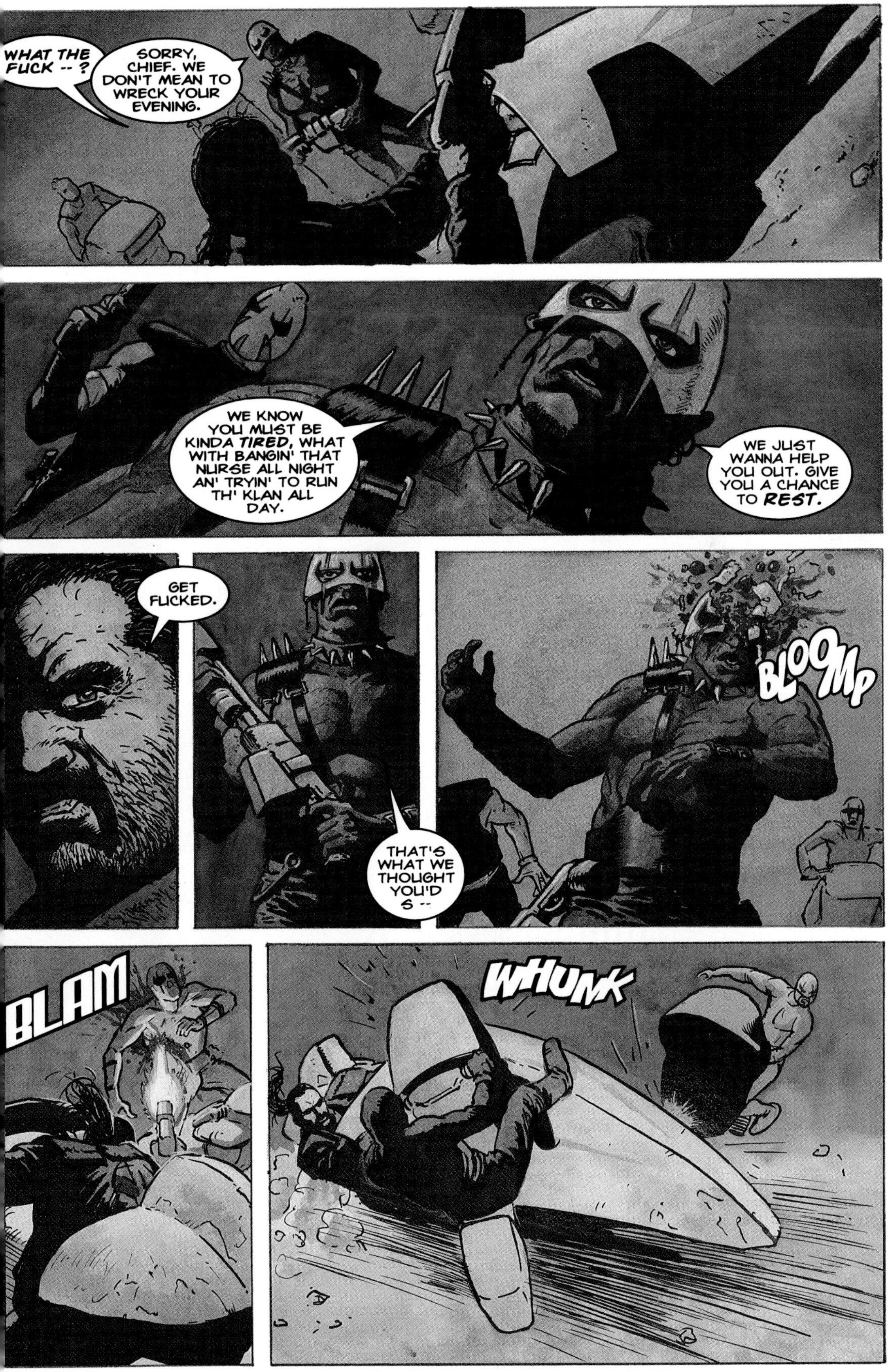

WHAT THE FUCK -- ?
SORRY, CHIEF. WE DON'T MEAN TO WRECK YOUR EVENING.
WE KNOW YOU MUST BE KINDA TIRED, WHAT WITH BANGIN' THAT NURSE ALL NIGHT AN' TRYIN' TO RUN TH' KLAN ALL DAY.
WE JUST WANNA HELP YOU OUT. GIVE YOU A CHANCE TO REST.
GET FUCKED.
THAT'S WHAT WE THOUGHT YOU'D S --
BLOOMP
BLAM
WHUNK

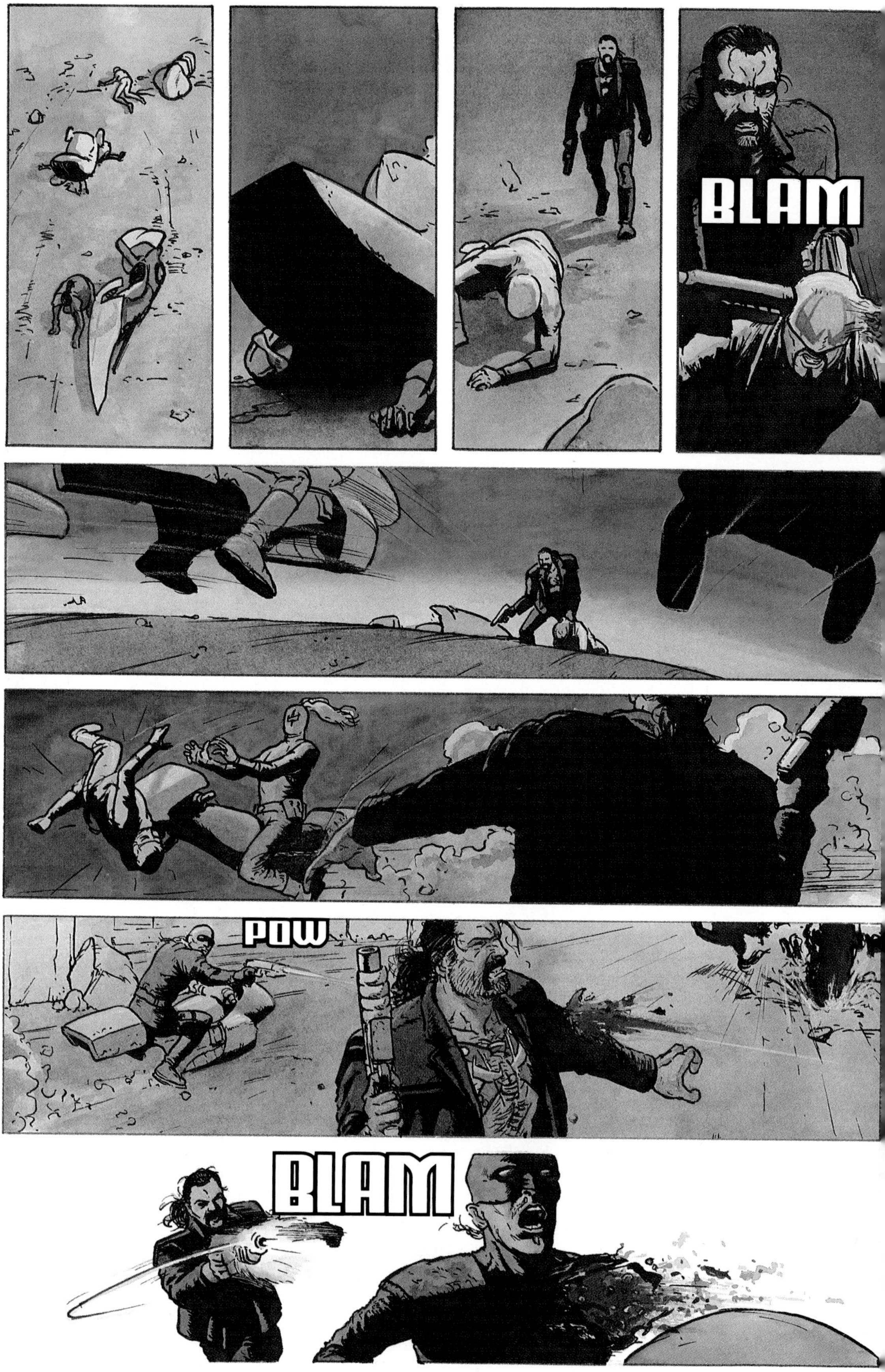
BLAM
POW
BLAM

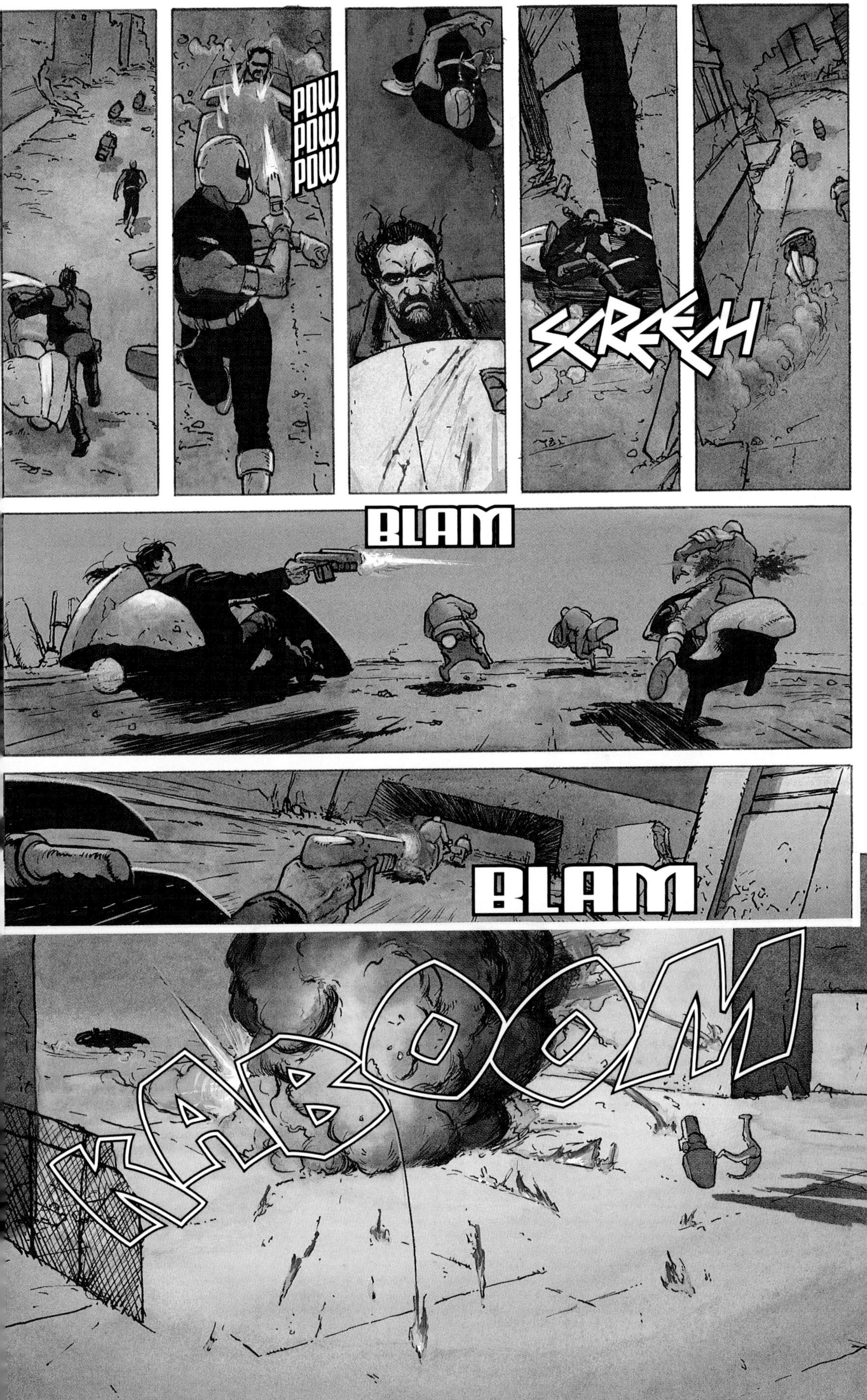
POW
POW
POW
SCREECH
BLAM
BLAM
KABOOM

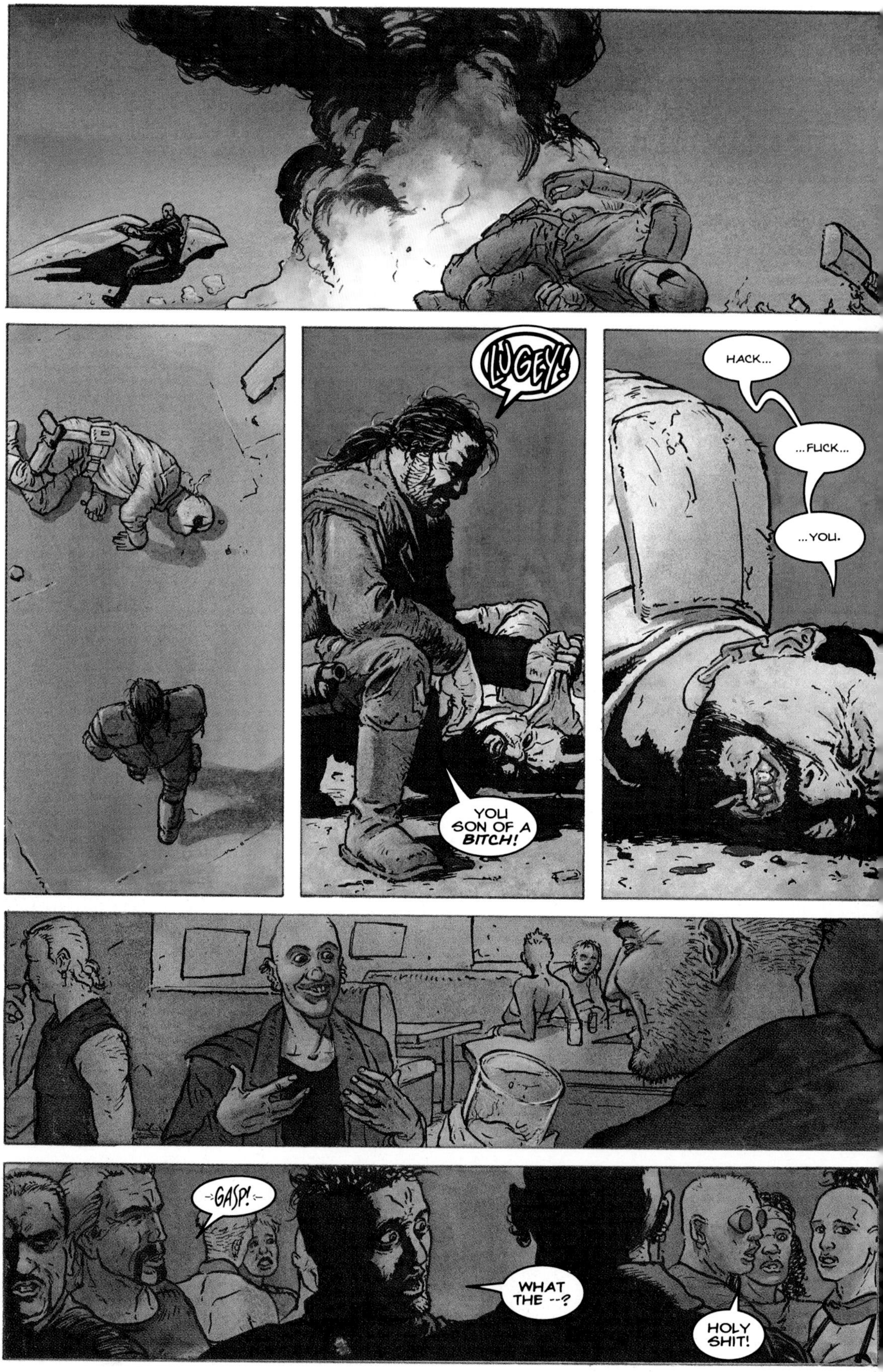

LUGEY!
YOU SON OF A BITCH!
HACK...
...FUCK...
...YOU.
-GASP!-
WHAT THE --?
HOLY SHIT!

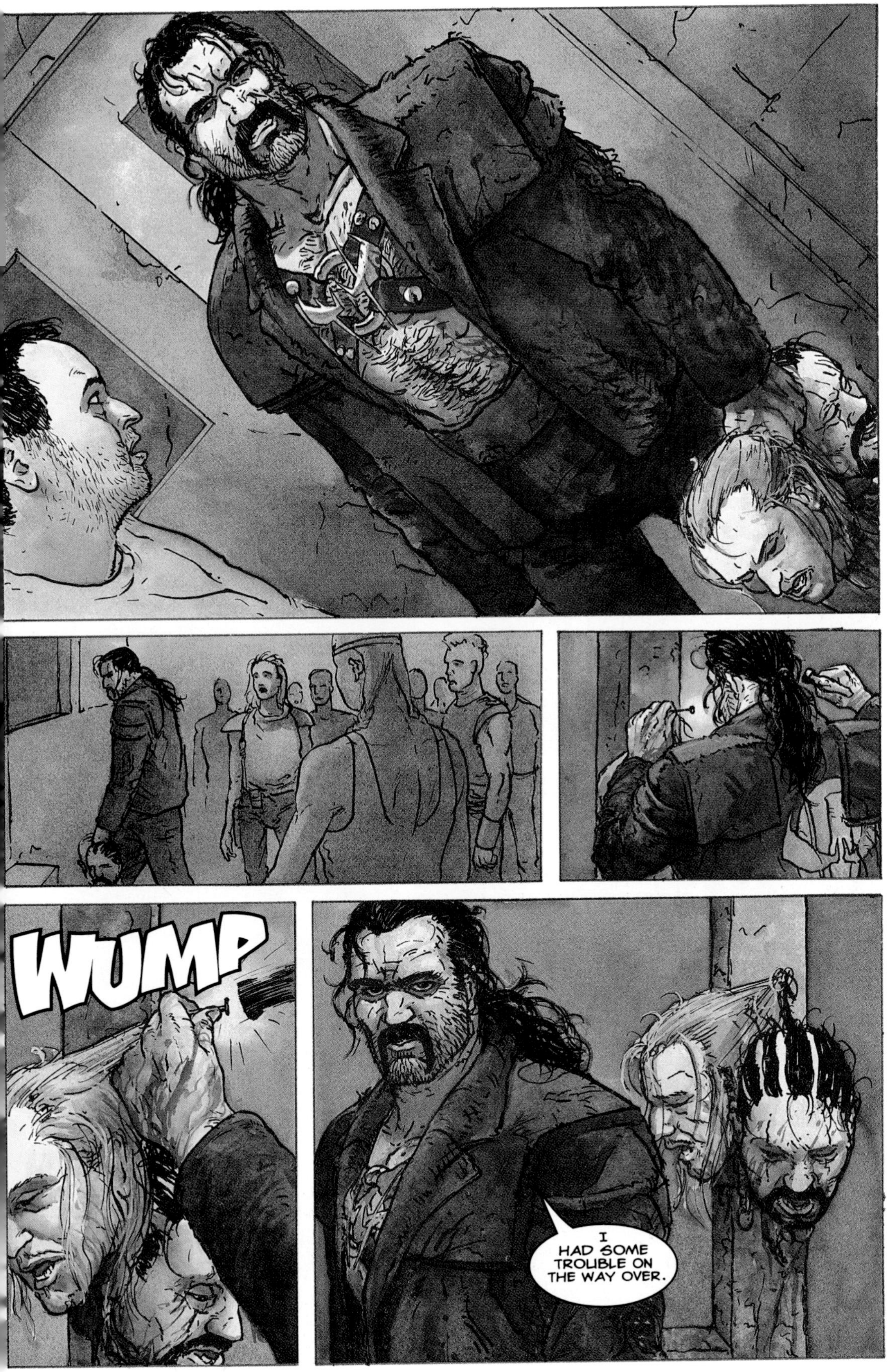
WUMP
I HAD SOME TROUBLE ON THE WAY OVER.

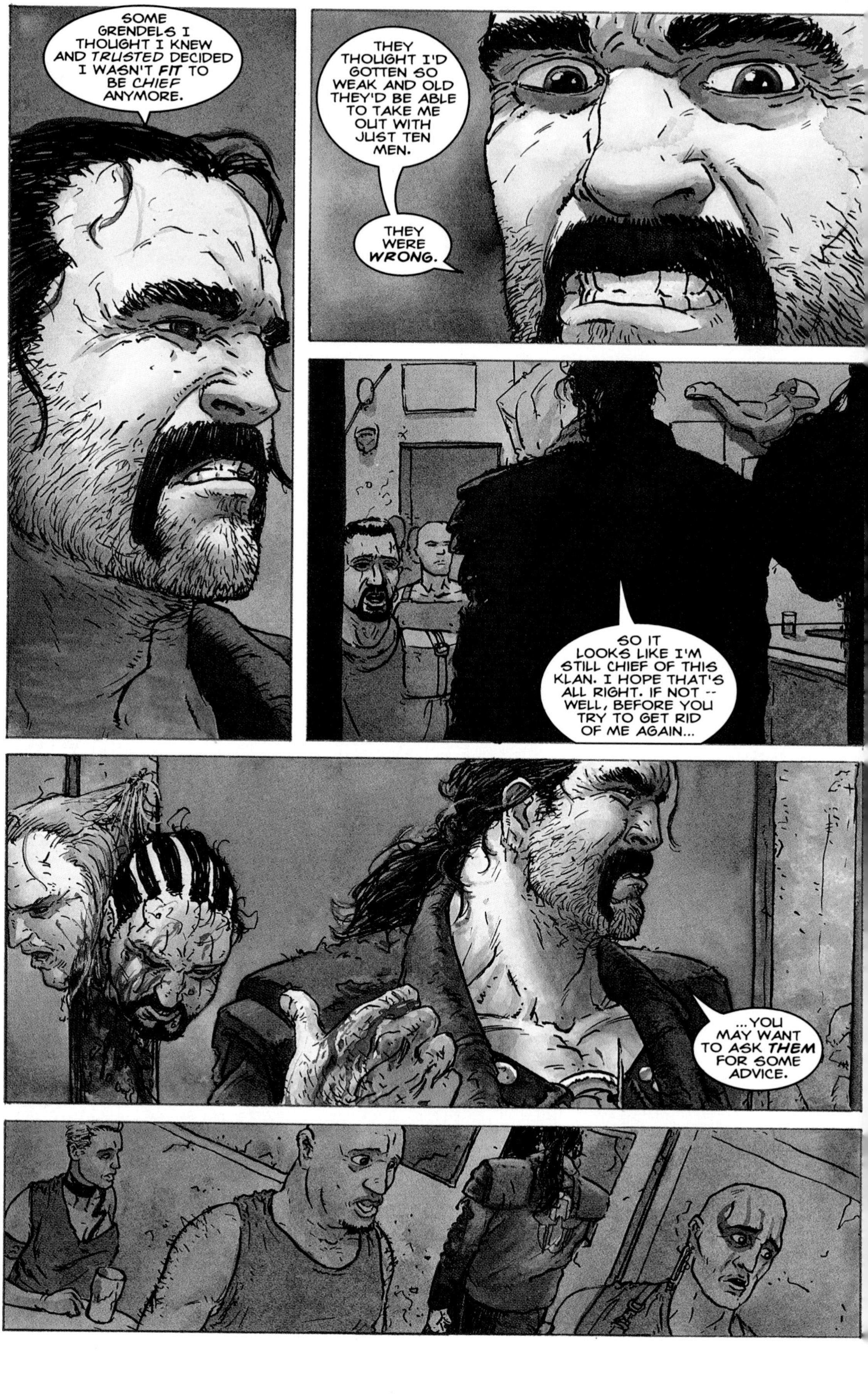
SOME GRENDELS I THOUGHT I KNEW AND TRUSTED DECIDED I WASN'T FIT TO BE CHIEF ANYMORE.
THEY THOUGHT I'D GOTTEN SO WEAK AND OLD THEY'D BE ABLE TO TAKE ME OUT WITH JUST TEN MEN.
THEY WERE WRONG.
SO IT LOOKS LIKE I'M STILL CHIEF OF THIS KLAN. I HOPE THAT'S ALL RIGHT. IF NOT -- WELL, BEFORE YOU TRY TO GET RID OF ME AGAIN...
...YOU MAY WANT TO ASK THEM FOR SOME ADVICE.

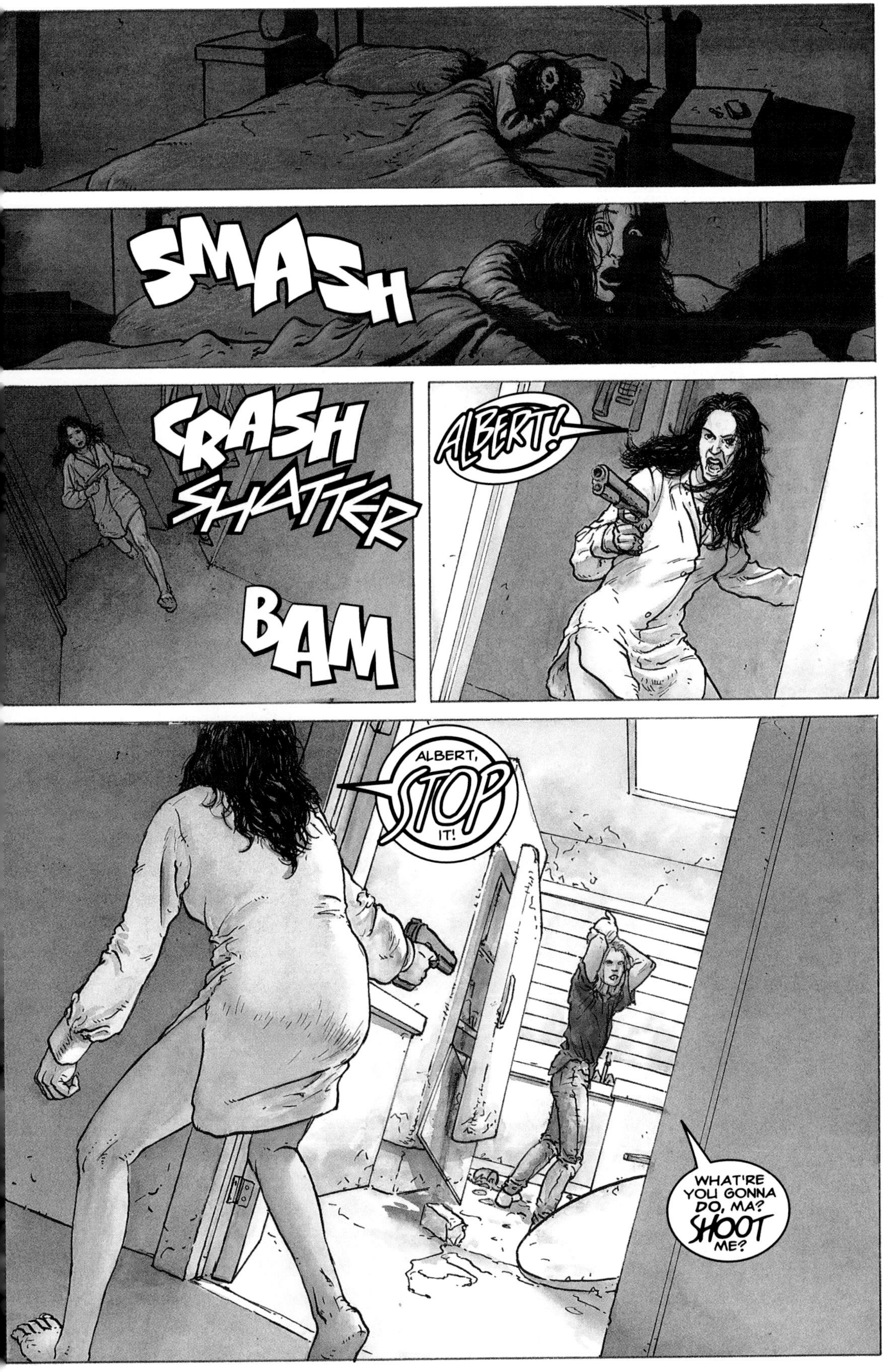
SMASH
CRASH
SHATTER
BAM
ALBERT!
ALBERT, STOP IT!
WHAT'RE YOU GONNA DO, MA? SHOOT ME?

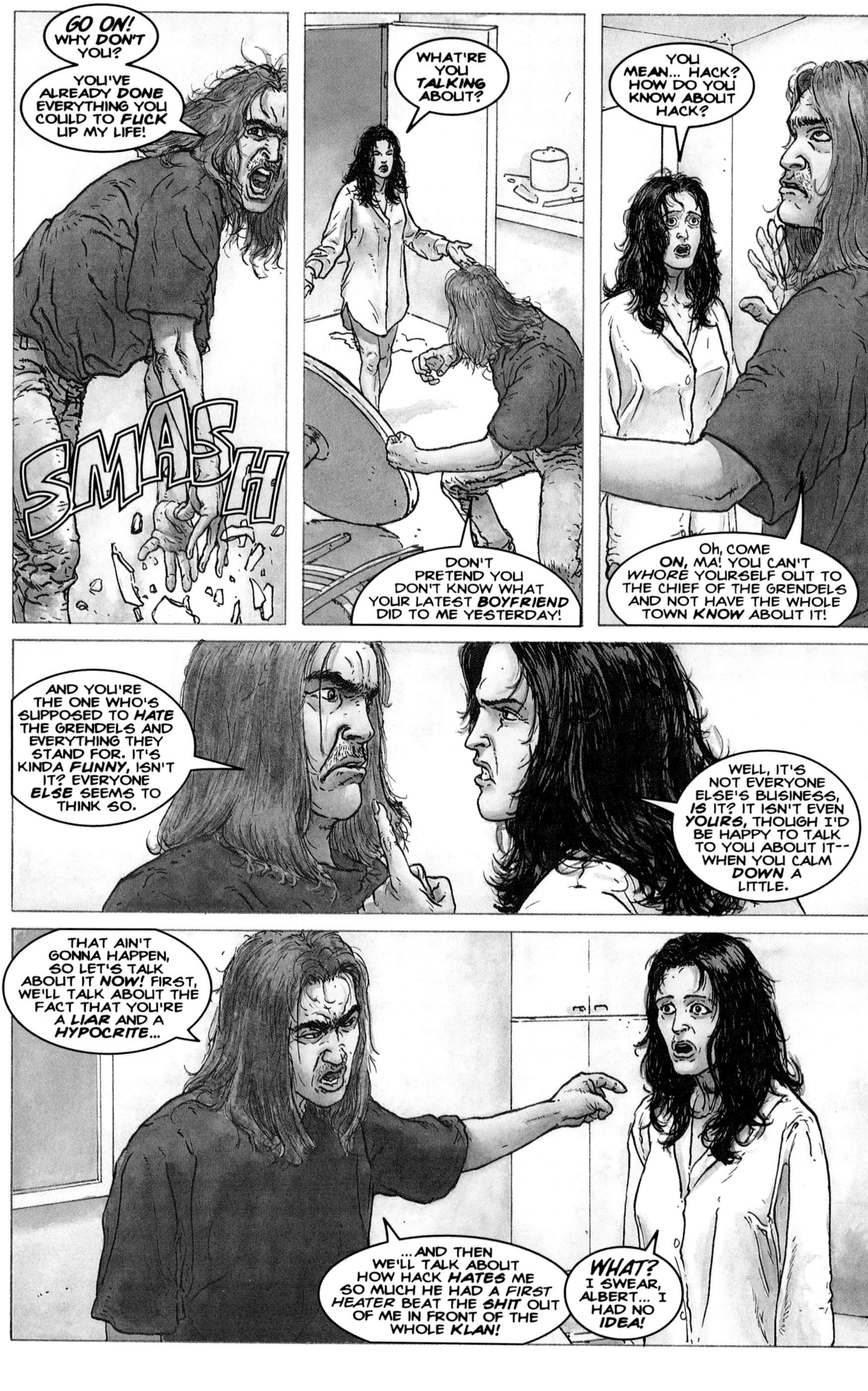
GO ON! WHY DON'T YOU?
YOU'VE ALREADY DONE EVERYTHING YOU COULD TO FUCK UP MY LIFE!
SMASH
WHAT'RE YOU TALKING ABOUT?
DON'T PRETEND YOU DON'T KNOW WHAT YOUR LATEST BOYFRIEND DID TO ME YESTERDAY!
YOU MEAN... HACK? HOW DO YOU KNOW ABOUT HACK?
Oh, COME ON, MA! YOU CAN'T WHORE YOURSELF OUT TO THE CHIEF OF THE GRENDELS AND NOT HAVE THE WHOLE TOWN KNOW ABOUT IT!
AND YOU'RE THE ONE WHO'S SUPPOSED TO HATE THE GRENDELS AND EVERYTHING THEY STAND FOR. IT'S KINDA FUNNY, ISN'T IT? EVERYONE ELSE SEEMS TO THINK SO.
WELL, IT'S NOT EVERYONE ELSE'S BUSINESS, IS IT? IT ISN'T EVEN YOURS, THOUGH I'D BE HAPPY TO TALK TO YOU ABOUT IT-- WHEN YOU CALM DOWN A LITTLE.
THAT AIN'T GONNA HAPPEN, SO LET'S TALK ABOUT IT NOW! FIRST, WE'LL TALK ABOUT THE FACT THAT YOU'RE A LIAR AND A HYPOCRITE...
...AND THEN WE'LL TALK ABOUT HOW HACK HATES ME SO MUCH HE HAD A FIRST HEATER BEAT THE SHIT OUT OF ME IN FRONT OF THE WHOLE KLAN!
WHAT? I SWEAR, ALBERT... I HAD NO IDEA!

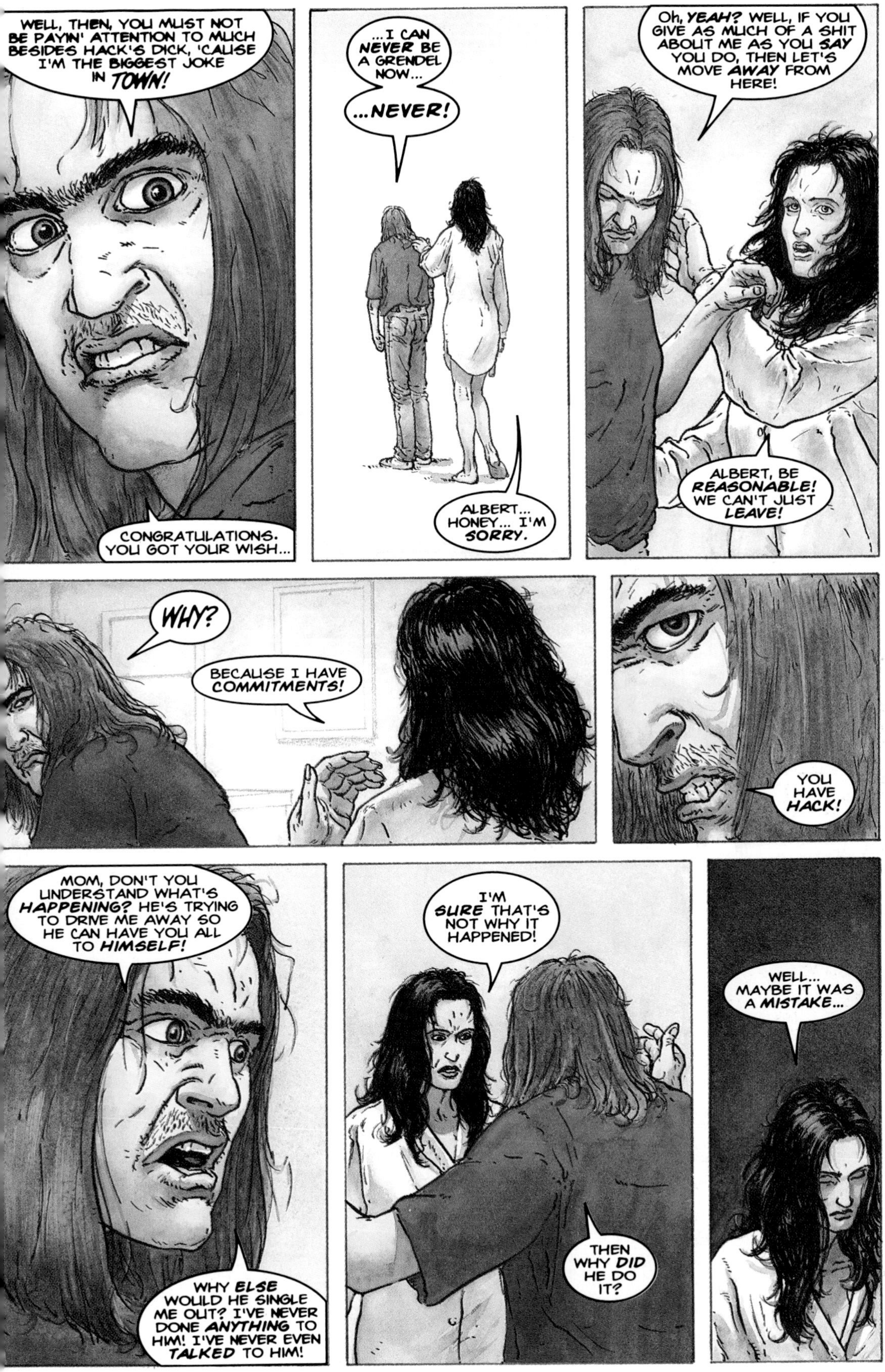
WELL, THEN, YOU MUST NOT BE PAYIN' ATTENTION TO MUCH BESIDES HACK'S DICK, 'CAUSE I'M THE BIGGEST JOKE IN TOWN!
CONGRATULATIONS. YOU GOT YOUR WISH...
...I CAN NEVER BE A GRENDEL NOW...
...NEVER!
ALBERT... HONEY... I'M SORRY.
Oh, YEAH? WELL, IF YOU GIVE AS MUCH OF A SHIT ABOUT ME AS YOU SAY YOU DO, THEN LET'S MOVE AWAY FROM HERE!
ALBERT, BE REASONABLE! WE CAN'T JUST LEAVE!
WHY?
BECAUSE I HAVE COMMITMENTS!
YOU HAVE HACK!
MOM, DON'T YOU UNDERSTAND WHAT'S HAPPENING? HE'S TRYING TO DRIVE ME AWAY SO HE CAN HAVE YOU ALL TO HIMSELF!
WHY ELSE WOULD HE SINGLE ME OUT? I'VE NEVER DONE ANYTHING TO HIM! I'VE NEVER EVEN TALKED TO HIM!
I'M SURE THAT'S NOT WHY IT HAPPENED!
THEN WHY DID HE DO IT?
WELL... MAYBE IT WAS A MISTAKE...

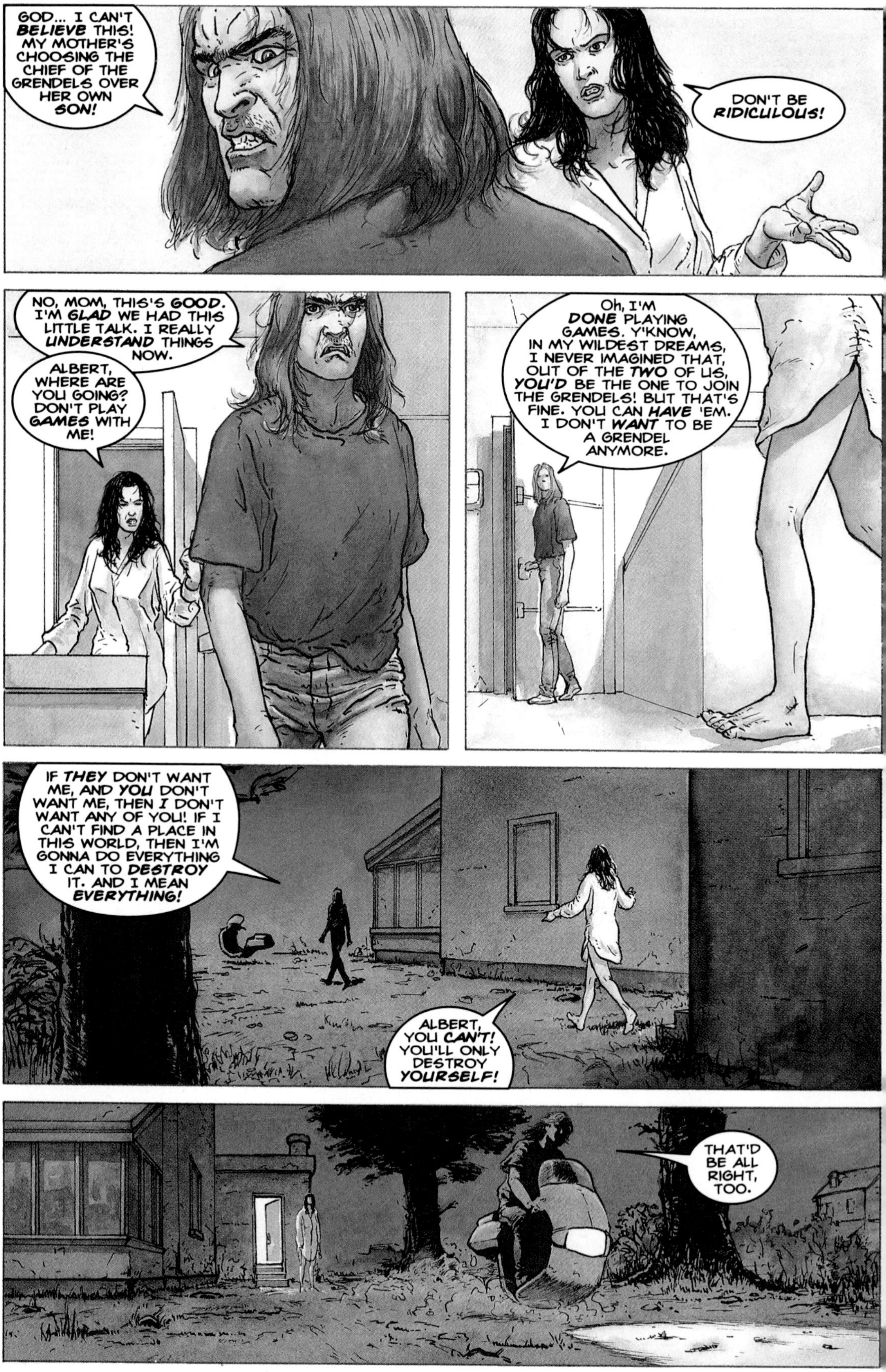
GOD... I CAN'T BELIEVE THIS! MY MOTHER'S CHOOSING THE CHIEF OF THE GRENDELS OVER HER OWN SON!
DON'T BE RIDICULOUS!
NO, MOM, THIS'S GOOD. I'M GLAD WE HAD THIS LITTLE TALK. I REALLY UNDERSTAND THINGS NOW.
ALBERT, WHERE ARE YOU GOING? DON'T PLAY GAMES WITH ME!
Oh, I'M DONE PLAYING GAMES. Y'KNOW, IN MY WILDEST DREAMS, I NEVER IMAGINED THAT, OUT OF THE TWO OF US, YOU'D BE THE ONE TO JOIN THE GRENDELS! BUT THAT'S FINE. YOU CAN HAVE 'EM. I DON'T WANT TO BE A GRENDEL ANYMORE.
IF THEY DON'T WANT ME, AND YOU DON'T WANT ME, THEN I DON'T WANT ANY OF YOU! IF I CAN'T FIND A PLACE IN THIS WORLD, THEN I'M GONNA DO EVERYTHING I CAN TO DESTROY IT. AND I MEAN EVERYTHING!
ALBERT, YOU CAN'T! YOU'LL ONLY DESTROY YOURSELF!
THAT'D BE ALL RIGHT, TOO.

CHAPTER FOUR

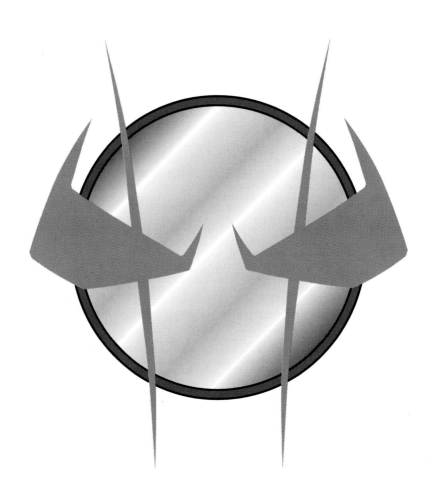

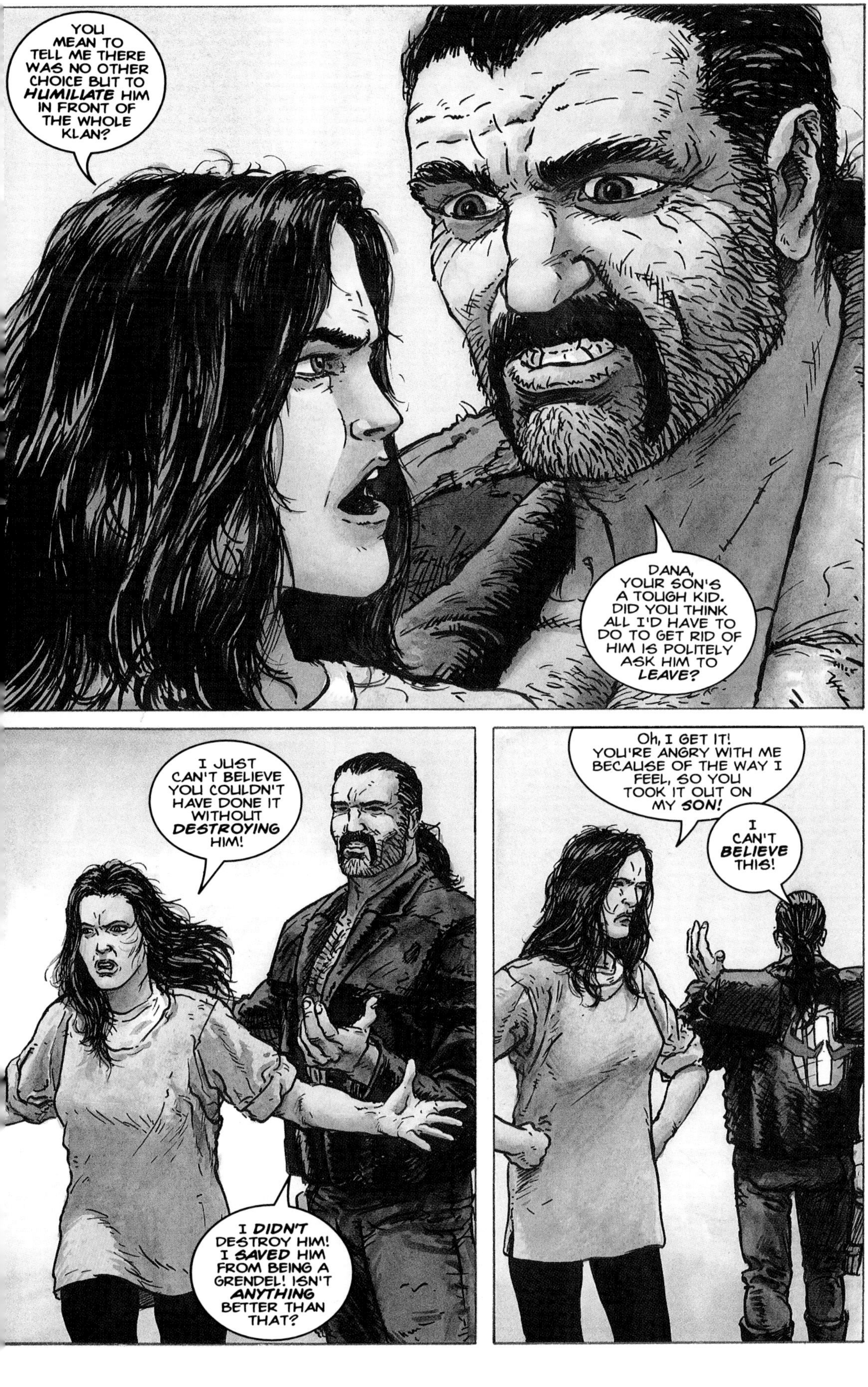
YOU MEAN TO TELL ME THERE WAS NO OTHER CHOICE BUT TO HUMILIATE HIM IN FRONT OF THE WHOLE KLAN?
DANA, YOUR SON'S A TOUGH KID. DID YOU THINK ALL I'D HAVE TO DO TO GET RID OF HIM IS POLITELY ASK HIM TO LEAVE?
I JUST CAN'T BELIEVE YOU COULDN'T HAVE DONE IT WITHOUT DESTROYING HIM!
I DIDN'T DESTROY HIM! I SAVED HIM FROM BEING A GRENDEL! ISN'T ANYTHING BETTER THAN THAT?
Oh, I GET IT! YOU'RE ANGRY WITH ME BECAUSE OF THE WAY I FEEL, SO YOU TOOK IT OUT ON MY SON!
I CAN'T BELIEVE THIS!

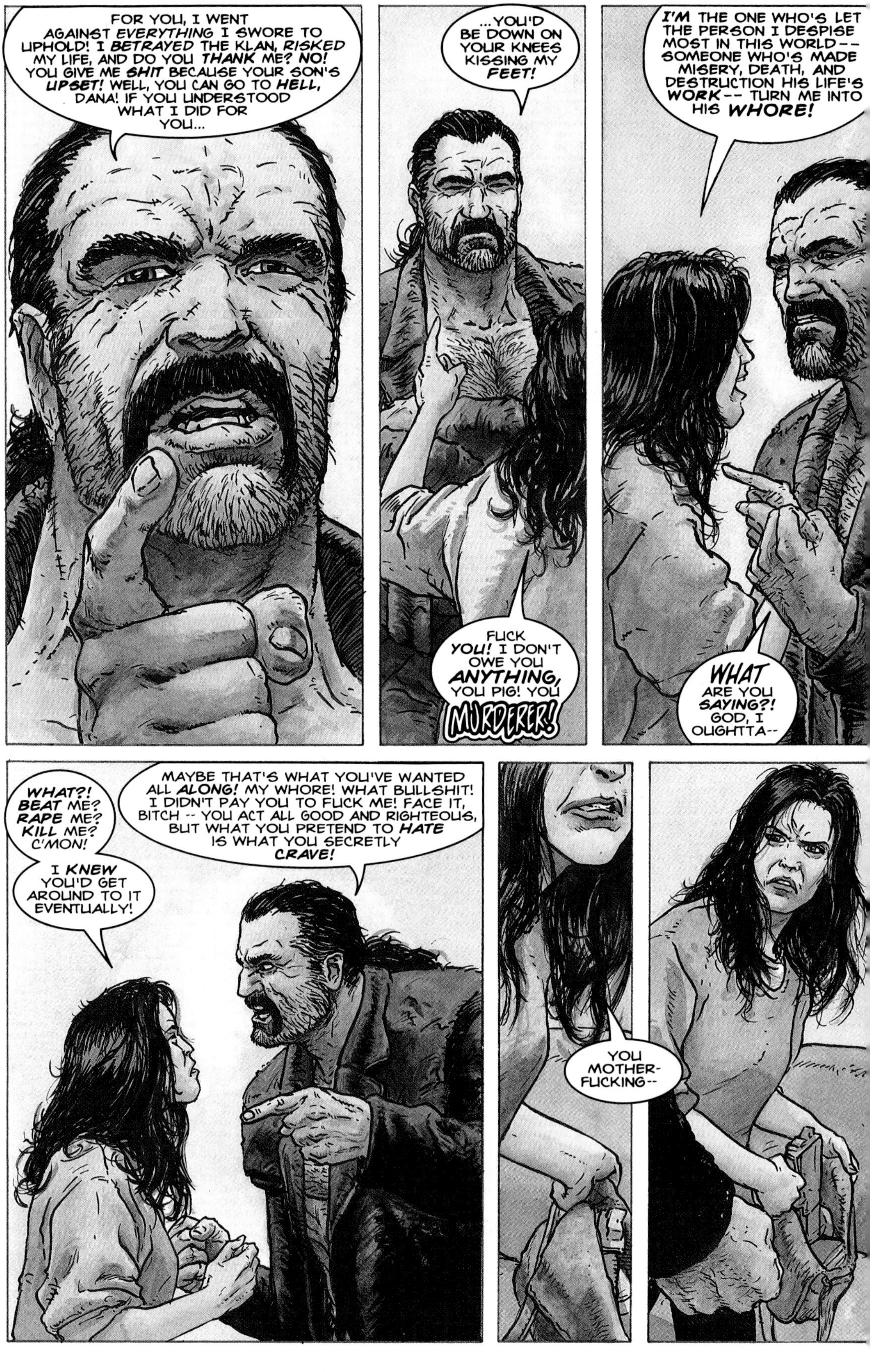
FOR YOU, I WENT AGAINST EVERYTHING I SWORE TO UPHOLD! I BETRAYED THE KLAN, RISKED MY LIFE, AND DO YOU THANK ME? NO! YOU GIVE ME SHIT BECAUSE YOUR SON'S UPSET! WELL, YOU CAN GO TO HELL, DANA! IF YOU UNDERSTOOD WHAT I DID FOR YOU...
...YOU'D BE DOWN ON YOUR KNEES KISSING MY FEET!
FUCK YOU! I DON'T OWE YOU ANYTHING, YOU PIG! YOU MURDERER!
I'M THE ONE WHO'S LET THE PERSON I DESPISE MOST IN THIS WORLD-- SOMEONE WHO'S MADE MISERY, DEATH, AND DESTRUCTION HIS LIFE'S WORK-- TURN ME INTO HIS WHORE!
WHAT ARE YOU SAYING?! GOD, I OUGHTTA--
WHAT?! BEAT ME? RAPE ME? KILL ME? C'MON!
I KNEW YOU'D GET AROUND TO IT EVENTUALLY!
MAYBE THAT'S WHAT YOU'VE WANTED ALL ALONG! MY WHORE! WHAT BULLSHIT! I DIDN'T PAY YOU TO FUCK ME! FACE IT, BITCH -- YOU ACT ALL GOOD AND RIGHTEOUS, BUT WHAT YOU PRETEND TO HATE IS WHAT YOU SECRETLY CRAVE!
YOU MOTHER-FUCKING--

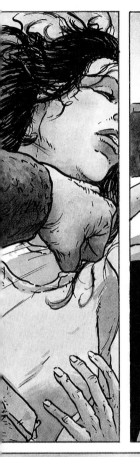

DANA! I'M *SORRY!* I DIDN'T WANT TO HIT YOU!

Oh, SHIT!

IT WAS... AUTOMATIC! I SAW THE GUN AND...DANA, *TALK* TO ME! CAN'T YOU *SAY* SOMETHING?

GET OUT.

JUST GET OUT.

MALKA, WOULD YOU GET ME ANOTHER FUCKIN' DRINK?

IF YOU WANT. BUT... ARE YOU FEELIN' OKAY? IT'S NOT LIKE YOU TO DRINK SO MUCH.

I FEEL *GREAT!* FUCKIN' *GREAT!* BETTER'N I FELT IN A *LONG* TIME. I'M ONE *MEAN* SON OF A BITCH, MALKA! AIN'T I A MEAN MOTHER-FUCKER?

YOU'RE A GRENDEL *CHIEF*, HACK. YOU CAN'T GET ANY *MEANER* THAN THAT.

THAT'S GOD-DAMN RIGHT. I DON'T GIVE A *FUCK* ABOUT ANYTHING OR ANY-BODY. REMEMBER SKID AND LUGEY? I RODE WITH THOSE FUCKERS TWENTY, THIRTY YEARS, BUT WHEN I HAD TO, I KILLED 'EM LIKE FUCKIN' *BUGS!*

THEY DESERVED IT.

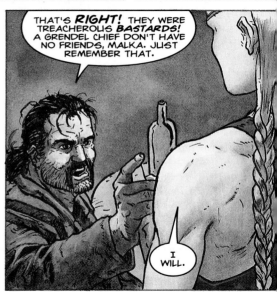

THAT'S *RIGHT!* THEY WERE TREACHEROUS *BASTARDS!* A GRENDEL CHIEF DON'T HAVE NO FRIENDS, MALKA. JUST REMEMBER THAT.

I WILL.

BUT A GRENDEL CHIEF CAN HAVE *FUN!* LOTS OF FUCKIN' *FUN!* I WANNA HAVE SOME FUN *TONIGHT,* GODDAMMIT! MALKA, GET THE KLAN TOGETHER!

IT'S BEEN A LONG TIME SINCE WE *REALLY* FUCKED ANYONE UP!

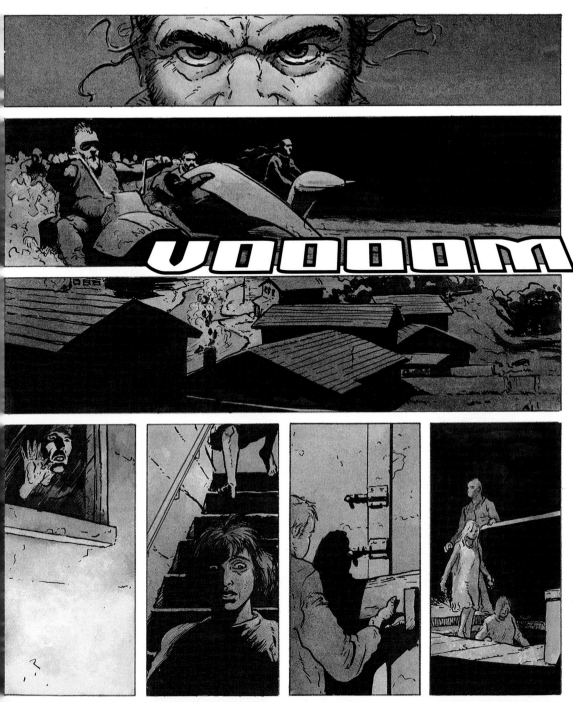

VOOOOM

SMASH

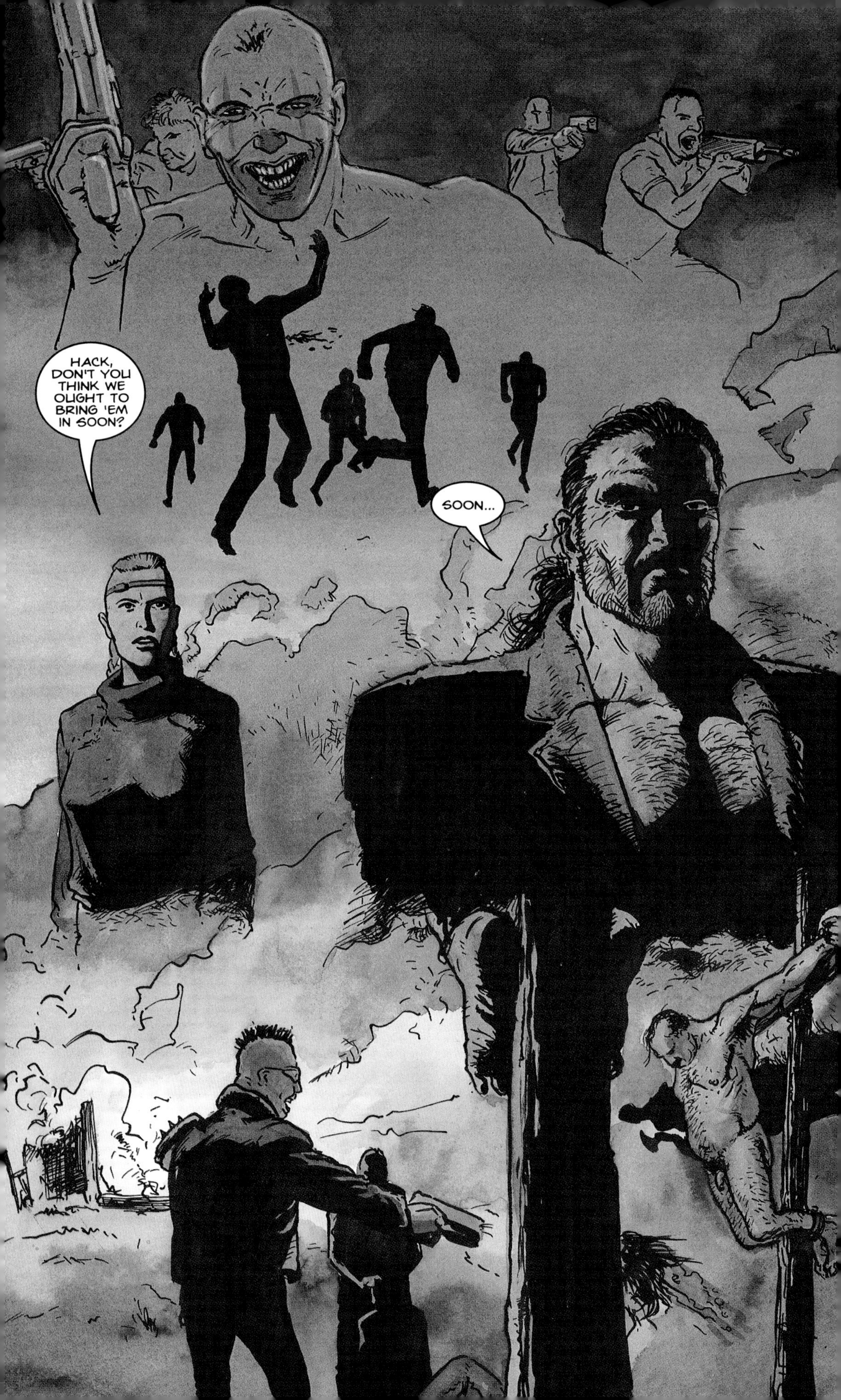
HACK, DON'T YOU THINK WE OUGHT TO BRING 'EM IN SOON?
SOON...

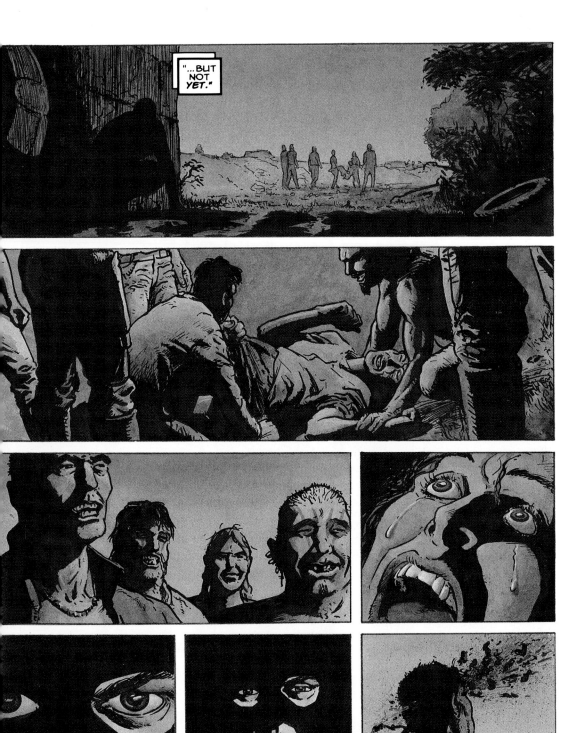

"...BUT NOT YET."

PTOOM

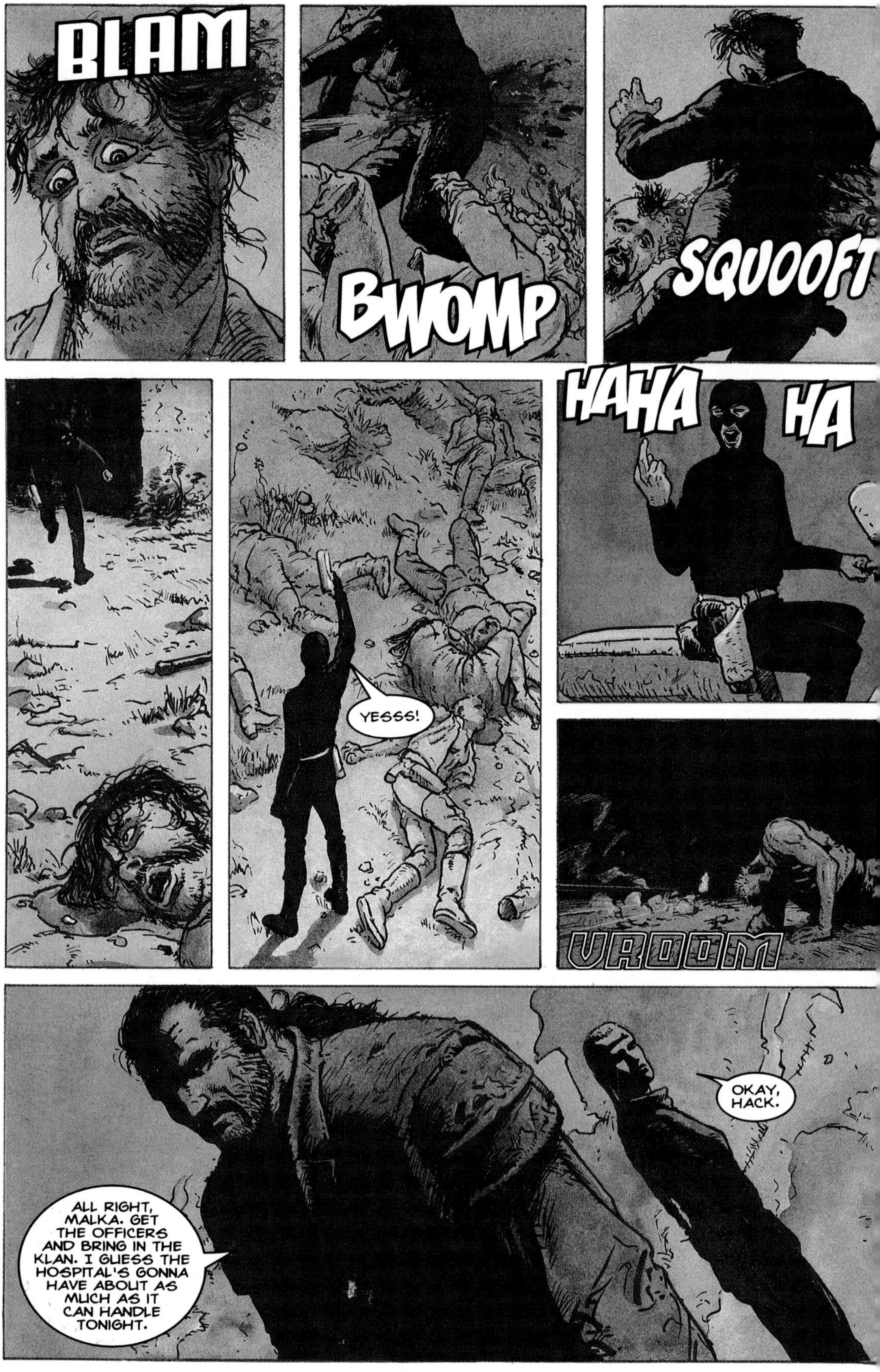
BLAM
BWOMP
SQUOOFT
YESSS!
HAHA
HA
HA
VROOM
OKAY, HACK.
ALL RIGHT, MALKA. GET THE OFFICERS AND BRING IN THE KLAN. I GUESS THE HOSPITAL'S GONNA HAVE ABOUT AS MUCH AS IT CAN HANDLE TONIGHT.

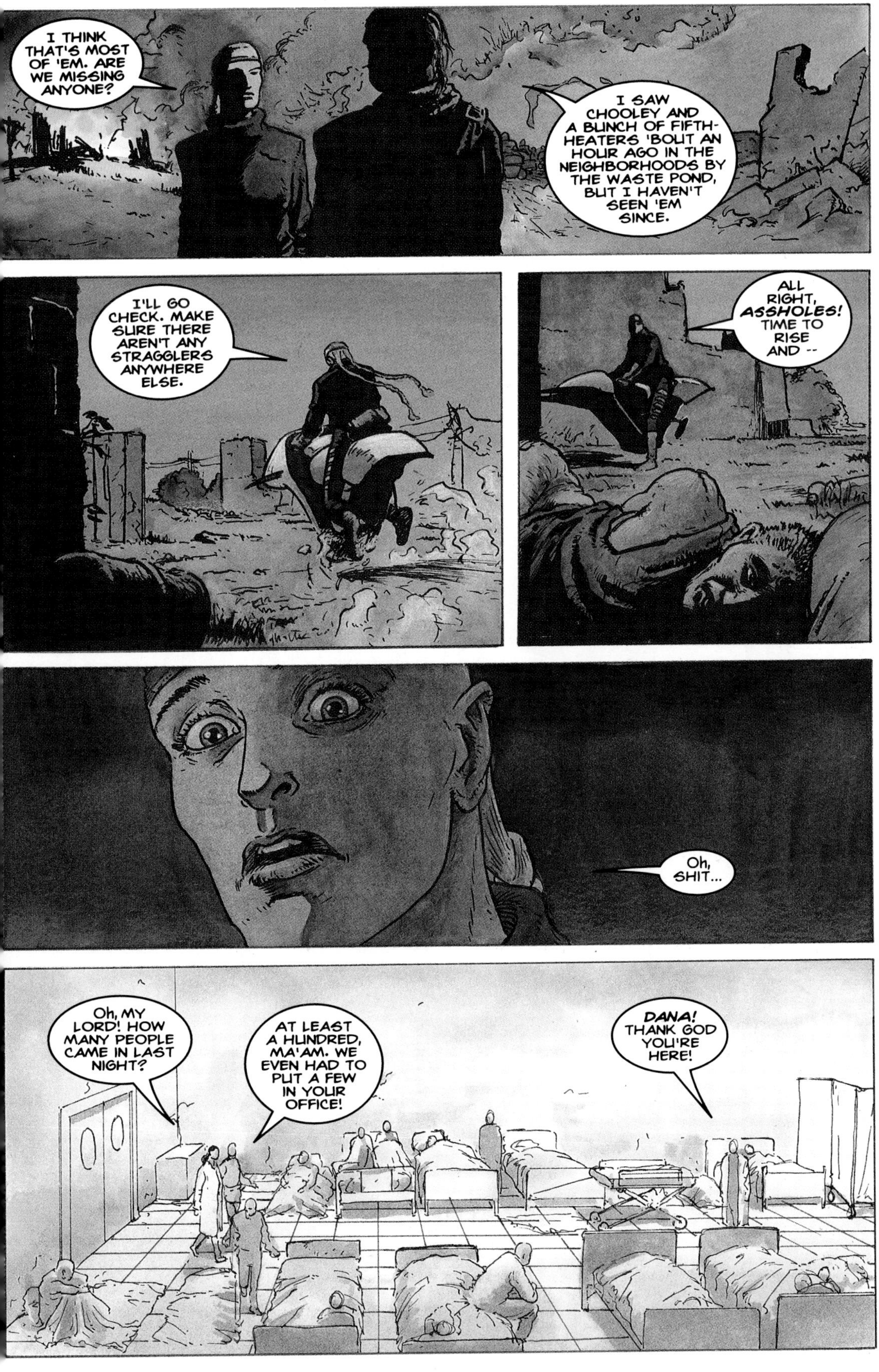

I THINK THAT'S MOST OF 'EM. ARE WE MISSING ANYONE?
I SAW CHOOLEY AND A BUNCH OF FIFTH-HEATERS 'BOUT AN HOUR AGO IN THE NEIGHBORHOODS BY THE WASTE POND, BUT I HAVEN'T SEEN 'EM SINCE.
I'LL GO CHECK. MAKE SURE THERE AREN'T ANY STRAGGLERS ANYWHERE ELSE.
ALL RIGHT, ASSHOLES! TIME TO RISE AND --
Oh, SHIT...
Oh, MY LORD! HOW MANY PEOPLE CAME IN LAST NIGHT?
AT LEAST A HUNDRED, MA'AM. WE EVEN HAD TO PUT A FEW IN YOUR OFFICE!
DANA! THANK GOD YOU'RE HERE!

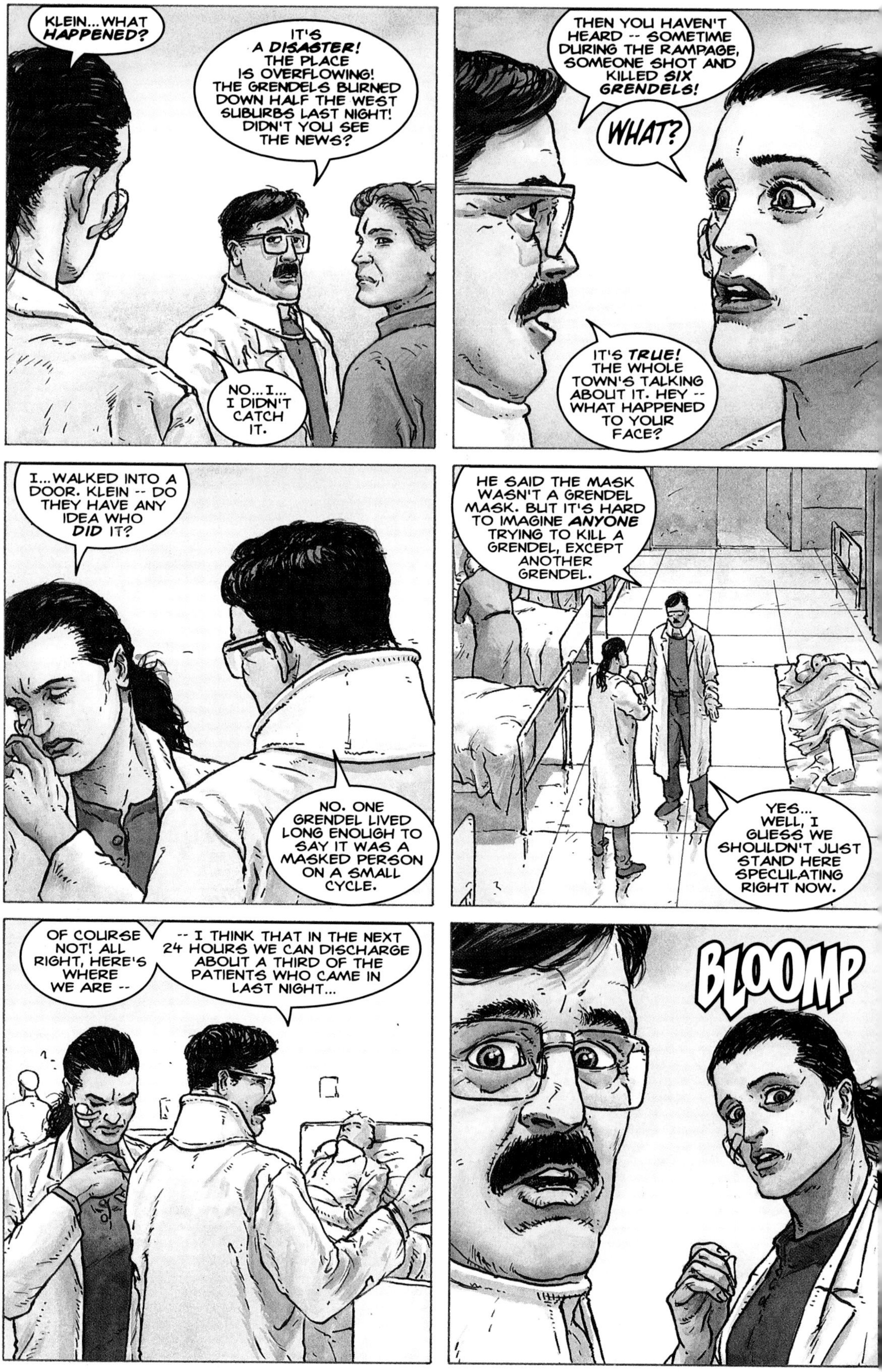
KLEIN...WHAT HAPPENED?
IT'S A DISASTER! THE PLACE IS OVERFLOWING! THE GRENDELS BURNED DOWN HALF THE WEST SUBURBS LAST NIGHT! DIDN'T YOU SEE THE NEWS?
NO... I... I DIDN'T CATCH IT.
THEN YOU HAVEN'T HEARD -- SOMETIME DURING THE RAMPAGE, SOMEONE SHOT AND KILLED SIX GRENDELS!
WHAT?
IT'S TRUE! THE WHOLE TOWN'S TALKING ABOUT IT. HEY -- WHAT HAPPENED TO YOUR FACE?
I...WALKED INTO A DOOR. KLEIN -- DO THEY HAVE ANY IDEA WHO DID IT?
NO. ONE GRENDEL LIVED LONG ENOUGH TO SAY IT WAS A MASKED PERSON ON A SMALL CYCLE.
HE SAID THE MASK WASN'T A GRENDEL MASK. BUT IT'S HARD TO IMAGINE ANYONE TRYING TO KILL A GRENDEL, EXCEPT ANOTHER GRENDEL.
YES... WELL, I GUESS WE SHOULDN'T JUST STAND HERE SPECULATING RIGHT NOW.
OF COURSE NOT! ALL RIGHT, HERE'S WHERE WE ARE --
-- I THINK THAT IN THE NEXT 24 HOURS WE CAN DISCHARGE ABOUT A THIRD OF THE PATIENTS WHO CAME IN LAST NIGHT...
BLOOMP

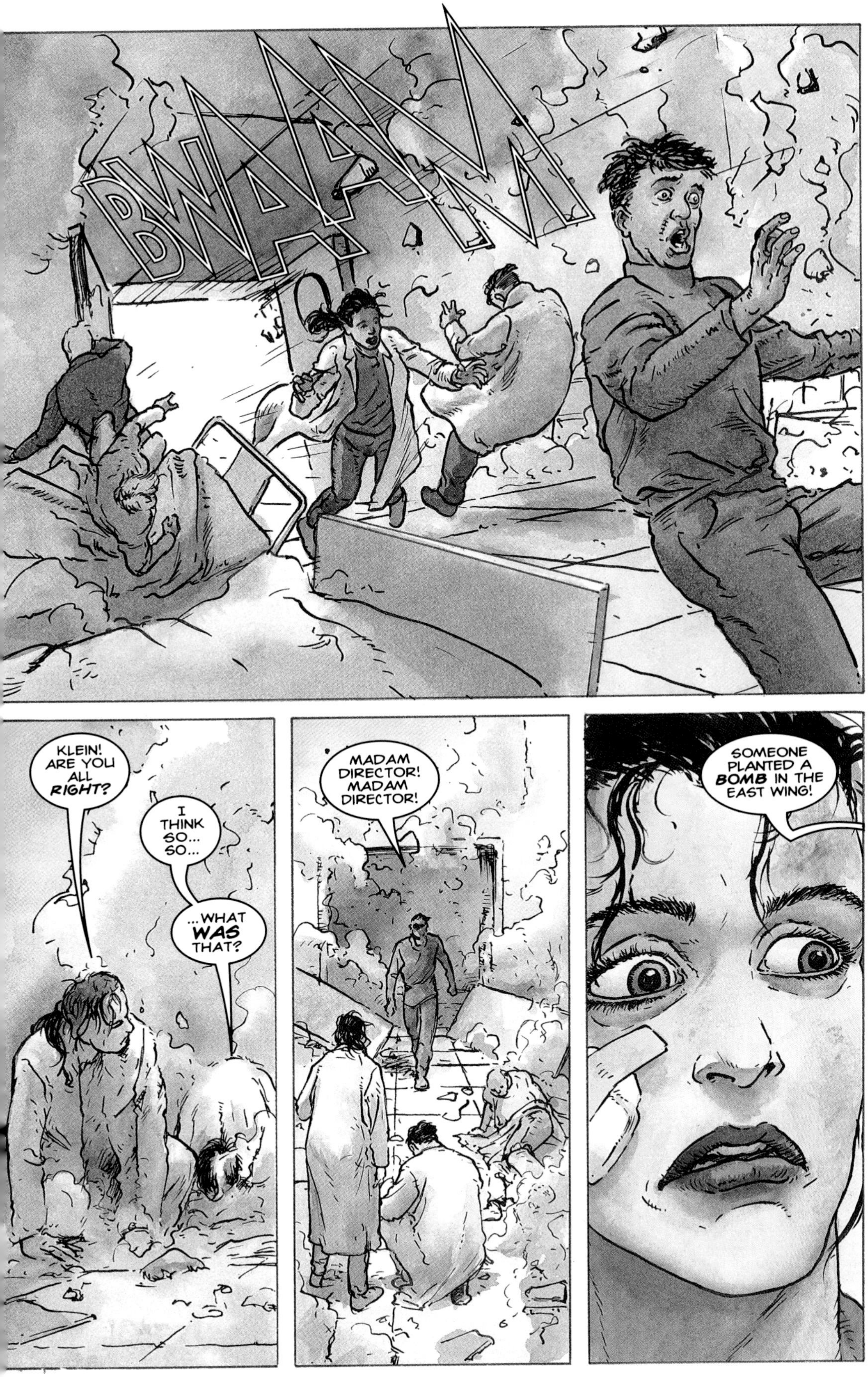
BWAAAM
KLEIN! ARE YOU ALL RIGHT?
I THINK SO... SO...
...WHAT WAS THAT?
MADAM DIRECTOR! MADAM DIRECTOR!
SOMEONE PLANTED A BOMB IN THE EAST WING!

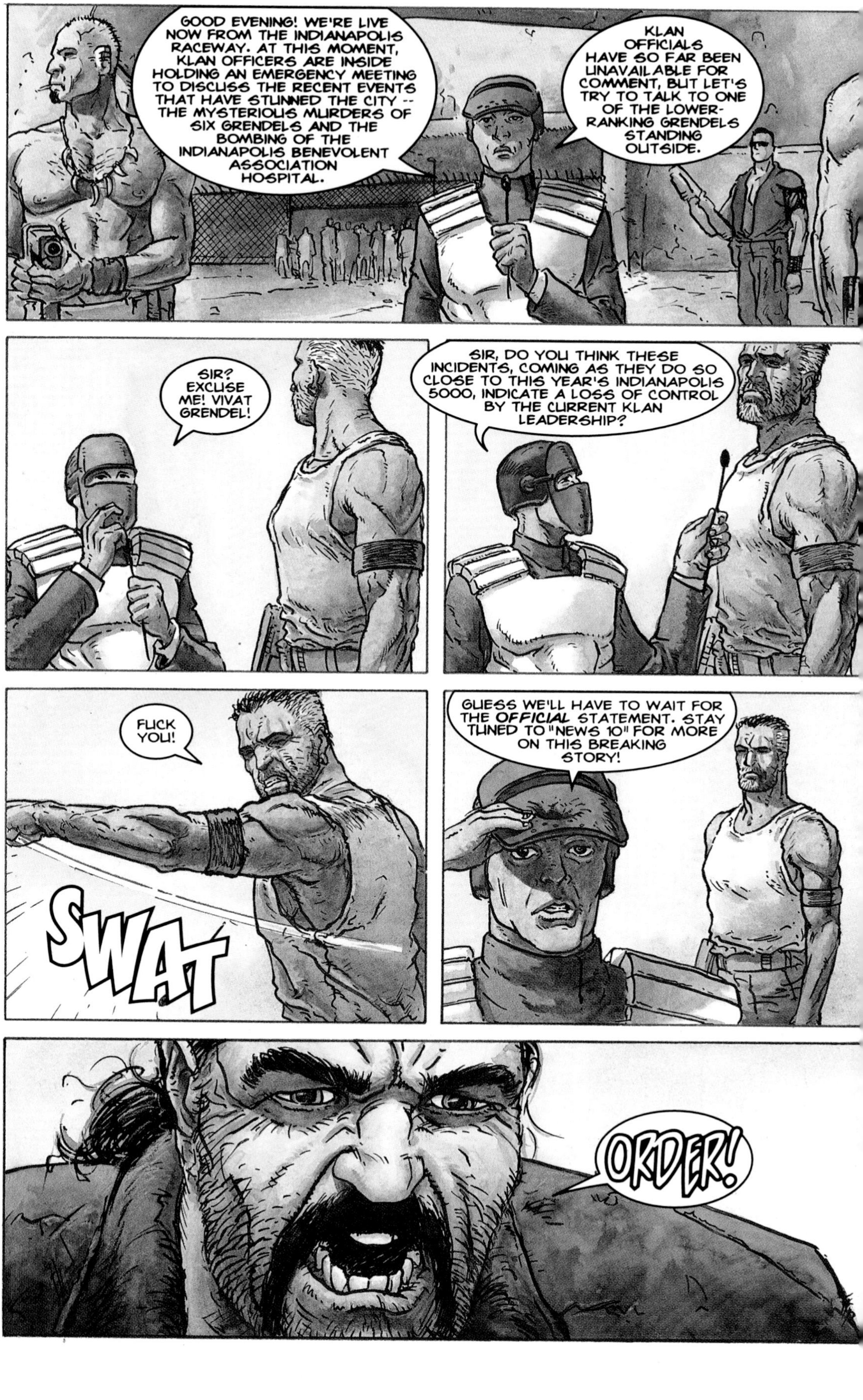
GOOD EVENING! WE'RE LIVE NOW FROM THE INDIANAPOLIS RACEWAY. AT THIS MOMENT, KLAN OFFICERS ARE INSIDE HOLDING AN EMERGENCY MEETING TO DISCUSS THE RECENT EVENTS THAT HAVE STUNNED THE CITY -- THE MYSTERIOUS MURDERS OF SIX GRENDELS AND THE BOMBING OF THE INDIANAPOLIS BENEVOLENT ASSOCIATION HOSPITAL.
KLAN OFFICIALS HAVE SO FAR BEEN UNAVAILABLE FOR COMMENT, BUT LET'S TRY TO TALK TO ONE OF THE LOWER-RANKING GRENDELS STANDING OUTSIDE.
SIR? EXCUSE ME! VIVAT GRENDEL!
SIR, DO YOU THINK THESE INCIDENTS, COMING AS THEY DO SO CLOSE TO THIS YEAR'S INDIANAPOLIS 5000, INDICATE A LOSS OF CONTROL BY THE CURRENT KLAN LEADERSHIP?
FUCK YOU!
SWAT
GUESS WE'LL HAVE TO WAIT FOR THE *OFFICIAL* STATEMENT. STAY TUNED TO "NEWS 10" FOR MORE ON THIS BREAKING STORY!
ORDER!

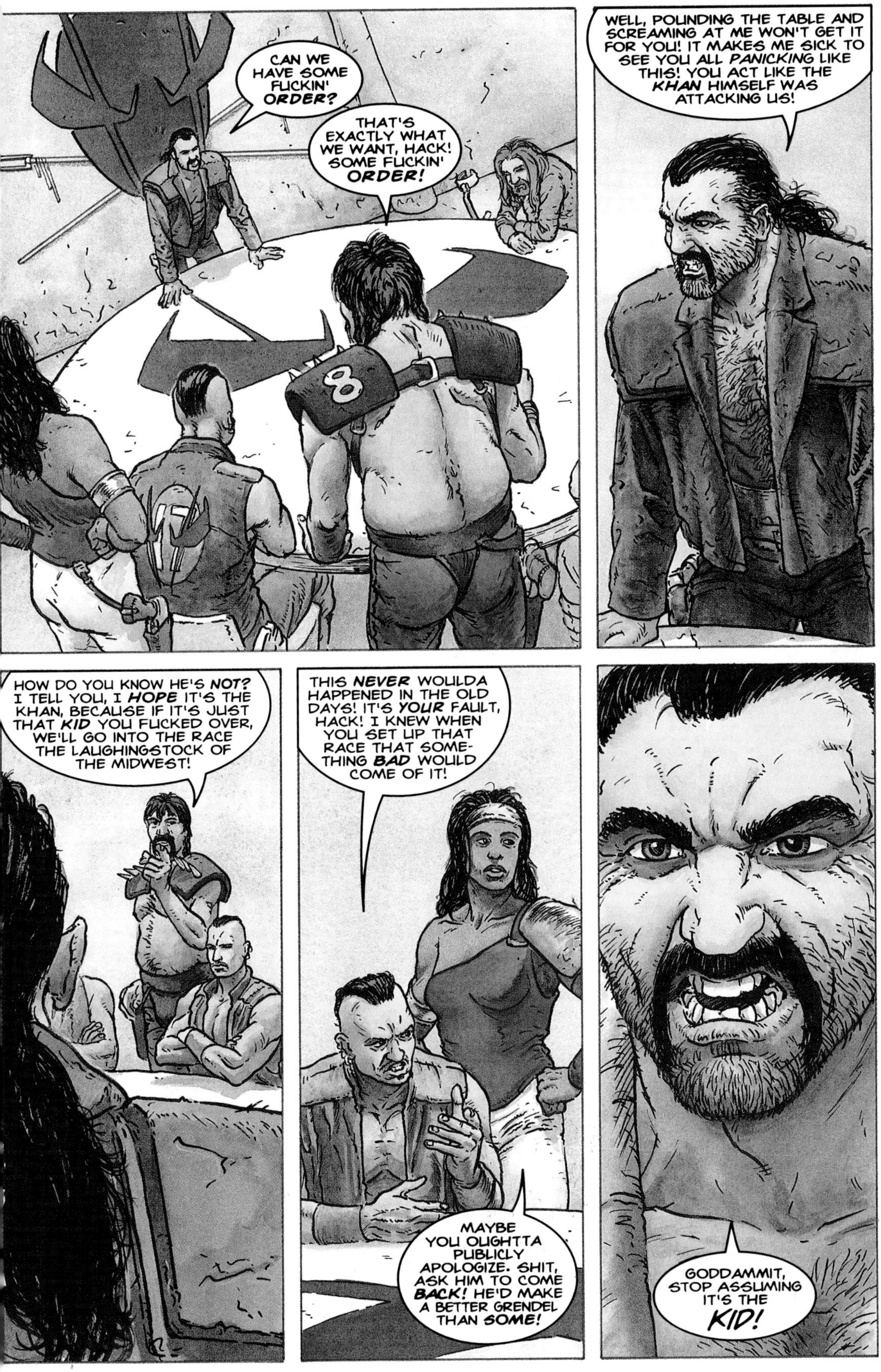
CAN WE HAVE SOME FUCKIN' ORDER?
THAT'S EXACTLY WHAT WE WANT, HACK! SOME FUCKIN' ORDER!
WELL, POUNDING THE TABLE AND SCREAMING AT ME WON'T GET IT FOR YOU! IT MAKES ME SICK TO SEE YOU ALL PANICKING LIKE THIS! YOU ACT LIKE THE KHAN HIMSELF WAS ATTACKING US!
HOW DO YOU KNOW HE'S NOT? I TELL YOU, I HOPE IT'S THE KHAN, BECAUSE IF IT'S JUST THAT KID YOU FUCKED OVER, WE'LL GO INTO THE RACE THE LAUGHINGSTOCK OF THE MIDWEST!
THIS NEVER WOULDA HAPPENED IN THE OLD DAYS! IT'S YOUR FAULT, HACK! I KNEW WHEN YOU SET UP THAT RACE THAT SOME-THING BAD WOULD COME OF IT!
MAYBE YOU OUGHTTA PUBLICLY APOLOGIZE. SHIT, ASK HIM TO COME BACK! HE'D MAKE A BETTER GRENDEL THAN SOME!
GODDAMMIT, STOP ASSUMING IT'S THE KID!

WELL, YOU RULED *OUT* THE KHAN, AND WE'RE NOT FEUDING WITH ANY OTHER KLANS. IF IT'S *NOT* THE KID, WHO IS IT?

MAYBE IT'S HIS *MOM.*

GODDAMMIT, YOU...

WHOP

ANYONE *ELSE* GOT ANYTHING FUNNY TO SAY? OR MAYBE YOU JUST WANNA GET RID OF ME RIGHT *NOW.* C'MON -- I TOOK OUT TEN LAST WEEK!

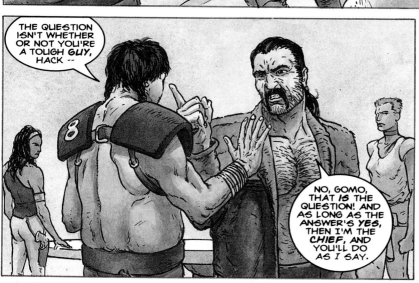

THE QUESTION ISN'T WHETHER OR NOT YOU'RE A TOUGH *GUY,* HACK --

NO, GOMO, THAT *IS* THE QUESTION! AND AS LONG AS THE ANSWER'S *YES,* THEN I'M THE *CHIEF,* AND YOU'LL DO AS I SAY.

NOW, LET'S LOOK AT THIS *REASONABLY.*

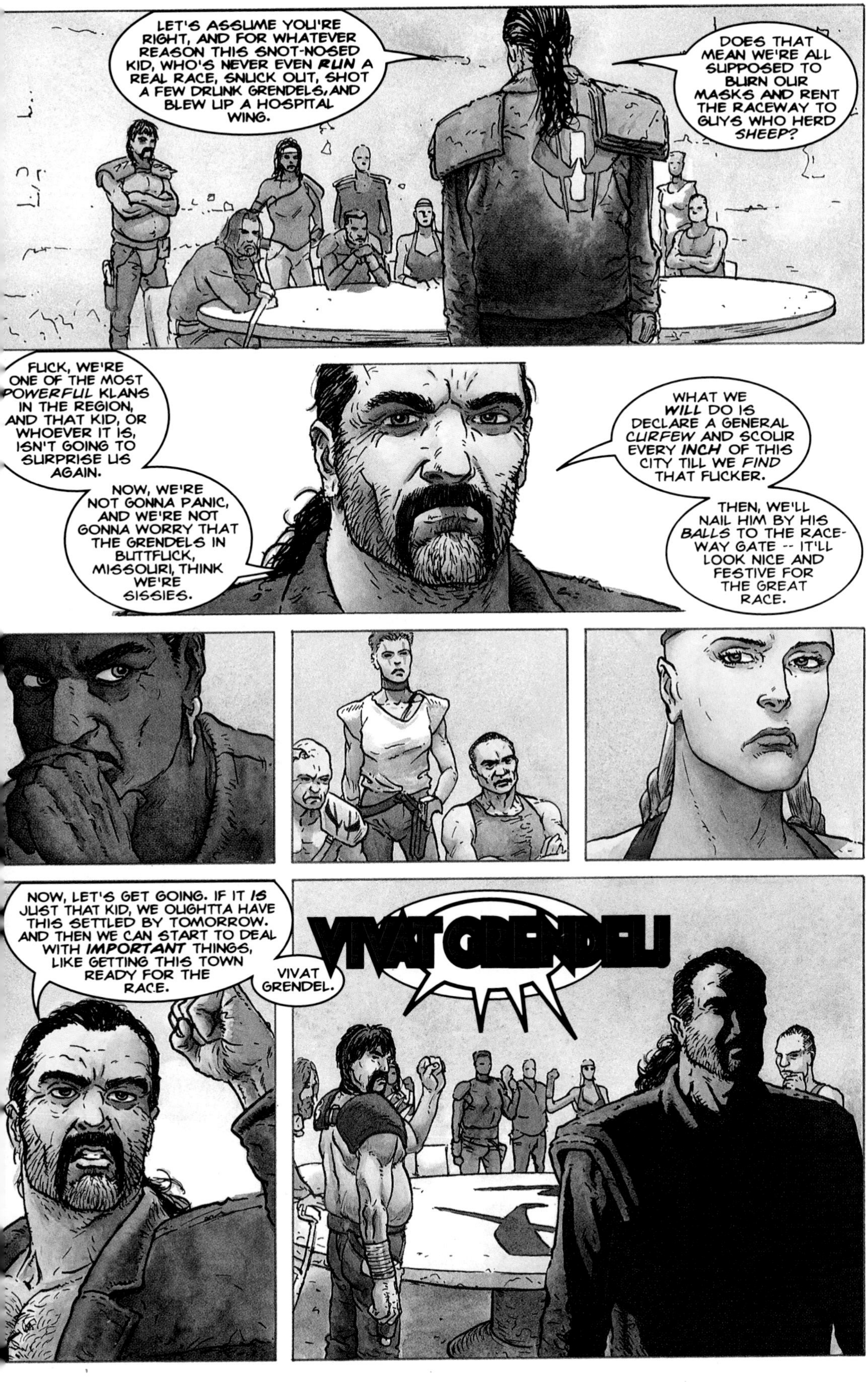
LET'S ASSUME YOU'RE RIGHT, AND FOR WHATEVER REASON THIS SNOT-NOSED KID, WHO'S NEVER EVEN *RUN* A REAL RACE, SNUCK OUT, SHOT A FEW DRUNK GRENDELS, AND BLEW UP A HOSPITAL WING.
DOES THAT MEAN WE'RE ALL SUPPOSED TO BURN OUR MASKS AND RENT THE RACEWAY TO GUYS WHO HERD *SHEEP?*
FUCK, WE'RE ONE OF THE MOST *POWERFUL* KLANS IN THE REGION, AND THAT KID, OR WHOEVER IT IS, ISN'T GOING TO SURPRISE US AGAIN.
NOW, WE'RE NOT GONNA PANIC, AND WE'RE NOT GONNA WORRY THAT THE GRENDELS IN BUTTFUCK, MISSOURI, THINK WE'RE SISSIES.
WHAT WE *WILL* DO IS DECLARE A GENERAL *CURFEW* AND SCOUR EVERY *INCH* OF THIS CITY TILL WE *FIND* THAT FUCKER.
THEN, WE'LL NAIL HIM BY HIS *BALLS* TO THE RACE-WAY GATE -- IT'LL LOOK NICE AND FESTIVE FOR THE GREAT RACE.
NOW, LET'S GET GOING. IF IT *IS* JUST THAT KID, WE OUGHTTA HAVE THIS SETTLED BY TOMORROW. AND THEN WE CAN START TO DEAL WITH *IMPORTANT* THINGS, LIKE GETTING THIS TOWN READY FOR THE RACE.
VIVAT GRENDEL.
VIVAT GRENDEL!

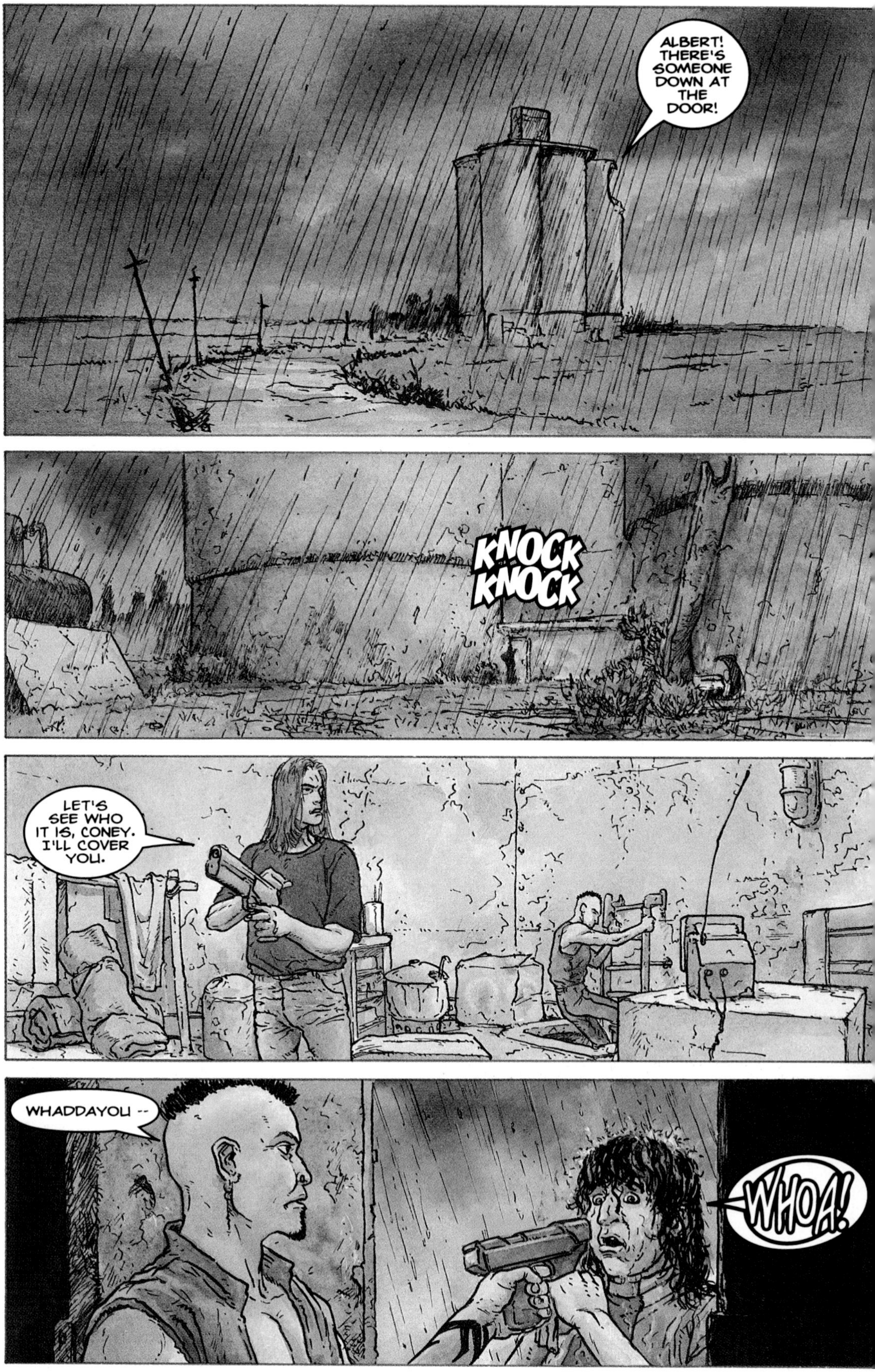
ALBERT! THERE'S SOMEONE DOWN AT THE DOOR!
KNOCK KNOCK
LET'S SEE WHO IT IS, CONEY. I'LL COVER YOU.
WHADDAYOU --
WHOA!

CONEY, MAN, IT'S *ME* -- PUG!

I ALMOST *SHOT* YOU, ASSHOLE! WHY DIDN'T YOU DO THE *KNOCK?*

SORRY, I FORGOT. BUT LOOK -- I GOT A *TON* OF FOOD, AND I STOLE A BUNCHA *AMMO* FROM THE MUNITIONS DUMP NEAR THE POWER PLANT!

YOU DID GOOD, PUG. LET'S GET THIS STUFF UPSTAIRS.

WHAT'VE YOU GUYS BEEN DOIN'?

WATCHIN' THE NEWS. THEY'VE BEEN GOIN' APESHIT IN TOWN. ME AN' ALBERT HAVE BEEN LAUGHIN' LIKE CRAZY.

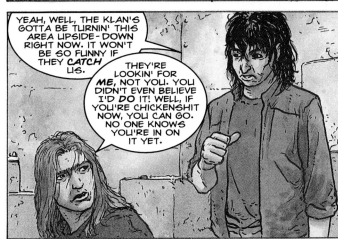

YEAH, WELL, THE KLAN'S GOTTA BE TURNIN' THIS AREA UPSIDE-DOWN RIGHT NOW. IT WON'T BE SO FUNNY IF THEY *CATCH* US.

THEY'RE LOOKIN' FOR *ME*, NOT YOU. YOU DIDN'T EVEN BELIEVE I'D *DO* IT! WELL, IF YOU'RE CHICKENSHIT NOW, YOU CAN GO. NO ONE KNOWS YOU'RE IN ON IT YET.

I'M *NOT* CHICKENSHIT, ALBERT! I'M STILL AS INTO IT AS I WAS WHEN WE TALKED THE OTHER NIGHT IN THAT BAR. I'M JUST BEIN' *PRACTICAL.* ANYWAY, YOU'D KILL ME IF I LEFT, RATHER THAN TAKE A CHANCE SOMEONE'D FIND OUT FROM ME WHERE YOU ARE.

THAT'S TRUE. BUT WE'D DO IT BECAUSE YOU WERE CHICKENSHIT, *NOT* BECAUSE WE'RE AFRAID OF THE KLAN.

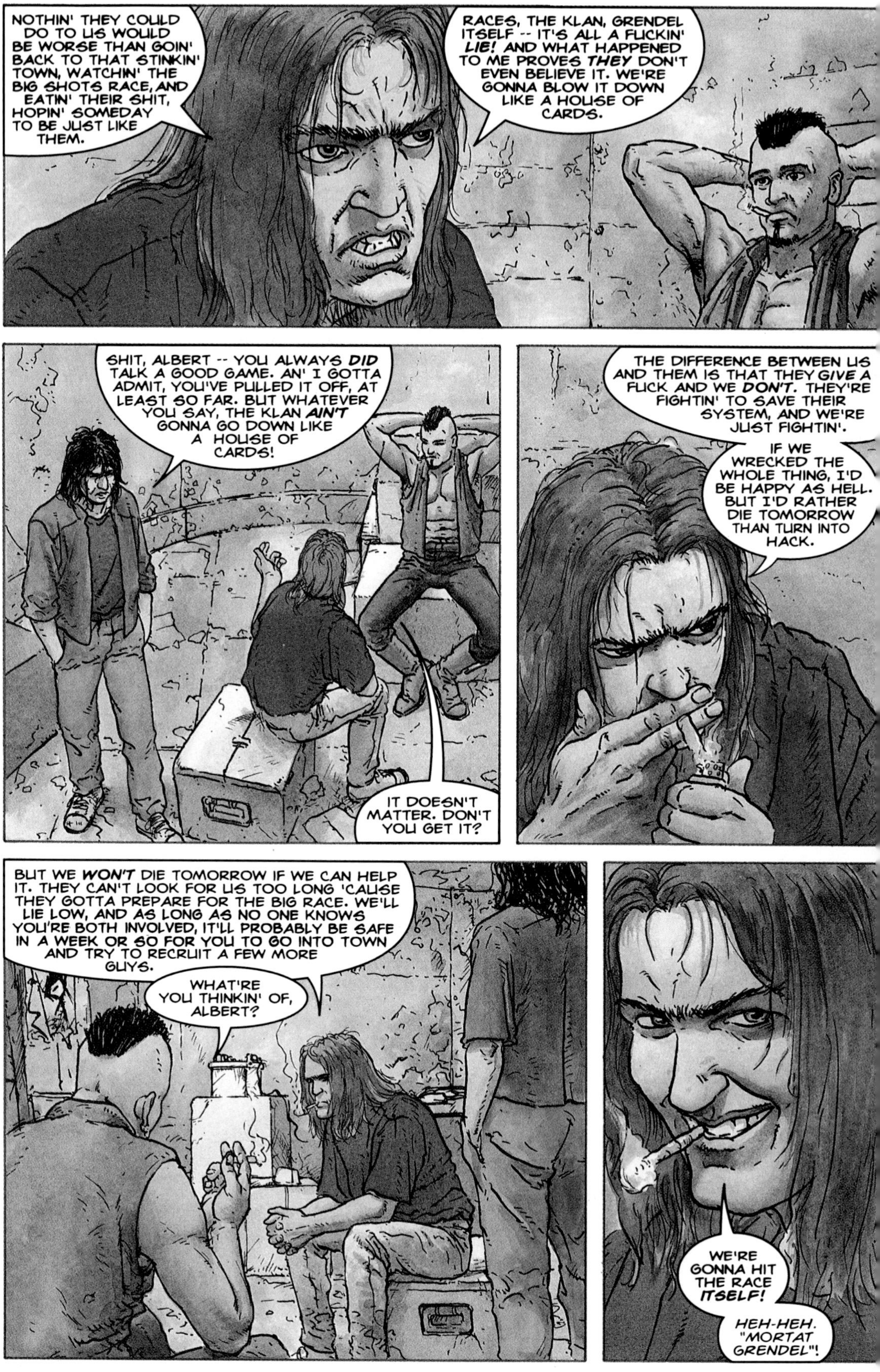
NOTHIN' THEY COULD DO TO US WOULD BE WORSE THAN GOIN' BACK TO THAT STINKIN' TOWN, WATCHIN' THE BIG SHOTS RACE, AND EATIN' THEIR SHIT, HOPIN' SOMEDAY TO BE JUST LIKE THEM.
RACES, THE KLAN, GRENDEL ITSELF -- IT'S ALL A FUCKIN' *LIE!* AND WHAT HAPPENED TO ME PROVES *THEY* DON'T EVEN BELIEVE IT. WE'RE GONNA BLOW IT DOWN LIKE A HOUSE OF CARDS.
SHIT, ALBERT -- YOU ALWAYS *DID* TALK A GOOD GAME. AN' I GOTTA ADMIT, YOU'VE PULLED IT OFF, AT LEAST SO FAR. BUT WHATEVER YOU SAY, THE KLAN *AIN'T* GONNA GO DOWN LIKE A HOUSE OF CARDS!
IT DOESN'T MATTER. DON'T YOU GET IT?
THE DIFFERENCE BETWEEN US AND THEM IS THAT THEY *GIVE* A FUCK AND WE *DON'T.* THEY'RE FIGHTIN' TO SAVE THEIR SYSTEM, AND WE'RE JUST FIGHTIN'.
IF WE WRECKED THE WHOLE THING, I'D BE HAPPY AS HELL. BUT I'D RATHER DIE TOMORROW THAN TURN INTO HACK.
BUT WE *WON'T* DIE TOMORROW IF WE CAN HELP IT. THEY CAN'T LOOK FOR US TOO LONG 'CAUSE THEY GOTTA PREPARE FOR THE BIG RACE. WE'LL LIE LOW, AND AS LONG AS NO ONE KNOWS YOU'RE BOTH INVOLVED, IT'LL PROBABLY BE SAFE IN A WEEK OR SO FOR YOU TO GO INTO TOWN AND TRY TO RECRUIT A FEW MORE GUYS.
WHAT'RE YOU THINKIN' OF, ALBERT?
WE'RE GONNA HIT THE RACE *ITSELF!*
HEH-HEH. "MORTAT GRENDEL"!

KLAN OFFICIALS REFUSED TO COMMENT ON WHETHER THEY WERE ANY CLOSER TO RESOLVING THE INCIDENT, WHICH HAS ROCKED BOTH THE CITY AND THE KLAN AT THE HIGHEST LEVELS...

THE SEARCH FOR THOSE RESPONSIBLE FOR THE MURDER OF SIX GRENDELS AND THE BOMBING OF THE INDIANAPOLIS BENEVOLENT ASSOCIATION CONTINUED TODAY, WITH GRENDELS PICKING UP SEVERAL SUSPECTS.

KNOCK KNOCK

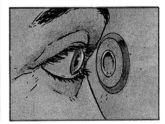

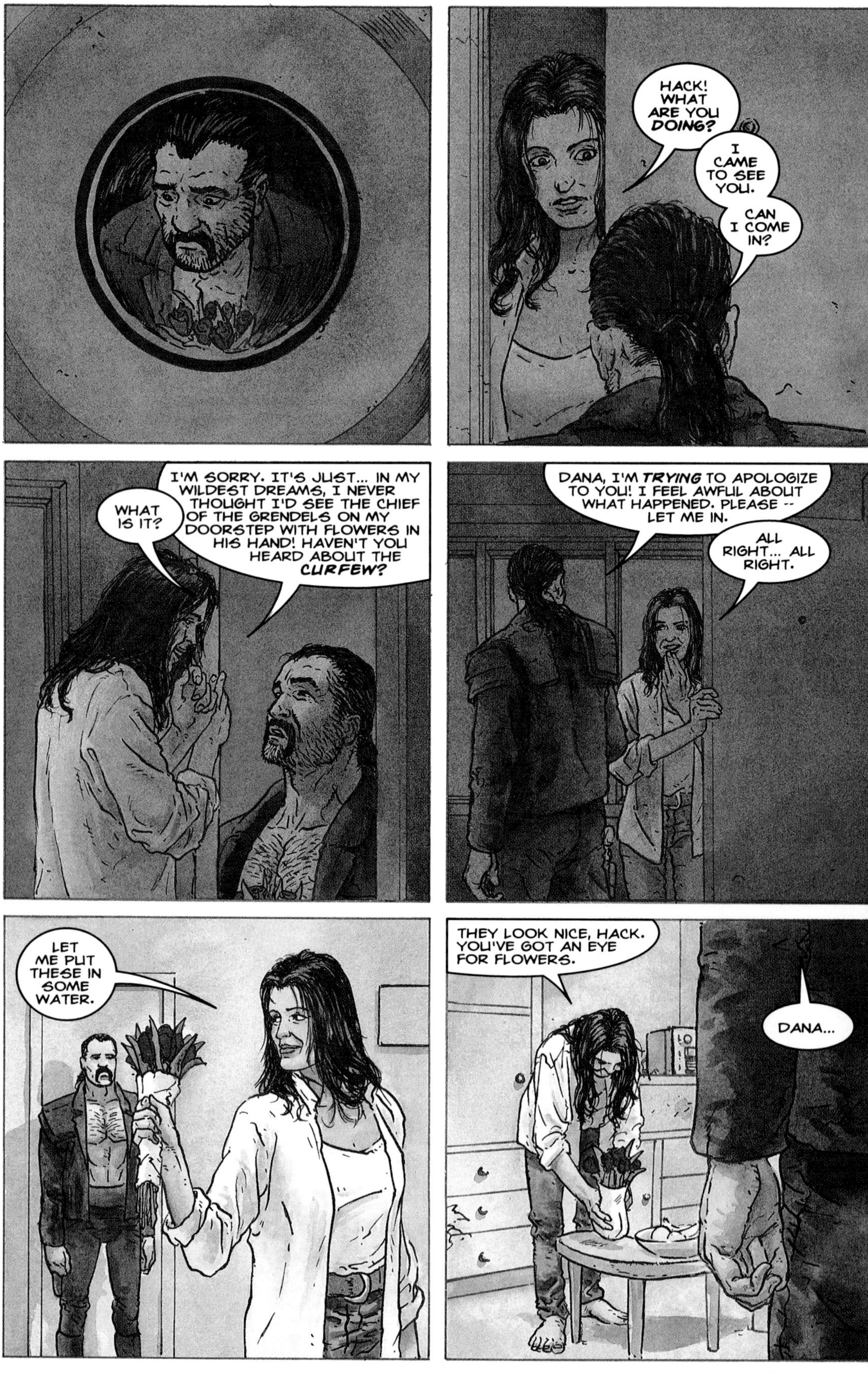

HACK! WHAT ARE YOU DOING?
I CAME TO SEE YOU.
CAN I COME IN?
WHAT IS IT?
I'M SORRY. IT'S JUST... IN MY WILDEST DREAMS, I NEVER THOUGHT I'D SEE THE CHIEF OF THE GRENDELS ON MY DOORSTEP WITH FLOWERS IN HIS HAND! HAVEN'T YOU HEARD ABOUT THE CURFEW?
DANA, I'M TRYING TO APOLOGIZE TO YOU! I FEEL AWFUL ABOUT WHAT HAPPENED. PLEASE -- LET ME IN.
ALL RIGHT... ALL RIGHT.
LET ME PUT THESE IN SOME WATER.
THEY LOOK NICE, HACK. YOU'VE GOT AN EYE FOR FLOWERS.
DANA...

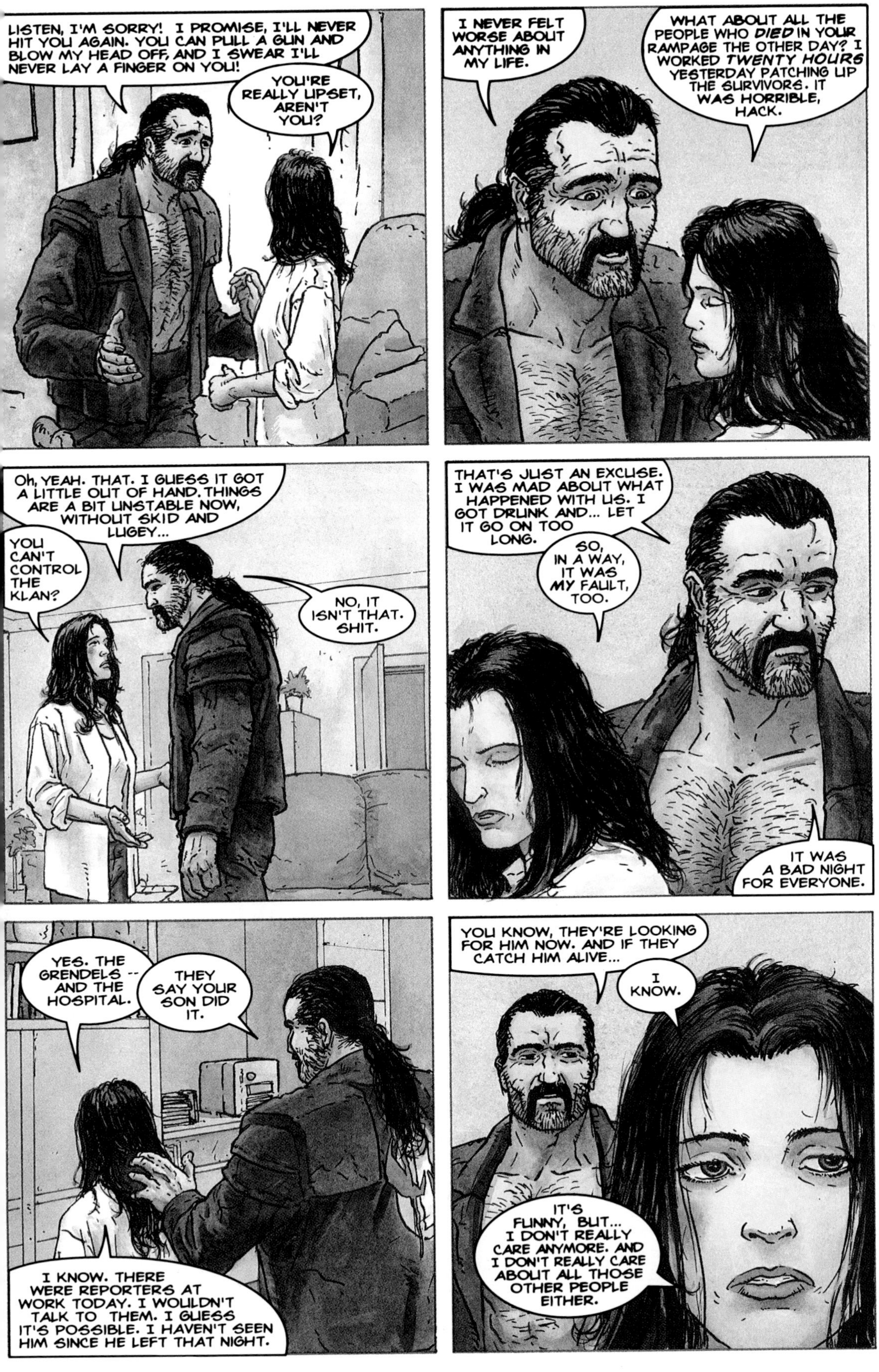
LISTEN, I'M SORRY! I PROMISE, I'LL NEVER HIT YOU AGAIN. YOU CAN PULL A GUN AND BLOW MY HEAD OFF, AND I SWEAR I'LL NEVER LAY A FINGER ON YOU!
YOU'RE REALLY UPSET, AREN'T YOU?
I NEVER FELT WORSE ABOUT ANYTHING IN MY LIFE.
WHAT ABOUT ALL THE PEOPLE WHO DIED IN YOUR RAMPAGE THE OTHER DAY? I WORKED TWENTY HOURS YESTERDAY PATCHING UP THE SURVIVORS. IT WAS HORRIBLE, HACK.
Oh, YEAH. THAT. I GUESS IT GOT A LITTLE OUT OF HAND. THINGS ARE A BIT UNSTABLE NOW, WITHOUT SKID AND LUGEY...
YOU CAN'T CONTROL THE KLAN?
NO, IT ISN'T THAT. SHIT.
THAT'S JUST AN EXCUSE. I WAS MAD ABOUT WHAT HAPPENED WITH US. I GOT DRUNK AND... LET IT GO ON TOO LONG.
SO, IN A WAY, IT WAS MY FAULT, TOO.
IT WAS A BAD NIGHT FOR EVERYONE.
YES. THE GRENDELS -- AND THE HOSPITAL.
THEY SAY YOUR SON DID IT.
I KNOW. THERE WERE REPORTERS AT WORK TODAY. I WOULDN'T TALK TO THEM. I GUESS IT'S POSSIBLE. I HAVEN'T SEEN HIM SINCE HE LEFT THAT NIGHT.
YOU KNOW, THEY'RE LOOKING FOR HIM NOW. AND IF THEY CATCH HIM ALIVE...
I KNOW.
IT'S FUNNY, BUT... I DON'T REALLY CARE ANYMORE. AND I DON'T REALLY CARE ABOUT ALL THOSE OTHER PEOPLE EITHER.

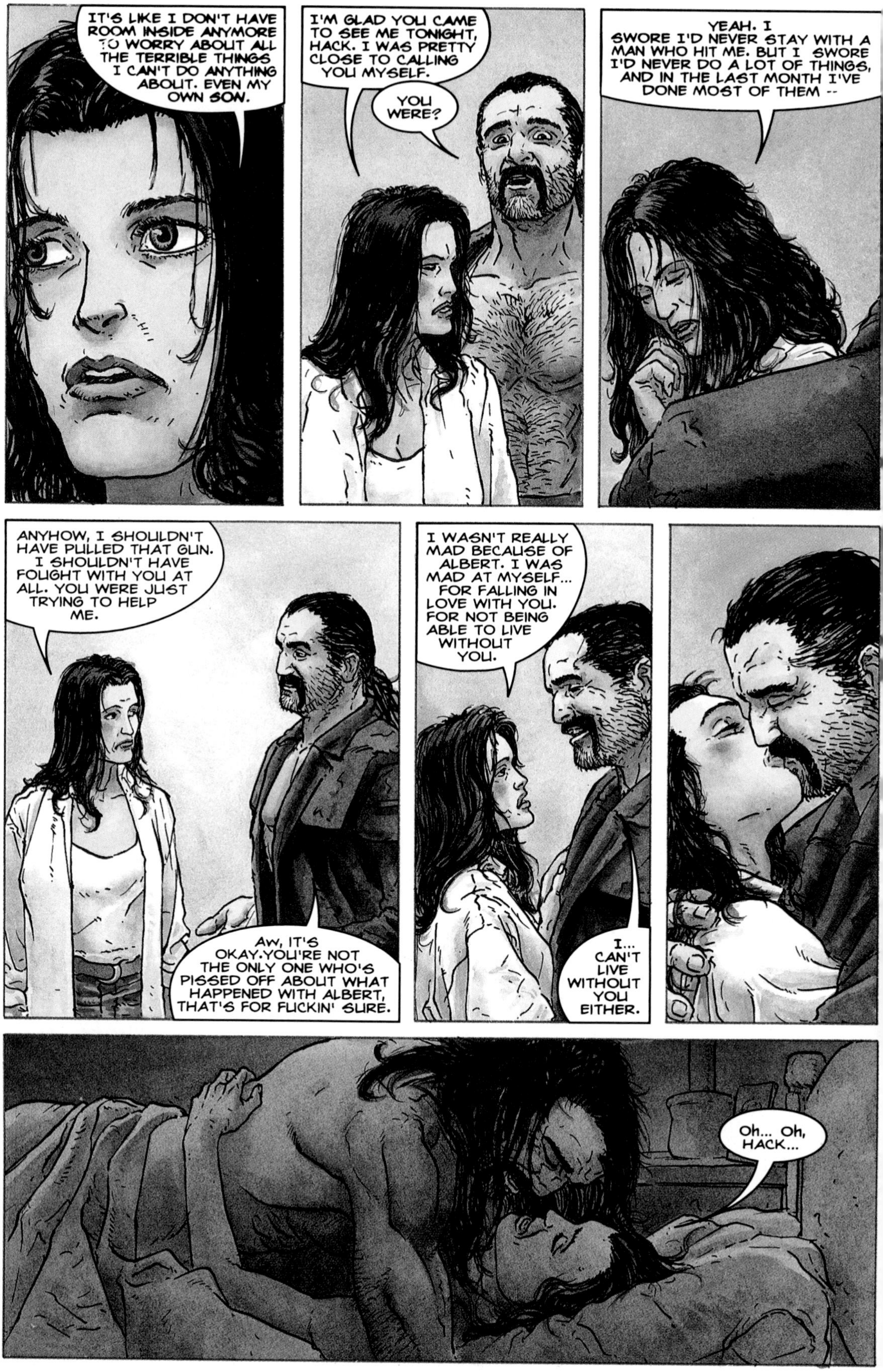
IT'S LIKE I DON'T HAVE ROOM INSIDE ANYMORE TO WORRY ABOUT ALL THE TERRIBLE THINGS I CAN'T DO ANYTHING ABOUT. EVEN MY OWN SON.
I'M GLAD YOU CAME TO SEE ME TONIGHT, HACK. I WAS PRETTY CLOSE TO CALLING YOU MYSELF.
YOU WERE?
YEAH. I SWORE I'D NEVER STAY WITH A MAN WHO HIT ME. BUT I SWORE I'D NEVER DO A LOT OF THINGS, AND IN THE LAST MONTH I'VE DONE MOST OF THEM --
ANYHOW, I SHOULDN'T HAVE PULLED THAT GUN. I SHOULDN'T HAVE FOUGHT WITH YOU AT ALL. YOU WERE JUST TRYING TO HELP ME.
AW, IT'S OKAY. YOU'RE NOT THE ONLY ONE WHO'S PISSED OFF ABOUT WHAT HAPPENED WITH ALBERT, THAT'S FOR FUCKIN' SURE.
I WASN'T REALLY MAD BECAUSE OF ALBERT. I WAS MAD AT MYSELF... FOR FALLING IN LOVE WITH YOU. FOR NOT BEING ABLE TO LIVE WITHOUT YOU.
I... CAN'T LIVE WITHOUT YOU EITHER.
Oh... Oh, HACK...

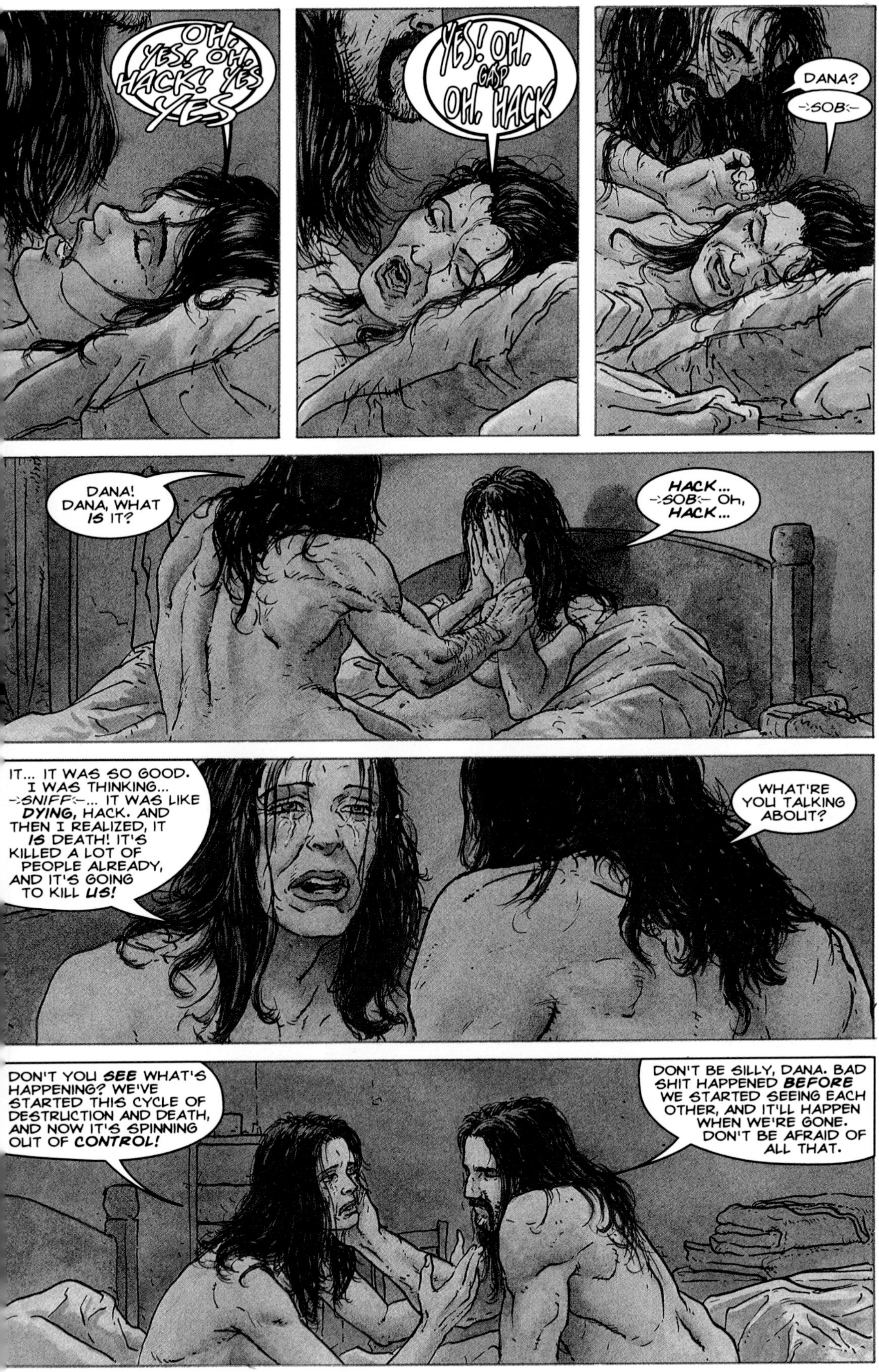
OH. YES! OH, HACK! YES YES
YES! OH, GASP OH, HACK
DANA?
SOB
DANA! DANA, WHAT IS IT?
HACK... SOB Oh, HACK...
IT... IT WAS SO GOOD. I WAS THINKING... SNIFF... IT WAS LIKE DYING, HACK. AND THEN I REALIZED, IT IS DEATH! IT'S KILLED A LOT OF PEOPLE ALREADY, AND IT'S GOING TO KILL US!
WHAT'RE YOU TALKING ABOUT?
DON'T YOU SEE WHAT'S HAPPENING? WE'VE STARTED THIS CYCLE OF DESTRUCTION AND DEATH, AND NOW IT'S SPINNING OUT OF CONTROL!
DON'T BE SILLY, DANA. BAD SHIT HAPPENED BEFORE WE STARTED SEEING EACH OTHER, AND IT'LL HAPPEN WHEN WE'RE GONE. DON'T BE AFRAID OF ALL THAT.

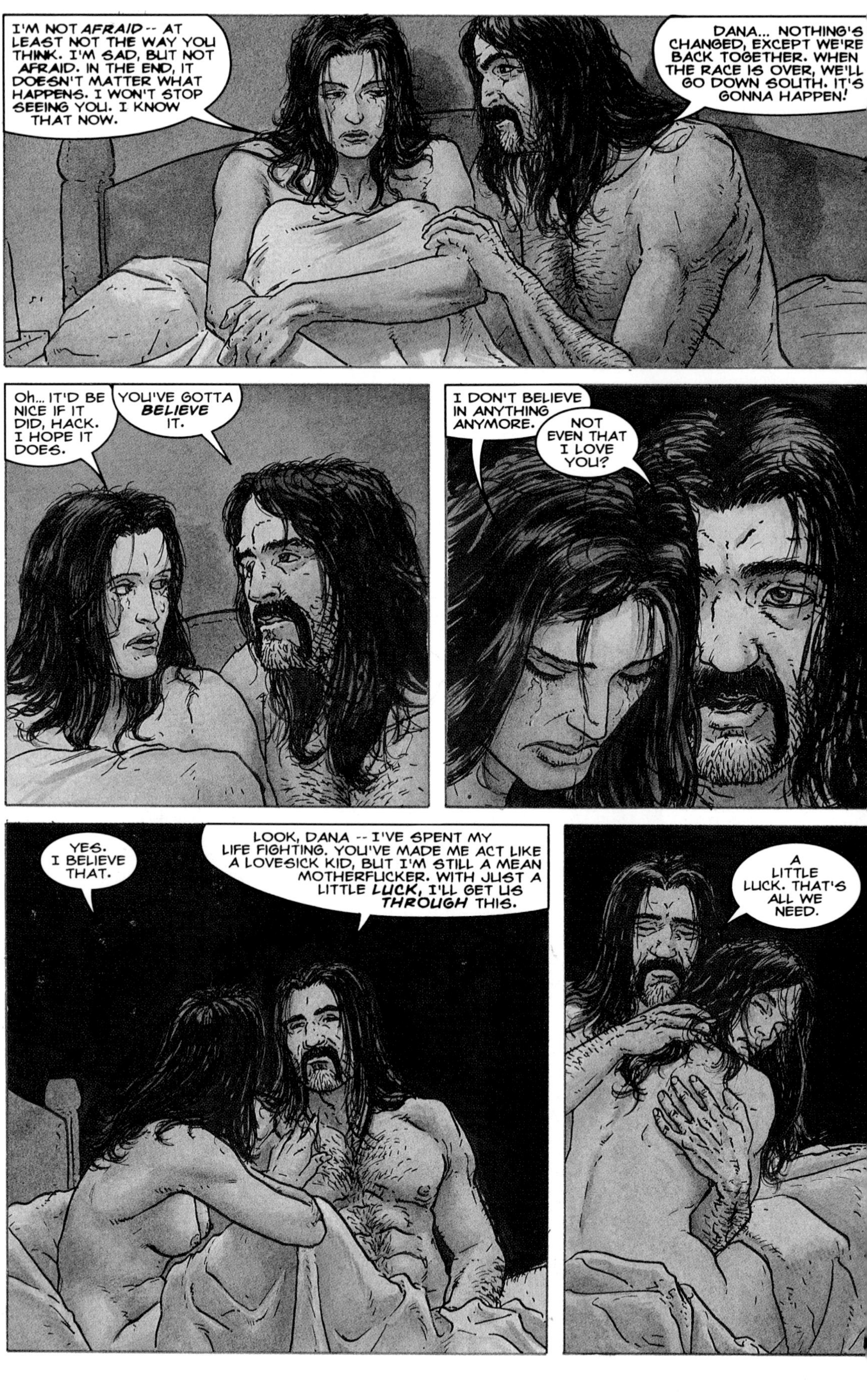
I'M NOT *AFRAID* -- AT LEAST NOT THE WAY YOU THINK. I'M SAD, BUT NOT *AFRAID*. IN THE END, IT DOESN'T MATTER WHAT HAPPENS. I WON'T STOP SEEING YOU. I KNOW THAT NOW.
DANA... NOTHING'S CHANGED, EXCEPT WE'RE BACK TOGETHER. WHEN THE RACE IS OVER, WE'LL GO DOWN SOUTH. IT'S GONNA HAPPEN!
Oh... IT'D BE NICE IF IT DID, HACK. I HOPE IT DOES.
YOU'VE GOTTA *BELIEVE* IT.
I DON'T BELIEVE IN ANYTHING ANYMORE.
NOT EVEN THAT I LOVE YOU?
YES. I BELIEVE THAT.
LOOK, DANA -- I'VE SPENT MY LIFE FIGHTING. YOU'VE MADE ME ACT LIKE A LOVESICK KID, BUT I'M STILL A MEAN MOTHERFUCKER. WITH JUST A LITTLE *LUCK*, I'LL GET US *THROUGH* THIS.
A LITTLE LUCK. THAT'S ALL WE NEED.

CHAPTER FIVE

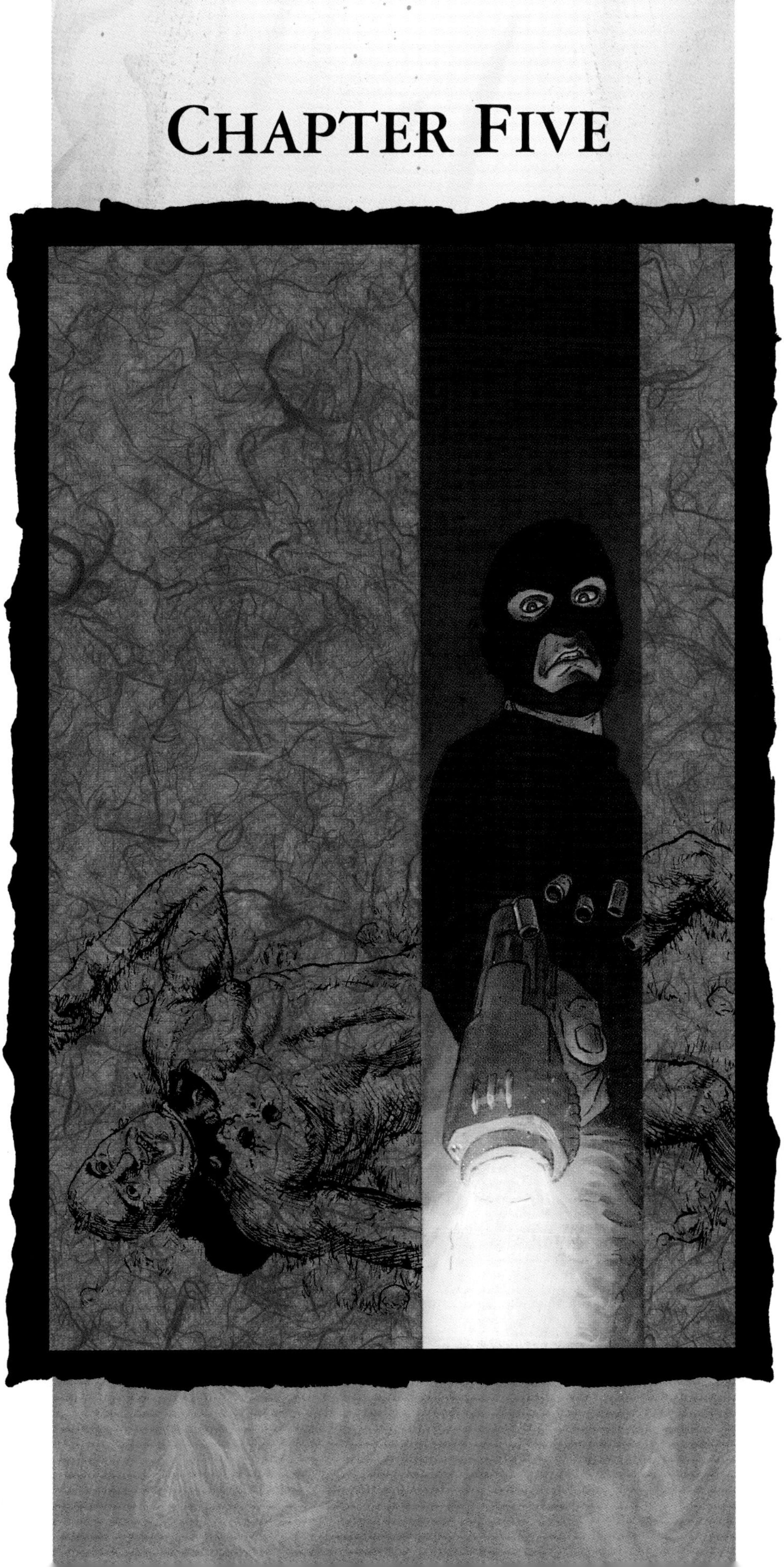

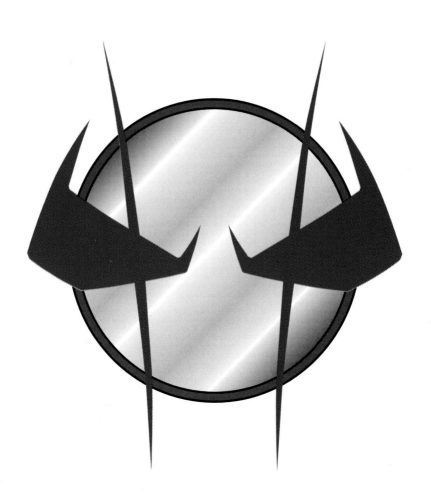

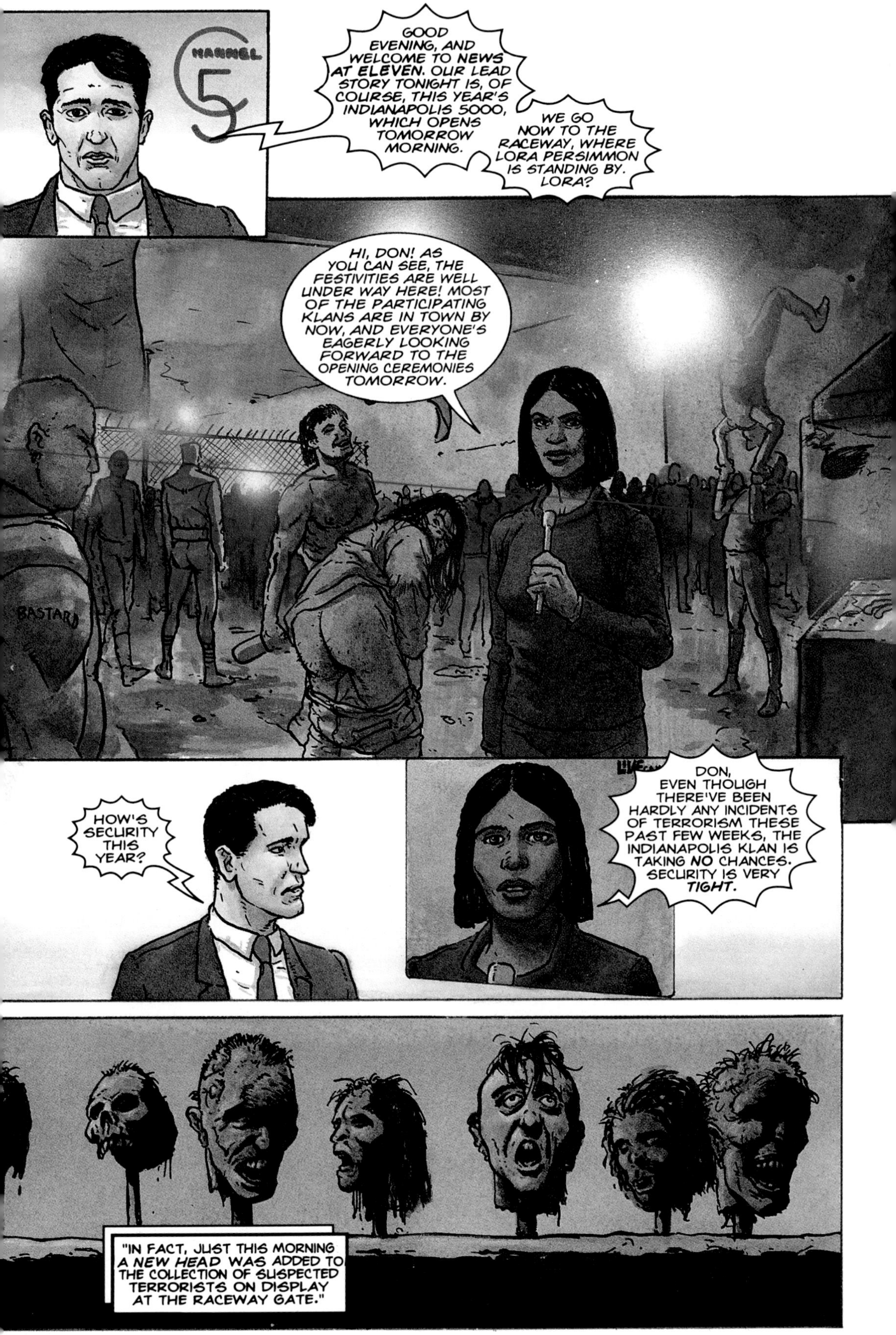
GOOD EVENING, AND WELCOME TO NEWS AT ELEVEN. OUR LEAD STORY TONIGHT IS, OF COURSE, THIS YEAR'S INDIANAPOLIS 5000, WHICH OPENS TOMORROW MORNING.
WE GO NOW TO THE RACEWAY, WHERE LORA PERSIMMON IS STANDING BY. LORA?
HI, DON! AS YOU CAN SEE, THE FESTIVITIES ARE WELL UNDER WAY HERE! MOST OF THE PARTICIPATING KLANS ARE IN TOWN BY NOW, AND EVERYONE'S EAGERLY LOOKING FORWARD TO THE OPENING CEREMONIES TOMORROW.
BASTARD
HOW'S SECURITY THIS YEAR?
DON, EVEN THOUGH THERE'VE BEEN HARDLY ANY INCIDENTS OF TERRORISM THESE PAST FEW WEEKS, THE INDIANAPOLIS KLAN IS TAKING NO CHANCES. SECURITY IS VERY TIGHT.
"IN FACT, JUST THIS MORNING A NEW HEAD WAS ADDED TO THE COLLECTION OF SUSPECTED TERRORISTS ON DISPLAY AT THE RACEWAY GATE."

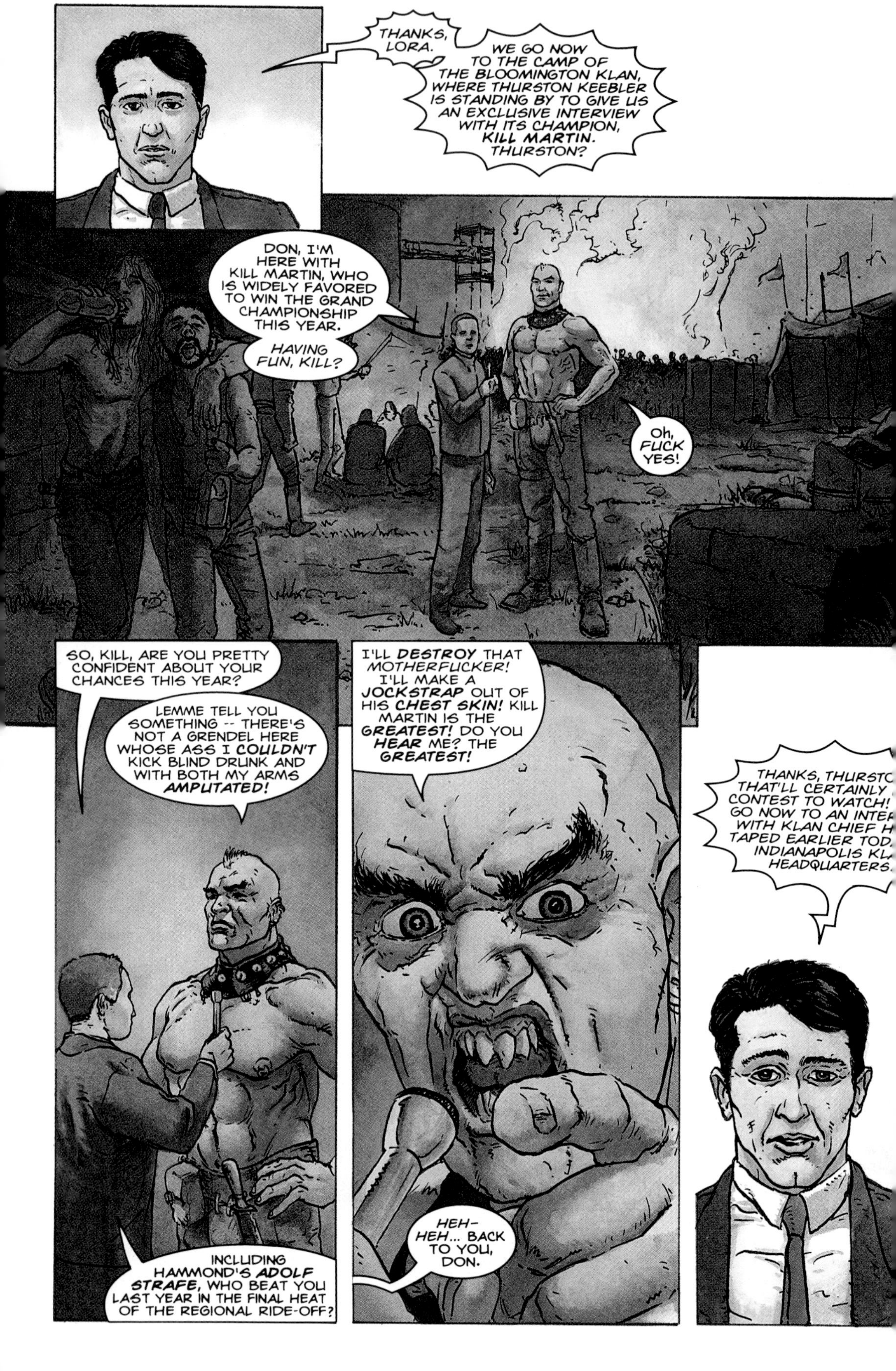

THANKS, LORA.
WE GO NOW TO THE CAMP OF THE BLOOMINGTON KLAN, WHERE THURSTON KEEBLER IS STANDING BY TO GIVE US AN EXCLUSIVE INTERVIEW WITH ITS CHAMPION, KILL MARTIN. THURSTON?
DON, I'M HERE WITH KILL MARTIN, WHO IS WIDELY FAVORED TO WIN THE GRAND CHAMPIONSHIP THIS YEAR.
HAVING FUN, KILL?
Oh, FUCK YES!
SO, KILL, ARE YOU PRETTY CONFIDENT ABOUT YOUR CHANCES THIS YEAR?
LEMME TELL YOU SOMETHING -- THERE'S NOT A GRENDEL HERE WHOSE ASS I COULDN'T KICK BLIND DRUNK AND WITH BOTH MY ARMS AMPUTATED!
INCLUDING HAMMOND'S ADOLF STRAFE, WHO BEAT YOU LAST YEAR IN THE FINAL HEAT OF THE REGIONAL RIDE-OFF?
I'LL DESTROY THAT MOTHERFUCKER! I'LL MAKE A JOCKSTRAP OUT OF HIS CHEST SKIN! KILL MARTIN IS THE GREATEST! DO YOU HEAR ME? THE GREATEST!
HEH-HEH... BACK TO YOU, DON.
THANKS, THURSTO THAT'LL CERTAINLY CONTEST TO WATCH! GO NOW TO AN INTER WITH KLAN CHIEF H TAPED EARLIER TOD INDIANAPOLIS KL HEADQUARTERS.

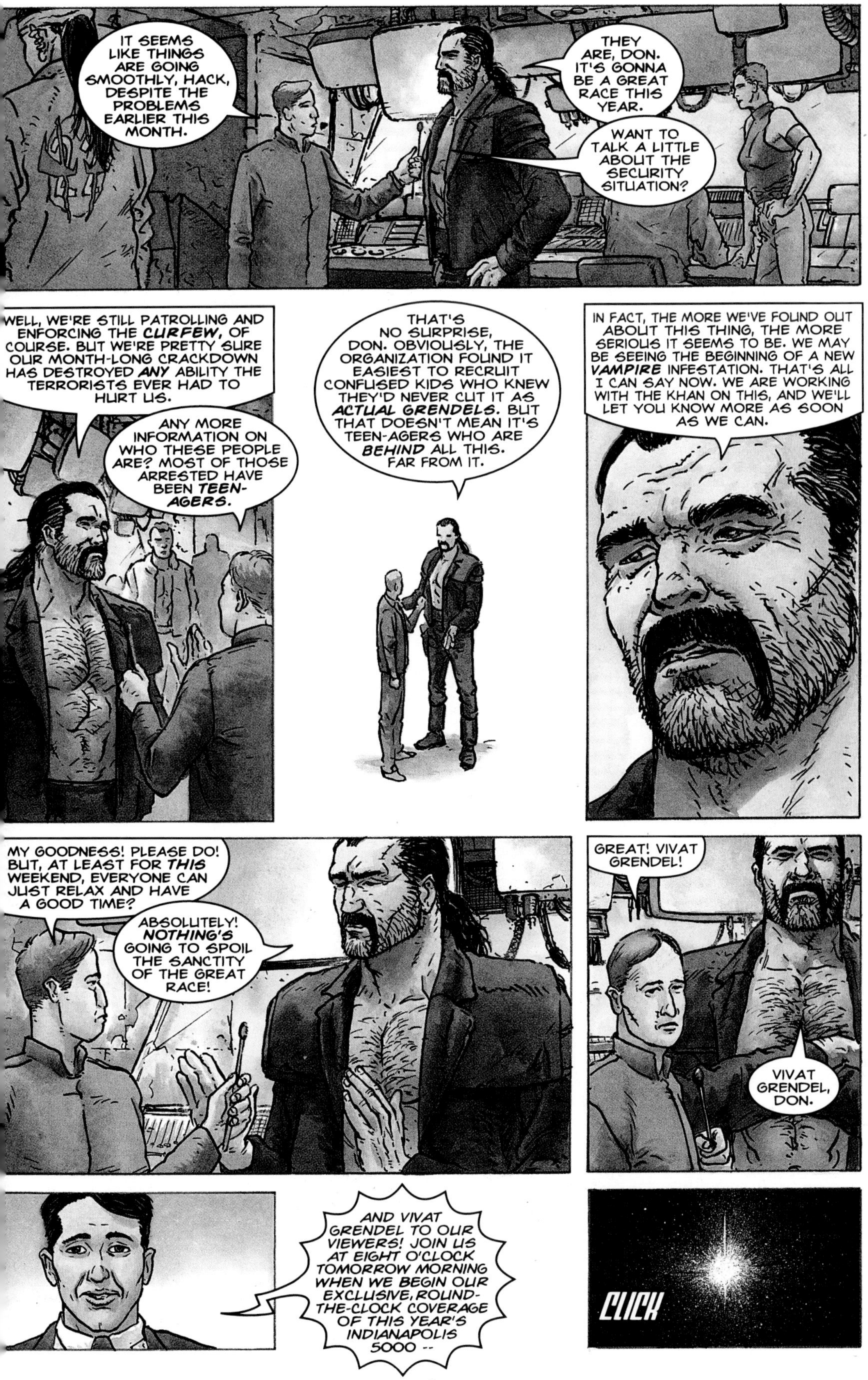
IT SEEMS LIKE THINGS ARE GOING SMOOTHLY, HACK, DESPITE THE PROBLEMS EARLIER THIS MONTH.
THEY ARE, DON. IT'S GONNA BE A GREAT RACE THIS YEAR.
WANT TO TALK A LITTLE ABOUT THE SECURITY SITUATION?
WELL, WE'RE STILL PATROLLING AND ENFORCING THE CURFEW, OF COURSE. BUT WE'RE PRETTY SURE OUR MONTH-LONG CRACKDOWN HAS DESTROYED ANY ABILITY THE TERRORISTS EVER HAD TO HURT US.
ANY MORE INFORMATION ON WHO THESE PEOPLE ARE? MOST OF THOSE ARRESTED HAVE BEEN TEEN-AGERS.
THAT'S NO SURPRISE, DON. OBVIOUSLY, THE ORGANIZATION FOUND IT EASIEST TO RECRUIT CONFUSED KIDS WHO KNEW THEY'D NEVER CUT IT AS ACTUAL GRENDELS. BUT THAT DOESN'T MEAN IT'S TEEN-AGERS WHO ARE BEHIND ALL THIS. FAR FROM IT.
IN FACT, THE MORE WE'VE FOUND OUT ABOUT THIS THING, THE MORE SERIOUS IT SEEMS TO BE. WE MAY BE SEEING THE BEGINNING OF A NEW VAMPIRE INFESTATION. THAT'S ALL I CAN SAY NOW. WE ARE WORKING WITH THE KHAN ON THIS, AND WE'LL LET YOU KNOW MORE AS SOON AS WE CAN.
MY GOODNESS! PLEASE DO! BUT, AT LEAST FOR THIS WEEKEND, EVERYONE CAN JUST RELAX AND HAVE A GOOD TIME?
ABSOLUTELY! NOTHING'S GOING TO SPOIL THE SANCTITY OF THE GREAT RACE!
GREAT! VIVAT GRENDEL!
VIVAT GRENDEL, DON.
AND VIVAT GRENDEL TO OUR VIEWERS! JOIN US AT EIGHT O'CLOCK TOMORROW MORNING WHEN WE BEGIN OUR EXCLUSIVE, ROUND-THE-CLOCK COVERAGE OF THIS YEAR'S INDIANAPOLIS 5000 --
CLICK

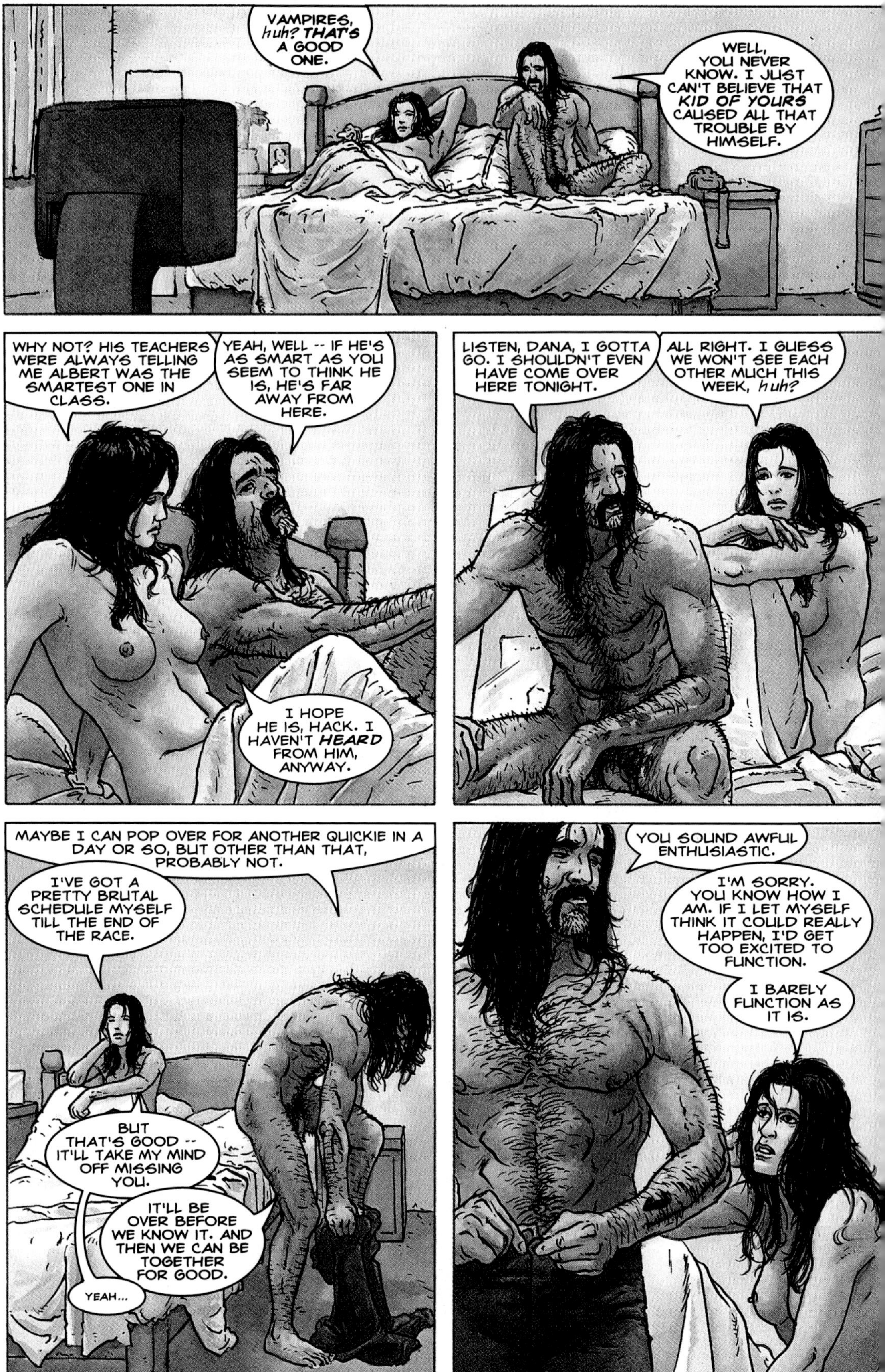

VAMPIRES, huh? THAT'S A GOOD ONE.
WELL, YOU NEVER KNOW. I JUST CAN'T BELIEVE THAT KID OF YOURS CAUSED ALL THAT TROUBLE BY HIMSELF.
WHY NOT? HIS TEACHERS WERE ALWAYS TELLING ME ALBERT WAS THE SMARTEST ONE IN CLASS.
YEAH, WELL -- IF HE'S AS SMART AS YOU SEEM TO THINK HE IS, HE'S FAR AWAY FROM HERE.
I HOPE HE IS, HACK. I HAVEN'T HEARD FROM HIM, ANYWAY.
LISTEN, DANA, I GOTTA GO. I SHOULDN'T EVEN HAVE COME OVER HERE TONIGHT.
ALL RIGHT. I GUESS WE WON'T SEE EACH OTHER MUCH THIS WEEK, huh?
MAYBE I CAN POP OVER FOR ANOTHER QUICKIE IN A DAY OR SO, BUT OTHER THAN THAT, PROBABLY NOT.
I'VE GOT A PRETTY BRUTAL SCHEDULE MYSELF TILL THE END OF THE RACE.
BUT THAT'S GOOD -- IT'LL TAKE MY MIND OFF MISSING YOU.
IT'LL BE OVER BEFORE WE KNOW IT. AND THEN WE CAN BE TOGETHER FOR GOOD.
YEAH...
YOU SOUND AWFUL ENTHUSIASTIC.
I'M SORRY. YOU KNOW HOW I AM. IF I LET MYSELF THINK IT COULD REALLY HAPPEN, I'D GET TOO EXCITED TO FUNCTION.
I BARELY FUNCTION AS IT IS.

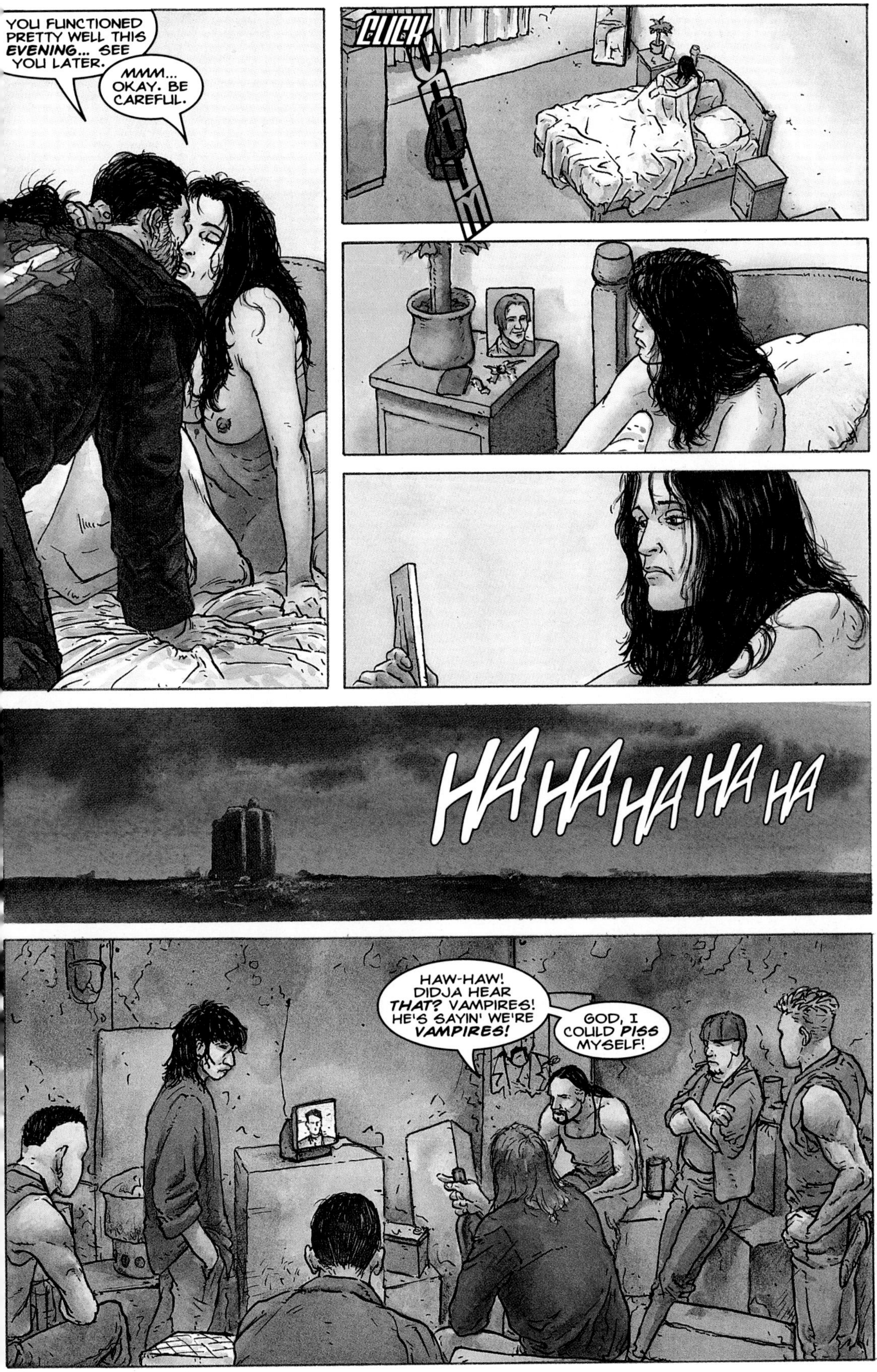
YOU FUNCTIONED PRETTY WELL THIS EVENING... SEE YOU LATER.
MMM... OKAY. BE CAREFUL.
CLICK
HA HA HA HA HA HA
HAW-HAW! DIDJA HEAR THAT? VAMPIRES! HE'S SAYIN' WE'RE VAMPIRES!
GOD, I COULD PISS MYSELF!

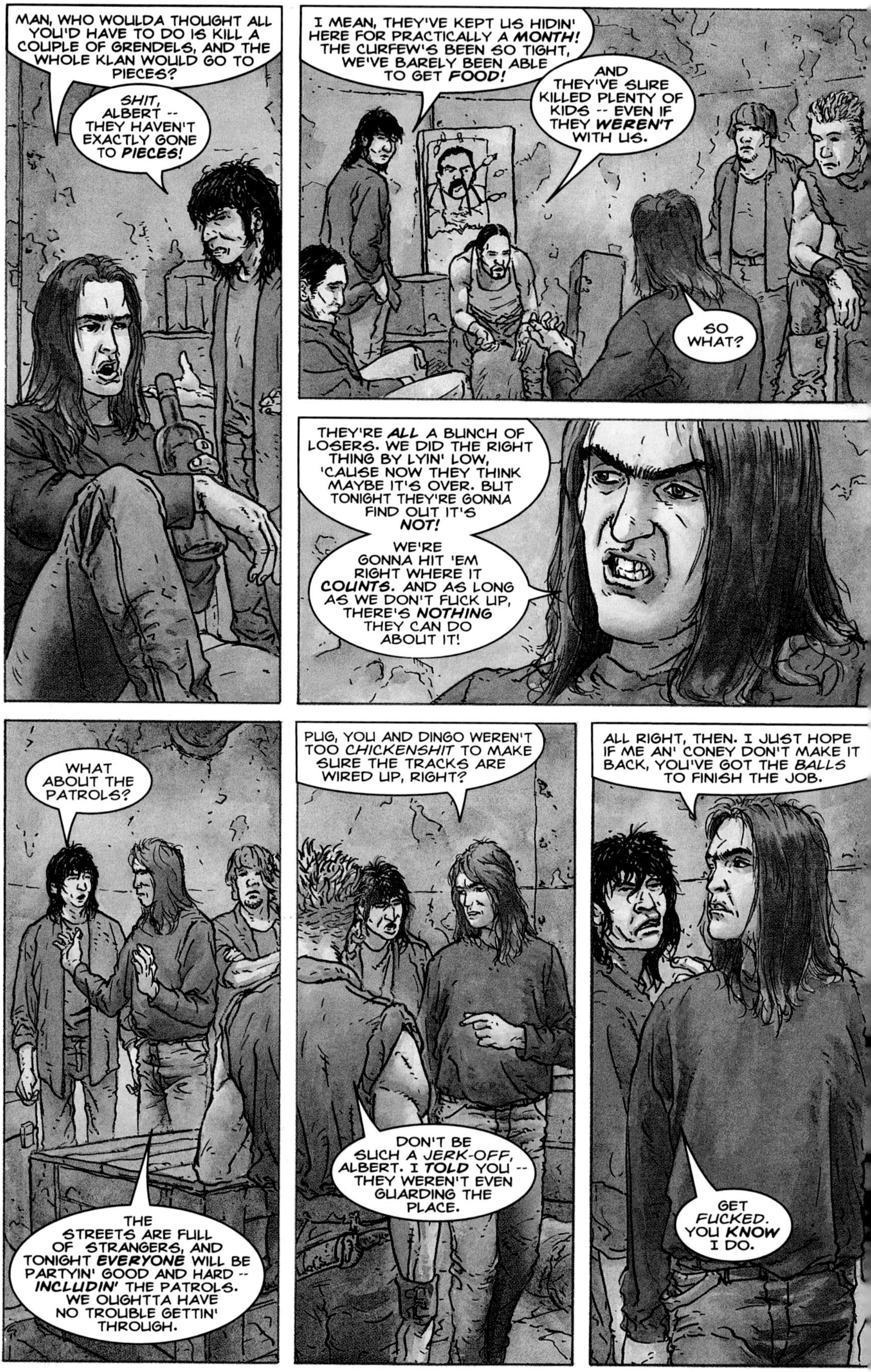
MAN, WHO WOULDA THOUGHT ALL YOU'D HAVE TO DO IS KILL A COUPLE OF GRENDELS, AND THE WHOLE KLAN WOULD GO TO PIECES?
SHIT, ALBERT -- THEY HAVEN'T EXACTLY GONE TO PIECES!
I MEAN, THEY'VE KEPT US HIDIN' HERE FOR PRACTICALLY A MONTH! THE CURFEW'S BEEN SO TIGHT, WE'VE BARELY BEEN ABLE TO GET FOOD!
AND THEY'VE SURE KILLED PLENTY OF KIDS -- EVEN IF THEY WEREN'T WITH US.
SO WHAT?
THEY'RE ALL A BUNCH OF LOSERS. WE DID THE RIGHT THING BY LYIN' LOW, 'CAUSE NOW THEY THINK MAYBE IT'S OVER. BUT TONIGHT THEY'RE GONNA FIND OUT IT'S NOT!
WE'RE GONNA HIT 'EM RIGHT WHERE IT COUNTS. AND AS LONG AS WE DON'T FUCK UP, THERE'S NOTHING THEY CAN DO ABOUT IT!
WHAT ABOUT THE PATROLS?
THE STREETS ARE FULL OF STRANGERS, AND TONIGHT EVERYONE WILL BE PARTYIN' GOOD AND HARD -- INCLUDIN' THE PATROLS. WE OUGHTTA HAVE NO TROUBLE GETTIN' THROUGH.
PUG, YOU AND DINGO WEREN'T TOO CHICKENSHIT TO MAKE SURE THE TRACKS ARE WIRED UP, RIGHT?
DON'T BE SUCH A JERK-OFF, ALBERT. I TOLD YOU -- THEY WEREN'T EVEN GUARDING THE PLACE.
ALL RIGHT, THEN. I JUST HOPE IF ME AN' CONEY DON'T MAKE IT BACK, YOU'VE GOT THE BALLS TO FINISH THE JOB.
GET FUCKED. YOU KNOW I DO.

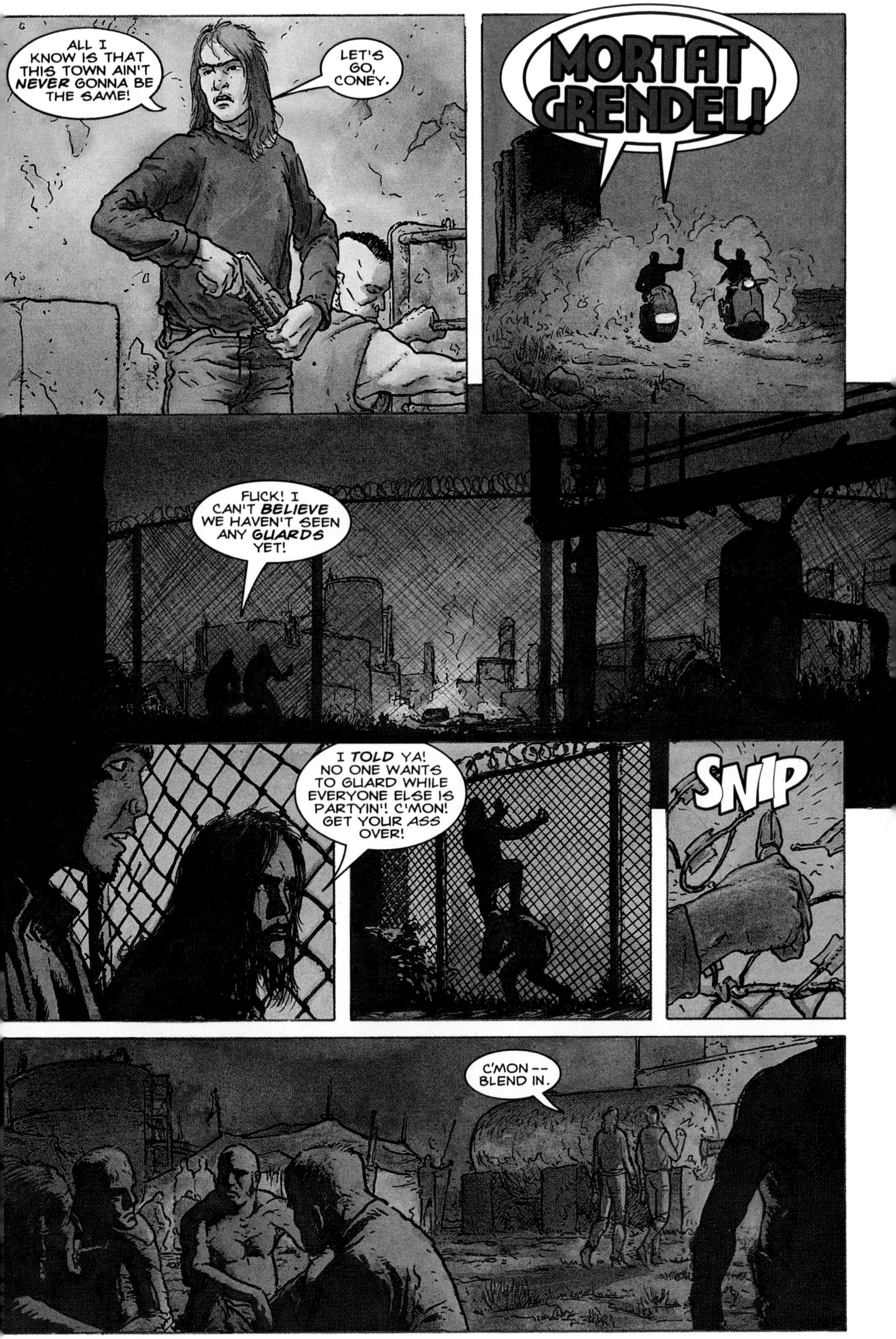
ALL I KNOW IS THAT THIS TOWN AIN'T NEVER GONNA BE THE SAME!
LET'S GO, CONEY.
MORTAT GRENDEL!
FUCK! I CAN'T BELIEVE WE HAVEN'T SEEN ANY GUARDS YET!
I TOLD YA! NO ONE WANTS TO GUARD WHILE EVERYONE ELSE IS PARTYIN'! C'MON! GET YOUR ASS OVER!
SNIP
C'MON -- BLEND IN.

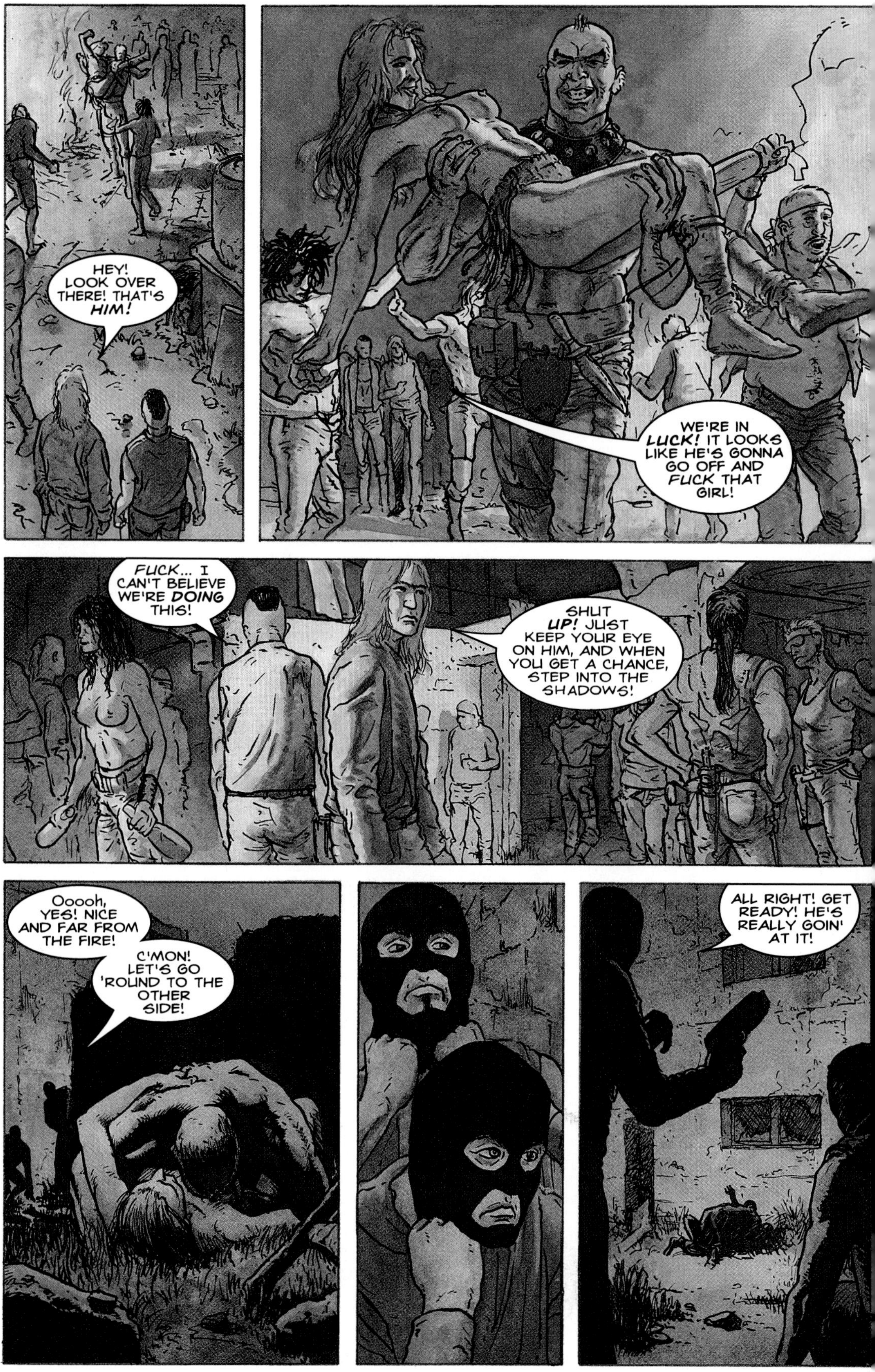
HEY! LOOK OVER THERE! THAT'S HIM!
WE'RE IN LUCK! IT LOOKS LIKE HE'S GONNA GO OFF AND FUCK THAT GIRL!
FUCK... I CAN'T BELIEVE WE'RE DOING THIS!
SHUT UP! JUST KEEP YOUR EYE ON HIM, AND WHEN YOU GET A CHANCE, STEP INTO THE SHADOWS!
Ooooh, YES! NICE AND FAR FROM THE FIRE!
C'MON! LET'S GO 'ROUND TO THE OTHER SIDE!
ALL RIGHT! GET READY! HE'S REALLY GOIN' AT IT!

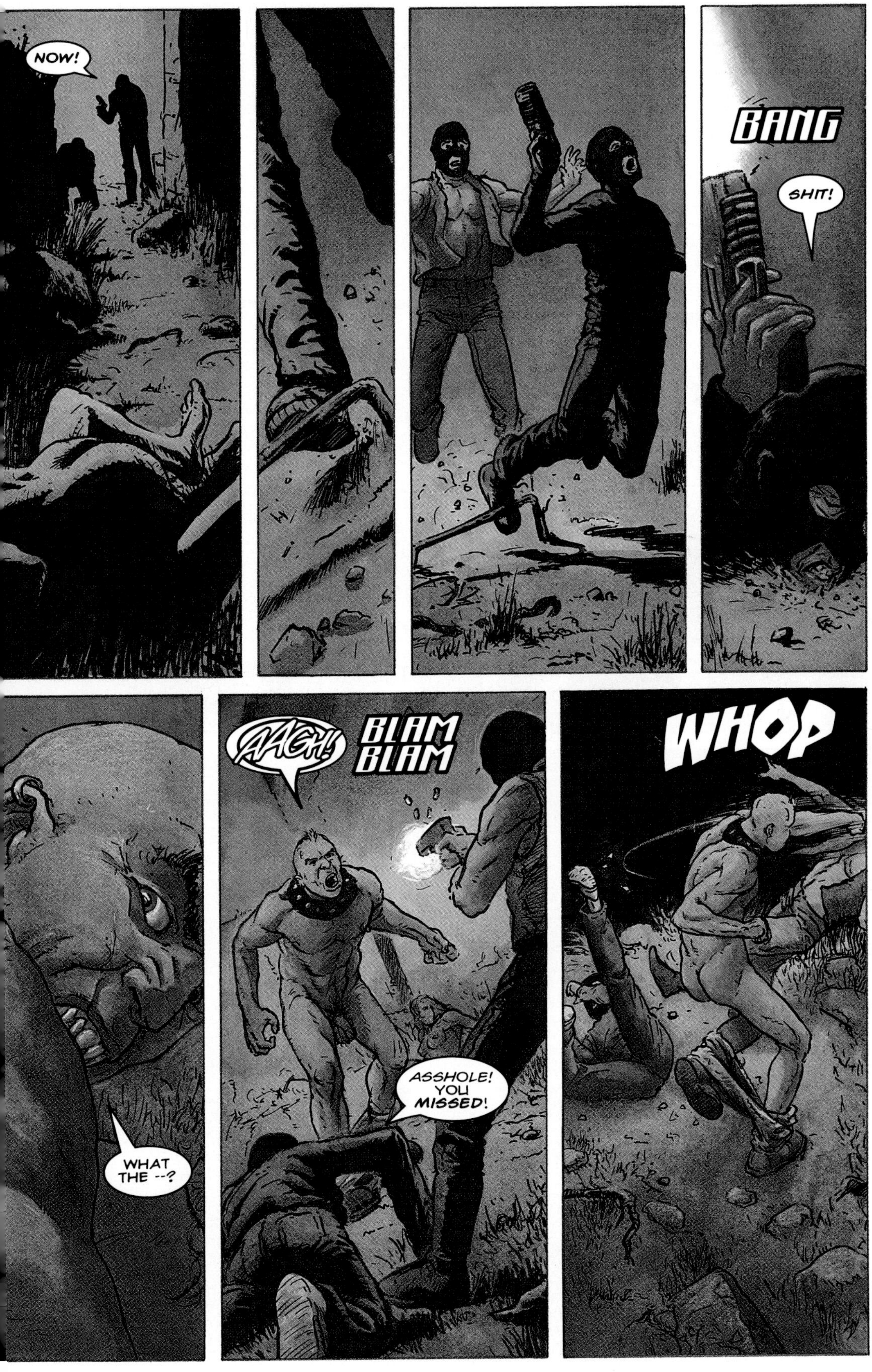
NOW!
BANG
SHIT!
WHAT THE --?
AAGH!
BLAM BLAM
ASSHOLE! YOU MISSED!
WHOP

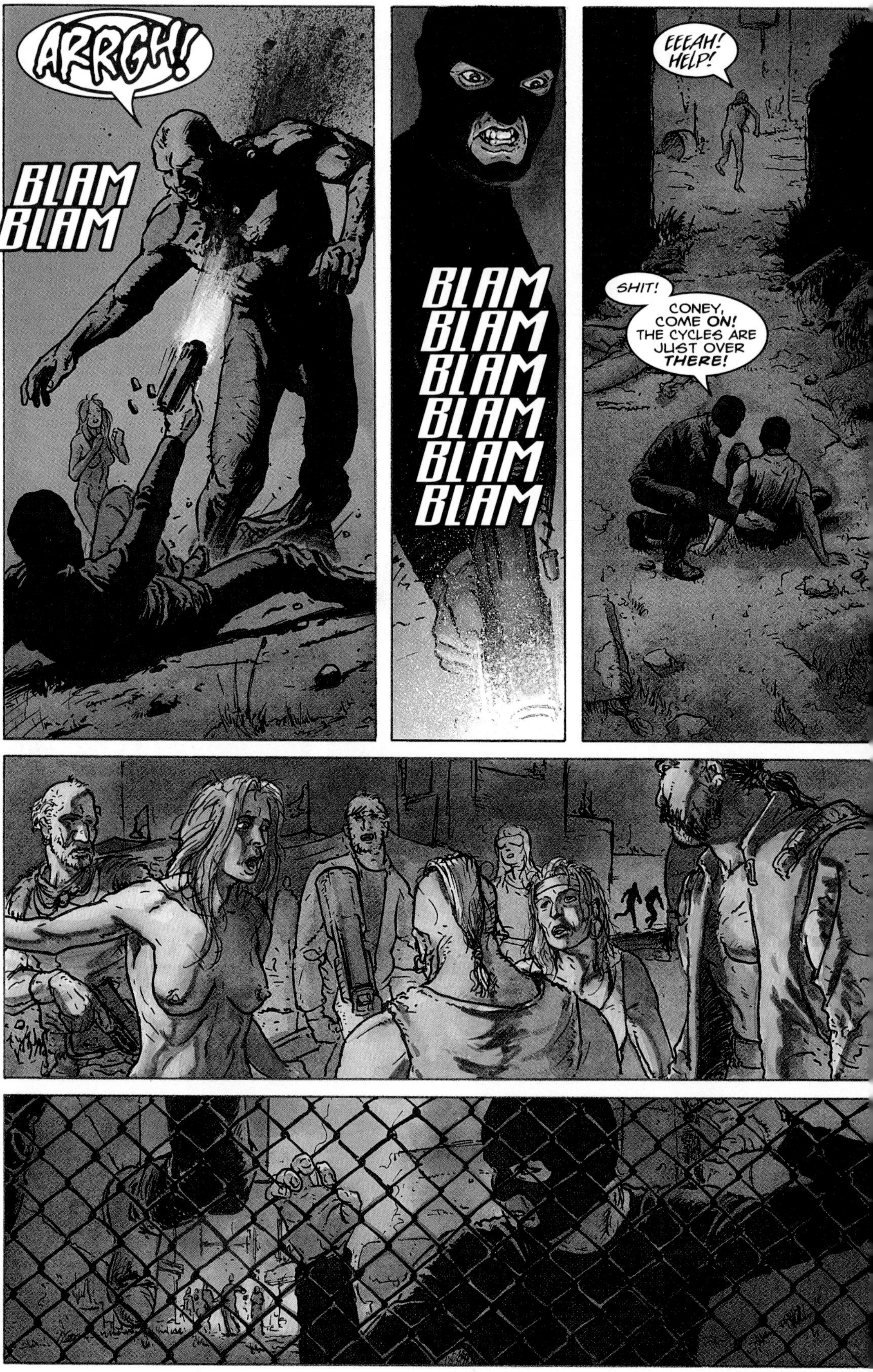
ARRGH!
BLAM BLAM
BLAM BLAM BLAM BLAM BLAM BLAM
EEEAH! HELP!
SHIT!
CONEY, COME ON! THE CYCLES ARE JUST OVER THERE!

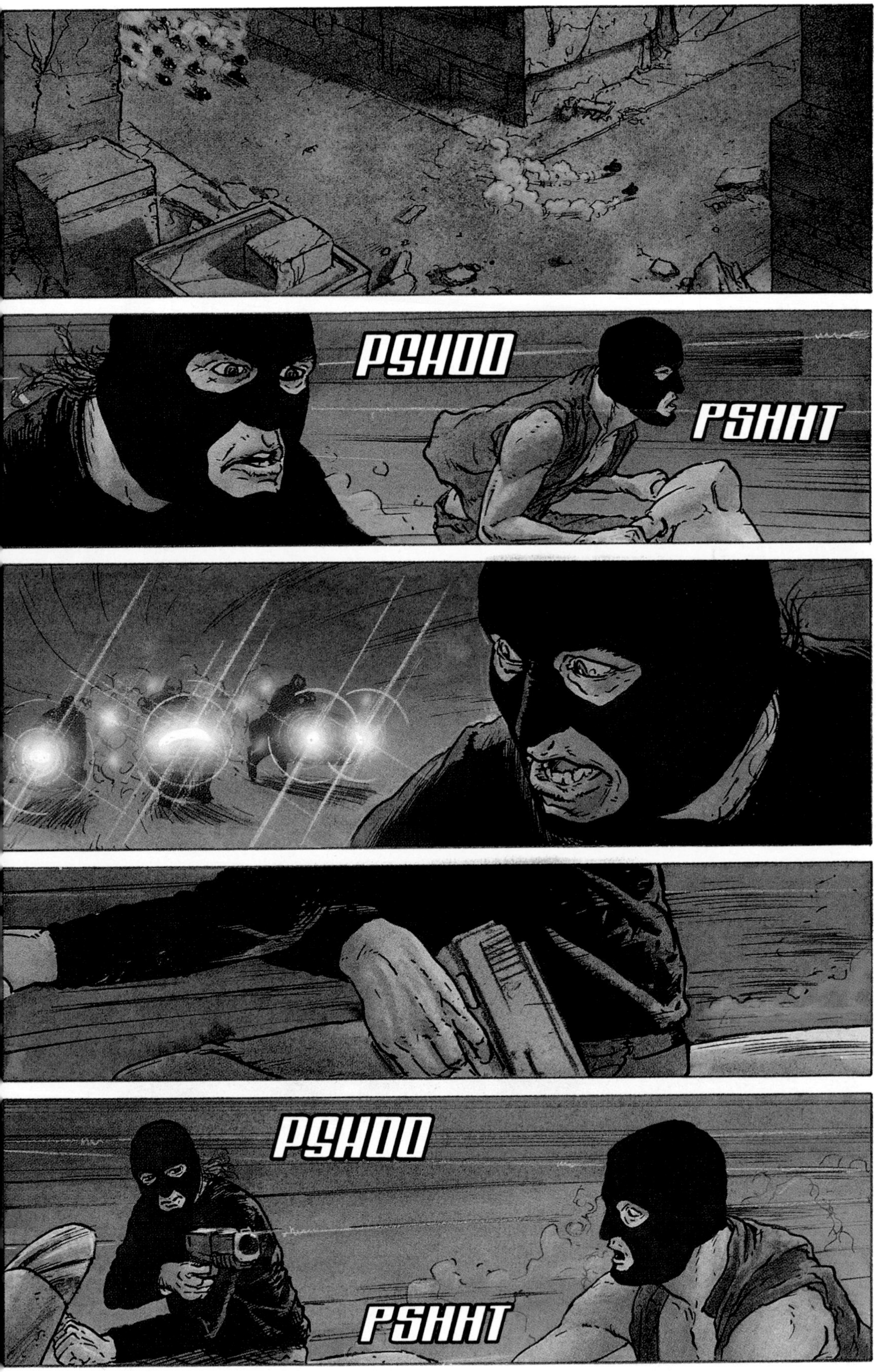
PSHOO
PSHHT
PSHOO
PSHHT

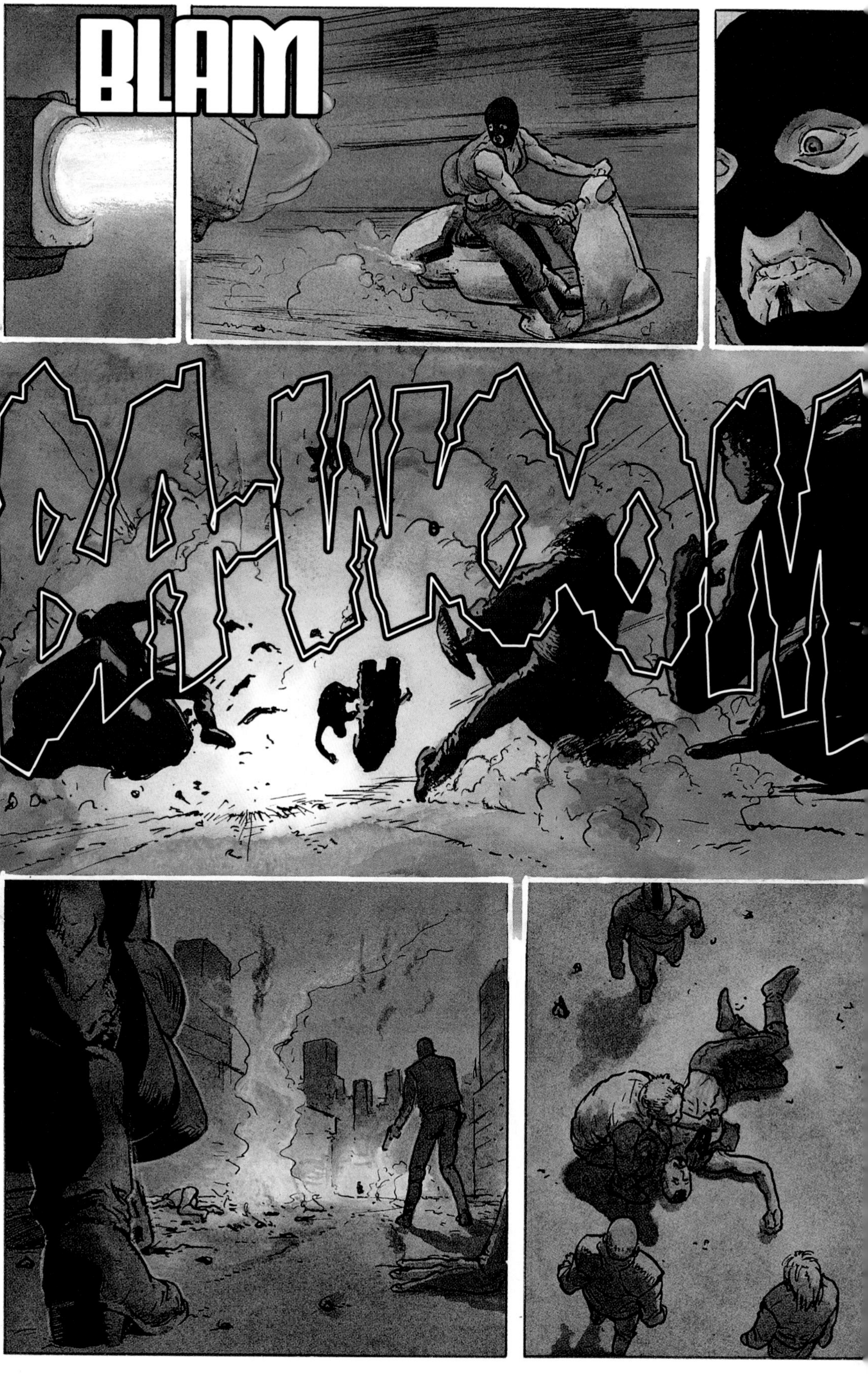
BLAM
BRAWOOM

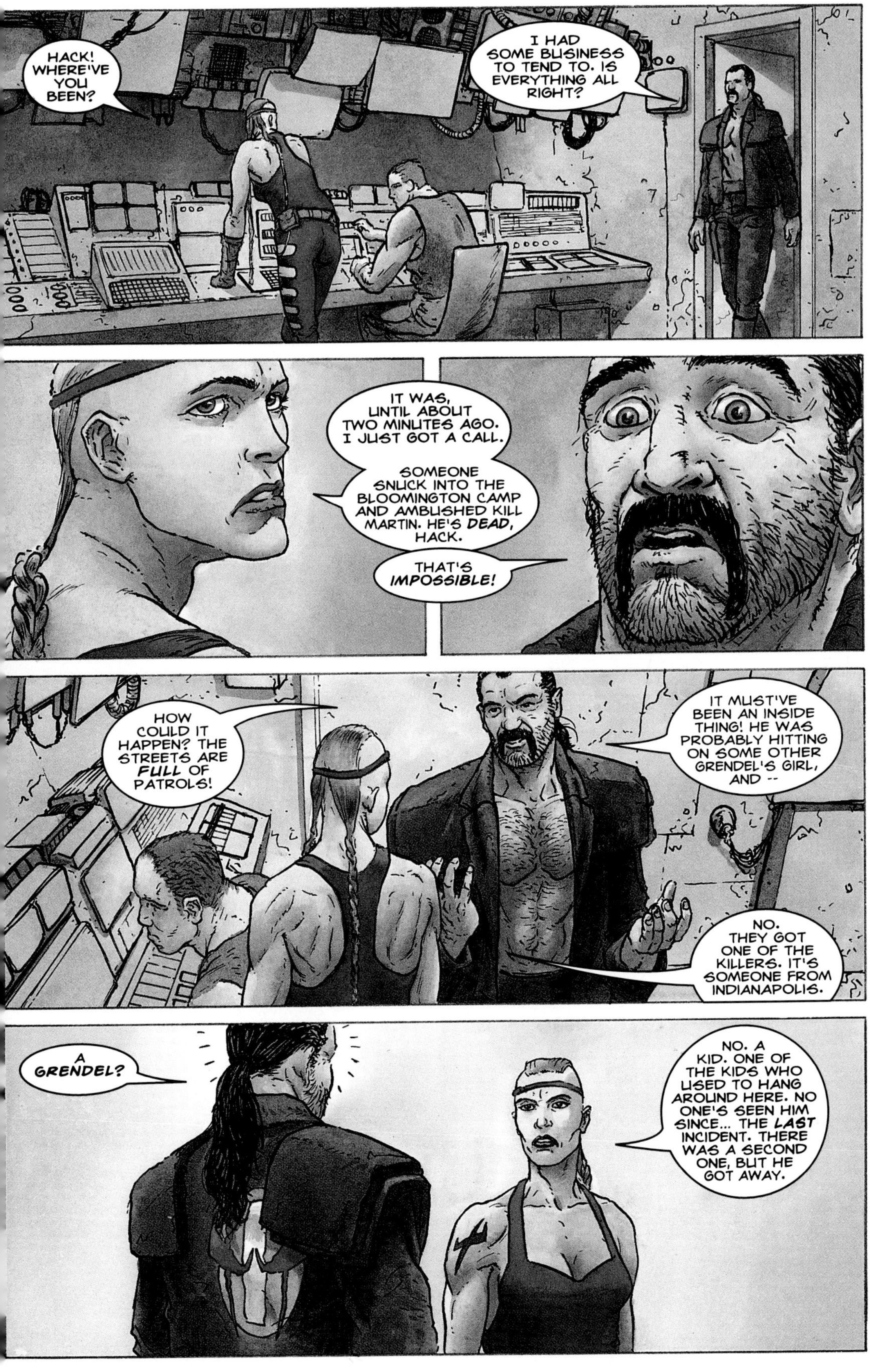
HACK! WHERE'VE YOU BEEN?
I HAD SOME BUSINESS TO TEND TO. IS EVERYTHING ALL RIGHT?
IT WAS, UNTIL ABOUT TWO MINUTES AGO. I JUST GOT A CALL.
SOMEONE SNUCK INTO THE BLOOMINGTON CAMP AND AMBUSHED KILL MARTIN. HE'S *DEAD*, HACK.
THAT'S *IMPOSSIBLE!*
HOW COULD IT HAPPEN? THE STREETS ARE *FULL* OF PATROLS!
IT MUST'VE BEEN AN INSIDE THING! HE WAS PROBABLY HITTING ON SOME OTHER GRENDEL'S GIRL, AND --
NO. THEY GOT ONE OF THE KILLERS. IT'S SOMEONE FROM INDIANAPOLIS.
A *GRENDEL?*
NO. A KID. ONE OF THE KIDS WHO USED TO HANG AROUND HERE. NO ONE'S SEEN HIM SINCE... THE *LAST* INCIDENT. THERE WAS A SECOND ONE, BUT HE GOT AWAY.

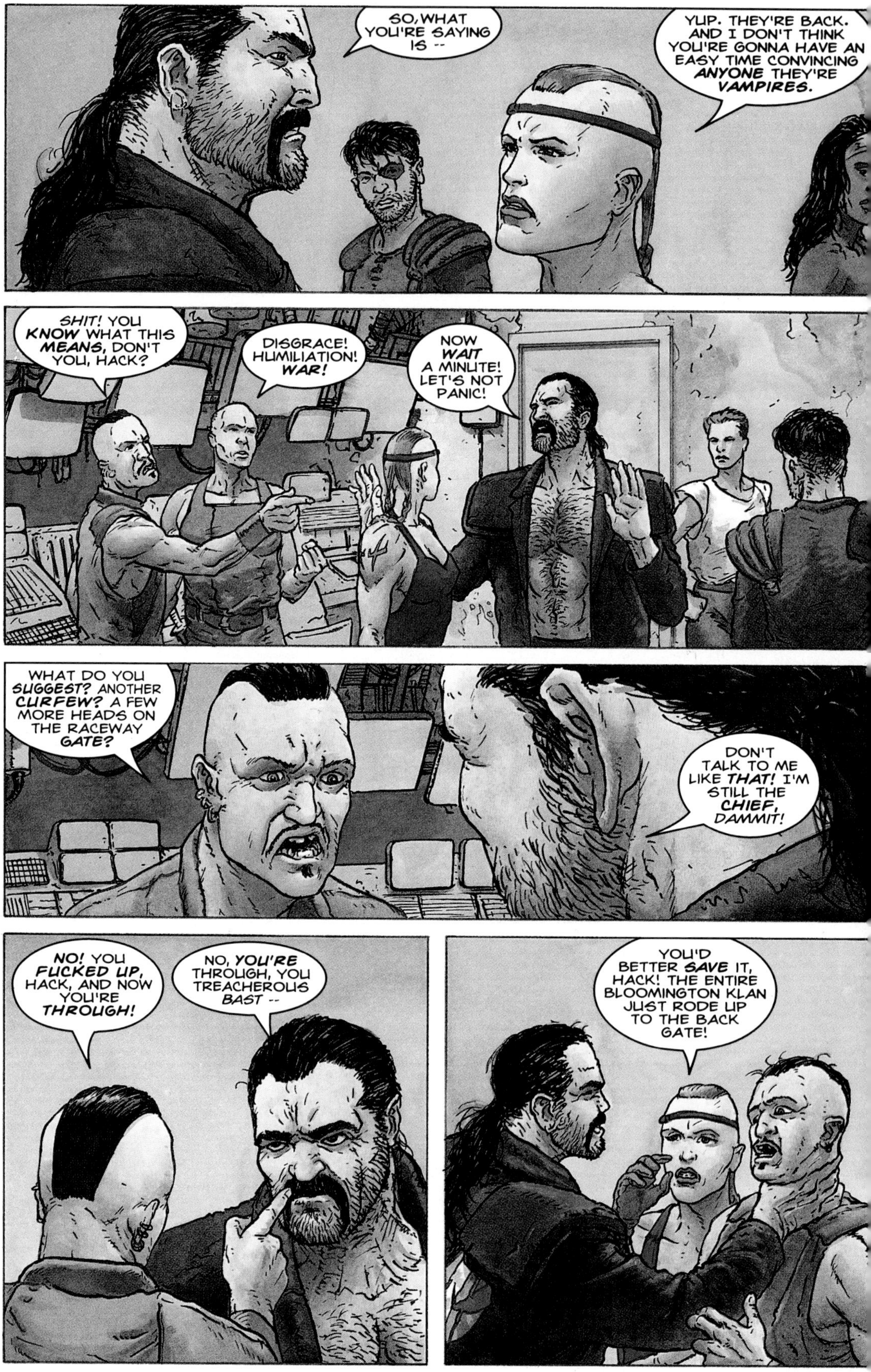
SO, WHAT YOU'RE SAYING IS --
YUP. THEY'RE BACK. AND I DON'T THINK YOU'RE GONNA HAVE AN EASY TIME CONVINCING ANYONE THEY'RE VAMPIRES.
SHIT! YOU KNOW WHAT THIS MEANS, DON'T YOU, HACK?
DISGRACE! HUMILIATION! WAR!
NOW WAIT A MINUTE! LET'S NOT PANIC!
WHAT DO YOU SUGGEST? ANOTHER CURFEW? A FEW MORE HEADS ON THE RACEWAY GATE?
DON'T TALK TO ME LIKE THAT! I'M STILL THE CHIEF, DAMMIT!
NO! YOU FUCKED UP, HACK, AND NOW YOU'RE THROUGH!
NO, YOU'RE THROUGH, YOU TREACHEROUS BAST --
YOU'D BETTER SAVE IT, HACK! THE ENTIRE BLOOMINGTON KLAN JUST RODE UP TO THE BACK GATE!

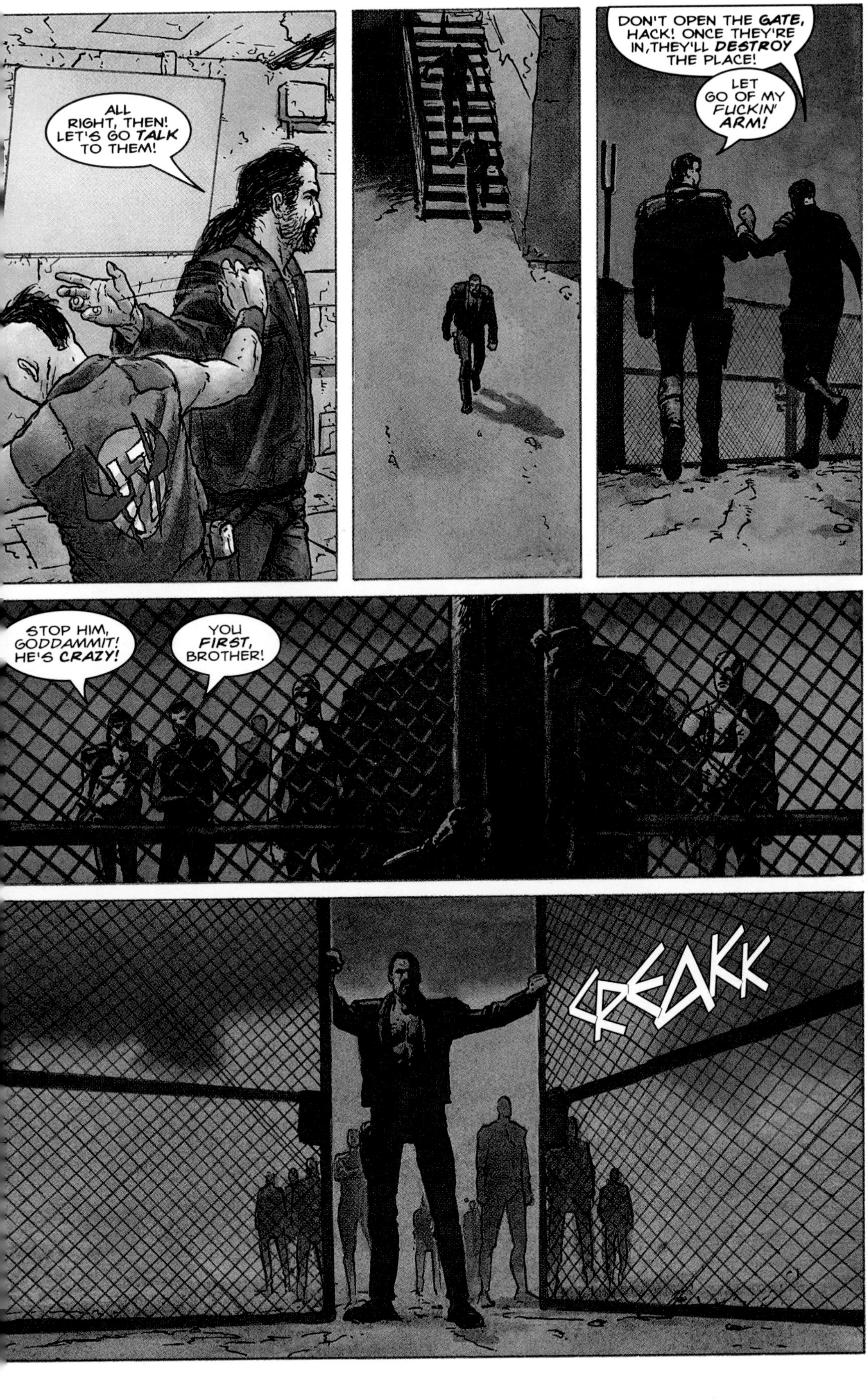

ALL RIGHT, THEN! LET'S GO TALK TO THEM!
DON'T OPEN THE GATE, HACK! ONCE THEY'RE IN, THEY'LL DESTROY THE PLACE!
LET GO OF MY FUCKIN' ARM!
STOP HIM, GODDAMMIT! HE'S CRAZY!
YOU FIRST, BROTHER!
CREAKK

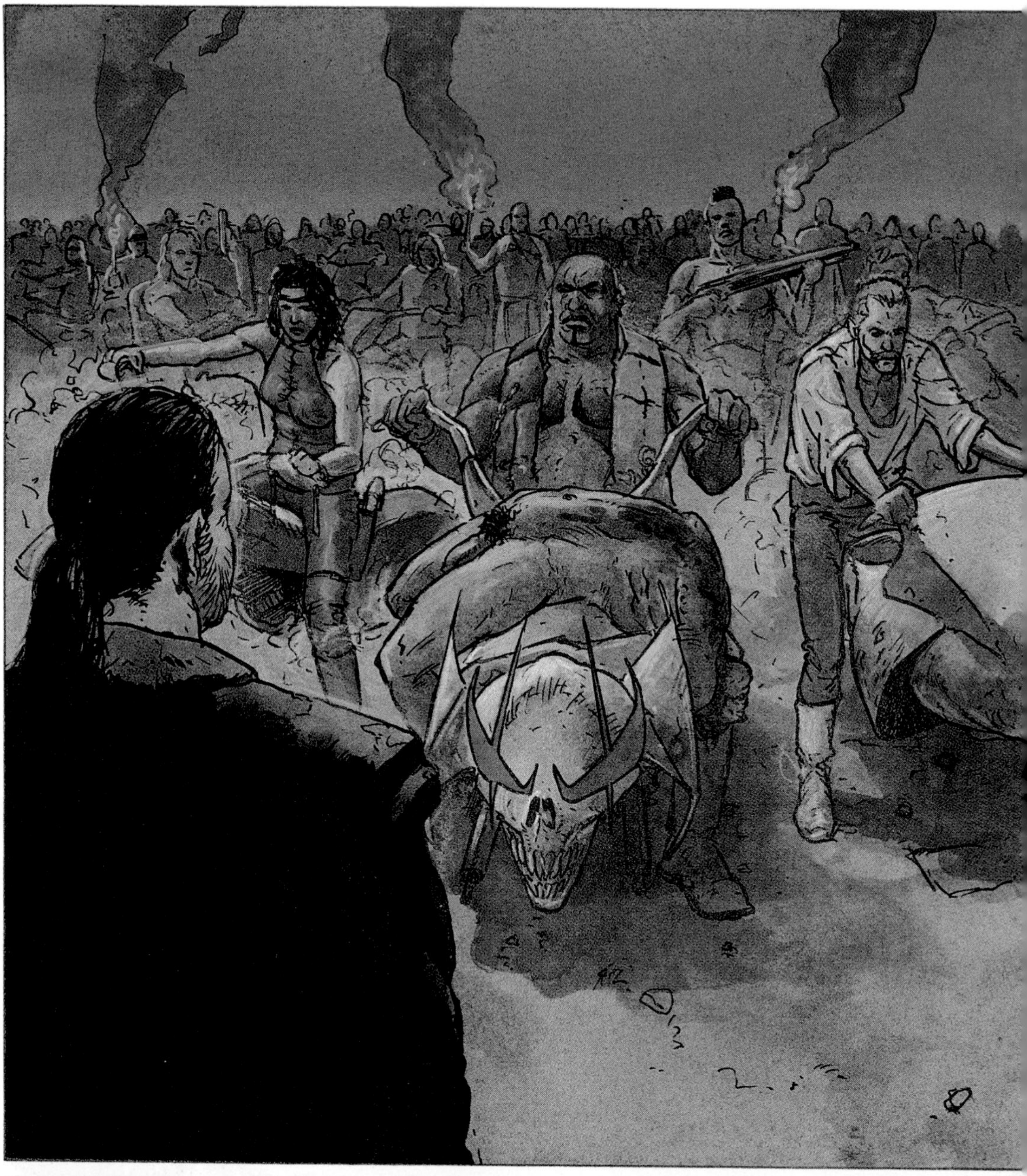

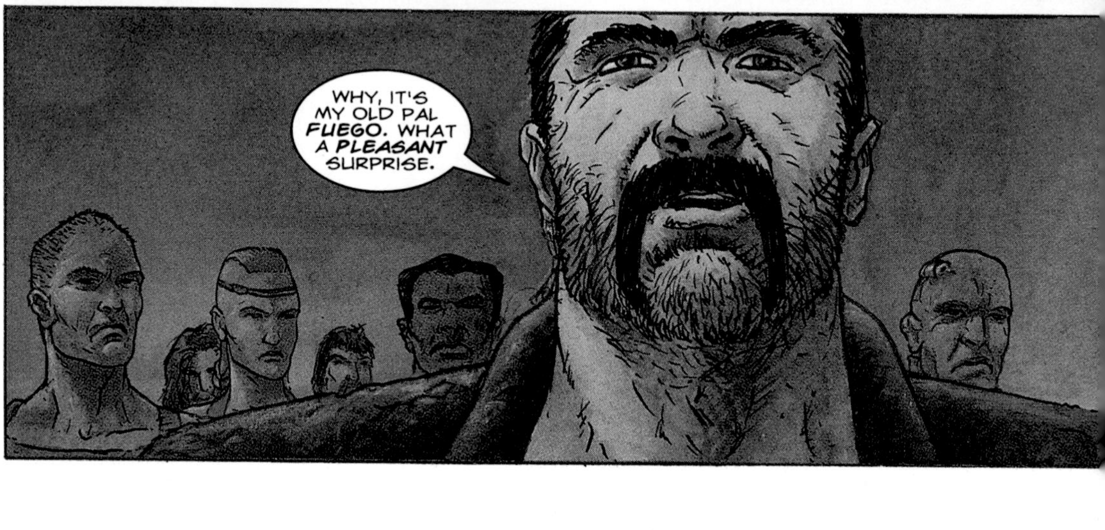
WHY, IT'S MY OLD PAL **FUEGO**. WHAT A **PLEASANT** SURPRISE.

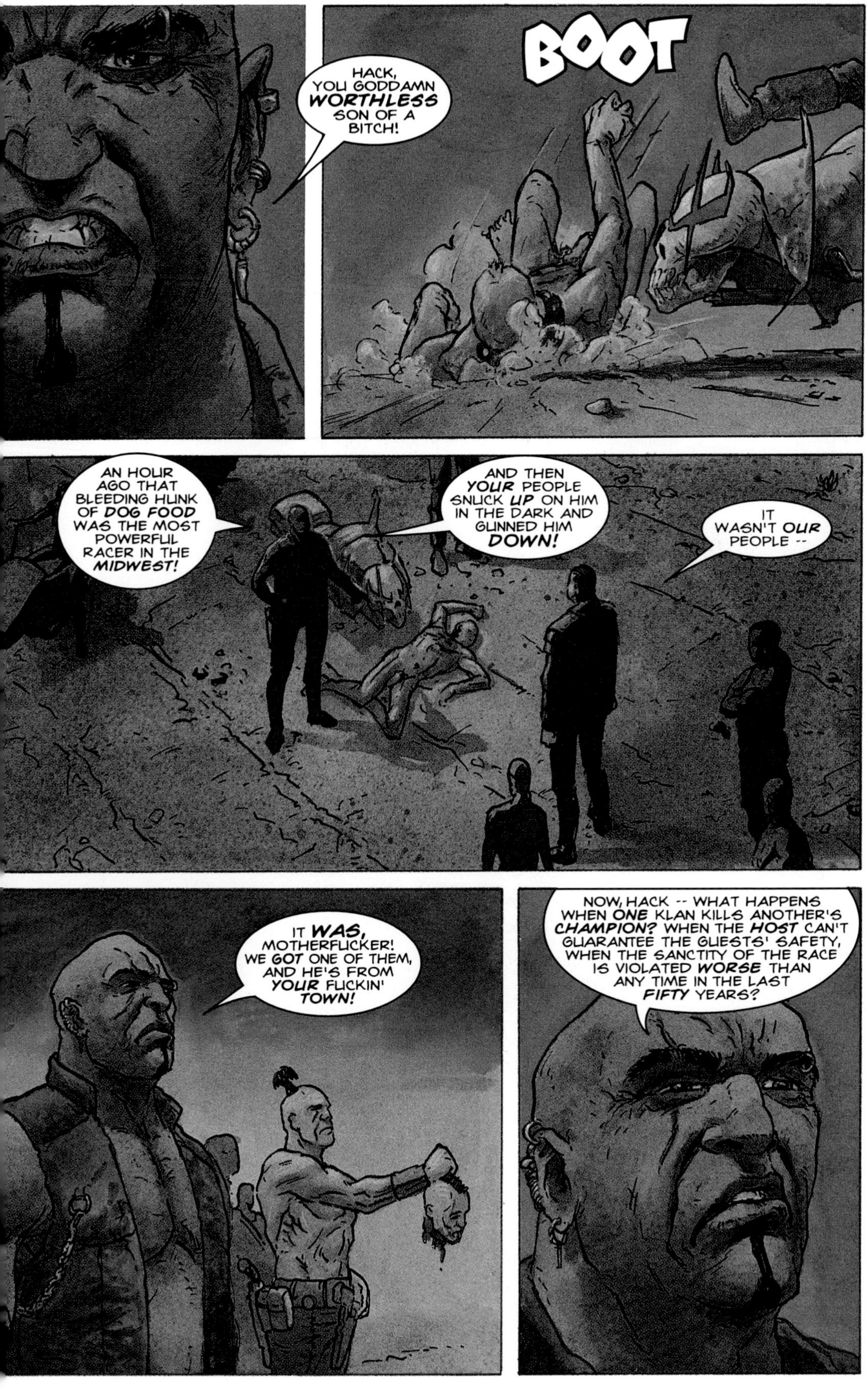
HACK, YOU GODDAMN WORTHLESS SON OF A BITCH!
BOOT
AN HOUR AGO THAT BLEEDING HUNK OF DOG FOOD WAS THE MOST POWERFUL RACER IN THE MIDWEST!
AND THEN YOUR PEOPLE SNUCK UP ON HIM IN THE DARK AND GUNNED HIM DOWN!
IT WASN'T OUR PEOPLE --
IT WAS, MOTHERFUCKER! WE GOT ONE OF THEM, AND HE'S FROM YOUR FUCKIN' TOWN!
NOW, HACK -- WHAT HAPPENS WHEN ONE KLAN KILLS ANOTHER'S CHAMPION? WHEN THE HOST CAN'T GUARANTEE THE GUESTS' SAFETY, WHEN THE SANCTITY OF THE RACE IS VIOLATED WORSE THAN ANY TIME IN THE LAST FIFTY YEARS?

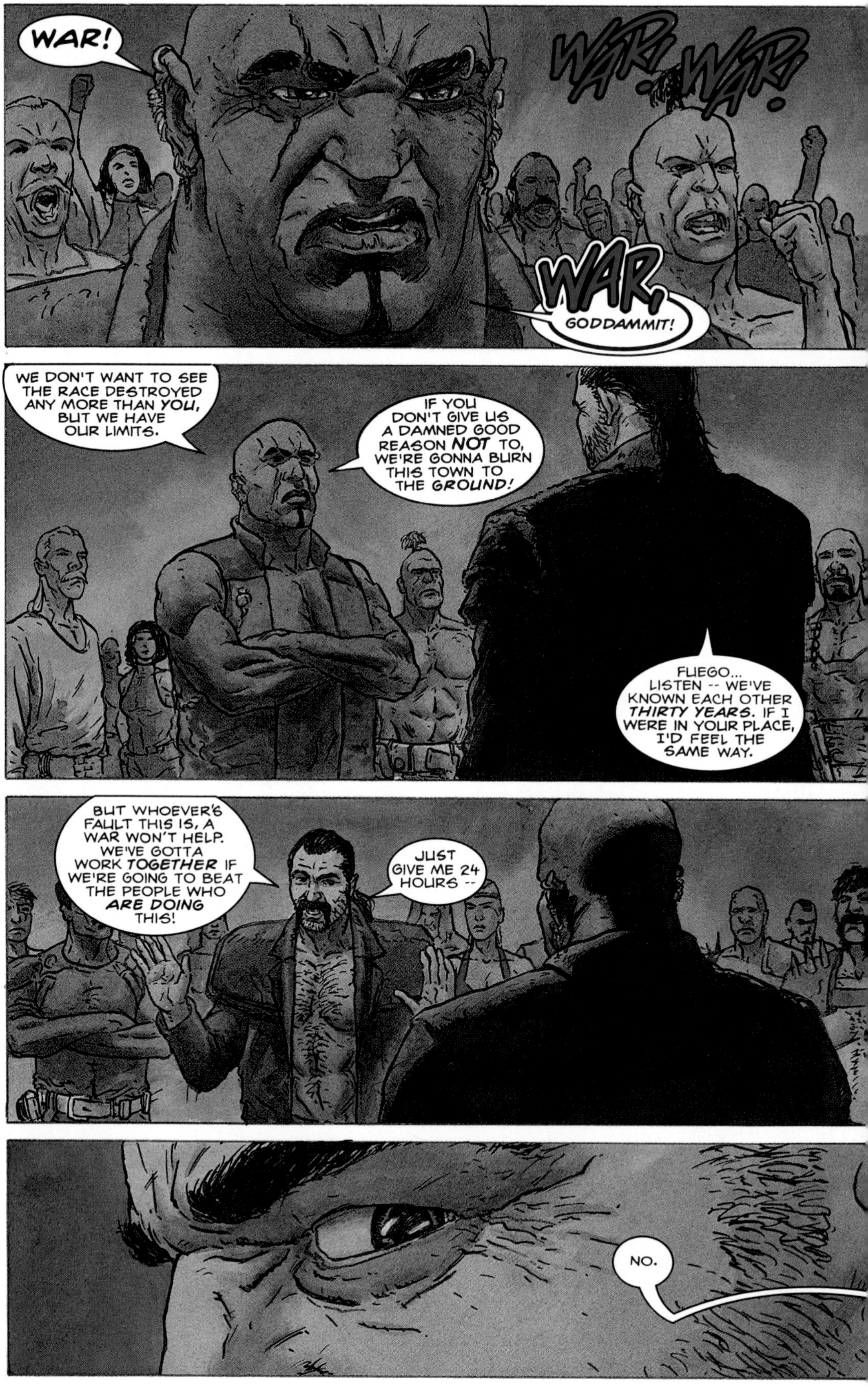
WAR!
WAR! WAR!
WAR, GODDAMMIT!
WE DON'T WANT TO SEE THE RACE DESTROYED ANY MORE THAN YOU, BUT WE HAVE OUR LIMITS.
IF YOU DON'T GIVE US A DAMNED GOOD REASON NOT TO, WE'RE GONNA BURN THIS TOWN TO THE GROUND!
FUEGO... LISTEN -- WE'VE KNOWN EACH OTHER THIRTY YEARS. IF I WERE IN YOUR PLACE, I'D FEEL THE SAME WAY.
BUT WHOEVER'S FAULT THIS IS, A WAR WON'T HELP. WE'VE GOTTA WORK TOGETHER IF WE'RE GOING TO BEAT THE PEOPLE WHO ARE DOING THIS!
JUST GIVE ME 24 HOURS --
NO.

BLOOMINGTON GRENDELS -- THE INDIANAPOLIS KLAN, AS GUARDIAN OF THE RACE, STANDS BEFORE YOU HUMILIATED AND WITHOUT *HONOR*. WE FAILED TO PROTECT YOU, OUR GUESTS...

...AND WE'VE LET OURSELVES BE BADLY LED.

WHAT?

LET HER *SPEAK*, HACK!

HEAR-HEAR! YES!

WHAT I WANT TO SAY IS: WE CAN'T REPLACE YOUR CHAMPION. BUT WE RECOGNIZE THAT YOU'VE BEEN WRONGED, AND WE'D LIKE TO MAKE A GESTURE OF *PEACE*.

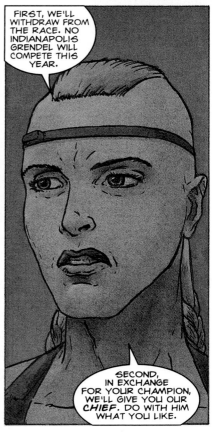

FIRST, WE'LL WITHDRAW FROM THE RACE. NO INDIANAPOLIS GRENDEL WILL COMPETE THIS YEAR.

SECOND, IN EXCHANGE FOR YOUR CHAMPION, WE'LL GIVE YOU OUR *CHIEF*. DO WITH HIM WHAT YOU LIKE.

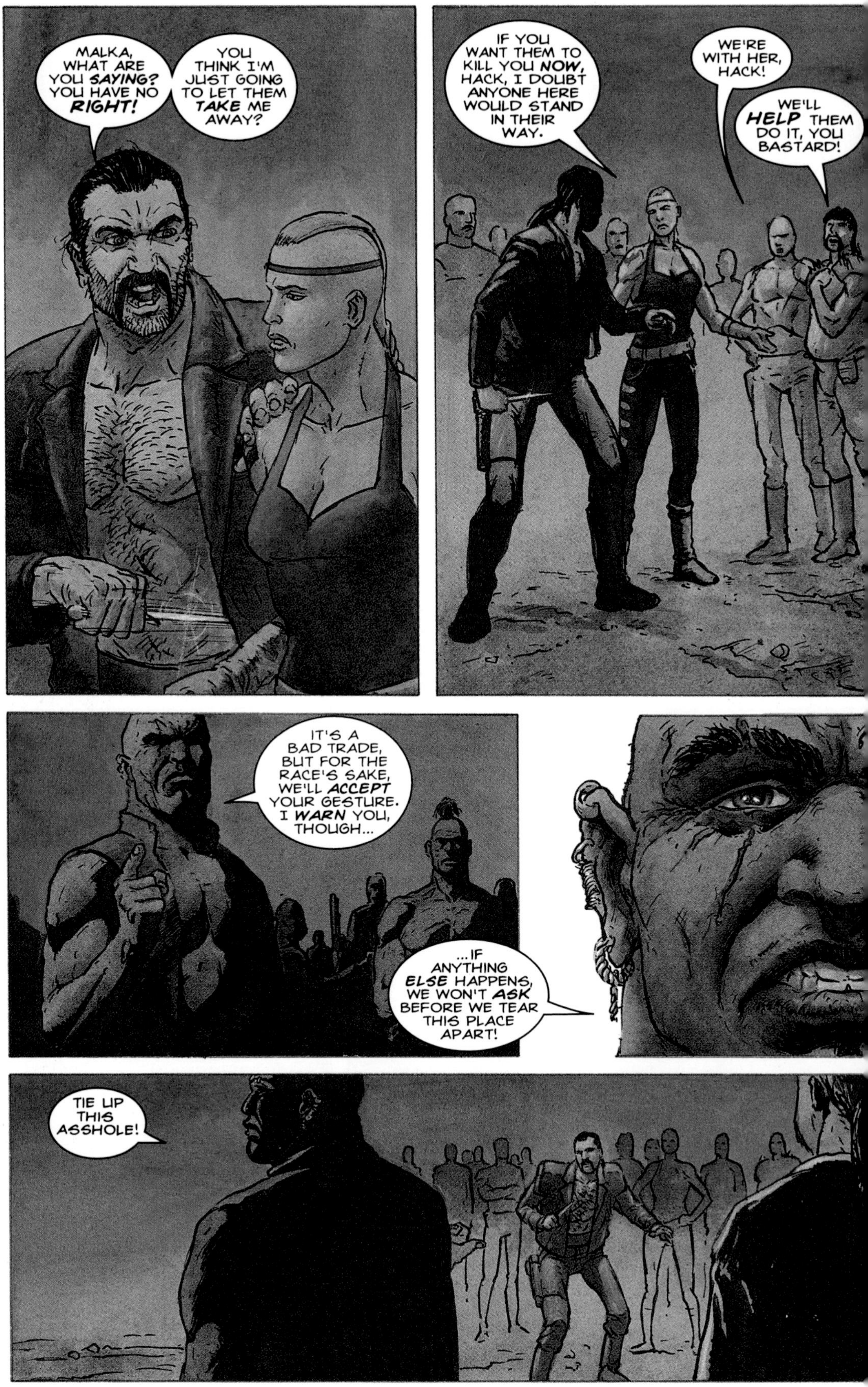
MALKA, WHAT ARE YOU SAYING? YOU HAVE NO RIGHT!
YOU THINK I'M JUST GOING TO LET THEM TAKE ME AWAY?
IF YOU WANT THEM TO KILL YOU NOW, HACK, I DOUBT ANYONE HERE WOULD STAND IN THEIR WAY.
WE'RE WITH HER, HACK!
WE'LL HELP THEM DO IT, YOU BASTARD!
IT'S A BAD TRADE, BUT FOR THE RACE'S SAKE, WE'LL ACCEPT YOUR GESTURE. I WARN YOU, THOUGH...
...IF ANYTHING ELSE HAPPENS, WE WON'T ASK BEFORE WE TEAR THIS PLACE APART!
TIE UP THIS ASSHOLE!

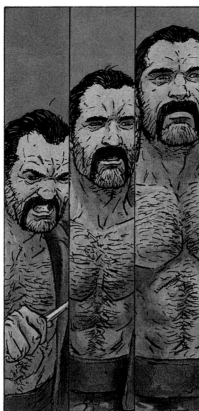

THUCK

VAROOOM

LOOK AT THAT. HE JUST LET 'EM KICK HIM AROUND!

I KNEW HE'D TURN OUT TO BE A COWARD IN THE END!

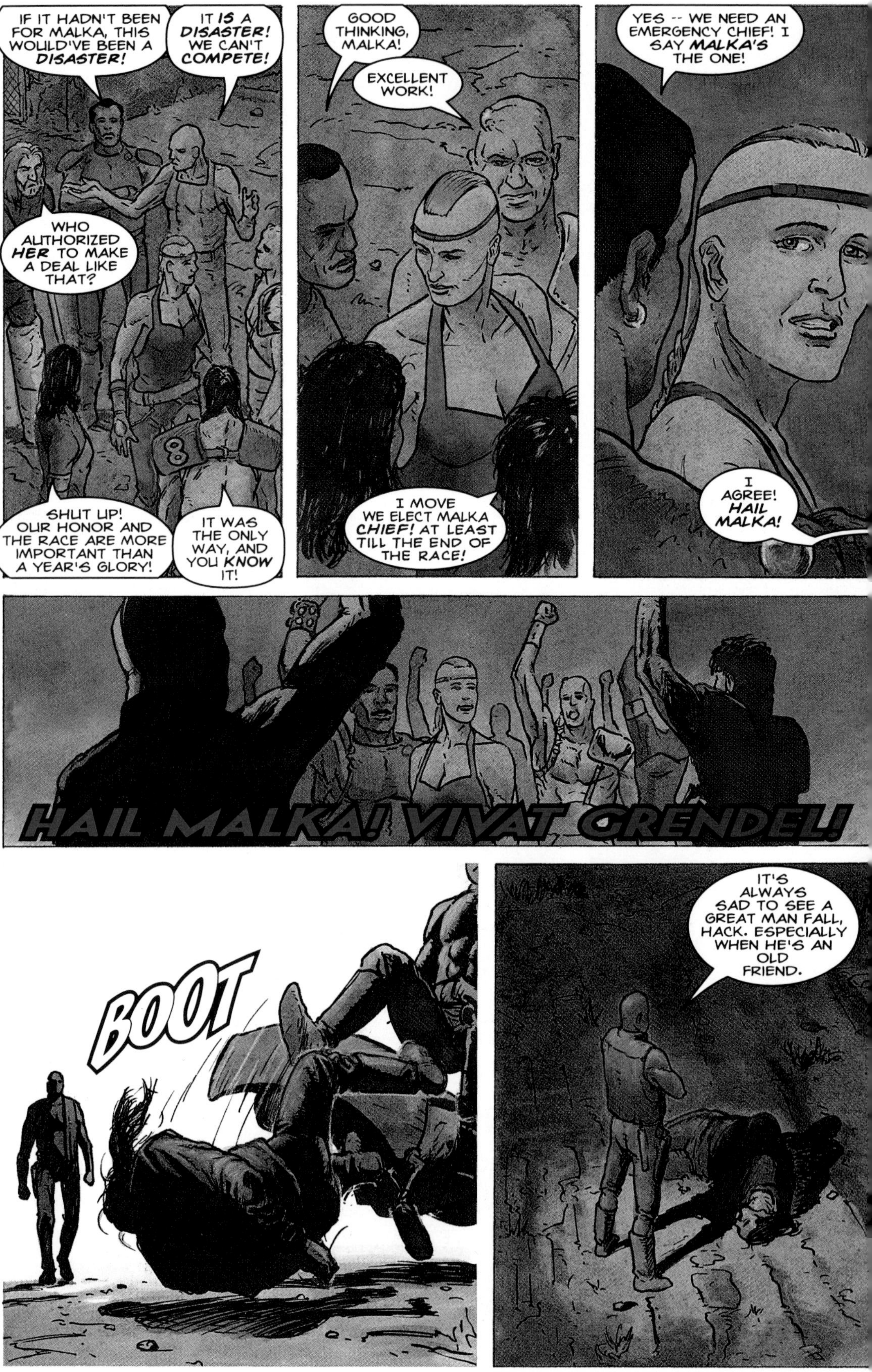

IF IT HADN'T BEEN FOR MALKA, THIS WOULD'VE BEEN A DISASTER!
IT IS A DISASTER! WE CAN'T COMPETE!
WHO AUTHORIZED HER TO MAKE A DEAL LIKE THAT?
SHUT UP! OUR HONOR AND THE RACE ARE MORE IMPORTANT THAN A YEAR'S GLORY!
IT WAS THE ONLY WAY, AND YOU KNOW IT!
GOOD THINKING, MALKA!
EXCELLENT WORK!
I MOVE WE ELECT MALKA CHIEF! AT LEAST TILL THE END OF THE RACE!
YES -- WE NEED AN EMERGENCY CHIEF! I SAY MALKA'S THE ONE!
I AGREE! HAIL MALKA!
HAIL MALKA! VIVAT GRENDEL!
BOOT
IT'S ALWAYS SAD TO SEE A GREAT MAN FALL, HACK. ESPECIALLY WHEN HE'S AN OLD FRIEND.

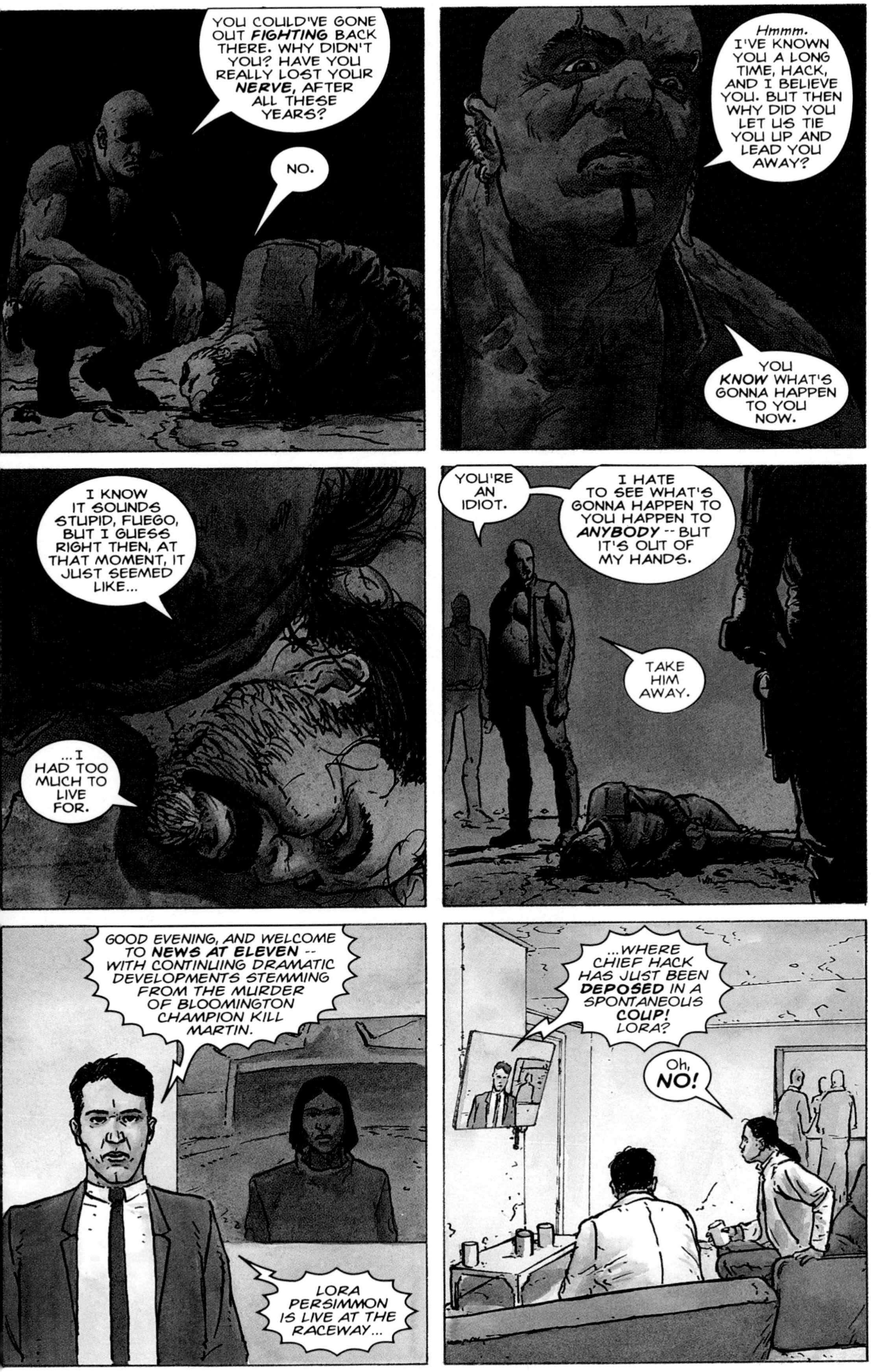
YOU COULD'VE GONE OUT FIGHTING BACK THERE. WHY DIDN'T YOU? HAVE YOU REALLY LOST YOUR NERVE, AFTER ALL THESE YEARS?
NO.
Hmmm. I'VE KNOWN YOU A LONG TIME, HACK, AND I BELIEVE YOU. BUT THEN WHY DID YOU LET US TIE YOU UP AND LEAD YOU AWAY?
YOU KNOW WHAT'S GONNA HAPPEN TO YOU NOW.
I KNOW IT SOUNDS STUPID, FUEGO, BUT I GUESS RIGHT THEN, AT THAT MOMENT, IT JUST SEEMED LIKE...
...I HAD TOO MUCH TO LIVE FOR.
YOU'RE AN IDIOT.
I HATE TO SEE WHAT'S GONNA HAPPEN TO YOU HAPPEN TO ANYBODY -- BUT IT'S OUT OF MY HANDS.
TAKE HIM AWAY.
GOOD EVENING, AND WELCOME TO NEWS AT ELEVEN -- WITH CONTINUING DRAMATIC DEVELOPMENTS STEMMING FROM THE MURDER OF BLOOMINGTON CHAMPION KILL MARTIN.
LORA PERSIMMON IS LIVE AT THE RACEWAY...
...WHERE CHIEF HACK HAS JUST BEEN DEPOSED IN A SPONTANEOUS COUP! LORA?
Oh, NO!

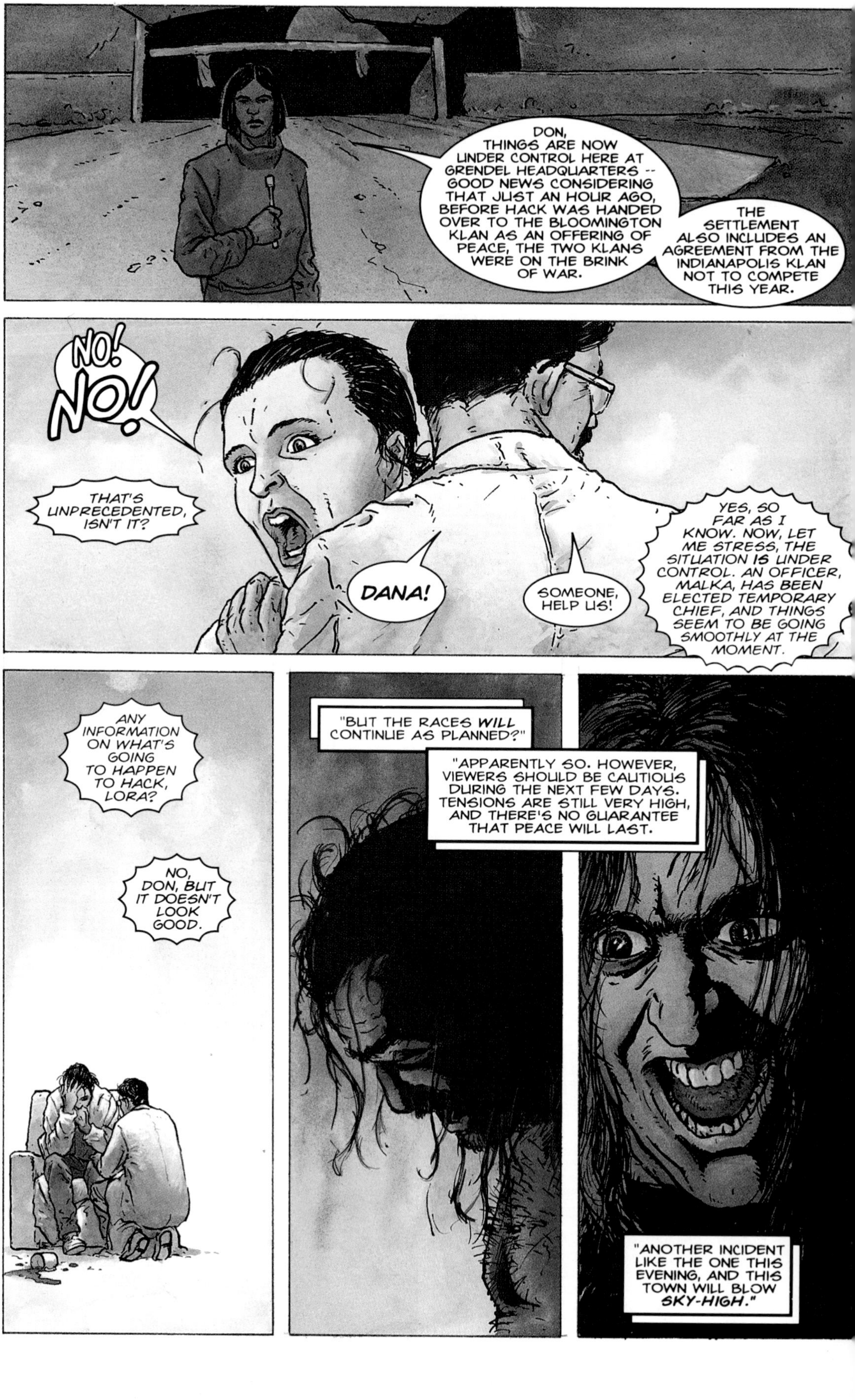
DON, THINGS ARE NOW UNDER CONTROL HERE AT GRENDEL HEADQUARTERS -- GOOD NEWS CONSIDERING THAT JUST AN HOUR AGO, BEFORE HACK WAS HANDED OVER TO THE BLOOMINGTON KLAN AS AN OFFERING OF PEACE, THE TWO KLANS WERE ON THE BRINK OF WAR.
THE SETTLEMENT ALSO INCLUDES AN AGREEMENT FROM THE INDIANAPOLIS KLAN NOT TO COMPETE THIS YEAR.
NO! NO!
THAT'S UNPRECEDENTED, ISN'T IT?
DANA!
SOMEONE, HELP US!
YES, SO FAR AS I KNOW. NOW, LET ME STRESS, THE SITUATION IS UNDER CONTROL. AN OFFICER, MALKA, HAS BEEN ELECTED TEMPORARY CHIEF, AND THINGS SEEM TO BE GOING SMOOTHLY AT THE MOMENT.
ANY INFORMATION ON WHAT'S GOING TO HAPPEN TO HACK, LORA?
NO, DON, BUT IT DOESN'T LOOK GOOD.
"BUT THE RACES WILL CONTINUE AS PLANNED?"
"APPARENTLY SO. HOWEVER, VIEWERS SHOULD BE CAUTIOUS DURING THE NEXT FEW DAYS. TENSIONS ARE STILL VERY HIGH, AND THERE'S NO GUARANTEE THAT PEACE WILL LAST.
"ANOTHER INCIDENT LIKE THE ONE THIS EVENING, AND THIS TOWN WILL BLOW SKY-HIGH."

Chapter Six

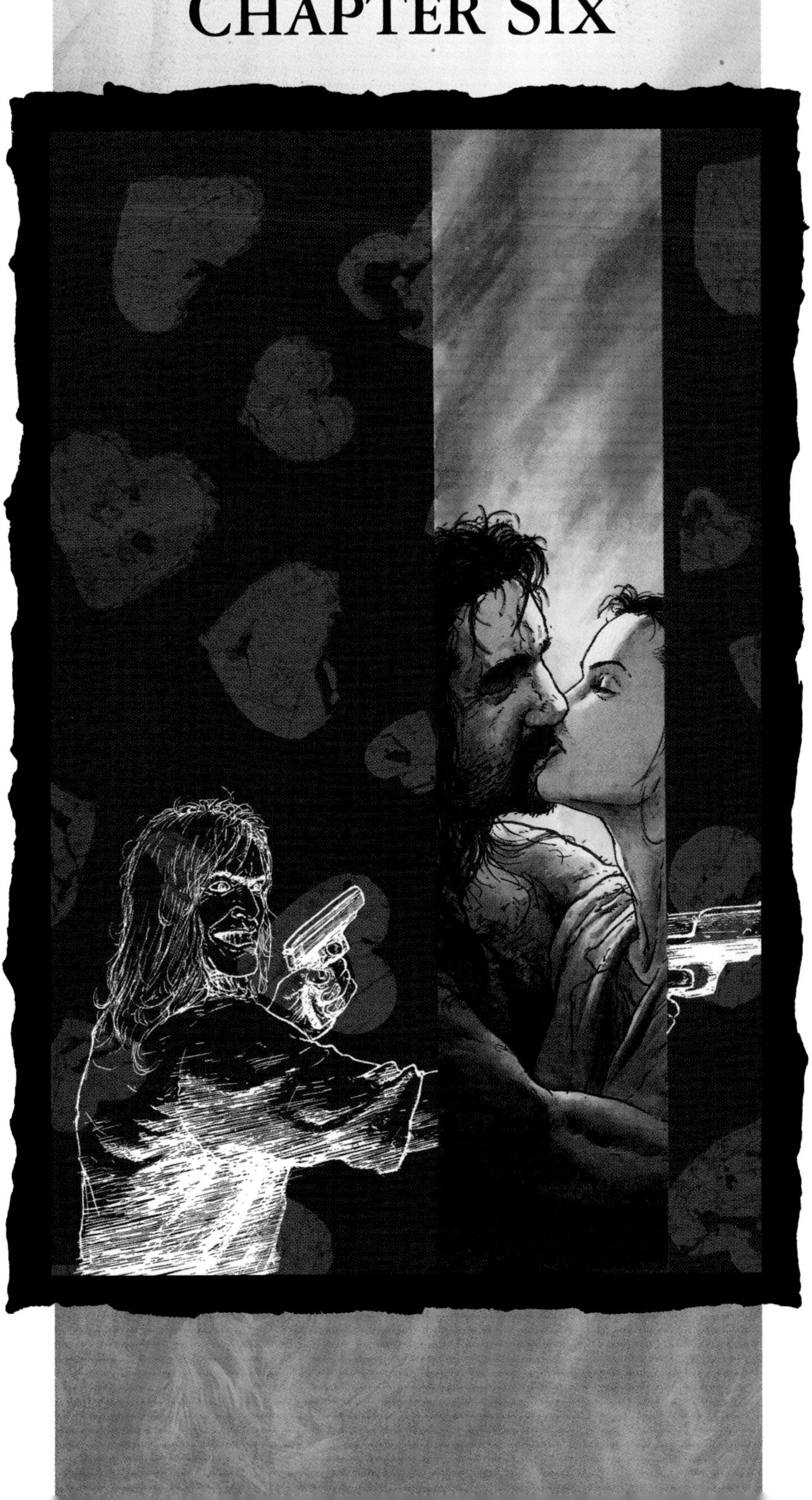

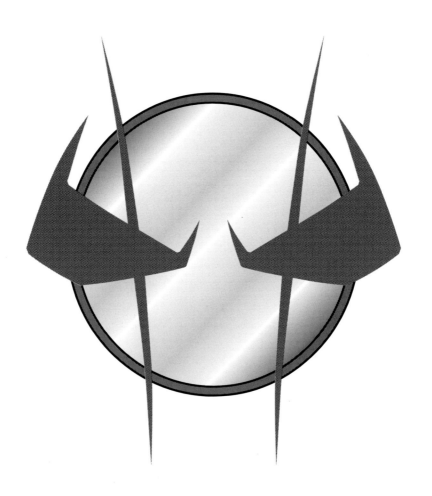

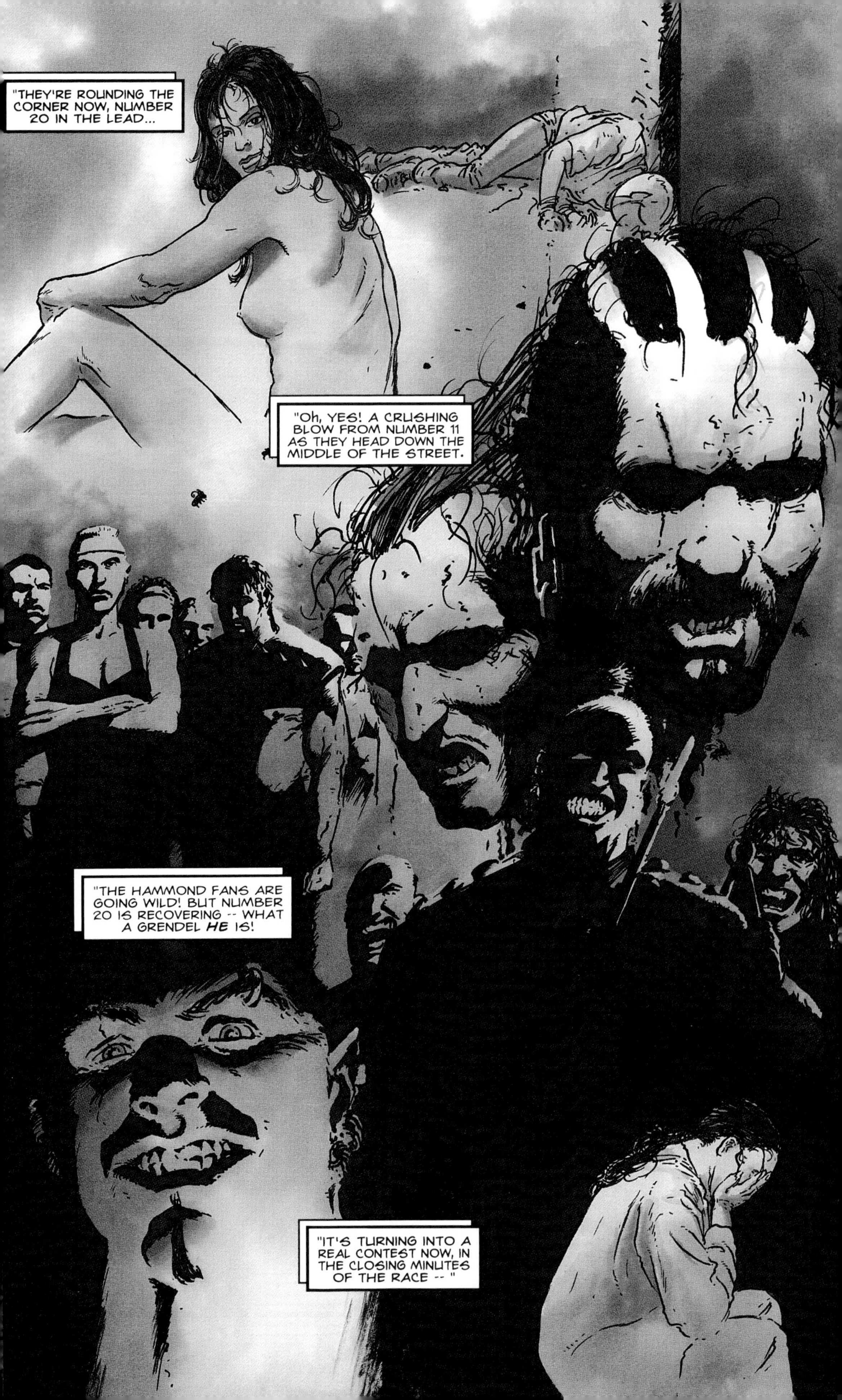
"THEY'RE ROUNDING THE CORNER NOW, NUMBER 20 IN THE LEAD...
"Oh, YES! A CRUSHING BLOW FROM NUMBER 11 AS THEY HEAD DOWN THE MIDDLE OF THE STREET.
"THE HAMMOND FANS ARE GOING WILD! BUT NUMBER 20 IS RECOVERING -- WHAT A GRENDEL HE IS!
"IT'S TURNING INTO A REAL CONTEST NOW, IN THE CLOSING MINUTES OF THE RACE -- "

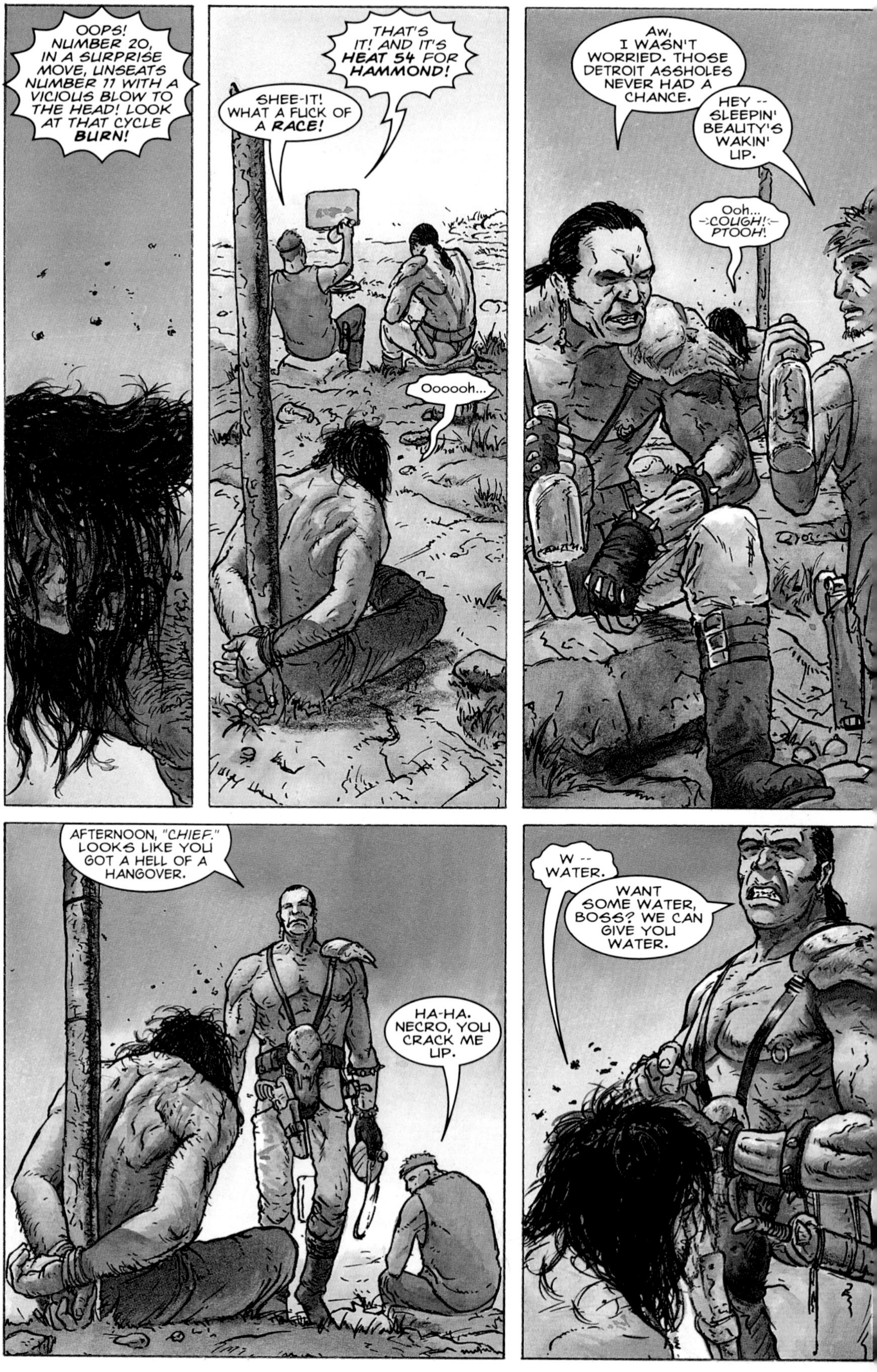
OOPS! NUMBER 20, IN A SURPRISE MOVE, UNSEATS NUMBER 11 WITH A VICIOUS BLOW TO THE HEAD! LOOK AT THAT CYCLE BURN!
THAT'S IT! AND IT'S HEAT 54 FOR HAMMOND!
SHEE-IT! WHAT A FUCK OF A RACE!
Oooooh...
Aw, I WASN'T WORRIED. THOSE DETROIT ASSHOLES NEVER HAD A CHANCE.
HEY -- SLEEPIN' BEAUTY'S WAKIN' UP.
Ooh... —COUGH!— PTOOH!
AFTERNOON, "CHIEF." LOOKS LIKE YOU GOT A HELL OF A HANGOVER.
HA-HA. NECRO, YOU CRACK ME UP.
W -- WATER.
WANT SOME WATER, BOSS? WE CAN GIVE YOU WATER.

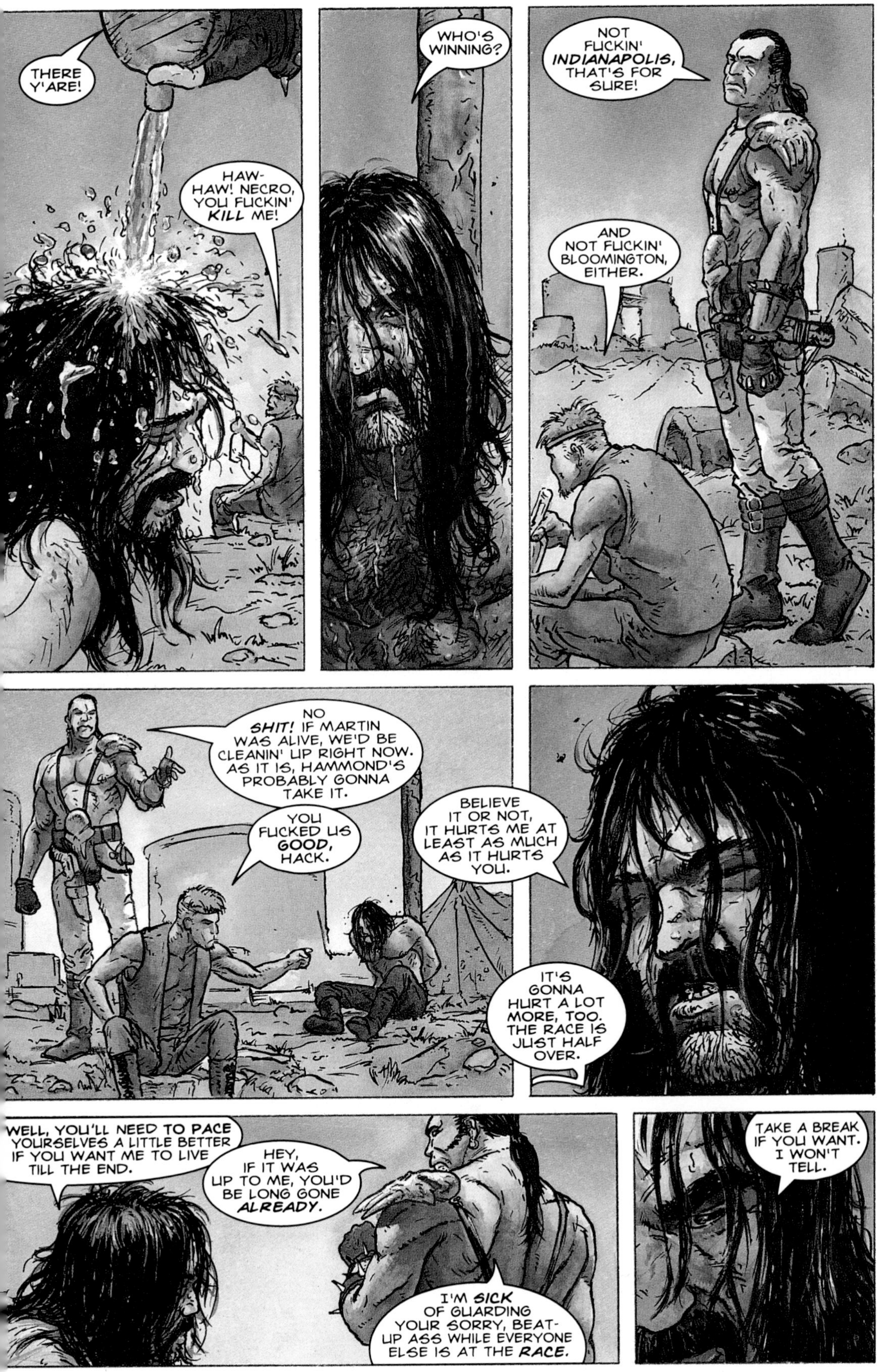
THERE Y'ARE!
HAW-HAW! NECRO, YOU FUCKIN' KILL ME!
WHO'S WINNING?
NOT FUCKIN' INDIANAPOLIS, THAT'S FOR SURE!
AND NOT FUCKIN' BLOOMINGTON, EITHER.
NO SHIT! IF MARTIN WAS ALIVE, WE'D BE CLEANIN' UP RIGHT NOW. AS IT IS, HAMMOND'S PROBABLY GONNA TAKE IT.
YOU FUCKED US GOOD, HACK.
BELIEVE IT OR NOT, IT HURTS ME AT LEAST AS MUCH AS IT HURTS YOU.
IT'S GONNA HURT A LOT MORE, TOO. THE RACE IS JUST HALF OVER.
WELL, YOU'LL NEED TO PACE YOURSELVES A LITTLE BETTER IF YOU WANT ME TO LIVE TILL THE END.
HEY, IF IT WAS UP TO ME, YOU'D BE LONG GONE ALREADY.
I'M SICK OF GUARDING YOUR SORRY, BEAT-UP ASS WHILE EVERYONE ELSE IS AT THE RACE.
TAKE A BREAK IF YOU WANT. I WON'T TELL.

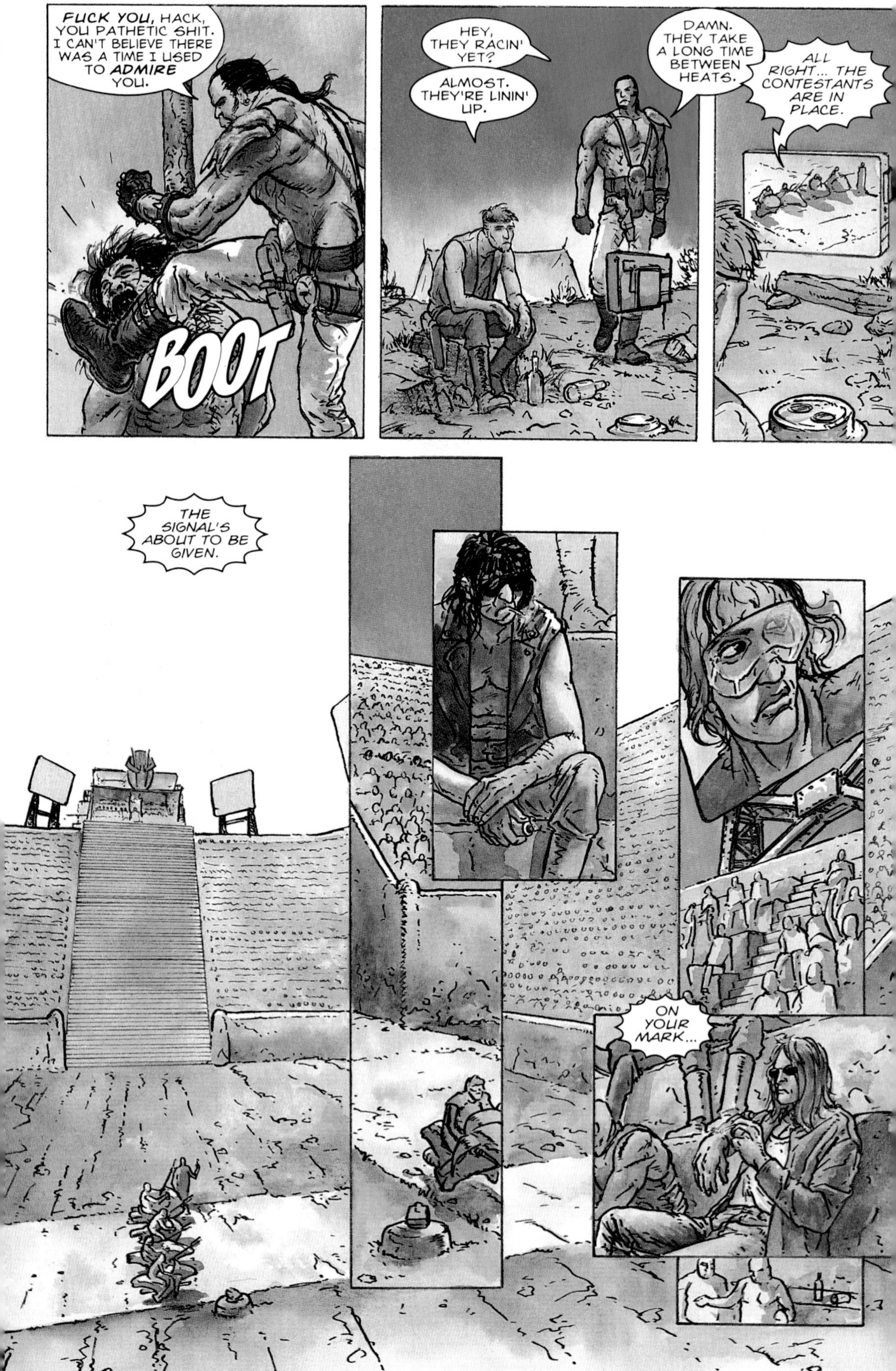

FUCK YOU, HACK, YOU PATHETIC SHIT. I CAN'T BELIEVE THERE WAS A TIME I USED TO ADMIRE YOU.
BOOT
HEY, THEY RACIN' YET?
ALMOST. THEY'RE LININ' UP.
DAMN. THEY TAKE A LONG TIME BETWEEN HEATS.
ALL RIGHT... THE CONTESTANTS ARE IN PLACE.
THE SIGNAL'S ABOUT TO BE GIVEN.
ON YOUR MARK...

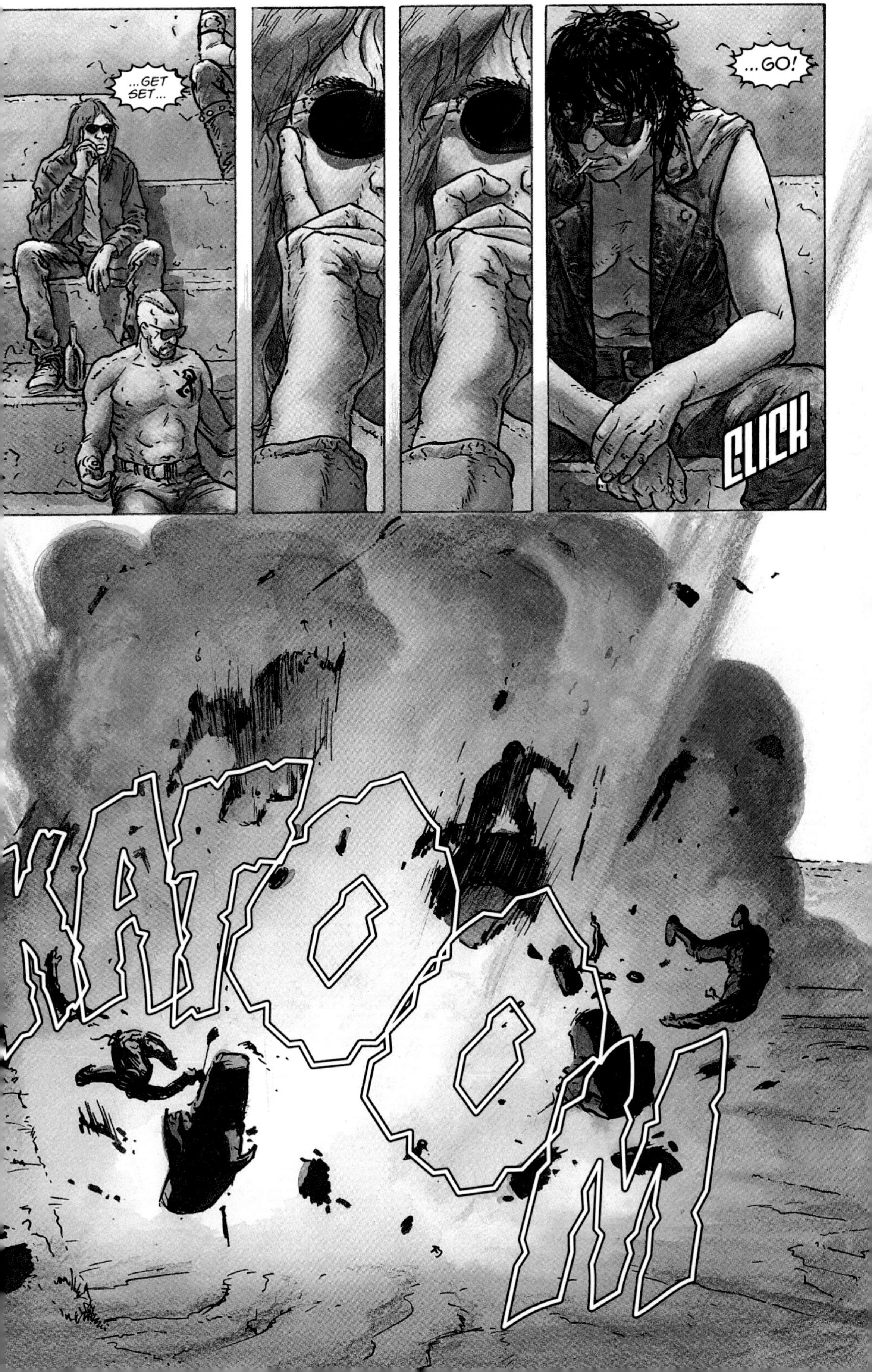
...GET SET...
...GO!
CLICK
KATOOM

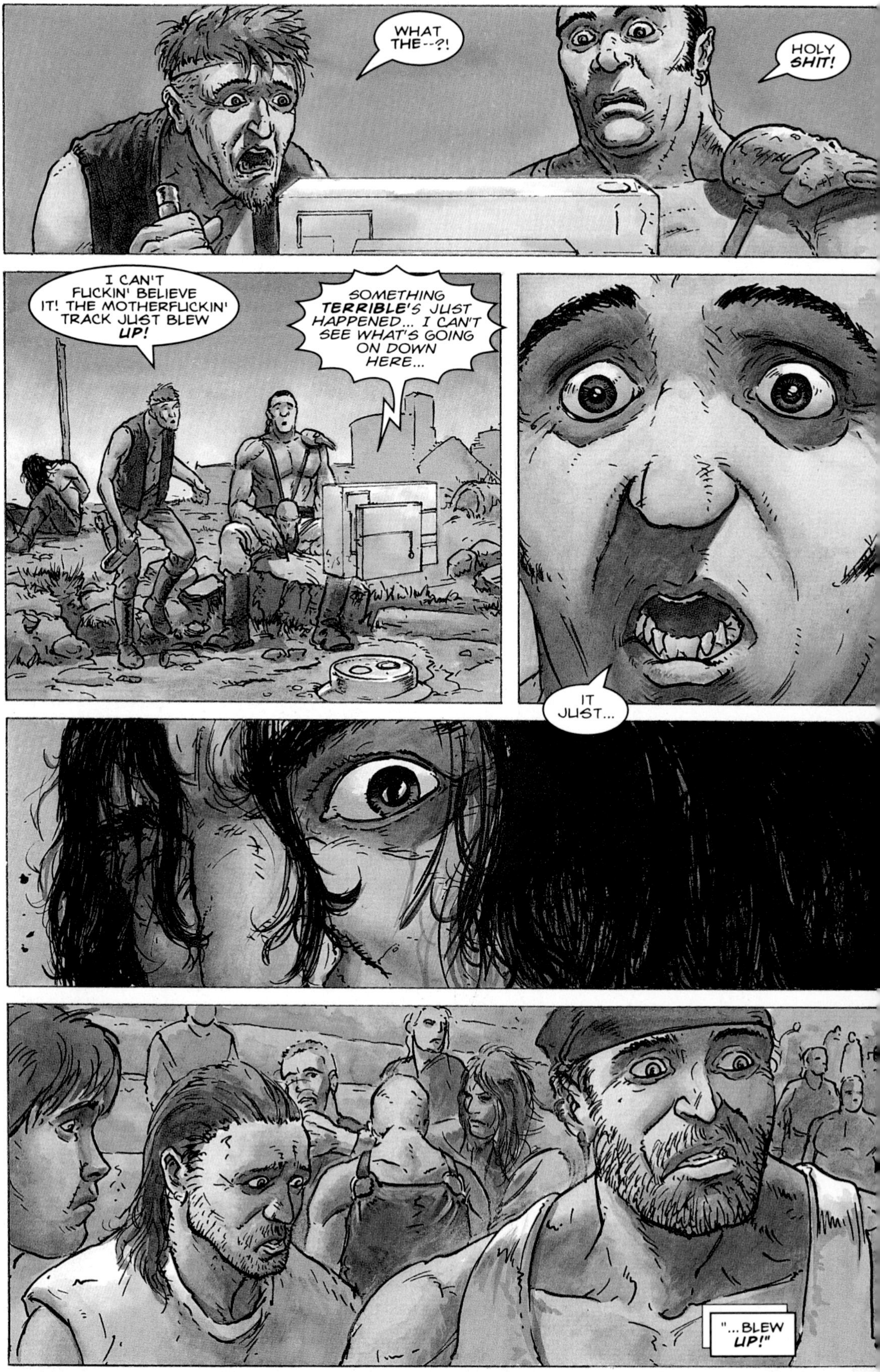
WHAT THE--?!
HOLY SHIT!
I CAN'T FUCKIN' BELIEVE IT! THE MOTHERFUCKIN' TRACK JUST BLEW UP!
SOMETHING TERRIBLE'S JUST HAPPENED... I CAN'T SEE WHAT'S GOING ON DOWN HERE...
IT JUST...
"...BLEW UP!"

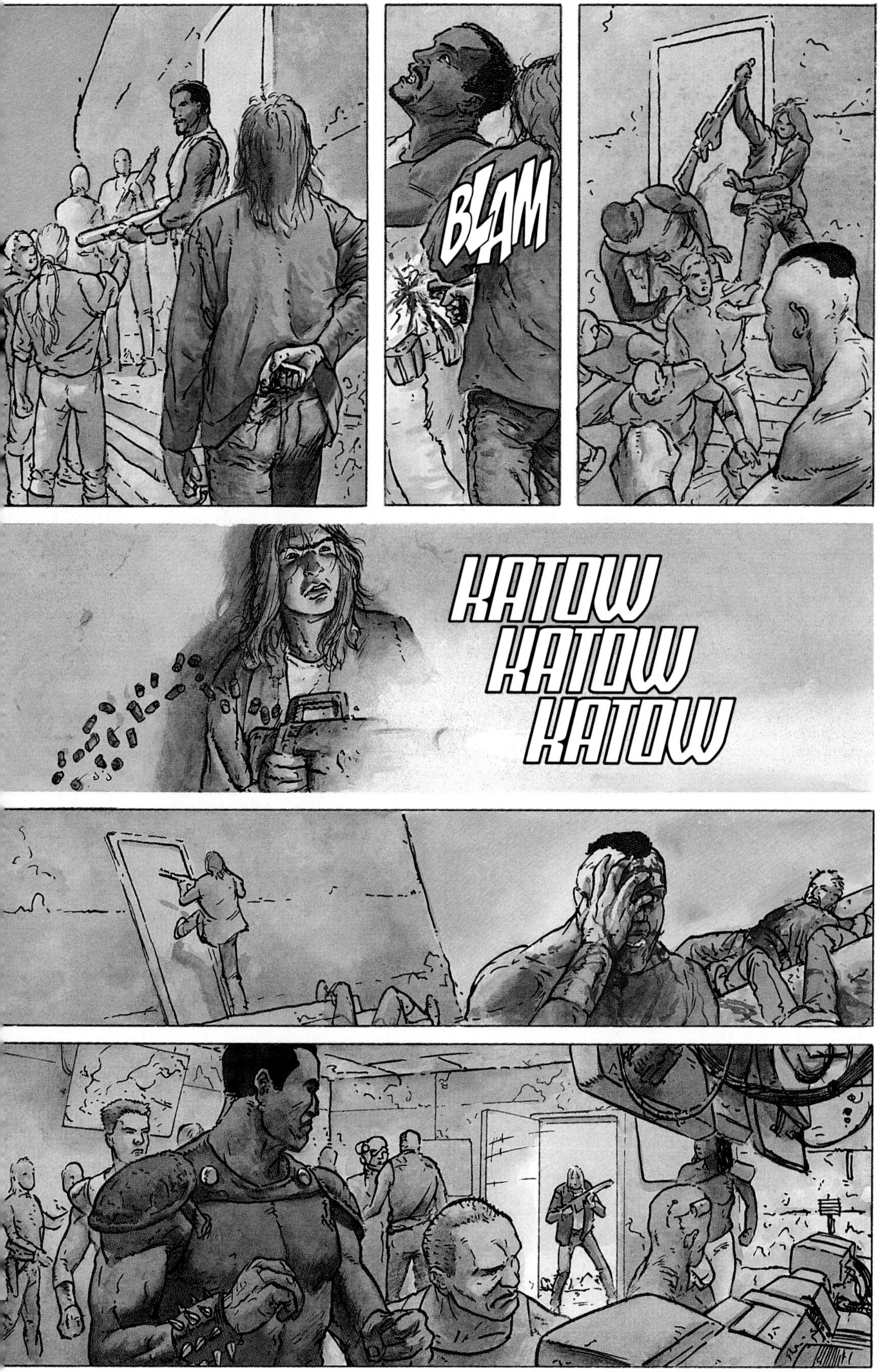
BLAM
KATOW
KATOW
KATOW

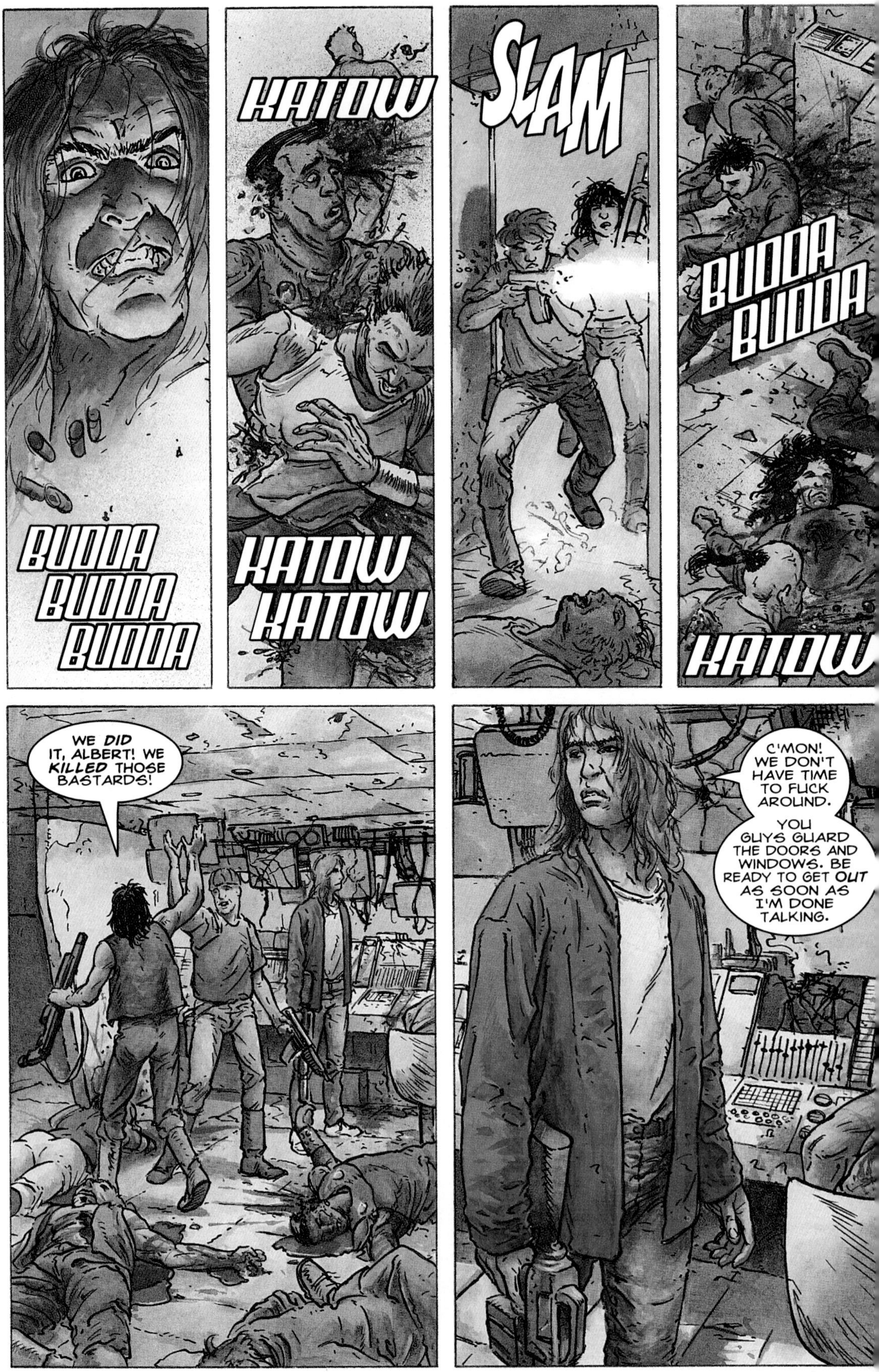
BUDDA
BUDDA
BUDDA
KATOW
KATOW
KATOW
SLAM
BUDDA
BUDDA
KATOW
WE DID IT, ALBERT! WE KILLED THOSE BASTARDS!
C'MON! WE DON'T HAVE TIME TO FUCK AROUND.
YOU GUYS GUARD THE DOORS AND WINDOWS. BE READY TO GET OUT AS SOON AS I'M DONE TALKING.

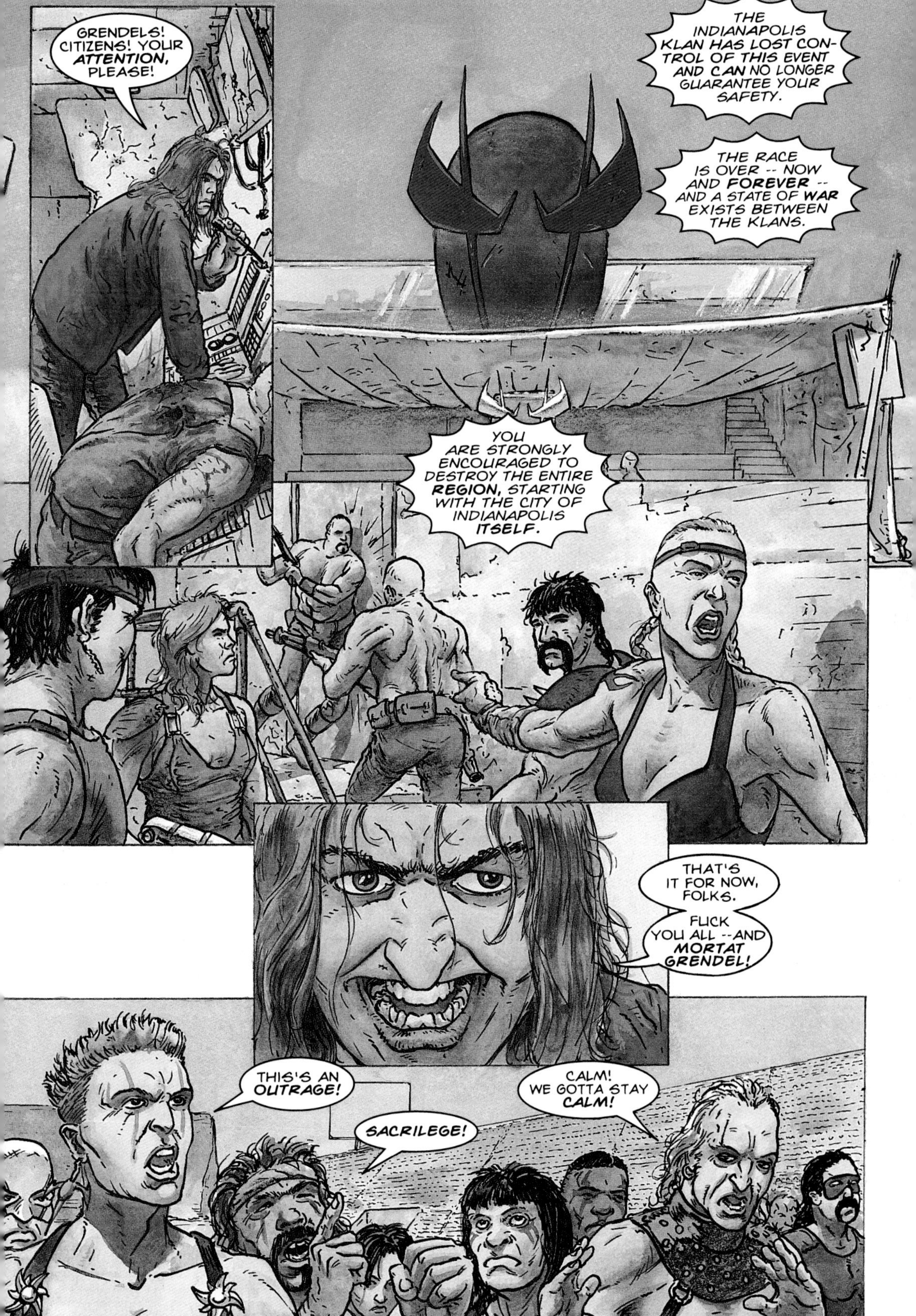
GRENDELS! CITIZENS! YOUR ATTENTION, PLEASE!
THE INDIANAPOLIS KLAN HAS LOST CONTROL OF THIS EVENT AND CAN NO LONGER GUARANTEE YOUR SAFETY.
THE RACE IS OVER -- NOW AND FOREVER -- AND A STATE OF WAR EXISTS BETWEEN THE KLANS.
YOU ARE STRONGLY ENCOURAGED TO DESTROY THE ENTIRE REGION, STARTING WITH THE CITY OF INDIANAPOLIS ITSELF.
THAT'S IT FOR NOW, FOLKS.
FUCK YOU ALL --AND MORTAT GRENDEL!
THIS'S AN OUTRAGE!
SACRILEGE!
CALM! WE GOTTA STAY CALM!

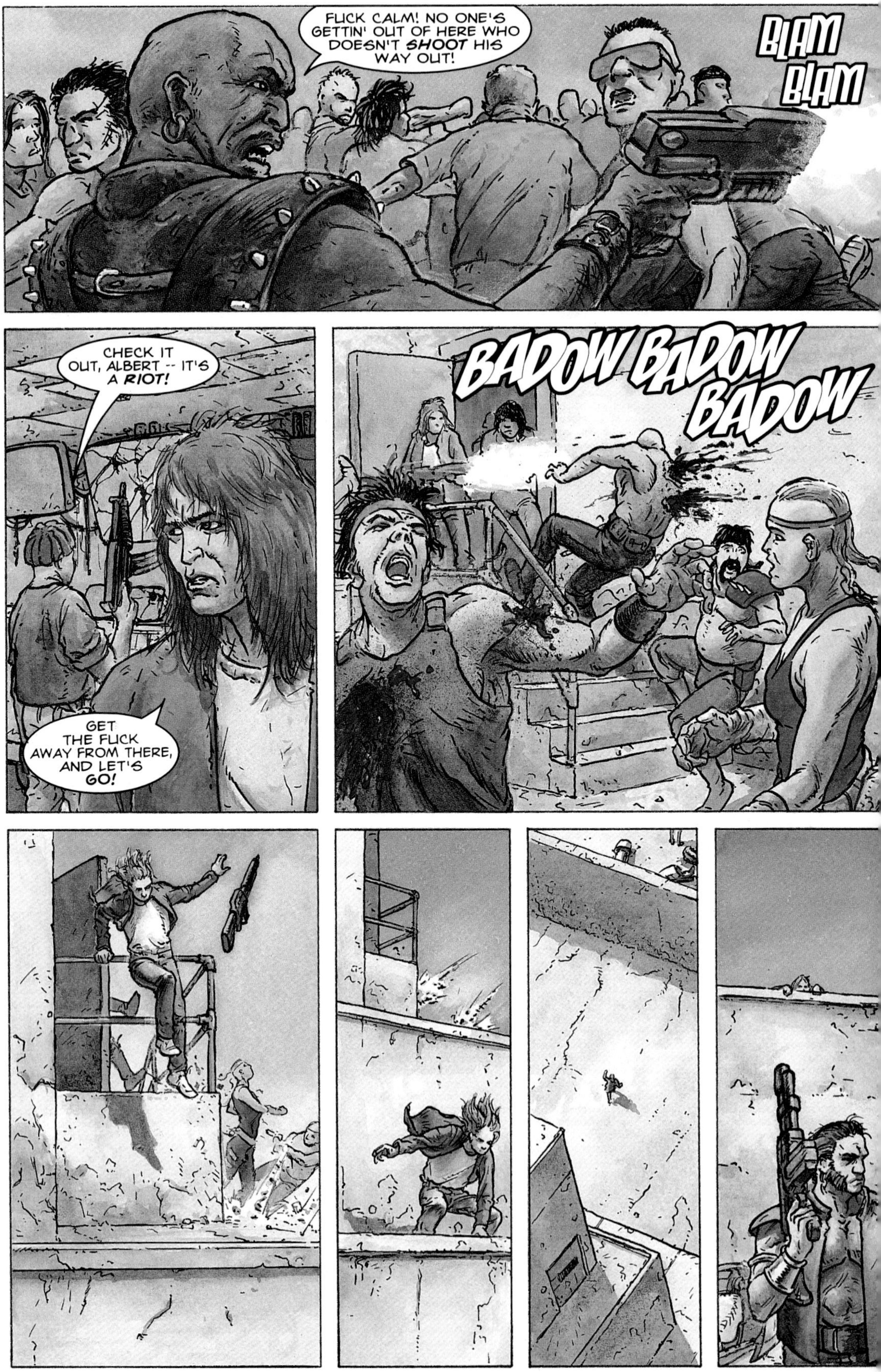

FUCK CALM! NO ONE'S GETTIN' OUT OF HERE WHO DOESN'T SHOOT HIS WAY OUT!
BLAM BLAM
CHECK IT OUT, ALBERT -- IT'S A RIOT!
GET THE FUCK AWAY FROM THERE, AND LET'S GO!
BADOW BADOW BADOW

BANG

HOLY SHIT! WE LOST THE PICTURE!

SOMETHING *BAD'S* HAPPENING! WE GOTTA GET OVER THERE.

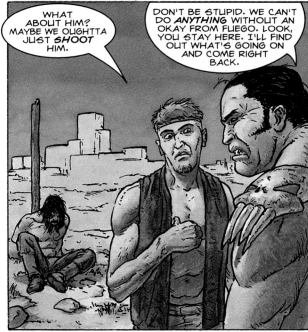

WHAT ABOUT HIM? MAYBE WE OUGHTTA JUST *SHOOT* HIM.

DON'T BE STUPID. WE CAN'T DO *ANYTHING* WITHOUT AN OKAY FROM FUEGO. LOOK, YOU STAY HERE. I'LL FIND OUT WHAT'S GOING ON AND COME RIGHT BACK.

FLICK...

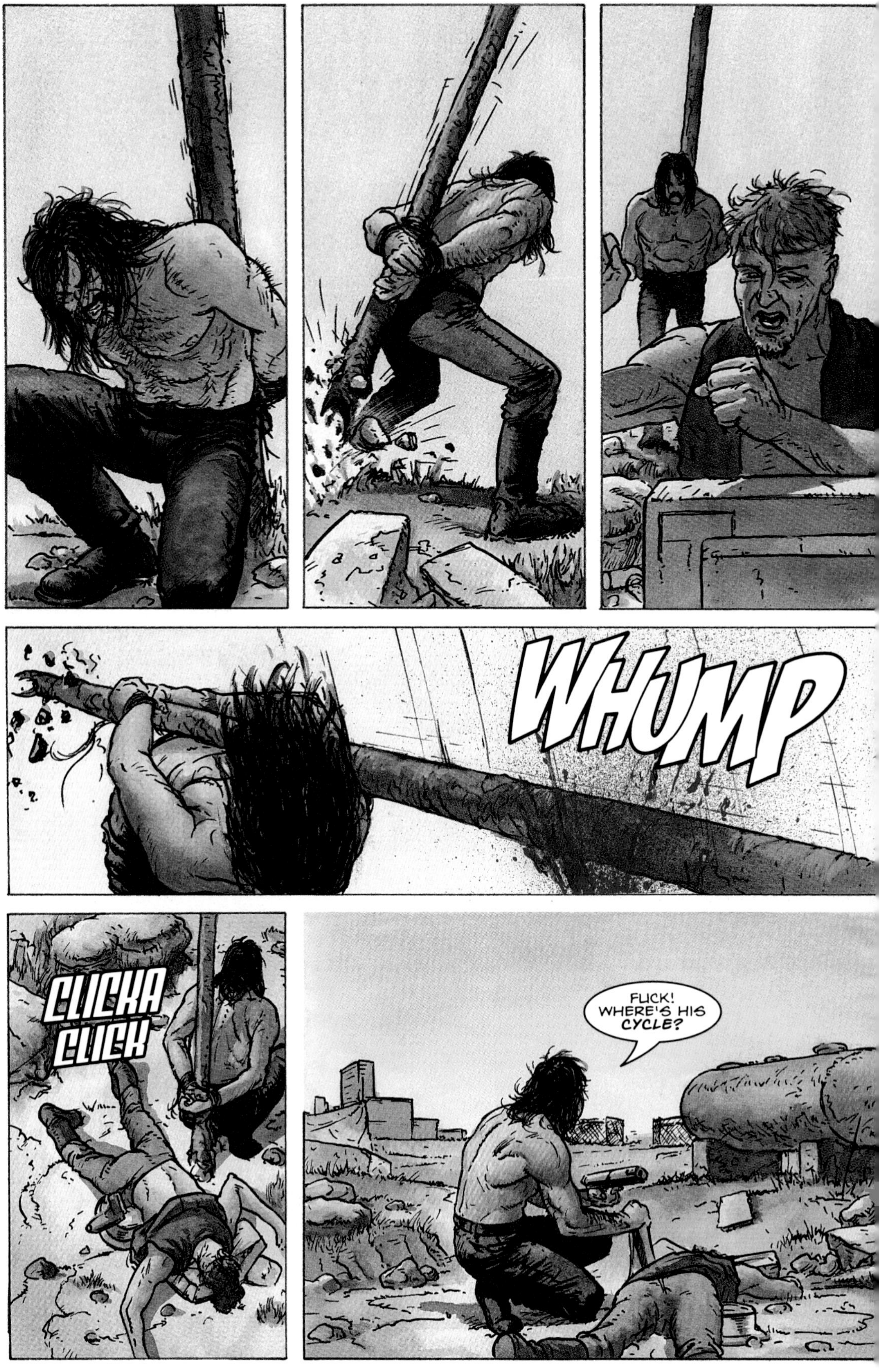
WHUMP
CLICKA CLICK
FUCK! WHERE'S HIS CYCLE?

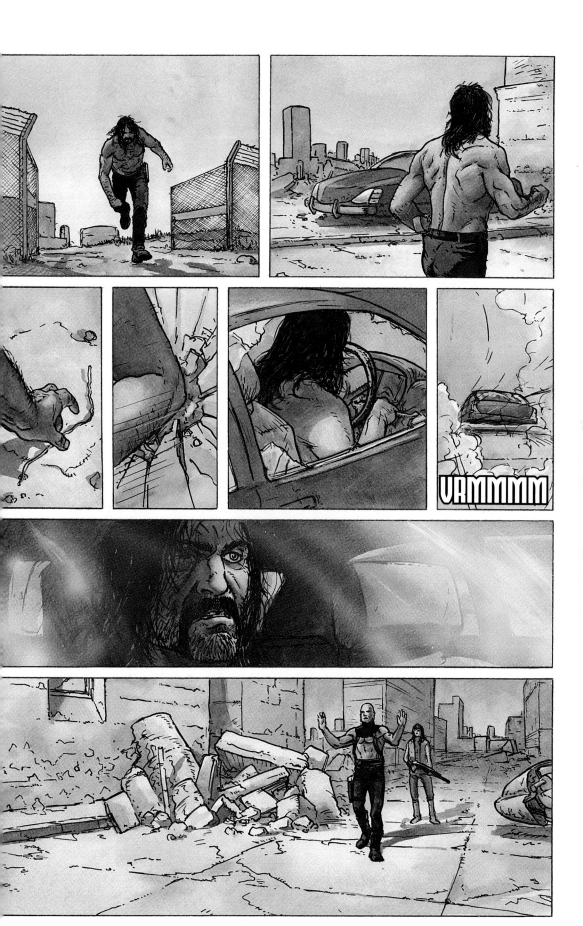

VRMMMM

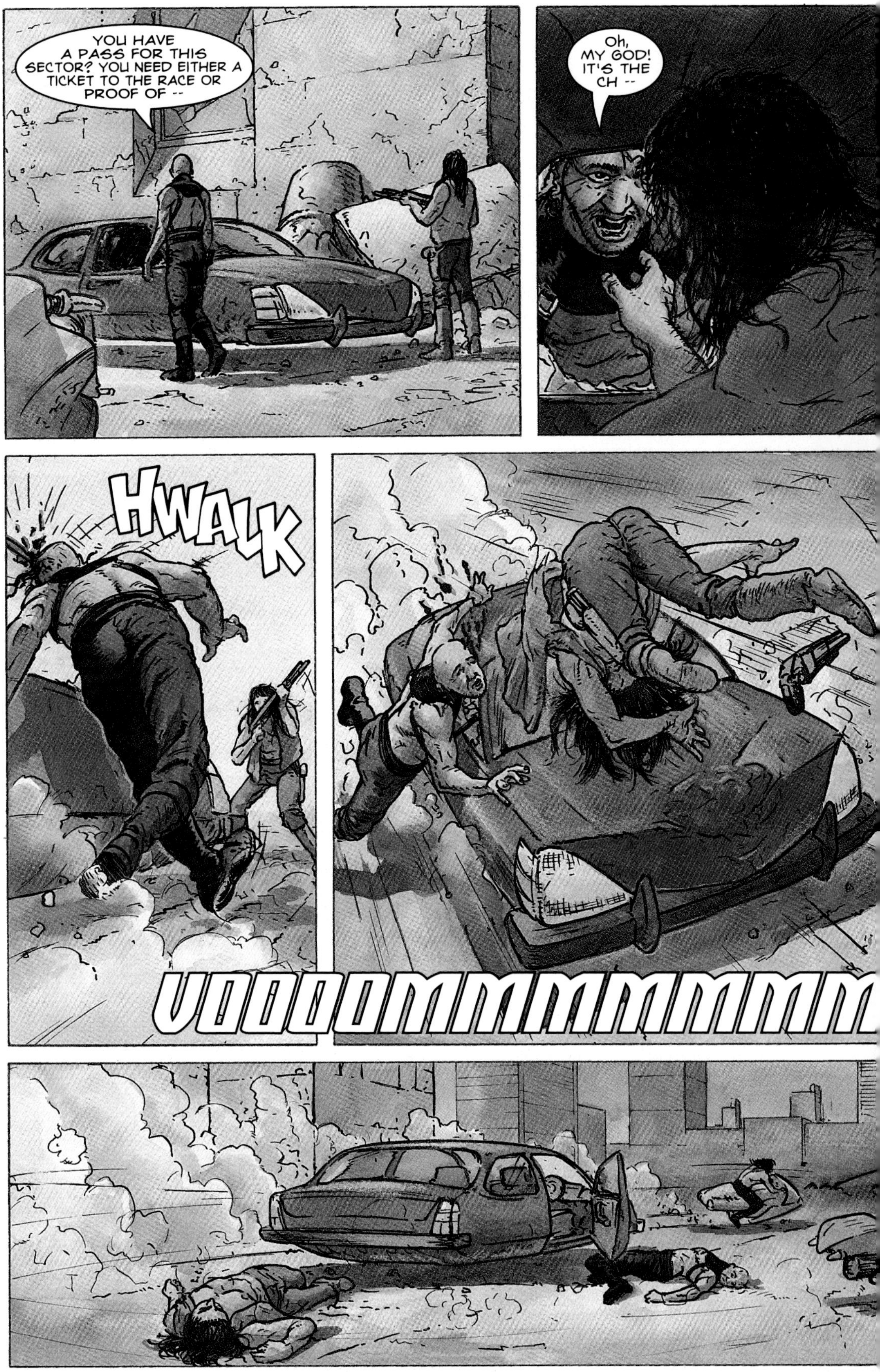
YOU HAVE A PASS FOR THIS SECTOR? YOU NEED EITHER A TICKET TO THE RACE OR PROOF OF --
Oh, MY GOD! IT'S THE CH --
HWALK
VOOOOMMMMMMMMMM

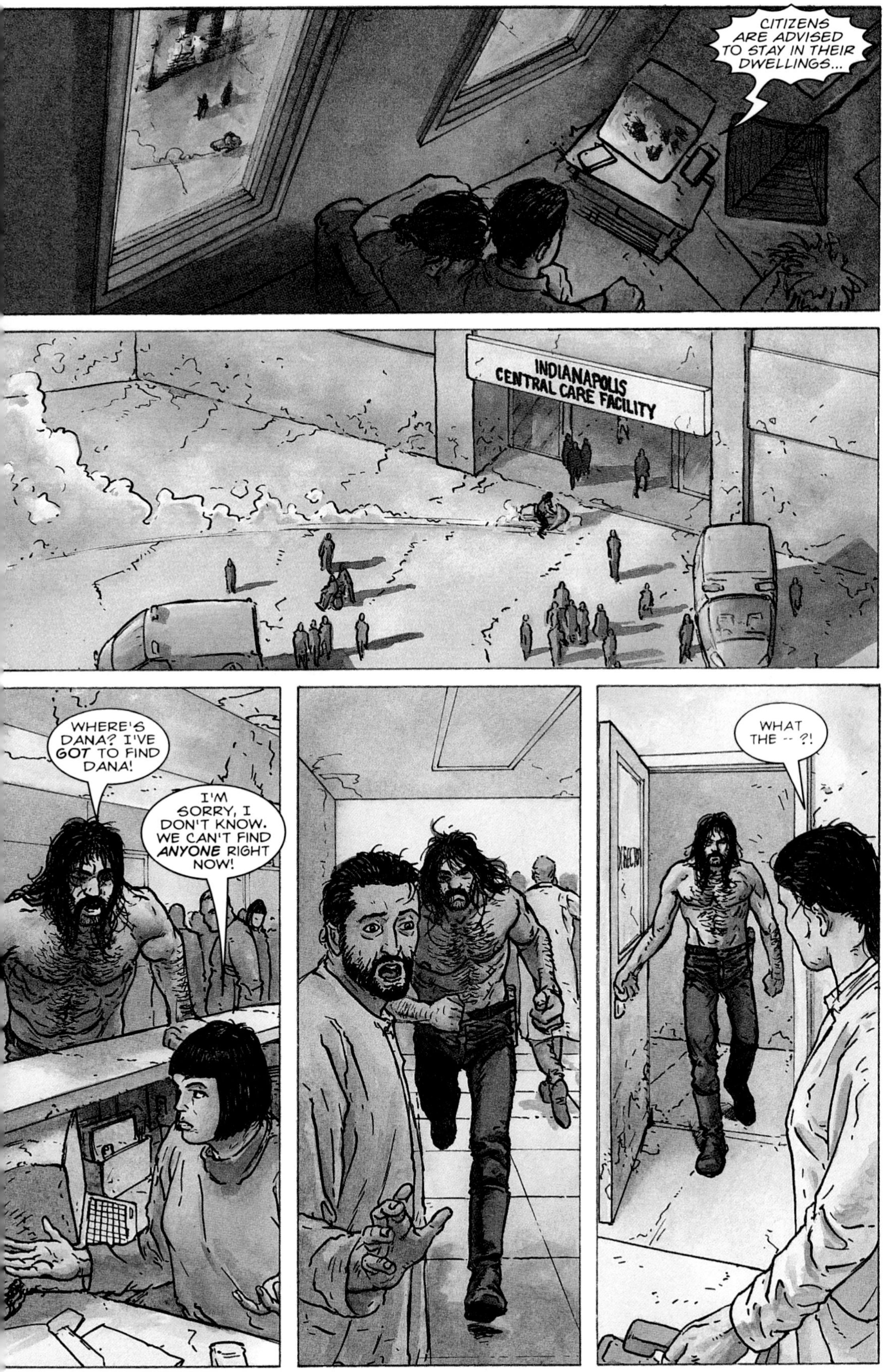
CITIZENS ARE ADVISED TO STAY IN THEIR DWELLINGS...
INDIANAPOLIS CENTRAL CARE FACILITY
WHERE'S DANA? I'VE **GOT** TO FIND DANA!
I'M SORRY, I DON'T KNOW. WE CAN'T FIND ***ANYONE*** RIGHT NOW!
WHAT THE -- ?!

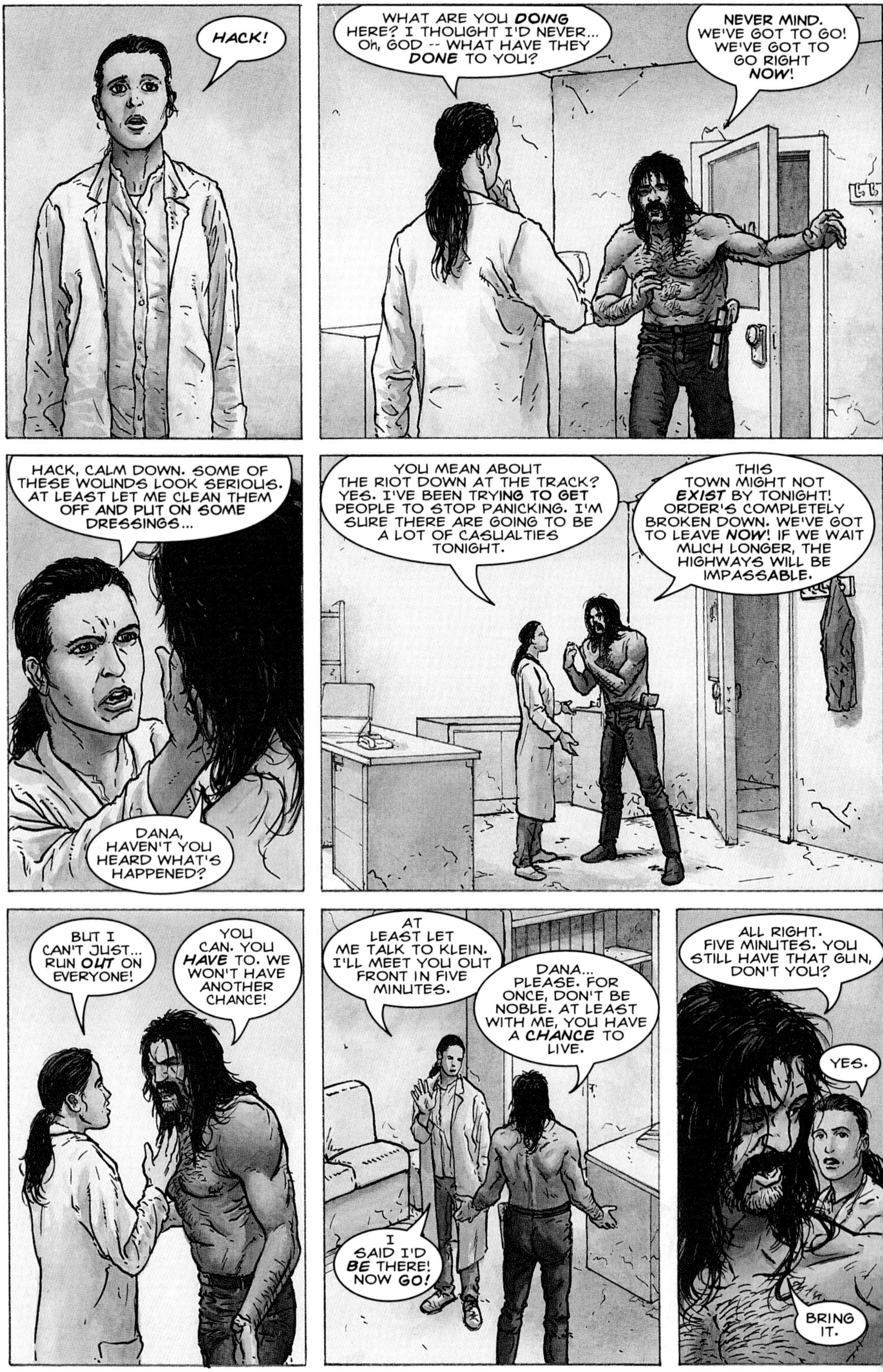

HACK!
WHAT ARE YOU DOING HERE? I THOUGHT I'D NEVER... Oh, GOD -- WHAT HAVE THEY DONE TO YOU?
NEVER MIND. WE'VE GOT TO GO! WE'VE GOT TO GO RIGHT NOW!
HACK, CALM DOWN. SOME OF THESE WOUNDS LOOK SERIOUS. AT LEAST LET ME CLEAN THEM OFF AND PUT ON SOME DRESSINGS...
DANA, HAVEN'T YOU HEARD WHAT'S HAPPENED?
YOU MEAN ABOUT THE RIOT DOWN AT THE TRACK? YES. I'VE BEEN TRYING TO GET PEOPLE TO STOP PANICKING. I'M SURE THERE ARE GOING TO BE A LOT OF CASUALTIES TONIGHT.
THIS TOWN MIGHT NOT EXIST BY TONIGHT! ORDER'S COMPLETELY BROKEN DOWN. WE'VE GOT TO LEAVE NOW! IF WE WAIT MUCH LONGER, THE HIGHWAYS WILL BE IMPASSABLE.
BUT I CAN'T JUST... RUN OUT ON EVERYONE!
YOU CAN. YOU HAVE TO. WE WON'T HAVE ANOTHER CHANCE!
AT LEAST LET ME TALK TO KLEIN. I'LL MEET YOU OUT FRONT IN FIVE MINUTES.
DANA... PLEASE. FOR ONCE, DON'T BE NOBLE. AT LEAST WITH ME, YOU HAVE A CHANCE TO LIVE.
I SAID I'D BE THERE! NOW GO!
ALL RIGHT. FIVE MINUTES. YOU STILL HAVE THAT GUN, DON'T YOU?
YES.
BRING IT.

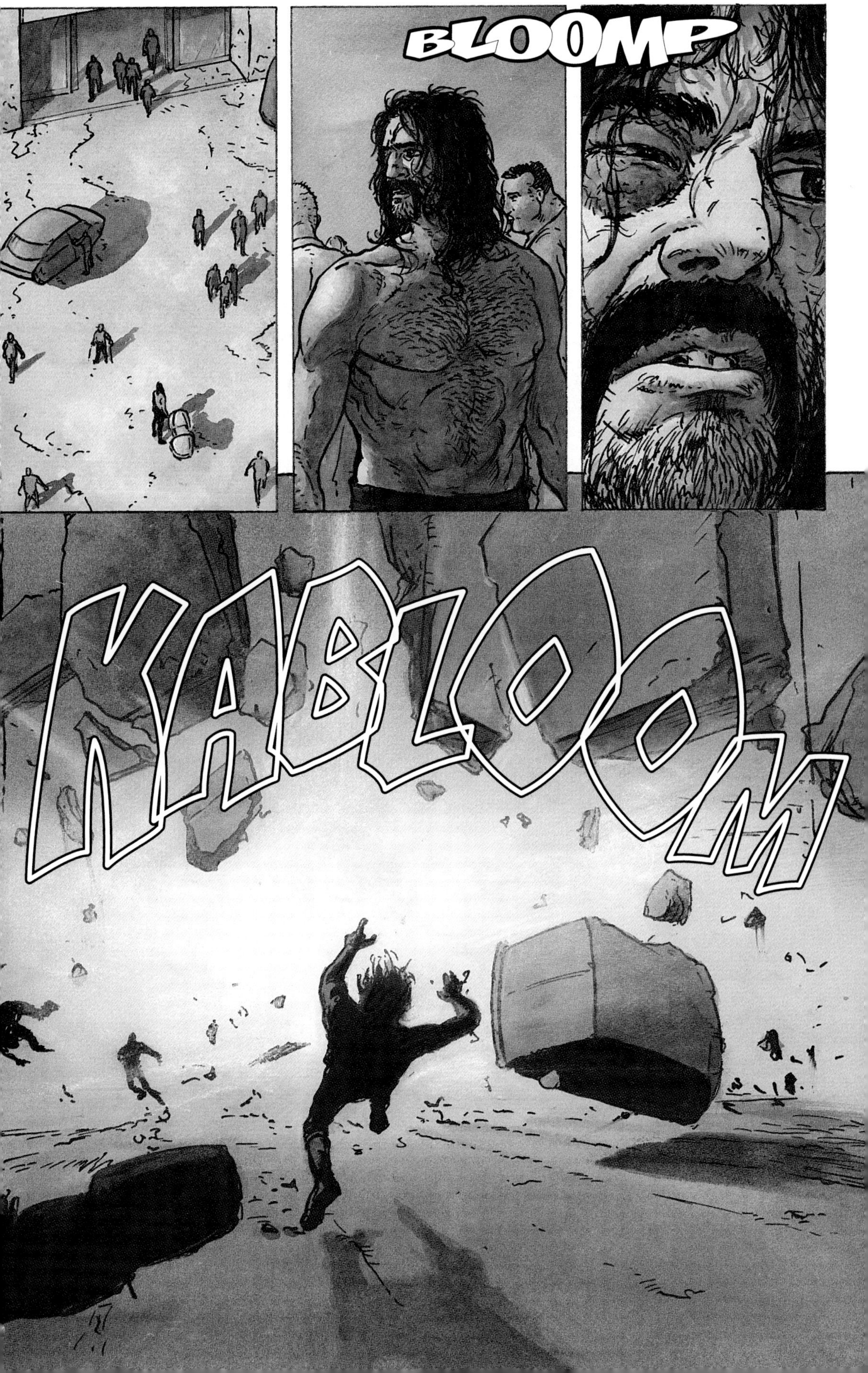
BLOOMP
KABLOOM

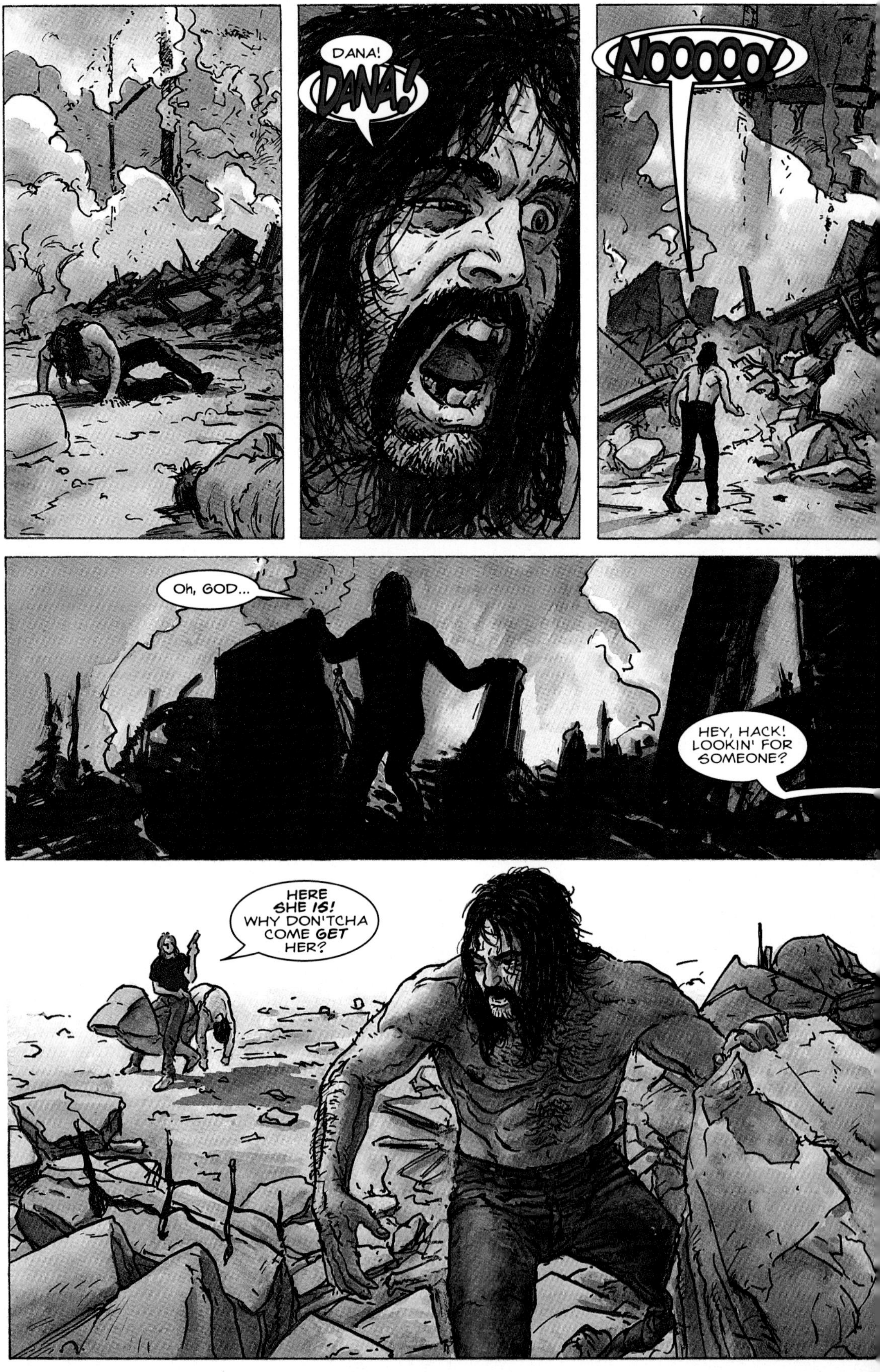
DANA!
DANA!
NOOOOO!
Oh, GOD...
HEY, HACK! LOOKIN' FOR SOMEONE?
HERE SHE IS! WHY DON'TCHA COME GET HER?

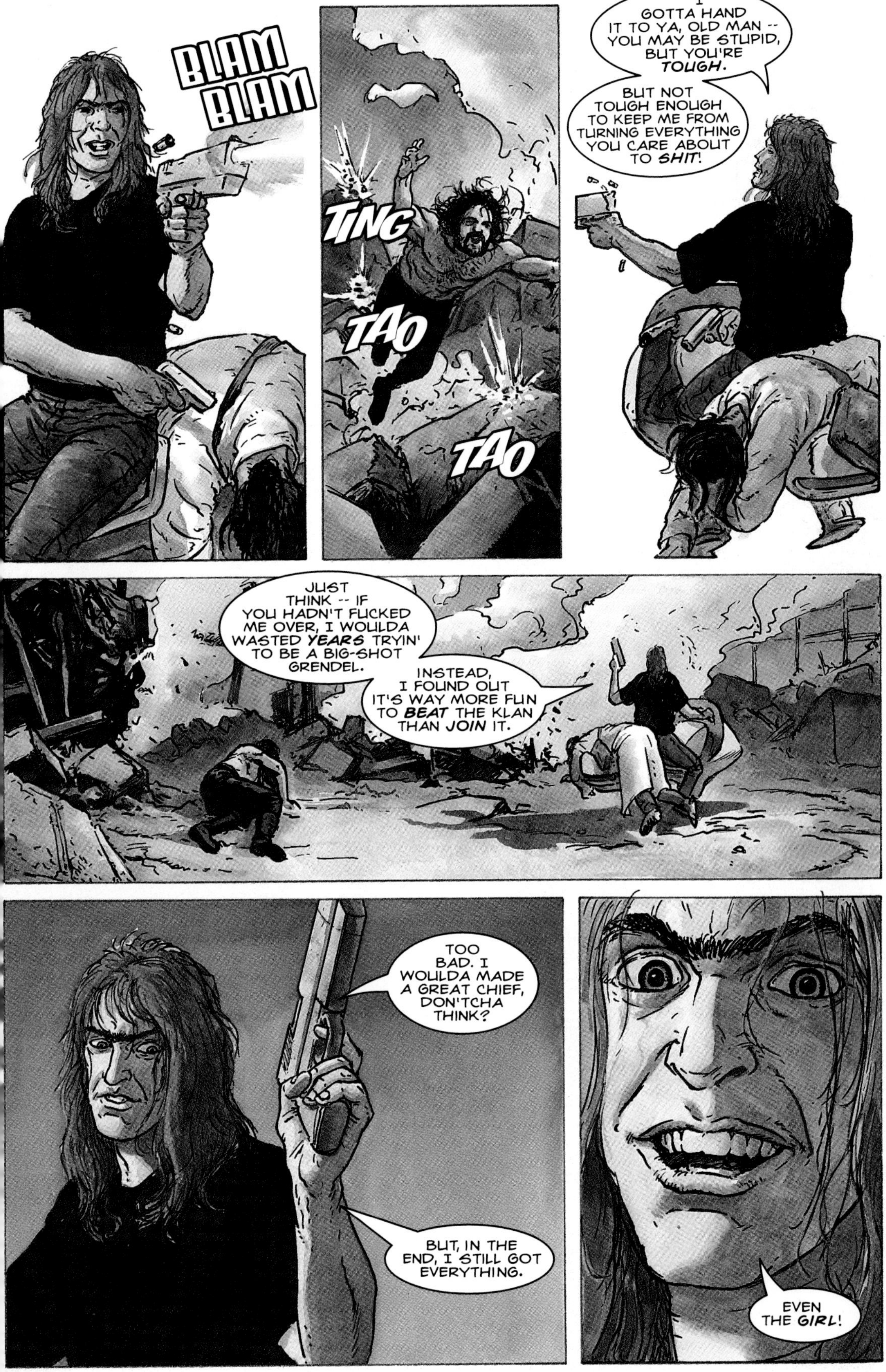
BLAM BLAM
TING
TAO
TAO
I GOTTA HAND IT TO YA, OLD MAN -- YOU MAY BE STUPID, BUT YOU'RE TOUGH.
BUT NOT TOUGH ENOUGH TO KEEP ME FROM TURNING EVERYTHING YOU CARE ABOUT TO SHIT!
JUST THINK -- IF YOU HADN'T FUCKED ME OVER, I WOULDA WASTED YEARS TRYIN' TO BE A BIG-SHOT GRENDEL.
INSTEAD, I FOUND OUT IT'S WAY MORE FUN TO BEAT THE KLAN THAN JOIN IT.
TOO BAD. I WOULDA MADE A GREAT CHIEF, DON'TCHA THINK?
BUT, IN THE END, I STILL GOT EVERYTHING.
EVEN THE GIRL!

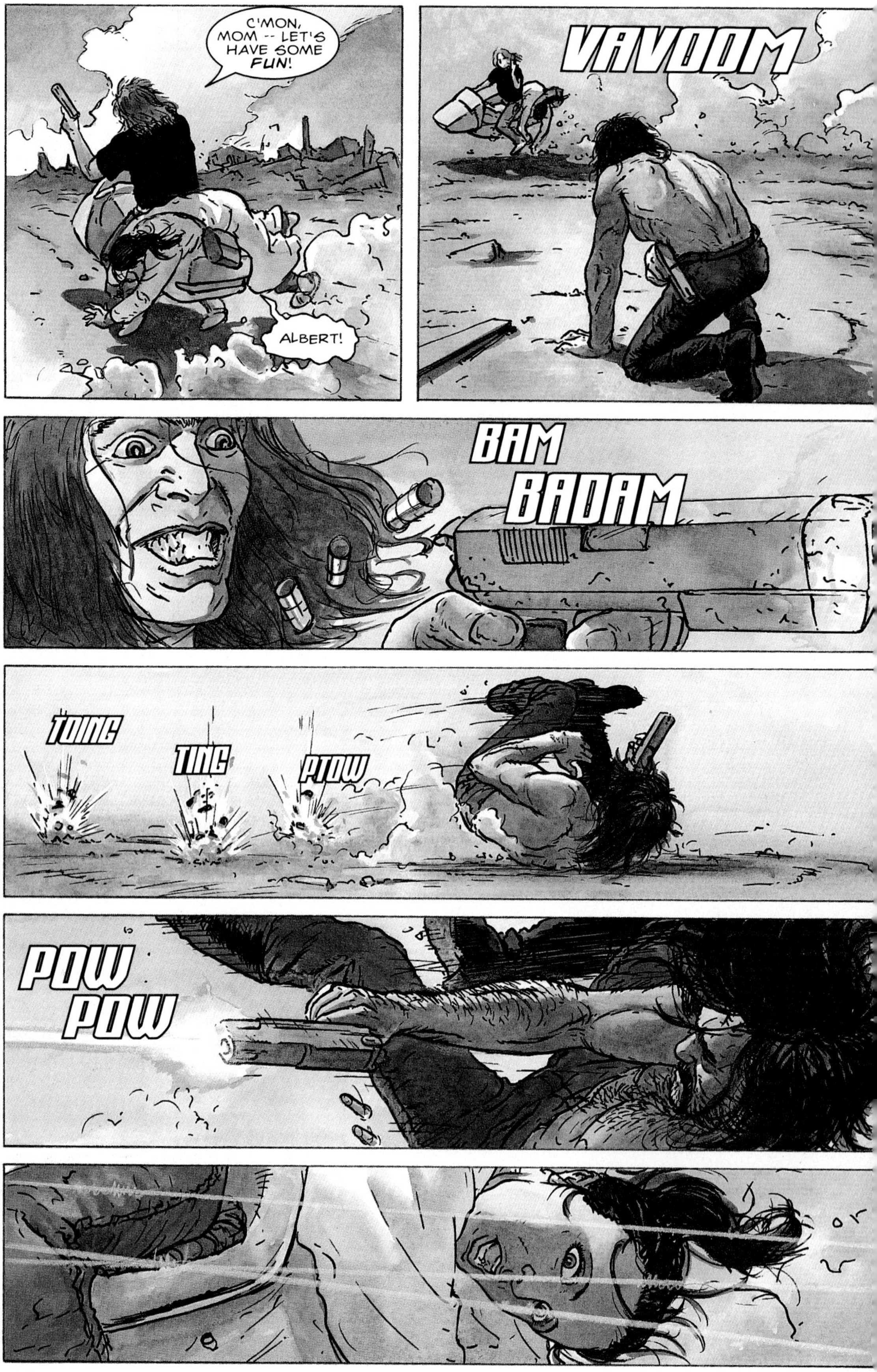
C'MON, MOM -- LET'S HAVE SOME FUN!
ALBERT!
VAVOOM
BAM
BADAM
TOING
TING
PTOW
POW
POW

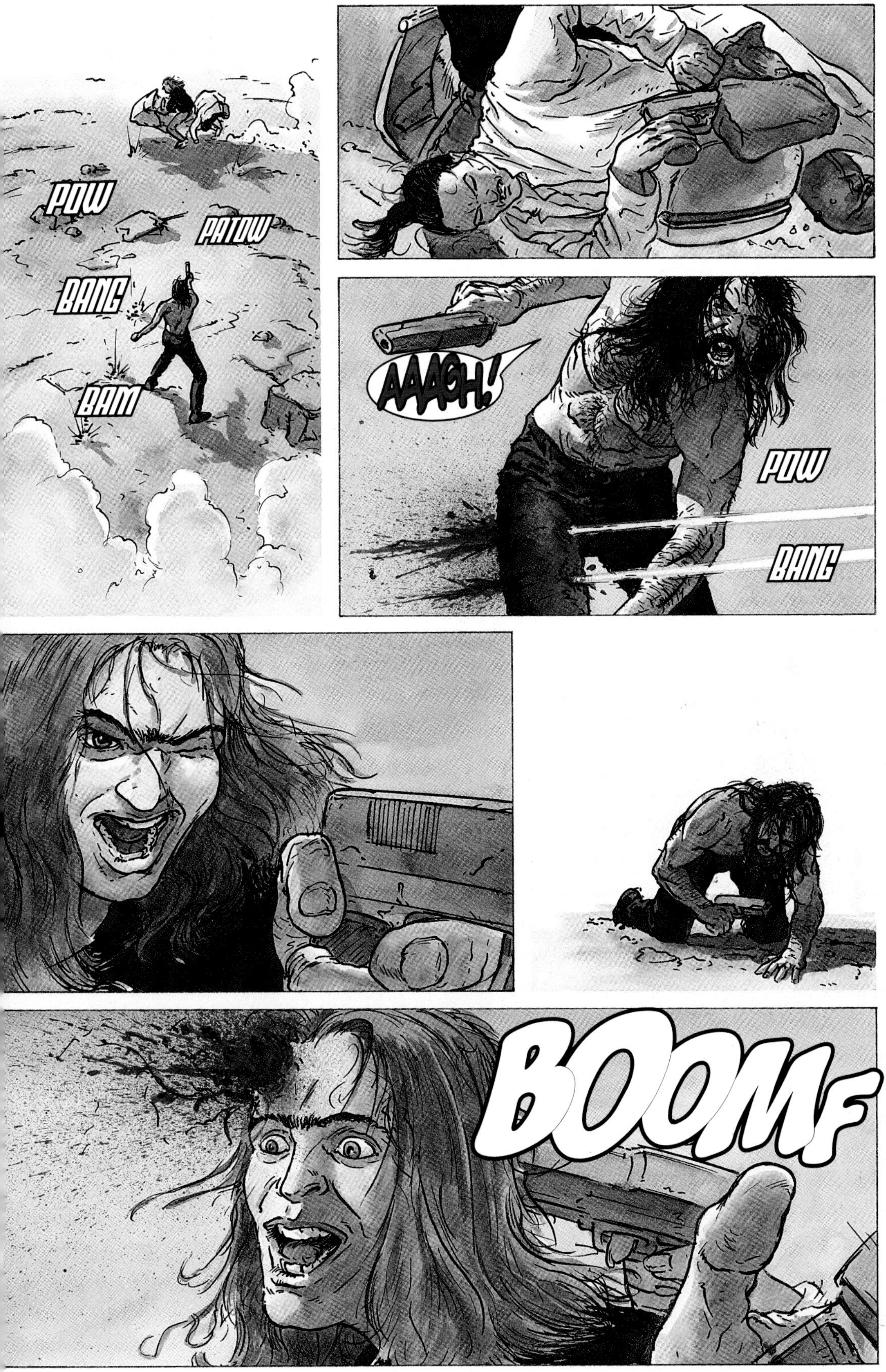
POW
PATOW
BANG
BAM
AAAGH!
POW
BANG
BOOMF

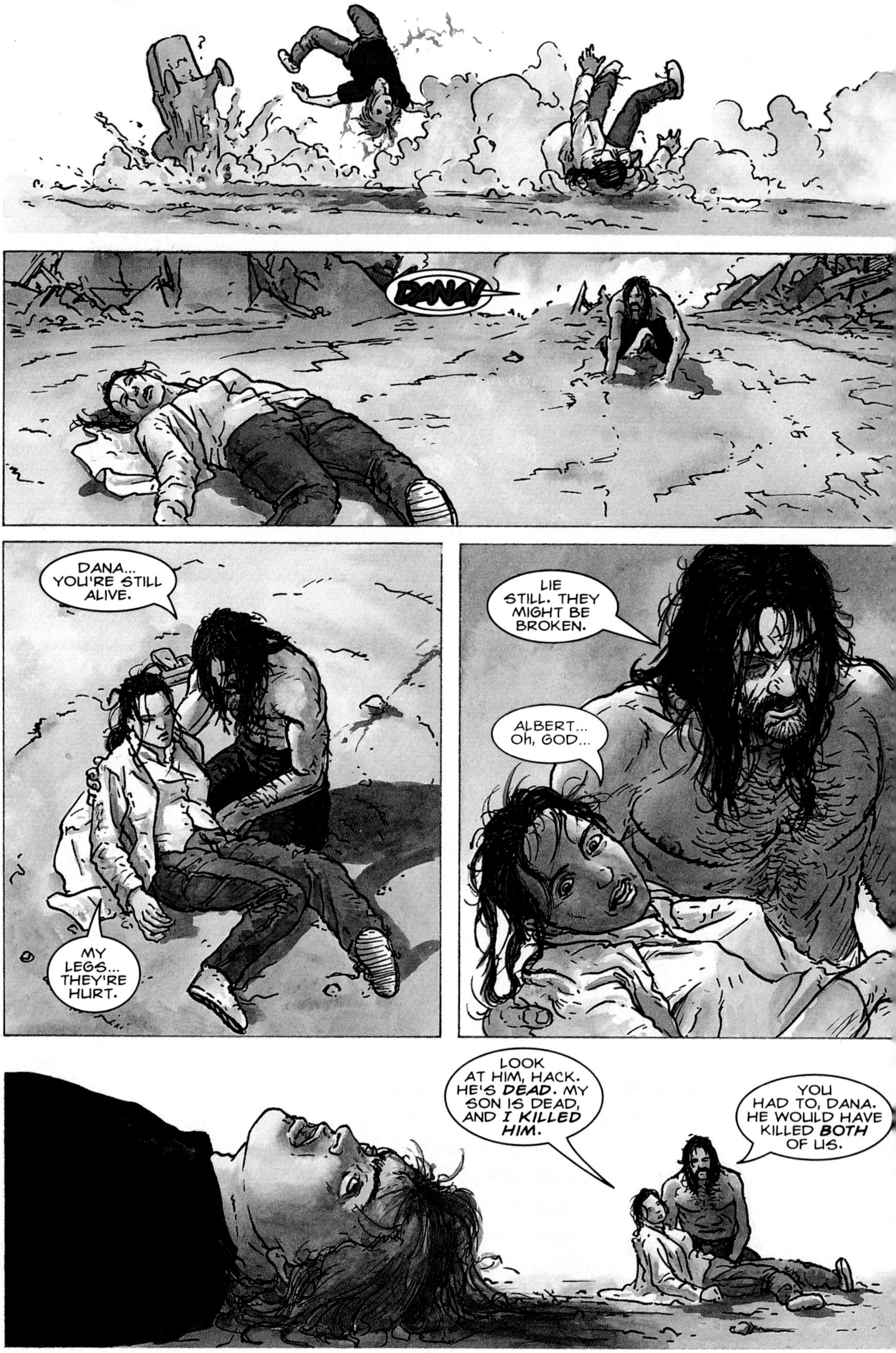
DANA!
DANA... YOU'RE STILL ALIVE.
MY LEGS... THEY'RE HURT.
LIE STILL. THEY MIGHT BE BROKEN.
ALBERT... OH, GOD...
LOOK AT HIM, HACK. HE'S DEAD. MY SON IS DEAD, AND I KILLED HIM.
YOU HAD TO, DANA. HE WOULD HAVE KILLED BOTH OF US.

EVERY-
THING'S
GONE! *EVERY-
THING!*

NO, DANA.
WE'RE STILL HERE.
WE'RE STILL ALIVE.
WE CAN BE
TOGETHER!

HACK,
LOOK AROUND.
IT'S *OVER.*

DON'T
TALK LIKE
THAT. WE CAN STILL
LIVE! WE CAN STILL
HAVE A LIFE
TOGETHER!

NO. WE
CAN'T HAVE
ANYTHING, EXCEPT
THIS. IT'S AS IF WE
CAME TOGETHER TO
PULL EVERYTHING
ELSE APART.

DANA,
STOP IT. WE
CAME TOGETHER
BECAUSE WE
FELL IN
LOVE.

IS
THAT WHY? I'VE
BEEN ASKING MYSELF
FOR A LONG TIME HOW A
FEELING SO GOOD COULD
LEAD TO SO MUCH BAD.
NOW I THINK I
KNOW.

WHAT
WE HAVE ISN'T
LOVE. IT'S LOVE'S
REVENGE ON A
WORLD THAT
WORSHIPS
HATE.

YOU'RE TALKING
CRAZY. YOU'RE IN SHOCK.
LET ME GET YOU SOMEWHERE
SAFE. YOU NEED A
CHANCE TO REST.

I'D...
LIKE TO GO
SOMEWHERE
SAFE.

WHERE
I CAN BE
WITH YOU...
AND IT
WON'T *HURT*
ANYTHING.
IF
YOU LOVE
ME, HACK, KISS
ME FOR A
MOMENT.

JUST
KISS ME.

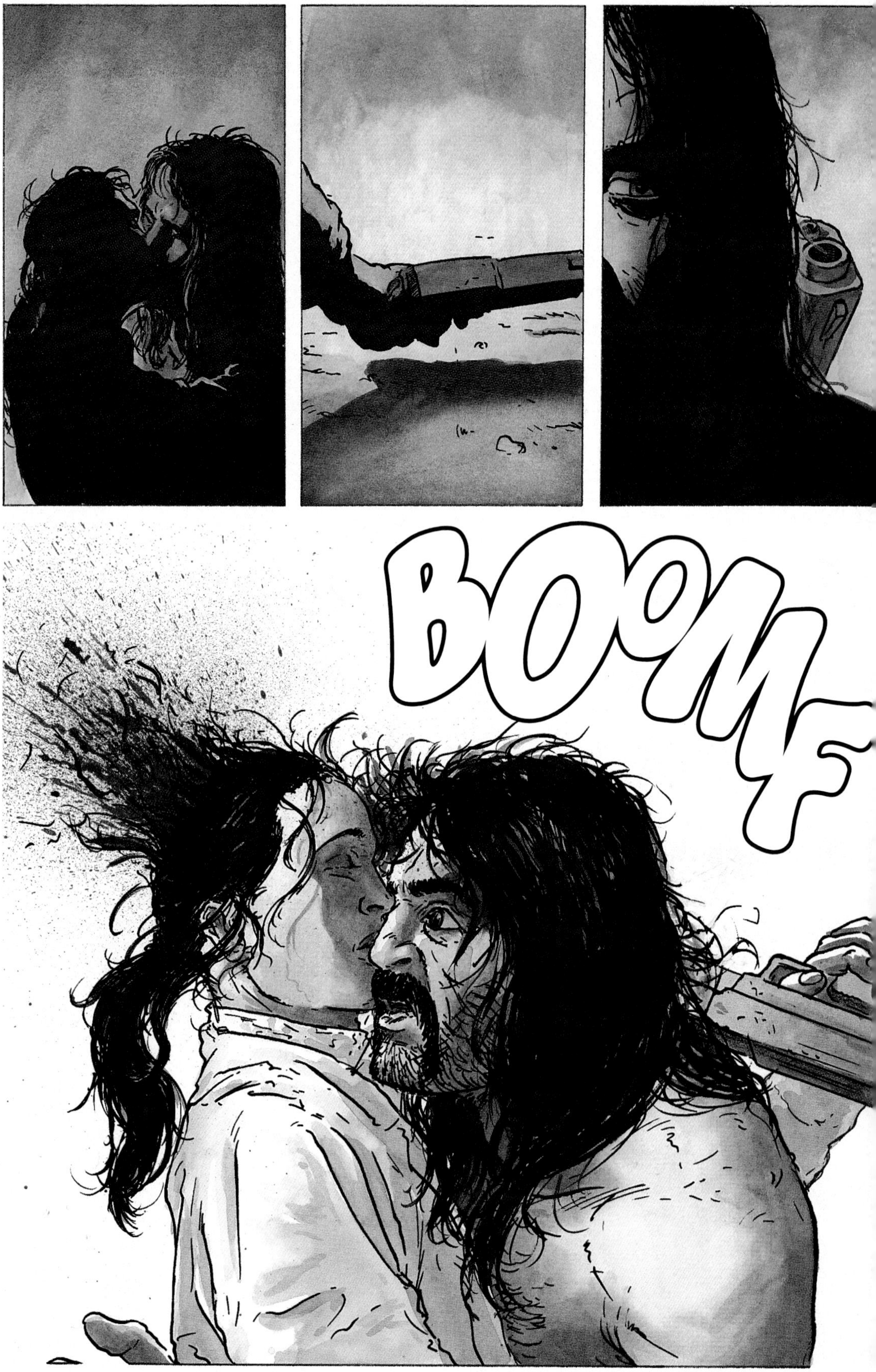
BOOMF

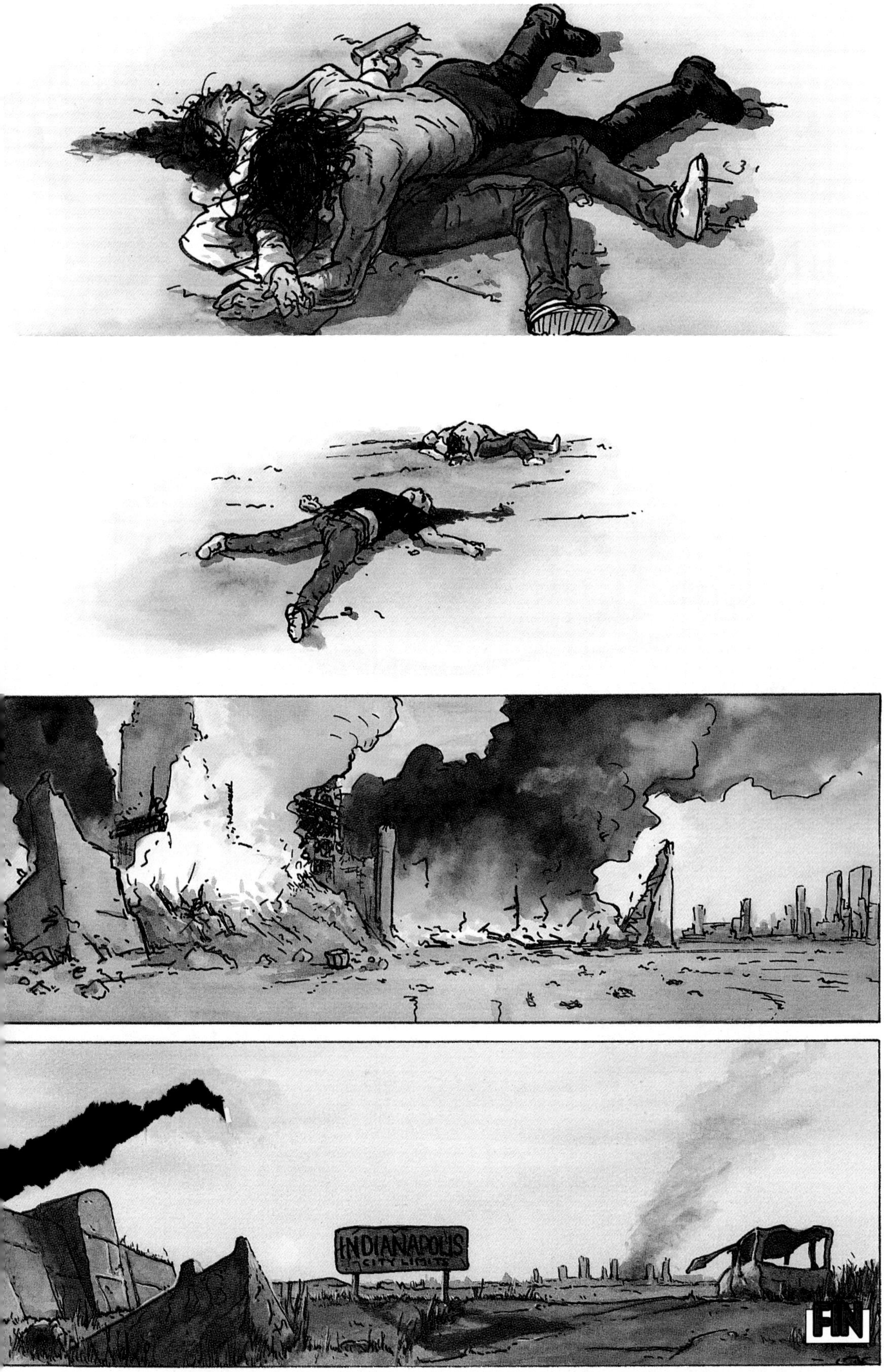
INDIANAPOLIS
CITY LIMITS
FIN

ALSO AVAILABLE

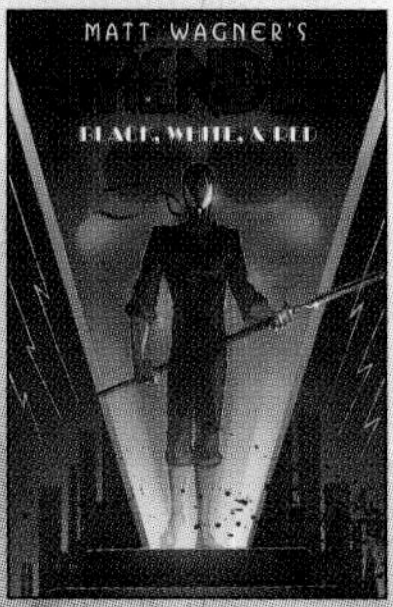
MATT WAGNER'S
BLACK, WHITE, & RED

GRENDEL: BLACK, WHITE, & RED
Matt Wagner • various artists
200-page two-color paperback
ISBN: 1-56971-493-2 $18.95

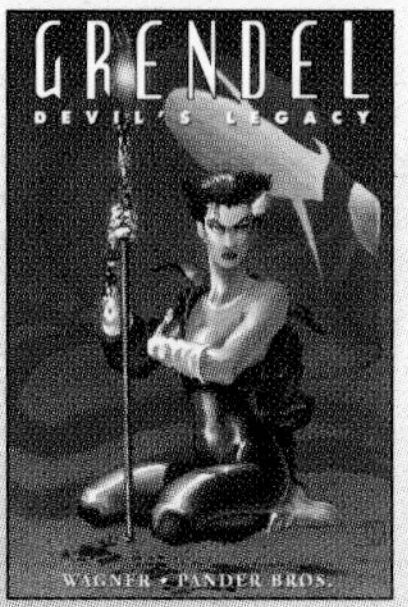
GRENDEL
DEVIL'S LEGACY
WAGNER • PANDER BROS.

GRENDEL: DEVIL'S LEGACY
Matt Wagner • Pander Bros.
328-page color paperback
ISBN: 1-56971-261-1 $29.95

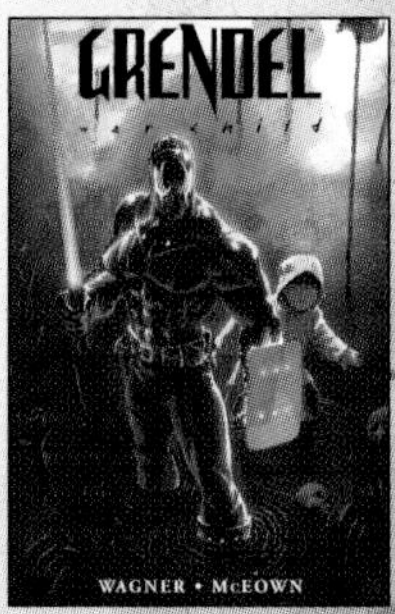
GRENDEL
WAGNER • McEOWN

GRENDEL: WAR CHILD
Matt Wagner • Pat McEown
304-page color paperback
ISBN: 1-878574-89-2 $24.95

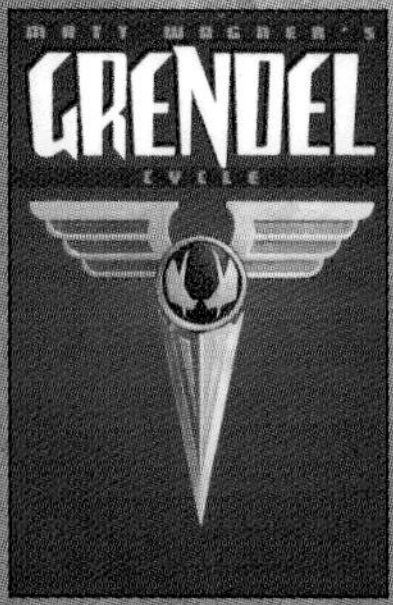
MATT WAGNER'S
GRENDEL

GRENDEL CYCLE
Matt Wagner • various artists
64-page color paperback
ISBN: 1-56971-138-0 $5.95

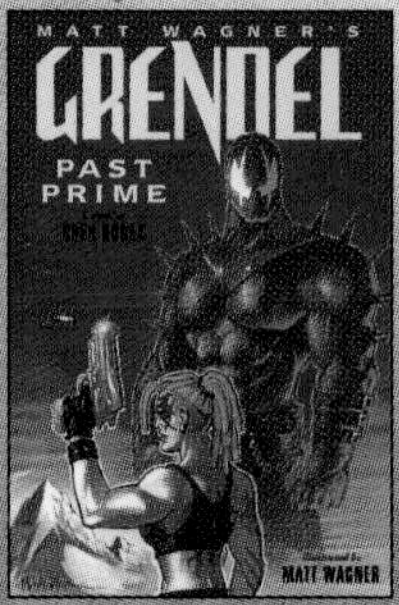
MATT WAGNER'S
GRENDEL
PAST
PRIME
MATT WAGNER

GRENDEL: PAST PRIME
Greg Rucka • Matt Wagner
208-page illustrated novel
ISBN: 1-56971-398-7 $14.95

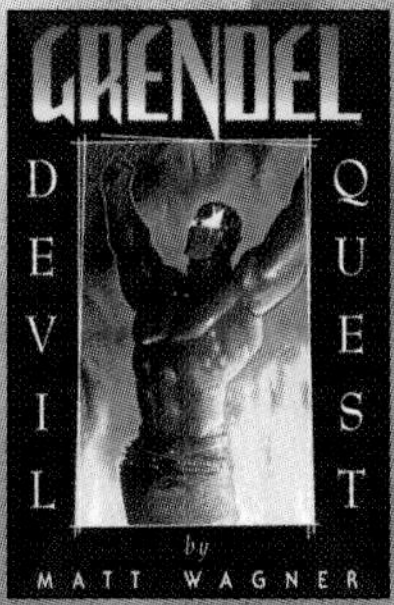
GRENDEL
DEVIL
QUEST
by
MATT WAGNER

GRENDEL: DEVIL QUEST
Matt Wagner
56-page color paperback
SOLD OUT!

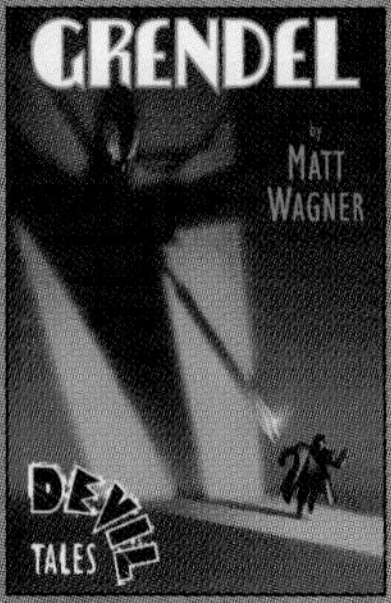
GRENDEL
by
MATT
WAGNER
DEVIL
TALES

GRENDEL: DEVIL TALES
Matt Wagner
96-page color paperback
ISBN: 1-56971-428-2 $9.95

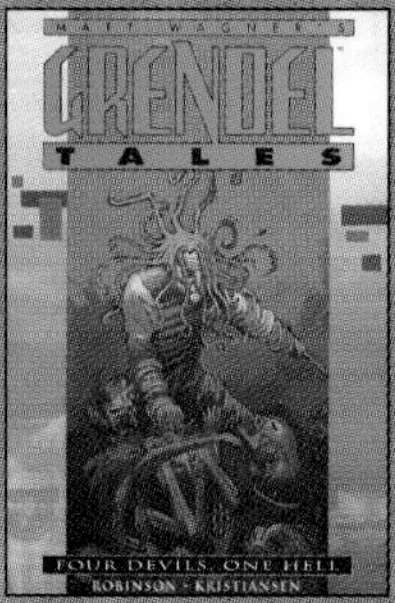
GRENDEL
TALES
FOUR DEVILS, ONE HELL
ROBINSON • KRISTIANSEN

GRENDEL TALES: FOUR DEVILS, ONE HELL
James Robinson • Teddy Kristiansen
168-page color paperback
ISBN: 1-56971-027-9 $17.95

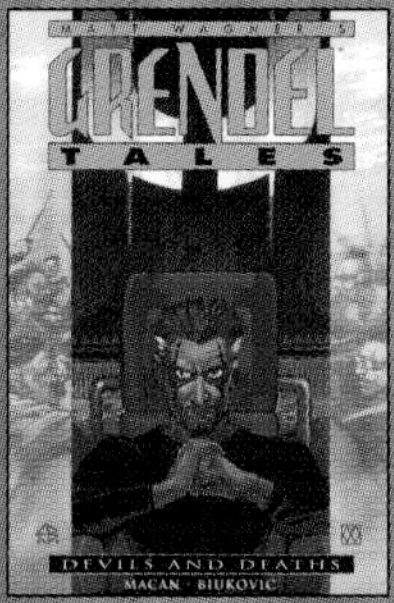
GRENDEL
TALES
DEVILS AND DEATHS
MACAN • BIUKOVIC

GRENDEL TALES: DEVILS AND DEATHS
Darko Macan • Edvin Biuković
160-page color paperback
ISBN: 1-56971-203-4 $16.95

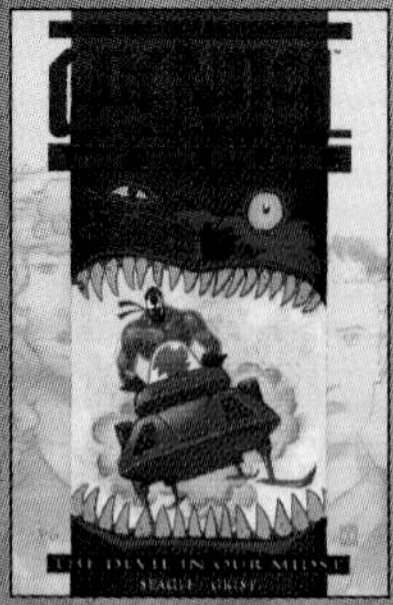

GRENDEL TALES: THE DEVIL IN OUR MIDST
Steven T. Seagle • Paul Grist
136-page color paperback
1-56971-312-X $15.95

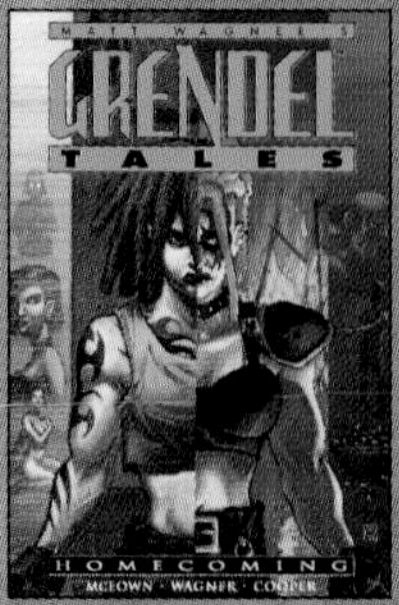
GRENDEL
TALES
HOMECOMING
McEOWN • WAGNER • COOPER

GRENDEL TALES: HOMECOMING
Pat McEown • Dave Cooper •
Matt Wagner
64-page color paperback
ISBN 1-56971-405-3 $7.95

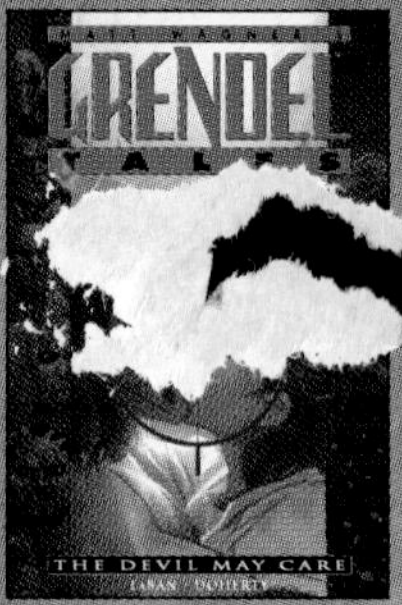
GRENDEL
THE DEVIL MAY CARE

GRENDEL TALES: THE DEVIL MAY CARE
Terry LaBan • Peter Doherty
160-page color paperback
ISBN 1-56971-796-6 $19.95